D0874278

Polish Catholics
in Chicago,
1850-1920

Polish Catholics in Chicago, 1850-1920

A Religious History

Joseph John Parot

NORTHERN ILLINOIS UNIVERSITY PRESS / DEKALB ILLINOIS

The translation of "Dawn" is from A. P. Coleman, "The Great Emigration," in *The Cambridge History of Poland*, ed. William F. Reddaway, 2 vols. (London: Cambridge University Press, 1941–50), 2: 323, and is reprinted here by permission of the Cambridge University Press.

Portions of Chapter Two originally appeared as "Sources of Community Conflict in Chicago Polonia: A Comparative Analysis and Historiographical Appraisal," *Ethnicity* 7 (December 1980): 333–48, and are reprinted here by permission of Academic Press, Inc.

Library of Congress Cataloging in Publication Data

Parot, Joseph John, 1940–
  Polish Catholics in Chicago, 1850–1920.

  Includes bibliographical references and index.
  1. Catholic Church—Illinois—Chicago region—History.
2. Polish Americans—Illinois—Chicago region—Religion.
3. Polish National Catholic Church of America—Illinois
—Chicago region—History. 4. Chicago region (Ill.)—
Church history. I. Title.
BX1418.C4P37   282'.0899185077311   81–11297
ISBN 0–87580–081–5   AACR2
ISBN 0–87580–527–2 (pbk.)

Copyright © 1981 by Northern Illinois University Press
Published by the Northern Illinois University Press, DeKalb, Illinois 60115
Manufactured in the United States of America
All Rights Reserved

For
my parents
John and Louise Parot

Contents

List of Maps

Preface

The religious and social history of Catholic immigrant groups and their subsequent impact on the development of American Catholicism and society has been a subject of growing interest in recent years. The emergence of the so-called "New Ethnicity" and the "New Catholic History" in the late sixties and early seventies can now be viewed not only as a concentrated effort to shake off the negative effects of a deeply ethnocentric "ghetto Catholic" life-pattern but also as a serious attempt to reaffirm positive values coming from the immigrant Catholic experience. Largely through an intensely self-critical appraisal of that past, both these intellectual movements have long since traversed the confines of the university and moved out into the public sphere. The grandchildren and great-grandchildren of the New Immigration are now, however so vaguely, aware of some sort of cultural "ethnic Catholic renaissance." In Polish circles, events of the past two years have in particular riveted public attention to the history and culture of the mother country. The election of a Polish pope and the rather sudden initiative taken by the Polish workers movement (Solidarity) have combined to subject Eastern Europe's largest Catholic country to an intense (and unaccustomed to) media scrutiny: now it is fashionable for John Paul II and Lech Walesa to make the cover of *Time* magazine. These events have not only changed the thinking of academicians and the general public alike but have also served to build new bridges of dialogue among the university, the church, and the working class.

But the exuberance of the New Ethnicity and the New Catholic History, as well as the euphoria brought on by media attention, have tended to gloss over a basic and, at this time, unresolved conflict between what are generally thought to be two complementary movements within "ethnic Catholicism" in America. Most analysts today speak of the immigrant past and the Catholic past in the same breath—and for good reason. For such groups as the Poles it would be unwise for observers to disassociate ethnicity from religion, or Polishness from Catholicism. John Paul II's triumphal tour of Poland in 1979 certainly reinforced in the public consciousness the marriage of nationality and religion in the lives of Polish Catholics. On the other hand, the New Ethnicity, unfortunately, has tended to exaggerate many of the more legitimate contributions made by such nationality (ethnic) groups as the Poles; the New Ethnicity has on any number of occasions given itself over to a stridency which has offended various sectors of society not belonging to the culture and past of a given ethnic group. In its dedication to assert the heritage of numerous southern and eastern European immigrant groups and in its continued efforts to gain what it feels are its rightful privileges in a widely diverse society, the New Ethnicity at times appears to revert to the old ethnocentrism. But this is not all. At the same time that other dynamic forces within

Catholicism attempt to reach out to all men via the ecumenical spirit engendered by Vatican II and through such admirable intellectual efforts as the New Catholic History, the New Ethnicity, which ironically traces its roots deep into the European Catholic past, attempts to reverse the forces of universalism and catholicity by arguing in favor of particularism. In this way the New Ethnicity not only contradicts itself but also refuses to face a dilemma that faces all cultural pluralists at one time or another: how does one reach out and give of oneself without losing one's own soul? Or to put the matter in terms relevant to this study, how is it possible to retain the ethnocentric character of Polish nationality while at the same time giving way to the centrifugal force of Catholic universality?

This study will attempt to trace the efforts of both the American Catholic hierarchy and the Polish Catholic community to deal with this central question. Whereas a vast literature produced by historians, sociologists, and anthropologists has concentrated on the assimilation of immigrant Catholic life into what is known as the American "mainstream," this study will instead concentrate on the tensions dealing with ethnicity and nationality in its harshest particularistic terms and those forces in American Catholicism which worked to integrate the American way of life into the universal, or catholic, aspects of the church. The book takes as its subject the religious life of Chicago's Polish-American Catholic community in the 1850–1920 period. This time span approximates the first two generations of Chicago Polonia, the formative years, so to speak, of the immigrant Catholic community in America. The study of the Polish group in Chicago is significant in a number of ways: first, for the past sixty years (1920–1980), the Poles have formed the largest white European ethnic group in the city; next, the Polish Catholics comprise the largest ethno-religious group in the Chicago Roman Catholic Archdiocese (which, too, is one of the largest dioceses in the world); finally, the Polish Catholics of Chicago are in many ways a microcosm of the immigrant Catholic ghetto way of life, which, to be sure, exhibits many of the primordial tensions already discussed. Moreover, locally, approximately one out of every five Roman Catholics in Chicago is Polish; and, on a national scale, one out of every eight American Catholics is of Polish descent. Hence the immigrant-Catholic "connection" here should be readily apparent.

The impact of Vatican II on the theologically conservative and relatively isolated Polish-American clergy takes on greater importance with each passing day. Leading Catholic intellectuals, with some support from the hierarchy, have already decided—for better or for worse—to cut off the American Catholic Church from its immigrant moorings. With Vatican II's emphasis on and encouragement of ecumenism in the daily spiritual and religious lives of Catholics, the immigrant ghetto Catholic parish, many would be prepared to argue, is an anachronism to say the least. Accordingly, this book will attempt to shed some light on the aspirations, accomplishments, and defeats experienced by the Polish Catholic clergy—the Congregation of the Resurrection of Our Lord, in particular—in raising to life a gigantic community-parish complex and structure which has stubbornly resisted encroachments of any kind. It is the personal conviction of this writer that the central role of the Resurrectionists in the development of the immigrant Catholic system may still be unappreciated by select readers of Polish-American history, the historical profession at large, and the general reading public. The role of the Congregation of the Resurrection in Chicago must be identified as precisely and in as detailed a fashion as possible before any larger questions dealing with the overall effects of immigration and ethnicity on the Catholic experience can take shape.

In doing so, this book will also aspire to grapple with several equally important questions: for instance, why is it that the Polish community in one American city after another engaged itself in some of the most bitter intragroup struggles ever to take place within any ethnic subsociety during its early years? How did this fratricidal struggle lead to the only major schism ever encountered by Roman Catholicism in the United States? What was the effect of the Americanization movement on the Polish group during the war years? Finally, what were the major differences dividing the Americanist hierarchy and the Polish Catholic clergy in Chicago and the United States, and how did the resolution of these differences ultimately affect the overall character of the American Catholic church?

The research that has gone into this book reflects a personal search to come to grips with the writer's own urban, Polish, "ghetto Catholic" past. Undoubtedly, some of the observations, arguments, and conclusions are the product of tensions coming from two radically different ways of life: immigrant Catholic working-class family life on Chicago's far south side and subsequent "uprootedness" in secular university life. My family's daily confrontation of those tensions may yet make this journey worthwhile. *Bądź wola twoja.*

Acknowledgments

First and foremost, I was greatly pleased to have been the beneficiary of the advice and insights provided by three leading scholars of Catholic, Protestant, and Jewish life in America: Reverend Dr. Menceslaus J. Madaj, Archivist of the Roman Catholic Archdiocese of Chicago; Professor Paul A. Carter of the University of Arizona; and Professor Moses Rischin of San Francisco State University. Of equal significance was the assistance provided by the clergy and the Polish language press, particularly the late Reverend Joseph Bednowicz, C.R., and Reverend Joseph Baker, C.R., of the *Dziennik Chicagoski*. Other Resurrectionists who attended to my project include the Reverend John Iwicki, Reverend Dennis Sanders, and Reverend Edmund Zygmunt, who granted me permission to use microfilmed records and collections of letters at the St. Joseph's Novitiate in Woodstock, Illinois. I am also grateful to Reverend Emil Seroka, O.F.M., of St. Roman's parish in Chicago, and to the late Reverend Anthony Balczun, pastor of my home parish of St. Casimir in Hammond, Indiana. I would also like to acknowledge the assistance of Mr. John Krawiec and the staff of the *Dziennik Związkowy* and *Zgoda*. I also owe special thanks to the priests, nuns, and parish staffs throughout Chicago Polonia, especially at St. Stanislaus Kostka, Holy Trinity, St. Hedwig's, St. John Cantius, St. Mary of the Angels, St. Stanislaus Bishop and Martyr, St. Hyacinth's, St. Augustine's (Back of the Yards), St. John of God, St. Casimir's, St. Adalbert's, St. Michael's (South Chicago), Immaculate Conception (South Chicago), St. Mary of Perpetual Help, and St. Florian's parishes.

Support from Polish-American organizations was also crucial throughout the research and writing. Accordingly, I am especially indebted to the past and present officers of the Polish Roman Catholic Union, the Polish National Alliance, the Polish Women's Alliance, and the Polish Alma Mater for extraordinary museum, archive, and library privileges. I received substantial support from Reverend Donald Bilinski, O.F.M., from Mr. George Walter and Mr. Joseph Zurawski of the Polish Roman Catholic Union Museum and Archives, and from Mrs. Bernice Rzewska, Head Librarian of the Polish National Alliance Library. I am equally appreciative of support by Miss Adele Lagodzinska, past president of the Polish Women's Alliance, and by the late Mrs. Anna Zych who served on the national board of directors of the Polish Women's Alliance. I would also like to thank my many colleagues and friends in the Polish American Historical Association, especially Professor Frank Renkiewicz, editor of *Polish American Studies*. Other scholars who have served as commentators on my work or who have offered constructive criticism along the way include: Professor Thaddeus Radzialowski of Southwest Minnesota State University; Professor Thaddeus Gromada of Jersey State College and Secretary-General of the Polish Institute of Arts and Sciences;

Dr. John Bodnar of the Pennsylvania Museum and Historical Commission; Professor Rudolph Vecoli of the University of Minnesota; Professor Andrew Greeley of the University of Arizona; and Professor John Bracey of the University of Massachusetts at Amherst.

The location and strategic use of archival and library materials saved me months, and even years, of valuable time. Accordingly, I am indebted to: Archie Motley, Dominic Pacyga, Larry Viskochil, Fannia Weingartner, and the entire staff of the Chicago Historical Society; Mrs. Gloria Sieben, Head Librarian at St. Mary of the Lake Seminary in Mundelein, Illinois, and her staff; the staff of *The Chicago Catholic* (formerly *The New World*), and Ellen Skerrett in particular, and the entire library staffs of St. Mary's College in Orchard Lake, Michigan, the Chicago Public Library, the University of Illinois at Champaign-Urbana, the University of Illinois at Chicago Circle, and the Regenstein Library at the University of Chicago. I also wish to express my gratitude to all my friends and colleagues at the Northern Illinois University Libraries, especially Dr. William R. DuBois, Professor of Language and Literature, Mrs. Eileen Dubin, Mr. Samuel Huang, and Mrs. Myrtie Podschwit, all of the Interlibrary Loan Department, Victor Schormann of the Serials Department, and Robert Fischer of the Bibliography and Reference Departments.

I am also grateful to my colleagues in the Department of History at Northern Illinois University, especially: Professor J. Carroll Moody, chairman, for his unqualified support on any number of occasions; Professors Paul Kleppner and W. Bruce Lincoln, for reading several preliminary chapter drafts; Professor Samuel Kinser for assistance in foreign language translations; the late Professor Jacob Hoptner, for sharing with me his many ideas regarding the political and social development of Poland and Eastern Europe; and Professor Emory Evans, now chairman of the Department of History at the University of Maryland.

I would also like to express my thanks to the Graduate School of Northern Illinois University for offering financial assistance, to the university as a whole for granting a sabbatical leave which enabled me to conduct further research and writing, and to the American Philosophical Society for providing additional funding during that sabbatical.

I would also like to recognize the secretarial expertise of Carla Lally Heister and the skillful bibliographic work of my student assistants—Mary Worden Maloney, Joanne Ellen Maloney, Rona Hunter, and Cynthia Argianas. Special thanks go to my niece Joanne Smith and my daughter Maribeth who spent much of one summer tracing addresses of ethnic parishes in the Chicago archdiocese through a maze of city and parish directories.

Finally, I want the entire family—*cała familja nasza*—to know that their spirit and love formed the bedrock of support for this project. My wife's mother, Mrs. Charlotte Przybysz of Hegewisch, kept her doors open throughout those many research trips into Chicago. To my parents—my father, John Joseph Parot, who died from leukemia shortly before the writing began, and my mother, Louise Klimek Parot—how does a son ever repay your solid faith, never-ending hope, and undying love? And to my wife, Barbara, and my children, Maribeth and John, I can offer no words in exchange for your patience and understanding. Through it all, these were by the grace of God happy years. Let us thank Him, this Happy Easter weekend of 19 April 1981, for it is finished.

Polish Catholics
in Chicago,
1850-1920

1

Catholicism and the Partitions: From *Ojczyzna* to *Nowy Świat*

> Before Your altars we in supplication
> Implore You, Lord, to free our nation.
> From *Boże Coś Polskę*

Ojczyzna

The Polish Partitions had a powerful bearing not only on the overall character of the Polish emigration to the United States but also on the peculiar religious structure and outlook brought over by Polish immigrants. If anything, it was the Partitions that contributed to Poland's weakened political and economic status in the nineteenth century and unleashed a massive Slavic Catholic exodus to *Nowy Świat*—the "New World." From the termination of the Napoleonic wars to the outbreak of World War I, approximately 1,500,000 Poles left the *ojczyzna*—the "homeland." In a political sense, the *ojczyzna* no longer even existed, if taken from the point of view of the partitioning powers; and if one were Polish, the *ojczyzna* was reduced to an idea rather than a place, something that could be romanticized rather than lived in. All things considered, Poland in the nineteenth century was a most unhappy place in a most unhappy time. The renowned Polish historian, Oscar Halecki, even while putting the finishing touches to his *History of Poland* in the horrendous aftermath of the Nazi *blitzkrieg* in World War II, still referred to the Partition as Poland's "saddest century." On three separate occasions in the 1772–1795 period and still once more at the Congress of Vienna, Poland was carved up by more powerful states adjacent to her borders—by Russia to the east, by Prussia to the west, and by Austria-Hungary to the south. After the aggrandizers had completed their respective takes, Poland was literally erased from the map of Europe.[1]

Prior to the First Partition in 1772, the Polish-Lithuanian Commonwealth—then referred to as the *Res Publica* or *Rzeczpospolita*—comprised some 760,000 square kilometers, a great state stretching from the Baltic Sea in the north to the

Dniester River and the Ottoman Empire in the south, and from the gates of the Russian cities of Kiev and Smolensk (both of which for a time were in the *Rzecz-pospolita*) all the way to Brandenburg in West Prussia. The Commonwealth was not only territorially vast but also quite heavily populated; in the late eighteenth century it was the fourth most densely populated state in all of Europe, behind France, the Holy Roman Empire, and Russia. But the First Partition reduced Polish territory by 29.2 percent and the population by 25.2 percent. Largely accomplished by the partitioning powers without any sustained political or military opposition from within Poland, future divisions of the *ojczyzna* now seemed inevitable.[2]

But the Polish *szlachta* (gentry) and intelligentsia finally roused the latent national impulses of the Commonwealth, and a twenty-year period of internal reform followed. Between 1772 and 1791 Poland was dominated by a resurgence of intense patriotism and national purpose. Political and social reforms, crisis-instigated to be sure, culminated with the adoption of the 3 May 1791 Constitution, a document highly praised by numerous American republicans. The new Polish Constitution essentially was an eleventh-hour attempt to strengthen the power of the state without infringing on personal liberties. The emerging burgher class now gained the franchise, and the notorious *liberum veto*, whereby a *szlachcic* could by a *single* negative vote abrogate the work of an entire *sejm* (Diet), was abolished—thus eliminating the monopoly of the *szlachta* over the newly formulated Polish "constitutional republic."

Nevertheless, such heroic efforts designed to bring new life to the Polish state met the disapproval of the partitioners, who were gravely concerned over Poland's resurrected nationalism. When Polish land magnates assembled the Targowica Confederation for the purpose of restoring the old social order, Catherine II sent Russian troops into Poland, and a Second Partition, one which a noted historian of the period termed the "death sentence of the Polish state," was immediately imposed. This time Poland's borders were pushed back so drastically that the old Commonwealth was no longer recognizable. Poland still survived on the map of Europe, but not for long.[3]

The Second Partition was met by full-scale resistance. In the spring of 1794, Tadeusz Kościuszko, a hero in the American Revolutionary War, assumed leadership of the Warsaw Insurrection, which temporarily raised hopes within Poland for a restoration of pre-Partition borders. Kościuszko's army swelled to more than 150,000 men, but renewed patriotism could not match the military prowess of the enemy's battle-hardened troops. The end for Kościuszko and the Polish cause came on the field of Maciejowice on 9 October 1794, when the Russian army went down to its last corps to defeat the exhausted Polish forces. In the spring of 1795, Catherine completed her policy of encirclement, and the Partitions entered their final phase. But for a brief interim in the Napoleonic era when the semi-independent Duchy of Warsaw was established, Poland, according to her greatest

Romantic poet, Adam Mickiewicz, was left to hang on the cross of national partition: Pomerania (Pomorze), Posen (Poznan), and Silesia (Śląsk) went over to Prussia; Galicia and the Górale region in the Carpathians were absorbed by Austria-Hungary; and Lithuania, Livonia, and the Ukraine were taken into the Russian Empire. The "saddest century" had indeed come to Poland.[4]

As each of the "three Polands" was left to fend for itself under these respective foreign regimes, an element of separatism inevitably rolled over the captive land. Polish *chłopi* (peasants) in the Galician sector, now governed from Vienna, were in both a political and social sense cut off from Silesian miners and their families in Prussian Poland. Coastal-dwelling Pomeranians in the Gdańsk region eventually lost contact with the urban cosmopolitanism of historic Cracow. Moreover, the Polish-Lithuanian Union effected back in 1569 was for all practical purposes terminated, as Wilno in Congress (Russian) Poland was severed from such cities as Lublin in Little Poland (*Małopolska*), where the Union came into being in the first place. This process of "regional separatism"[5] became more acute as the saddest century moved past its middle half. But the full impact of this phenomenon would also be felt far beyond the *ojczyzna*. Its effects would fracture the solidarity of dozens of Polish settlements in urban America as well, where thousands upon thousands of Polish immigrants coming from these separated regions of the *ojczyzna* would find themselves inadvertently reunited, only to discover that a century of political, social, and cultural separation had taken its toll. The Third Partition drastically altered the demographic construct of not only Poland but also American Polonia: with a thoroughness and suddenness never before experienced in Polish history, Russia annexed approximately 470,000 square kilometers of Polish territory housing a population of 6,300,000; Prussia absorbed close to 150,000 square kilometers, with a population of 4,200,000; and Austria took 240,000 square kilometers, with a population of 2,500,000.[6]

The Partitions also exacerbated other social divisions within Poland, and, as the historian Piotr Wandycz tells us, they also interrupted or arrested numerous processes of positive development. For one, the social sores between the *szlachta* and the landless *chłopi* were not given their proper healing time. And without a solid bridge constructed between the interests of the *szlachta* (who before the Partitions comprised nearly 25 percent of the Polish population) and the needs of the *chłopi* (who numbered approximately ten million), all hopes for reversing the Partitions via a united insurrectionary front would certainly be dashed. On the other hand, the Partitions may have magnified Poland's internal gentry-versus-peasant division beyond its actual significance, for recent Polish historiography has demonstrated that many thousands of gentry lived in as abject a state of poverty as the peasants themselves. Nevertheless, that such primordial social divisions in Partitioned Poland could, under the circumstances, hardly be narrowed certainly arrested the efforts of the intelligentsia and, later, the insurrectionists, to mold a truly comprehensive national consciousness in Poland—at least the kind of solidarity that would have inspired the *chłopi* to take up arms in the Insurrections of 1831 and 1863. This incomplete process of national development in Poland was likewise destined to produce numerous social tremors of a similar nature in the internal life of American Polonia. On any number of occasions, as shall later be seen, the Polish Catholic clergy, who were largely recruited from the burgher class in the pre-Partition period and who subsequently maintained a socially superior position in Polish society by virtue of closer ties with the *szlachta*, would find themselves seriously challenged "from below" by laity coming from the *chłopi* class. Such challenges to the clergy would occur throughout American Polonia in the late nineteenth century, with some of the more infamous incidents taking place in the archdiocese of Chicago. Aside from such challenges to their authority from within Polonia, the Polish Catholic clergy would also face the prospect of diminished status when confronting clergymen of more established nationality groups in the American Church, namely, the Irish-American and German-American clergy.[7]

The Partitions also interrupted the natural process of constitutional development in Poland. The 3 May 1791 effort at establishing a limited form of constitutional republicanism—one equating political power with property qualifications rather than merely gentry status—was, of course, prematurely aborted. Henceforth, politically active Polish émigrés throughout Europe and America would satisfy their need for constitutionalism on a severely restricted, local basis only. Hundreds of such local political action groups aimed at liberating the *ojczyzna* were to spring up throughout the nineteenth century, and each went about the business of drawing up complex "constitutions," even when small uncomplicated political groups were involved. It was as if each group wanted to prove to the world, and perhaps to itself, that Poland's rightful destiny was that of a constitutional republic. All in all, without engaging in the technicalities of a highly complex subject, it is the contention here that there was a direct correlation between the interruption of Polish political and patriotic development during the saddest century and the proliferation of secular/political organizations of all types in American Polonia, many of which would challenge the supremacy of the church and its clergy. The intensity of these challenges on the parish church level in American Polonia would in many ways rival the overall drive toward the national liberation of Poland.

But to untangle the relationship of Catholicism to the development of the Polish state in history is next to impossible, for the growth of the church and the state in Poland's early years is so nearly synchronized that one cannot discuss the power of the state without also considering the power of the church. Poland owed its very origins and existence to an intentional union of state and church. The Piast dynasty was in fact formed by a marriage in 966 A.D. between the pagan Polish Duke Mieszko and the Bohemian Christian Princess Dubravka, a union that not only served to introduce Poland to Christianity but also to seal the bond

between the two over the next four centuries. This Piast-Christian symbiosis enabled the fledgling Polish state to survive intact in times of great danger, when
many nearby aspirants to statehood could not. For whenever the stability of the
Polish state was threatened, at least within the *Res Publica Christiana*, the papacy
invariably pleaded Poland's case before the courts of Europe, and somehow Poland not only survived politically but also remained aboard the bark of Peter.
When the last of these Piasts, Casimir the Great, left no male heir to the Polish
throne during his reign in the fourteenth century, Poland's traditional policy of
tolerance to her neighbors appeared to have been paid back tenfold. Good relations with Lithuania in particular paved the way for a smooth transition of power
which brought about the so-called Golden Age of the Jagiellonians. Another dy-
nastic marriage, this one between Władisław (Ladislaus) Jagiełło, a Lithuanian
prince, and his beloved Jadwiga (Hedwig) of Anjou in 1386, perpetuated the
union of church and state and inaugurated the process which eventually culminated in the historic Polish-Lithuanian Union. When the saintly Jadwiga died at
the premature age of twenty-six, Jagiełło and his cousin Witold continued to
pursue a foreign policy designed to safeguard Polish frontiers and a domestic
policy aimed at strengthening the position of the church internally so that its
presence would immediately be made known in the spheres of education and
culture. During this Golden Age, Polish territory was vastly extended, coming to
encompass an area of 400,000 square miles, or more than three times the size of
present-day Poland. And throughout this period of expansion, the church kept
pace by creating additional dioceses and by assuming leadership over the educational system, first via Jesuit power and prestige and later through Piarist influence. By the eve of the First Partition, these two religious societies alone had
established a Catholic secondary school network totaling 115 institutions.[8]

By 1772, the Catholic church in Poland was already exerting an institutional
influence that would not be matched by the *entire* American Catholic church until
the early twentieth century. According to the Polish historian Jerzy Kloczowski,
the church in Poland before the Partitions tended to the spiritual needs of nearly
10.5 million Catholics, 6 million of whom belonged to the Latin rite and 4.5
million of whom were Uniates (Ruthenian and Ukrainian Catholics retaining the
Greek rite). In 1772, there existed in Poland eighteen Catholic dioceses, containing 4,985 Latin-rite and 9,300 Greek-rite parishes. The Catholic parish system in
Poland contained nearly *fifteen times* the total number of Polish parishes ever
founded on American soil.[9] Moreover, the Polish monastic system in the same
period already comprised 27 different religious orders and societies spread over
46 religious provinces, and these provinces contained at least 884 religious houses
to which belonged a total of 14,000 regular clergy (Latin rite). In addition, the
church in Poland also claimed some 10,000 secular (or diocesan) clergy, most of
whom were ordained at any one of the 34 diocesan-administered seminaries established throughout Poland. Because this institutional growth had been so wide-

spread, church-owned lands were nearly equal in acreage to crown-held territories. Prior to the First Partition, 9 percent of all available land in Poland was owned by the church, 13 percent was controlled by the crown, and 78 percent by the nobility.[10]

But beneath this impressive institutional topsoil nourished by the church lay several layers of rocky and shifting substratum, much of which would surface at unexpected intervals, causing the church great political, social, and spiritual difficulties. Since the Polish church on the eve of the Partitions had in every way assumed the character of a *national* church, almost every conceivable social and political division which affected the state would also shake the church. The cleavage between the *szlachta* and the *chłopi*, for one, forced the church to function on two levels in the late eighteenth and early nineteenth centuries. In a fashion paralleling that of the prevailing social structure, Polish Catholicism maintained an "upper" and a "lower" church.

In the "upper" church the higher-level *szlachta* and land magnates reserved for themselves and their clients the right to nominate candidates to the bishoprics and cathedral canons; in fact, it was not altogether uncommon for the *szlachta* to appoint themselves to the most highly prized bishoprics. Generally speaking, Poland's hiearchy was composed of men who combined gentry status, wealth, and land ownership with higher education, as exemplified by Bishop Kajetan Soltyk of the Cracow diocese in the mid-eighteenth century.

The "lower" church comprised millions of peasants and lower-class townspeople, and whatever clergy came from this sector of society. In many ways this was the "devotional" church in Poland—the type of church Thomas and Znaniecki discuss in detail in their classic study *The Polish Peasant in Europe and America*.[11] It was this "devotional lower church" that was given to excessive emotionalism in the liturgy, to belief in miracles, and to occasional superstition; it was this church that scrupulously obeyed the commandments, confessed sins when these commandments were broken, and enjoyed the liturgical calendar with its many-sided and colorful social events. And, according to Kloczowski, it was this church that, even given the modifications made by the Enlightenment, survived intact into the twentieth century.[12]

The Catholic church in Poland was also beset by other internal difficulties arising from its national church status, one of which concerned its inability to deal with religious pluralism and the Dissident question. Ironically, it was Poland's centuries-old policy of toleration toward various minority nationalities (Ruthenians and Ukrainians, for instance) and religious Dissidents (Protestant and Orthodox) which produced a conflict between the Latin-rite church and the Orthodox church in the mid-eighteenth century.

In 1596, via the Union of Brest, the Ruthenian and Ukrainian Catholics were given permission by Rome to retain their historic rites while still remaining in communion with Rome. As a result of this compromise, which did not come about without the usual ferment one might expect when substantive concessions had to be made by both sides in order to effect a Union, the Uniate church in Poland came into being. With Brest as an impetus, Poland by the end of the sixteenth century gave every indication of becoming not only a supranationality state, by its absorption of Lithuanians, Ruthenians, Belorussians, Ukrainians, and Germans, but also a suprareligious nation containing Latin-rite Catholics, Uniates, Jews, Protestants, and Greek Orthodox. Religious freedom for the Dissident Protestant and Greek Orthodox membership had already been agreed to at the Confederation of Warsaw in 1573 and was subsequently accepted by every Polish king until the late seventeenth century. But as Catholicism waxed in influence this historic policy of toleration gave way in the early eighteenth century to one of proselytism. The Catholic church of the Latin rite began making strenuous efforts to convert the Greek Orthodox membership in Poland to the Uniate church (which used the Greek rite). Moreover, a movement to abolish civil rights for the Dissidents gained momentum, much to the alarm of Catherine the Great in Russia. On the eve of the First Partition, the Dissident question became a major agenda item for the Polish *sejm*.[13]

At the Diet of the Polish-Lithuanian Commonwealth in October 1766, Kajetan Soltyk, Bishop of Cracow, with the support of Józef Zaluski, Bishop of Kiev, submitted for consideration to the Deputies and Senators present a controversial proposal entitled "Security of the Faith." "Desiring to secure as most fundamental our Holy Roman Catholic faith, for centuries dominant in our kingdom," the Bishop of Cracow proposed "as eternal law, that no citizen . . . under any title or pretense, on account of the Dissidents, venture to propose a constringent on the Roman Catholic religion, under the penalty of confiscation of his estates. . . ."[14] The fact that so strongly worded a motion was even considered at this Diet in the "Indian Summer of Polish Politics," let alone approved (in a modified form), demonstrated the power of the *kościot* (church) in the secular affairs of the *ojczyzna*.[15] The Soltyk motion also clearly indicated that the Polish hierarchy now viewed the Roman Catholic church as the state church—in *de jure* and *de facto* terms. Dissidents in the *ojczyzna* were no longer even to be tolerated, that is, until Catherine the Great, Empress of Russia, began using the religious ferment in Poland as a pretext for interfering in Polish affairs.

Hardly devoted to religious toleration, let alone ecumenism, Catherine, so as to make herself appear to her own people as a staunch defender of Orthodoxy, issued a "Declaration on Behalf of the Dissidents" on 4 November 1766. The Empress Catherine also pressed the Polish king, Stanislaus August Poniatowski, her favorite on the throne, to support proposals which would guarantee equal status for the *szlachta* of the Orthodox and Protestant faiths. When such stalwarts as Bishops Soltyk and Zaluski refused to accept Catherine's terms in favor of Catholic-Protestant-Orthodox civil equality and religious freedom, the Empress, under the veil of religious protector, sent Russian troops into Poland; Bishops

Soltyk and Zaluski and their supporters were arrested and deported to Russia. Bishop Adam Krasinski of Kamieniec, under the so-called Confederation of the Bar, attempted to redress the situation, but the Confederation was ultimately defeated by Russian troops.[16]

The significance of the Catholic response to the Dissident question prior to and during the Partitions has to do with the church's commitment to a policy of orthodoxy (with a small o) which would sustain itself well into the period of mass emigration to America. The deep commitment to a national church in Poland would, of course, be transferred into Polish Catholic settlements in the United States where Poles would strenuously argue in favor of national parishes housing one ethnic group as against territorial parishes which admitted numerous ethnic groups.

But there is yet another matter regarding the Polish Catholic church which calls for some elaboration here: the adjustment of Polish Catholicism to the Partitions themselves. As Wandycz has already succinctly stated, the most obvious effects of the Partitions involved the loss of church lands and related church income. Equally significant is the fact that in Prussia and Russia the church was forced to work under the jurisdiction of monarchs of different faiths.[17] Accommodation to the Catholic Maria Teresa of Austria was, to be sure, much easier; but in Prussia, where continued attempts at Prussianization (and later, Germanization) of the Polish church were made, the conduct of church affairs was a most difficult operation, calling for a great deal of skilled diplomacy. After the unification of the German nation under Bismarck, matters went from bad to worse: between 1871 and 1878, the German state attempted to subordinate control of the clergy to itself, and during 1878–1914 the German government actually coerced the Polish church into the work of Germanization of Polish areas.[18] Despite the failure of Bismarck's *kulturkampf*, the Germanization of the Polish hierarchy remained a constant threat to Polish Catholic autonomy. As late as 1892, Kaiser Wilhelm was directly involved in the nomination of Poland's primate, Archbishop Florian Stablewski.[19]

The Polish church suffered even more the agonies associated with governmental policies of Russianization in Congress Poland. Here the Uniates, in particular, were persistently persecuted if they did not join the Russian Orthodox church. By 1870, not a single Polish bishop remained in charge of his diocese, and the Uniate church, for all practical purposes, was destroyed. Moreover, Catholic Dissidents in Congress Poland now felt the lash of the *knout*, and imprisonment and deportation to the Siberian wastelands were commonplace. By comparison, Uniates in Austria-Hungary were given fair treatment, although here the motivation was political as Maria Teresa hoped to win over the Uniates in order to serve as a counterbalance to growing Russian influence and power. On the whole, modern Polish historians generally concede that Polish Catholics in Galicia were better off than in any of the other partitioned areas.[20]

Since the Catholic church in Poland throughout the nineteenth century was subordinated to the interests of these foreign powers, it faced an unenviable dilemma in each of the Polish insurrections—in 1831, in 1846–1848, and again in 1863. Each of these wide-scale revolts, if given the endorsement or full support of the church, could have destroyed whatever gains the church had made through diplomacy and accommodation. The first of Poland's ill-fated insurrections began on 29 November 1830, when a secret association of Polish cadets marched in the streets of Warsaw in open rebellion against the Russian Grand Duke Constantine Pavlovich, brother of Czar Nicholas I. Instead of meeting the resistance with military force, the Grand Duke retreated with his troops, and the insurgents under General Joseph Chłopicki captured the northern part of Warsaw. After a series of negotiations between the Czar and the insurgents broke down, pitched battles erupted, lasting until the summer of 1831, when the Russians drove the insurgents off Polish soil and into Prussia. The insurrection failed mainly because the widely anticipated support of the *chłopi* in the countryside never materialized; and the church, both at the hierarchical and parish levels, largely remained neutral.[21]

The scattered Polish insurgents—remnants of the once-proud aristocracy, disillusioned intellectuals, defeated army officers, and middle-class townspeople who had lost everything—formed the "Great Emigration" of 1831. Finding a temporary and sympathetic home in Paris, the Great Emigration soon broke into two factions: the aristocratic wing, under the leadership of Prince Adam Czartoryski, and the democratic wing, the reins of which were seized by Joachim Lelewel, a noted Polish historian. Czartoryski felt that it was in Poland's best interests to pursue liberation through diplomacy, on the assumption that the foreign powers, Great Britain in particular, would at the proper moment intervene on the side of Poland. Lelewel, on the other hand, considered Czartoryski's position to be delusional, and he continued to view the aristocracy as counterrevolutionary and even guilty of betraying the peasant masses. Rather than relying on foreign intervention, Lelewel, acting as President of the Permanent National Committee, argued for revolution from within, a position which Czartoryski obviously despised. Lelewel also opposed the use of Polish troops as mercenaries in foreign armies. In any event, the aristocratic-democratic debate was to be a decisive factor in forming the outlook of numerous ultranationalistic immigrant organizations in America during Polonia's formative years; and these ultranationalist groups would one day seriously challenge fraternal organizations in Polonia organized by the clergy solely on a religious and social rather than political basis.[22]

Of equal significance, too, was the tremendous outpouring of religiosity emanating from the Parisian debates. Many of the 1831 émigrés—regardless of political ideology, aristocrat or democrat—were at first convinced that their departure from the *ojczyzna* was only temporary, an emigration calculated only to gain time and support for the cause of Polish liberation. But as Czartoryski's efforts brought no positive results and as talks regarding the formation of a Polish

Legion of liberation broke down, a feeling of moody pessimism descended on this "cream of Poland" sitting in Paris hotel rooms. Recurring doubts about the decision to emigrate haunted both wings.

This crisis in the émigré consciousness was addressed by all of Poland's great Romantic poets—Adam Mickiewicz, Sigismund Krasiński, and Julius Słowacki. In his *Books of the Polish Nation and the Polish Pilgrimage* (1832), Adam Mickiewicz preached a new messianic gospel to his fellow refugees in Paris. Mickiewicz resolutely declared that the Polish *naród* (nation) was destined by the Father to suffer the role of His Only Begotten Son; that Poland's salvation was bound up in the torments and martyrdom by crucifixion; and that by this time on the cross Poland would gain expiation for the sins committed by the partitioning powers. The suffering and death of the Polish *naród* would, however, be followed by a resurrection into a new life, and it was this new life which would bring about a regenerated world of a higher moral order. Poland's life after death would be an unmistakable sign of God's Providence in the affairs of nations. The Great Emigration must therefore maintain the faith, Mickiewicz preached, for "two days" had already elapsed in the "tomb" of Partition (referring to the Insurrections of 1794–1795 and 1831). Past defeats, he prophesied, would lead to a time when "wars shall cease in Christendom," when "the third day shall begin . . . and not end." This, then, was Poland's true role in history: it was the will of the Father that Poland be the Christ of Nations.[23]

The dynamic spiritual message imbedded in the Romanticism of Mickiewicz's prose came to influence strongly the literary gospel of Słowacki, who in *Anhelli* fearlessly proclaimed that the hour of national martydom was already at hand. Słowacki's thunder, in turn, alerted all of Poland to the resounding movement and stormy power displayed by Sigismund Krasiński, who was the culmination of the messianic front sweeping over partitioned Poland. Krasiński's beautiful "Dawn" was intended to restore the émigré's faith in the role of divine election in the historical process, and it announced the glad tidings of Poland's coming resurrection from the graveyard of defeat with unmistakable clarity and startling poetic precision:

> . . . and I heard
> A voice that called in the eternal sky:
> As to the world I gave a Son,
> So to it, Poland, thee I give.
> My only Son he was—and shall be
> But in thee my purpose for Him lives,
> Be thou then the Truth, as He is, everywhere.
> Thee I make my daughter!
> When thou didst descend into the grave
> Thou wert, like Him, a part of mankind.

But now, this day of victory
Thy name is: All Humanity.[24]

But the national resurrection prophesied by the Romantics was not in Poland's immediate future. During the Poznan and Cracow riots of 1846 the insurrectionists faced defeat once again, largely because the *chłopi* remained the silent and unshaken monolith. Only at Tarnow were the peasants actively involved, and here, in one of the insurrection's bloodiest battles, the *chłopi* turned instead on the *szlachta* rather than against their Austrian captors. So shaken were the local clergy by this bloodshed that they immediately called for an end to the revolts.[25]

The battle at Tarnow was followed by yet another insurrectionary attempt in January 1863, when Polish soldiers in the Russian army initiated a general revolt in Congress Poland. More Polish blood was spilled, more insurrectionists were exiled to Siberia, and more civilian casualties were recorded than in any of the previous insurrections. But this time the insurrectionists were aided by the clergy, who served as army messengers, as harborers of refugees, and even as gun-runners. The carnage lasted for two years before the Czar's forces managed to brutally smother the last of the rebellion. So repressive and harsh were the measures adopted by the Czar in the wake of the insurrection that Poland would struggle no more in this saddest century.[26]

A new movement, known as "Warsaw Positivism," now came into prominence, filling the void left by the Romantics. While not absolving the partitioners of responsibility for Poland's loss of freedom, Positivists instead concentrated on repairing Poland's internal economic and cultural weaknesses. A more realistic strategy known as "triple loyalty" was invoked. Positivists such as the famed Polish novelist Henryk Sienkiewicz urged their partitioned countrymen to accommodate themselves to the political realities dictated by the foreign powers. Emphasis was now placed on *working* to secure the economic benefits enjoyed by the more technologically advanced European nations to the west of Poland. Universal education, the development of Polish industry and commerce, and the introduction into Polish society of the latest scientific and technological skills was now thought to be of greater long-range advantage to Poland than military insurgency. Only by bringing the separate parts of Poland into step with late nineteenth-century economic progress could the Poles be reunited once again.[27]

An entire generation of Poles in the 1863–1914 period was raised on the more secular values of the Organic Movement and on the *za chlebem* ("for bread only") instincts preached by the Positivists prior to the First World War. Where the gospel of the Romantics did much to shape the religious outlook of the Polish immigrants in America and elsewhere, the practical and more expedient lessons taught by the Positivists shared the stage in forming the economic outlook and values brought over by the immigrants. These dual legacies inherited by the Polish immigrant in the United States foreshadowed several basic and conflicting tensions of a structural nature between the Polish immigrant church and immigrant society. This intensive struggle over spiritual and temporal values and goals would commence shortly after the Polish immigrant's arrival in numerous "urban villages" throughout the United States. The largest and most prominent of these transplanted villages was *Stanisławowo*—the "Village of St. Stanislaus Kostka Parish"—located on the near northwest side of Chicago.

Nowy Świat

The city of Chicago by 1850 was already serving notice to its urban competitors in the Great Lakes region that it was determined to become the immigrant and industrial metropolis of the Midwest. According to the Seventh Census of the United States, Chicago had a population of 29,963, a seven-fold increase over the previous decennial census; of this total, 15,682 inhabitants (precisely 52.3 percent of the overall population) were foreign-born. The message for the city fathers was clear: Chicago already was a "foreign" city. And in many respects it always would be. In its bustling adolescent years Chicago was already revealing an insatiable appetite for the skills of foreign-born workers who were desperately needed to maintain the boom in the booster city on the prairie. When thousands upon thousands of unskilled workers were needed to sustain its industrial and commercial momentum, Chicago unhesitatingly devoured more than its fair share of unsuspecting foreign-born. Thus, a hundred years hence, Chicago came to house some of the largest immigrant concentrations in all of North America: for the Poles, Chicago became a "second Warsaw"; for Bohemians, another "Pilsen"; for Lithuanians, a new Wilno; for Serbs and Croatians, a haven from which to decide Old World political strategies; for the Scandinavians, an attraction even greater than Minneapolis-St. Paul. In addition, by the mid-twentieth century, Chicago would also absorb the second highest concentrations of Germans, Slovaks, Greeks, and Jews, as well as the third largest Italian settlement in the United States. When the great European migration to America slowed in the post–World War I period, a rapid influx of Blacks to the city's south side formed a massive Black Belt which competed with the white immigrant settlements for jobs, housing, and good schools. When, after three and even four generations, the immigrant settlements moved to the outer edges of the city and into the suburbs, their places were taken by Mexican and Puerto Rican migrants, who in the post–World War II period flooded the near northwest and near southwest sides, leading to the creation of *barrio* environments closely resembling those of South Los Angeles and Spanish Harlem.[28]

Why were so many immigrants drawn to Chicago? The primary reason was the city's advantageous geographic location. With the opening of the Erie Canal in 1825 and the inauguration of the Illinois and Michigan Canal in 1848, Chicago inadvertently became the "natural" center of the Eastern seaboard-Great Lakes-Mississippi River transportation and trade network. Furthermore, Chicago's central position was made even more commanding with the completion of the Michigan Central and Southern Michigan railroads, which connected the city to more highly developed eastern lines. As heir to this enormous canal-railroad windfall, Chicago, by the mid-nineteenth century, had already become the main point of departure for railroad expansions westward. Thus, in 1850, an immigrant traveller could complete the New York to Chicago journey in only five days for as little as five dollars. Overland travel by stage was also far less taxing via the newly built Chicago Road, connecting Chicago and Detroit, or via the historic Vincennes Trace, tying the burgeoning grain mills in Chicago to the rich farming country of the Wabash River basin of north central Indiana. On the western perimeter of the city, the Chicago Northwestern, Galena and Chicago, Rock Island, and Illinois Central railroads fanned out in three directions—north, west and south—to connect Chicago's emerging financial and commercial interests to the rich grain belts and cattle trade of the prairie grasslands. Import-export figures by mid-century certainly supported claims made by the city's boosters who heralded Chicago as the "Emporium of the West." When the last of the Fox and Sauk tribes made their final trek west of the Mississippi in the year 1836, Chicago's village-like economy sustained itself on imports alone: for every dollar exported, 325 dollars in goods was imported. But in the span of a single decade, Chicago was to prove to competing river cities in the nation's heartland, namely, Cincinnati and St. Louis, that it was destined to make the transition from village to metropolitan economy. By 1848, imports to the city were reported at $8,338,939, but exports leaped to the lofty sum of $10,709,333.[29]

This favorable trade ratio laid the foundation for Chicago's remarkable business and commercial growth. The *Norris Directory of Chicago* in 1846 listed a wide range of economic activity: the city could boast of its 64 wholesale and retail grocery stores; 23 hotels and taverns; 15 lumber yards; 15 insurance agencies; 12 furniture factories; 8 printing houses; 8 soap, oil, and candle factories; 7 drug stores; 6 auction commission firms; 4 foundaries; 3 breweries; and 2 ship-building concerns. Dozens of smaller businesses maintained by bakers, shoemakers, coopers, wagonmakers, blacksmiths, and shopkeepers coexisted with or supported the larger firms. The legal and financial services required by the boom economy were handled by a battery of 93 lawyers and 7 bankers, and the commercial advertising for Chicago's diverse economic interests in turn led to the foundation of 10 newspapers—7 dailies and 3 weeklies.[30]

This professional and commercial lifeblood stimulated even further the import of more capital investment, which hastened the process of highly centralized corporate growth. Chicago's newly developed economic muscle of 1850 made a deep impression on an assortment of government officials, business experts and investers, and foreign travellers, most of whom predicted long before Sandburg that

Chicago would gain preeminence in rails, grain, meatpacking, lumber, iron, and steel. This corporate diversity—a hallmark in Chicago's history—translated into thousands of jobs, many of which could be handled by unskilled and hungry *za chlebem* immigrants. Shrewd entrepreneurs along the lines of Cyrus Hall Mc-Cormick, Philip Armour, and Gustavus Swift would build their fortunes on cheap labor, and, consequently, each captain of industry invariably favored the relaxation of restrictions on the importation of foreign labor over the next two generations. In turn, the newly hired immigrant workers, finding abundant openings in the foundaries, stockyards, grain elevators, and steel mills, relayed the exciting news of "splendid opportunities" in Chicago to their kinfolk in the *ojczyzna* and other Old World villages. Unfortunately, the most recently arrived immigrants usually became the unwitting recruiters of competing cheap labor for their industrial masters, most of whom unscrupulously reduced wages whenever labor came at such bargain prices.[31]

On the political front, the Democratic Party by the mid-nineteenth century had emerged as the dominant political force in the city. Victorious over Whig opponents in eleven of the first fifteen mayoralty races and maintaining a clear majority in the city council throughout, Democrats easily established a political monopoly. The steady stream of victories was due, of course, to the party's popularity in foreign-born areas of the city; consequently, native-born Whigs were already accusing the Democrats of moving toward political "bossism" and "colonization" of the city's Irish wards in particular. According to dispirited Whigs, the newly formed Democratic-Irish alliance even conspired to control city elections, a charge that would become rather commonplace in Chicago politics.[32]

The transition from pioneer settlement to municipality forced Chicago's religious bodies to respond accordingly. The building of new churches and synagogues, or the buying and remodeling of older ones, was a major concern of every religious community. By 1850, twenty-seven houses of worship dominated the skyline of Chicago: twenty-two Protestant, four Catholic, and one Jewish. By the eve of the great Chicago fire, twenty years later, the number of church buildings had increased seven-fold to a total of 190. Because of Chicago's native-born American base, the Protestant denominations in pioneer Chicago were predominant: at mid-century, the Methodist Episcopal church formed the largest denomination with 688 members; it was followed by the New School Presbyterians with 642 believers; the Lutherans with 480 communicants; the Baptists with 452 members; and the Protestant Episcopal church with an enrollment of 380.[33] But as immigration to Chicago increased, the Jewish and Catholic groups made steady gains. On 3 October 1846 German Jews on the near west side founded the *Kehilath Anshe Mayriv* (Congregation of the People of the West) at 122 Lake Street, adjacent to the original downtown area of Chicago. It was the first Jewish settlement recorded in the city. Shortly thereafter a group of Jewish immigrants from the Poznan area of Prussian Poland founded another synagogue, the *Kehilath B'nai Sholom* (Congregation of the Children of Peace). Both these synagogues cooperated in the formation of the Hebrew Benevolent Society, a major social welfare force in the early life of Chicago's Jewish community, which grew to approximately 1,500 members on the eve of the American Civil War.[34]

The Catholic Church in Chicago, which would one day become the largest archdiocese in the United States and one of the largest in the world, owed its origins to a small, tightly-knit, French immigrant community that had settled along the Chicago River even before the Indian had vanished. Leadership here was exercised by the proprietor of the Sauganash Hotel, Mark Beaubien, and his brother, Jean Baptiste. Both were instrumental in founding the first Catholic parish in Chicago, St. Mary's, built on the corner of what are today State and Lake streets shortly after the incorporation of the city. The Beaubiens, on behalf "of almost one hundred Catholics" in the community, petitioned for the parish church to Bishop Rosati of St. Louis, whose authority at the time extended over the entire state of Illinois. Rosati ruled in favor of the Beaubien petition, and St. Mary's, under the pastoral care of the Reverend John St. Cyr, developed into an organizational base for all incoming Catholics in the late 1830s and early 1840s. When the Catholic population in Chicago expanded beyond the administrative capacities of faraway St. Louis, permission was granted by the Fifth Plenary Council of Baltimore for the erection of a diocesan see in Chicago during May 1843, an action which was formally approved by Pope Gregory XVI in his brief dated 30 September 1843.[35]

Responsible for the needs of approximately 50,000 Catholics in the state of Illinois, the Right Reverend William J. Quarter, first bishop of Chicago (1844–1848), embarked on an energetic building program primarily designed to handle the influx of Irish and German Catholics. In the center of the city, on Madison and Wabash streets, Quarter oversaw construction of St. Mary's Cathedral, completed in October 1845. Three new parish churches followed, one for each section of the city: St. Michael's, completed in 1846, for the west side Irish community; and St. Joseph's and St. Peter's, on the north and south sides respectively, for German immigrants. With the completion of this initial phase of his building program, Bishop Quarter had, in effect, laid the cornerstone for a diocesan policy which would forever remain unchanged: first and foremost, a Catholic "presence" was established in all parts of Chicago; next, and of equal importance, Catholic parishes were allowed to retain a marked ethnic quality which would persist as long as the host ethnic group remained in residence in a particular area of the city, and, in some unique instances, long after the original group had moved on. In such a fashion, certainly inadvertently, Quarter sanctioned the foundation of national parishes within a territorial parish framework—a practice which later "New Immigration" groups, especially the Poles, would take most seriously.

Bishop Quarter also set into motion activity which would one day culminate in another hallmark of Chicago Catholicism, parochial school education. A major seminary, St. Mary of the Lake, was established to alleviate the chronic shortage of priests in the diocese as well as to render numerous higher education courses. He also invited the Mercy Sisters from Pittsburgh to upgrade the quality of education for women in the diocese. The Mercy Sisters accepted Quarter's call and proceeded to establish St. Xavier's Academy, the first and oldest institution of higher education for women in the Northern Illinois area.[36]

Bishop Quarter died on 10 April 1848 after a brief illness, exhausted by the self-imposed rigors of his office. He was succeeded by the Right Reverend James Van de Velde, who continued to pursue vigorously the "brick and mortar" program initiated by his predecessor. In addition to supervising the construction of six more parish churches in the diocese—three within and three outside the city limits—Bishop Van de Velde looked to the development of diocesan parochial schools at the elementary and secondary levels. In 1848, the Free Schools of St. Joseph's (for boys) and St. Mary's (for girls) opened with enrollments of 40 and 140 respectively. Additional parochial schools at Holy Name and St. James followed.

The rapid parochial school development at all levels undertaken in the Van de Velde administration encouraged local Catholics to request public funding for their system, some indication that aspirations were outstripping the financial base of the diocese. The issue, almost overnight, galvanized native-born Protestant militants. Cries of "popery" became somewhat commonplace, and rumors about Catholic ignorance, superstition, and slavery circulated freely in the Know-Nothing climate of the day. Nativists also vigorously opposed the expenditure of public monies for the care of paupers, a majority of whom happened to be Irish Catholics, at the County Poor House. But diocesan investments in other social welfare programs such as the Free Asylum Orphanage on South Wabash Street did much to quiet many of the harsher nativist critics. And when Mercy Hospital effected an open-door policy in the aftermath of the 1848 cholera epidemic, nativism was dealt a sound defeat.[37] In any event, despite occasional skirmishes between Catholics and Nativists over lesser issues, none of which ever gained the notoriety of the Philadelphia riots and convent burnings, the Roman Catholic diocese of Chicago continued to prosper. By 1870, the Bishop of Chicago's jurisdiction extended to some 40,000 Catholics, 26 parishes, 50 parochial schools, and 142 priests. Such, in general, was the state of Catholicism in Chicago prior to the massive New Immigration years which would make this the most powerful diocese in America.[38]

There was no indication whatsoever in ante-bellum Chicago that the Polish community in the span of two generations would become not only the largest Catholic immigrant group but also the largest white ethnic group in the city. Unlike the unusually stormy period between 1870 and 1920 when Poles engaged in bitter intragroup conflict and the tense insurrectionary years in the *ojczyzna*, the period between 1837, when the first Pole is believed to have come to Chicago, and 1867, when the first Polish Catholic parish was founded, was inordinately calm. Census figures, despite their unreliability caused by Poles being counted as Germans, Austrians, or Russians, account for only 495 Poles in 1850; and the disproportionate male-to-female ratio (423:72) explains why no permanent Polish colony had been founded until then. In any event, even if one disputes the low census counts of Poles, as indeed many Polish scholars have, the revised estimates seldom vary significantly from the official tabulations made by the Treasury Department—at least for the ante-bellum period. The first significant Polish emigration, the famed Galveston Emigration, took place during 1851–1855 and led to the formation of the first permanent Polish settlement in the United States, at Panna Marya ("Village of Our Lady"), Texas, in 1854. The male-to-female ratio was more favorable for colonization than in the past—551 males and 272 females. But as tensions leading to the Insurrection of 1863 increased in the *ojczyzna* and as the complex set of questions surrounding states' rights and slavery went unresolved in the United States, Polish emigration slowed considerably until after the cessation of warfare in both the *ojczyzna* and *Nowy Świat*. The 1860 Census accounted for 7,298 Poles in the states and territories, 309 of whom settled in Illinois and 109 of whom resided in Chicago.[39]

Secondary accounts generally agree that Anthony Smarzewski-Schermann was the founder of Chicago Polonia (*Polonia* is a term that can either refer to a specific local Polish settlement or to the entire Polish-American community at-large, apart from numerous religious and sociological distinctions which will be discussed later). Born in Węgrowice in the Grand Duchy of Posen, Smarzewski-Schermann is believed to have emigrated to the United States in 1850 with his wife, Frederica, and their three children, Loisa, Dora, and Stanislaus. By occupation, according to the manuscript schedules of the 1860 Federal Census, he was a carpenter. But Smarzewski-Schermann was not the first Polish settler in Chicago. Preceding him was Captain John Napieralski, a veteran of the battle of Cross Mountain in the 1831 Insurrection, who is generally believed to be the first Pole to set foot in the city. Another early settler was Major Louis Chłopicki, nephew of the same General Joseph Chłopicki who had led the 1831 Insurrection. Other Poles preceding Smarzewski-Schermann included a certain A. Panakaske (Panakaski), who resided in the Second Ward in the 1830s, and J. Zoliski, who lived in the Sixth Ward; both were recorded as having cast ballots for William B. Ogden in the 1837 mayoralty race in Chicago. Other contemporaries of Smarzewski-Schermann were two Polish physicians, a Dr. Jacob Cert and a Dr. Edward Hartwich (Hartwitch), who immigrated to Chicago in 1852 and 1856, respectively. Joining these early settlers was Edward Wilkoszewski, who came to Chicago in 1861 and subsequently opened what was to become a successful picture frame factory, one which provided employment for hundreds of Poles in the

1860s and 1870s. Since no written evidence pertaining to Polonia's pioneers in Chicago has survived, one can only speculate about what motivated them to immigrate here. Henryk Sienkiewicz, the famed Polish novelist who was to visit Chicago Polonia in 1876, offers some clues in his novel *Za Chlebem* which indicate that Polonia's first two generations were mainly economically motivated. Smarzewski-Schermann appears to fit Sienkiewicz's description. One of his first ventures was to quit carpentry and open a grocery store on Noble and Bradley streets, where he sold to other Polish families moving into the near northwest side of Chicago. Moreover, in order to increase his business with the German immigrant community nearby, Smarzewski-Schermann changed his name to Schermann (Sherman), an indication that this Father of Chicago Polonia was no die-hard political nationalist.[40]

Schermann's property and surrounding environment must have reminded him of many Polish farming communities. From the still undeveloped and sparsely settled prairie on the outskirts of ante-bellum Chicago, he could see nothing but grassland stretching westward to the horizon. East of his land stood a thickly wooded area guarding both banks of the nearby North Branch of the Chicago River which swung noose-like around Goose Island. The virgin land between Schermann's settlement and the river was populated at the time only by chickens and cattle belonging to neighboring farms; fifty years later this same land would support the highest population density in the city—more than 450 Polish immigrants on each acre of land, packed into tenement houses. But in the 1850s Schermann's rural outpost was a picture of serenity. His only outlet to the Chicago downtown was Plank Road, a clumsily built highway actually constructed from wooden planks—a far cry from the bustling commercial thoroughfare later called Milwaukee Avenue along which Polish merchants in the 1920s built their own "Polish Downtown." Schermann's closest neighbors were other Polish settlers, perhaps landless tenant farmers, numbering approximately thirty families during the American Civil War.[41]

Available fragments of evidence indicate that Schermann's Polonia in its formative years suffered a severe case of Old World nostalgia, a phenomenon commonly associated with newly arrived immigrant groups. In Chicago Polonia, as in almost every other Polish settlement in the United States in the late nineteenth century, this nostalgia was most acutely expressed in the common desire to secure a Polish Catholic parish ministered to by a Polish-speaking priest. Many pioneer settlers worried greatly that their religious faith would be lost without the elementary social and cultural Catholicism of the *ojczyzna*. Reverend Joseph Dąbrowski, a prominent Polish clergyman in Wisconsin, remarked in a letter dated 16 March 1870 that

> Our Polish people are living without the Mass, confession, Sunday
> sermons, and adequate education. Some have settled in the large

cities and, because of the lack of priests and the preaching of the Word of God, do not attend church services. Without any religious formation, they will certainly be lost to the Church.[42]

Dąbrowski's sentiments were widely shared, not only by Polish but also by later German immigrants in America, who, under the leadership of Peter Cahensly, would use the "loss of immigrant faith" argument to its fullest in order to convince the Vatican that German priests be nominated to bishoprics in German-speaking areas. So there was nothing really unusual in Polonia's eagerness to fulfill her ancient socioreligious life-wishes. In hundreds of Old World villages, towering church steeples, well-tended crossroad shrines, colorful outdoor processions, and an emotionally moving liturgy was part of the normal landscape and rhythm of life. Both the brilliant literary tetralogy of Reymont in *The Peasants* and the highly original sociological investigations conducted by Thomas and Znaniecki in *The Polish Peasant in Europe and America* call attention, time and time again, to the close working relationship between the Polish church and society and between the priest and the peasant. These relationships had symbolized for centuries the basic unity between *castellum* (castle) and *kościoł* (church), words which the Polish language used interchangeably to show the indivisibility of the things that were God's and the things God gave to man. Civil holidays and religious feast-days were so interwoven into Polish society in the *ojczyzna* that unsuspecting visitors to Poland seldom were able to differentiate between the socioreligious, cultural, and civil spheres.

The accumulated effect of these historical factors helps explain why the lack of a Polish parish and priest bordered on the traumatic for Schermann's settlement. Later exchanges of letters by the Resurrectionist Fathers in Chicago indicate that many of the Polish settlers had not received the Sacrament of Penance ("Reconciliation" in post-Vatican II terminology) since their arrival in Chicago. Fears of living in mortal sin may have plagued the consciences of at least some scrupulous adults who had been unable to fulfill such canonical obligations as the Easter Duty. And even though Poles were welcomed at nearby parishes made up of culturally similar nationality groups—such as the Bohemian parish of St. Wenceslaus or the mixed nationality parish of St. Boniface—they were still in need of Polish-speaking confessors, a situation which was not remedied in any consistent way until the Jesuits sent the Polish-speaking Reverend Szulak to Chicago in the early 1860s.

In addition to the practical problem of sacramental communication—i.e., confessing to a priest who did not understand Polish—Poles attending the parishes of St. Wenceslaus or St. Boniface were not able to participate in the liturgy when non-Polish languages were used. This inability to participate no doubt precluded the emotional attachment which has always been a significant feature of the Polish Catholic liturgy—witness the somber power of *Gorzkie Żale* ("Bitter Lamentations") Lenten services, the shattering impact of the *Witaj Królowo* ("Hail, Queen of Heaven") funeral march, or the stunning beauty of *Serdeczna Matko* ("Dearest Mother") often sung during Marian May devotions. These are but a few examples from the vast Polish liturgy which demonstrate the indissoluble marriage of language and religious devotion in the nineteenth century and beyond.[43]

Interethnic parish cooperation, though in evidence, also was hampered or restricted at times due to tensions and hostilities of a social nature outside the immediate parish area. Uncomplimentary attitudes toward and stereotypes of the Polish working class were often transferred into parish affairs. This was especially true in later years (the mid 1880s in particular, again in 1905, and once again in the 1917–1919 period preceding the great Chicago race riot of July 1919) when the Poles, Bohemians, and Lithuanians engaged in heady competition with Irish and Blacks for jobs in the stockyards.[44]

Other Old World ways reinforced Chicago Polonia's, and later, American Polonia's search for single nationality parishes administered by native priests. Significant among these customs was the rather lofty status accorded the clergy by the Polish laity. In Poland, as in many Old World countries, a young man ordained a priest usually gained higher social standing for his immediate family. Occasionally, even among some of the wealthier landowning *szlachta*, one son would forgo personal ambitions in order to pursue the priesthood and maintain family honor.[45] These more favorable attitudes toward the clergy, generally speaking, protected Poles from some of the harsher aspects of anticlericalism which would later spread through Czech and Italian settlements in Chicago; although, as we shall later see, the Poles were hardly immune to every aspect of anticlericalism. Nevertheless, the traditional respect by the laity for the clergy appears to have been strengthened by the absence of priests in Schermann's Polonia, and indeed this factor may have contributed to later Polish generosity in contributing to the financial support of their churches. A contemporary's description of the emerging Chicago Polonia captures this feeling appropriately:

> Wherever there is a priest or church, wherever a parish is being created, there Polish life grows vigorously and numbers multiply, for people come willingly from all walks of life, feeling better among their own kind, feeling more secure under the protective wings of the parish with their own pastor, who in this foreign land is not only a representative of his brothers before the altar of God, but also leads them in all worldly matters. . . . The priest is in every sense of the word a social and national worker.[46]

But despite these noble sentiments neither Schermann nor any of his compatriots seemed capable of transforming such dreams into reality. Before a truly national parish could be established, diocesan approval would have to be obtained, a task that assumed formidable dimensions as the episcopal head, Bishop

James Duggan, was already on the verge of a mental breakdown. Next, funding for a parish church would have to be arranged and formally approved by the diocese, a process that would necessarily entail the services of non-Polish bankers whom the Poles were known to distrust (Polish religious orders in Chicago later started their own banks). Finally, the problem of procuring a Polish priest would have to be solved immediately. In any event, whether by accident or design—the evidence is not at all clear on this point—Chicago Polonia found a leader whose talents would mesh well with those of Schermann.[47]

He was Peter Kiolbassa, a handsome twenty-seven-year-old Union army officer who in the winter months of 1863–1864 came to Chicago Polonia to spend his furlough. Shortly after his arrival, Kiolbassa involved himself in the community's attempt to establish a national parish. With his colorful and varied background, Kiolbassa was cordially received by the settlers, on whom he made a positive first impression. Born in 1837 in Swib, a small Silesian town in Prussian Poland, Kiolbassa at age eighteen took part in the Galveston emigration, arriving in Texas with his parents and approximately one hundred other Polish families in the year 1855. Moving northward into central Texas with this *za chlebem* migration, Kiolbassa assisted in the establishment of the Panna Marya settlement—a small church, an even more modest schoolhouse, and several hastily constructed huts. Kiolbassa, an experienced horseman, found employment as a cowboy at a nearby ranch, but soon tired of this and moved to San Antonio where he got a job as a waiter, and enrolled at a German-American business college. In 1862 he returned to Panna Marya as an elementary school teacher and part-time organist at the village church. When the Civil War spread to the Southwest, Kiolbassa joined the Texas cavalry, was captured by Union forces shortly thereafter, and was taken to Illinois. Here the plucky Kiolbassa enlisted in the Sixteenth Illinois Volunteers and made First Sergeant of Company B. After passing an examination given by the Federal Board of Examiners, Kiolbassa was promoted to captain of Company E, Sixth U.S. Colored Cavalry.[48]

During his Chicago furlough, Kiolbassa contacted his close friend, the Reverend Leopold Moczygemba, who was pastor at Panna Marya, and bluntly suggested that the priest quit his Texas mission and come to Chicago instead. Accepting Kiolbassa's invitation, but only on a temporary basis, Moczygemba arrived in Chicago during the Easter season of 1864. A chronicler noted that "the Polish community received Father Leopold with vivid joy and in elevated spirits for the stay of this pastor in Chicago revived the desire for a stable and permanent organization."[49] The long sought after "permanent organization" referred to by the chronicler was the Society of Saint Stanislaus Kostka, formed at a community-wide meeting in the home of Smarzewski-Schermann. Named after Poland's youthful patron saint, the Society devoted itself to drawing up plans for what was to become the first Polish Catholic parish in Chicago, St. Stanislaus Kostka's, affectionately known to these Polish pioneers as *Stanisławowo*, that is, the village of St. Stanislaus. Officers elected to the Society were Smarzewski-Schermann, president; Peter Kiolbassa, vice-president; Joseph Niemczewski, secretary; and two committee members, John Arkuszewski and Andrew Kurr.[50]

Despite the spirited beginning of the Society, little was accomplished in the first three years. Kiolbassa had been called back to the front, and Smarzewski-Schermann, now saddled with the responsibilities of a large family, concerned himself mainly with increasing the family income. He became an agent for a local immigration agency which eventually became a base for transporting thousands of Polish immigrants to *Stanisławowo*. But despite this inauspicious beginning, the St. Stanislaus Society was described by the historian Kruszka as "omne vivens ex ovo," the "egg giving life" to all future parishes and religious organizations in Chicago Polonia. By the end of World War I, thirty-five Polish Roman Catholic parishes had been established in the Chicago archdiocese; by the end of World War II there were fifty-seven. Each retained features of the original Stanislawian model. But before all this would come to pass, Chicago Polonia was to be rocked by a series of violent internal divisions and disputes, the scars of which are still visible in our times.[51]

Map One: Partitioned Poland

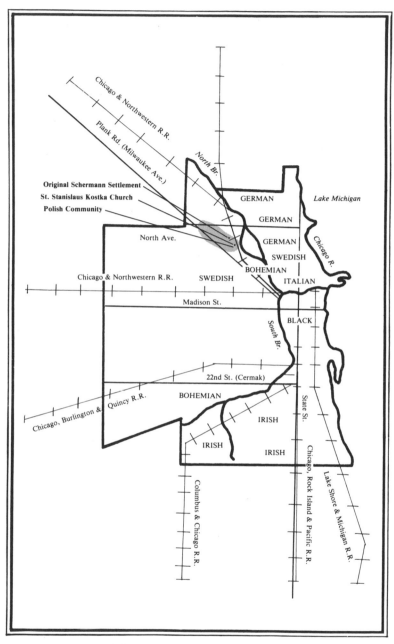

Map Two: Chicago Polonia in 1870

2

Intragroup Conflict:
Polish Catholics and Catholic Poles

The work in the parish of St. Stanislaus was very tiring . . . as it was necessary to struggle with a complex of social elements, parties absorbed in politics, headed mostly by men who were not worth much and who belonged to various American secret societies—some say even to Masonic lodges. To these pseudo-progressives the calm and noiseless domination of the Catholic Church and religious practices were undesirable.

The Golden Jubilee Album of
St. Stanislaus Kostka Parish

Historical testimony supplies abundant evidence of the waxing and waning cycle of conflict between nativistic "insiders" in American society, whoever and wherever they might be, and the millions of immigrant "outsiders" huddled in tightly construced enclaves in American cities during the period stretching from the end of the American Civil War to the end of World War II. In a succession of profoundly moving accounts, an entire generation of noted immigration historians, each of pre–New Ethnicity vintage, has consistently elected to tell the story of assimilation by emphasizing the power position of the insider and his ruthless manipulation of the helpless outsider. Ray Billington, for example, in his incisive examination of the origins of nativism,[1] has argued that the immigrant Catholic during the Jacksonian period was the chief target of ridicule, physical abuse, and unrestrained mob terror during the first of several Protestant Crusades bent on cleansing the Anglo-Saxon soul of any Catholic influence. Other students of the period and the movement have demonstrated conclusively that this era of bigotry perpetuated religious hatred for more than a century, all the while destroying sustained and meaningful religious and spiritual dialogue among ecumenical-minded Protestants, Catholics, and Jews. Nativism then, if one accepts the Billington portrayal, can be said to have contributed to one of America's widest and deepest chasms, one which cuts across the entire political, economic, and social landscape of American history. Not until the 1960s would men of good will, representing several denominations in American religious life, even attempt to cross the chasm of bigotry over newly constructed ecumenical bridges.

The historical record, largely due to Oscar Handlin's masterful touch, also incorporates the experience of "uprootedness" in immigrant life. No one before or after Handlin has so poignantly described the shock and aftershock of immigration. *The Uprooted* has cast a long shadow from which few historians escape. For who can now dismiss the tearful farewells endured by family members who were to separate themselves over an entire lifetime; or the cruel and sadistic exploitation of peasant migrants passing through foreign lands on their way to port cities of departure—witness the thousands of Poles who made their way to Hamburg in 1870–1914; or, all too frequently, the journeys made by inexperienced and unseasoned migrants who had never been outside a peasant village before, and who did not know how to light the way when the horizon suddenly darkened? And after Handlin, how can one ignore the plight of unsuspecting victims who faced the gauntlet of a long, arduous ocean voyage which sapped the spirits and dreams of even the most ardent of visionaries: where overcrowded quarters aboard ship made no allowances whatsoever for family privacy; where fever-wracked children cried endlessly to parents who could do no more than watch and pray; where grandparents were found dead in mid-passage; where life's savings disappeared in a matter of weeks into the pockets of the many con artists who knew when to gain the advantage? To the uprooted, such were daily and common occurrences. And when arriving at points of destination, what then? How was one supposed to prepare for the inevitable urban shock meted out to Jews on the Lower East Side of New York, to Sicilians in the "Little Italy" of Chicago's North Side, or to transplanted Polish coal miners now wallowing in the depths of Scranton's mines rather than Silesian ones? And how were "inferior" ethnic cultures supposed to defend against the savage "culture struggles" and attacks mounted by uncompromising nativists in their fight-to-the-death stands waged in the name of holy Americanization—once in the 1850s, again in the 1880s, and still again in the 1920s? As John Higham has vividly reminded all students of the subject, millions of immigrants were doomed, even before their arrival, to becoming permanent "strangers in the land."[2]

Because of these many solid and now well-absorbed historical studies, it is not necessary to elaborate further on the numerous burdens placed on the shoulders of immigrants by hostile insiders. What instead concerns us here is the wide variety of internal pressures *within* an immigrant subsociety *that were self-imposed*. More often than not, bitterly fought intragroup contests were far more revealing of the true nature of immigrant life in cities than were some of the more popularly known nativist-versus-immigrant confrontations. Specifically, we will concentrate in this chapter on the origins of such relatively unknown insider-versus-insider struggles as those waged between the *Gmina Polska* and the St.

Stanislaus Society in Chicago's Polish community in the 1865–1880 period. We shall then examine the repercussions of this conflict and see how the protagonists wrestled with questions and policies which were destined to have a lasting impact on the immigrant American mind.

Intraethnic conflict was, to be sure, by no means limited to the Polish group in America. It crossed all ethnic, religious, and racial boundaries and was a predominant factor in shaping the collective histories of various minority groups in American life. One does not have to probe very long, or very deeply, to uncover intragroup conflicts strikingly comparable to those in Chicago Polonia, although disentangling the complex sequences of cause and effect in each case can be a most time-consuming process. For the serious student and general reader alike, it is significant to recall that the forces of nationalism and romanticism, which added fuel to each intraethnic conflagration, were in the ascendency precisely when the great European emigration was taking place. Given this coincidence, it was not at all surprising to observe immigrant subsocieties and subcultures engaging in highly idealized and abstract versions of mother-country nationalism. And since the immigrant subsocieties in America were no longer intimately involved in the daily affairs of the homeland, it was inevitable that these "second-hand" romantic experiences in New World urban ghettoes would spawn philosophies and outlooks traversing a wide ideological spectrum. Accordingly, intra-ethnic group strife in America would not only center on the basic issue of allegiance to the homeland, but also on the degree of that allegiance. In Polish terms, it was not only a matter of proving one's allegiance to the cause of Partitioned Poland but also of clearly demonstrating to one's neighbors just how Polish *and* how Catholic one was. Applying this premise to the Polish situation in Chicago during the late nineteenth century, one can conclude that the Poles maintained their own "melting pot." Each Polish immigrant coming to Chicago was assimilated into the urban subsociety not on the basis of any identity crisis involving Americanization (that would only come about after World War I) but on the basis of determining that one was a Catholic Pole or a Polish Catholic. The degree of one's emphasis on God or Country—to paraphrase the dynamic pastor of St. Stanislaus Kostka, Vincent Barzynski—was what marked one's standing in the community. There was little question that one had to choose a side immediately upon arrival. One either had to become a "clerical" or a "national." That was the choice, and the crisis.

But this elemental crisis was by no means limited to Polonia. Other nationality groups suffered similar identity crises. Irish-American society, for example, was a widely diversified fraternal network of political, economic, and religious differences. Such organizations as the Irish Catholic Benevolent Association or the American-Irish Aid Society were largely devoted to social and cultural pursuits, whereas the Fenian Brotherhood and the Clan-na-Gael, which comprised some of the most militant radicals in all of immigrant America, remained fanatically de-

voted to the cause of Irish independence. And there is no question that the Fenians
and the Clan were far more prone to violence than their Polish counterparts, the
Gmina Polska. By the 1860s, this Irish brand of radicalism spread to the Pennsylvania anthracite region, where the Molly McGuires gained further notoriety
long before Polish miners from Silesia engaged in radical labor activity in that
area at the turn of the century. Eventually the Irish were able to bridge ideological
differences between their social/cultural benevolent associations and the radical-
political groups. Such a bridge was erected by the Ancient Order of Hibernians
(A.O.H.), an organization whose origins were cloaked in semisecrecy so as to
strengthen Irish militancy in mining areas. In all probability the A.O.H. and the
Molly McGuires offered their followers joint membership. Ties between the two
organizations remained extremely close during and immediately after the Civil
War. But as Irish radicalism waned at the close of the nineteenth century the
A.O.H. gradually shifted its emphasis to charity work and cultural pursuits more
suited to the interests of the "lace curtain Irish," who were in the process of
overshadowing the "shanty Irish" in the streets of Boston, New York, Philadelphia, and Chicago.[3]

The Greek-American experience, particularly in Chicago, offers other paral-
lels of a political nature. The historian of Greek immigration, Theodore Saloutos,
delineates at least two sharply defined intragroup disputes within Greek-American
society. Newly arrived Greeks in Chicago and elsewhere were forced to choose
between Venizelism (an Anglo-French-Greek alliance in World War I) and Roy-
alism (calling for wartime neutrality). After the war, new internal divisions
evolved between the American Hellenic Educational Progressive Association
(AHEPA) and the Greek American Progressive Association (GAPA); throughout
the 1920s AHEPA strongly emphasized the rapid Americanization of Greeks,
while GAPA stressed the persistence of Greekness in American society. But both
groups encouraged Greek immigrants to become permanent citizens of the United
States, a move surely prompted by the prevailing currents of nativist "tribalism"
sweeping across the land in the twenties.[4]

Old World regionalism and regional differences also accounted for intraethnic
disputes within an ethnic subsociety. Robert Foerster, in his classic study of
Northern and Southern Italian immigration, tells us that Northern Italian immigrants coming from the provinces of Venetia, Lombardy, and the Piedmont were
known to flaunt their urban cosmopolitanism at every opportunity, in sharp contrast to the alleged cultural backwardness of the *paisano* coming from Calabria,
Basilicata, and Sicily. Italians from Lombardy took pride in their "municipal history in which rural classes have never had a place" and where attitudes toward the
paisano reeked with "condescension and disesteem."[5] With such Old World regionalism brought to the forefront of the immigrant mind in daily life, it was not
at all surprising to witness the formation of the *Unione Siciliana* in Chicago, a
group which made regionalism a basis for social organization. Many Italian so-

cieties in the city named their organizations after towns, or patron saints of those towns, to which their ancestry could be traced: for example, the *Societa S. di Nicosia*, the *S. Cristtofero di Ricigliano*, the *Santo Stefano di Castiglione*, and the *San Vito di Rapone*.[6]

Geographical and cultural differences were also prominent in dividing German and Russian Jewry on New York's Lower East Side. Here, German Jewish businessmen frequently taunted their coreligionists from Russia; family members whose surnames ended in the familiar "ki" or "ski" were called "kikes," a stereotype which historian Moses Rischin claims originated within the New York Jewish community and which forced most Russian Jews to Germanize their names.[7] As shall later be seen, regionalism and the use of stereotypes were both powerful forces within Polish society in Chicago and contributed greatly to Polonia's internecine warfare.

Finally, no survey of the factors leading to the upcoming clerical-versus-nationalist struggle in Chicago would be complete without at least passing mention of the element of anticlericalism. Because anticlericalism, according to nineteenth-century Chicago Polonia's most prominent clergyman, Reverend Vincent Barzynski, was thought to be directly linked to numerous "irreligious" forces of the time—Freemasonry, freethinking, secular liberalism, athiestic humanism, and socialism—most of Polonia's clergy, perhaps recalling the anticlerical victories in Rome during Vatican I, rushed to the alarm whenever the faintest breezes of anticlericalism began blowing their way. Moreover, even when anticlericalism was tied to legitimate efforts at social reform, clergymen rarely sided with their nationalist counterparts because reform measures might have damaged the social status of the clergy. On the other hand, some opportunistic clergymen secretly welcomed the spectre of anticlericalism in their parishes, as the subject could easily be manipulated to drum up support for national parishes. Such was indeed the case in the Croatian-American community. Here the Croatian-American clergy soundly denounced the Croatian National Alliance (*Hrvatski Narodni Savez*) for its interference in the spiritual lives of the laity and for encouraging the laity to quit the Church in order to organize around the common purpose of freeing Croatia from foreign oppression.[8] Old World anticlerical forces also swept through Italian Chicago. In the densely populated Italian district of the city's Nineteenth Ward, a coalition of "nationalists, socialists and liberals" formed the Giordano Bruno Anti-Clerical Society in 1907 so as to "combat religious superstition and priestly exploitation."[9] So intent was the Giordano Bruno Society on accomplishing its objectives that it may have been the only immigrant society in Chicago to have used the term "Anti-Clerical" in its organizational name. Similar battle lines were also drawn in Czech-American society between secular Freethinkers and the Czech Catholic clergy. When the Czech Slavic Benevolent Society (*Cesko-Slovansky Poporujici Spolek*) arose in St. Louis in 1854 as an umbrella organization for such like-minded "liberal-humanistic" organizations as the Western Czech Fraternal Union and the Union of Czech Women, the clergy immediately countered with the Czech Roman Catholic First Central Union in the United States (*Ceska Rimski-Katolicka Prvni Ustredni Jednota ve Sp. St. Americkych*) and such clerical organizations as the Western Czech Catholic Union and the Central Union of Women in the United States. Such organizational splits between the Freethinkers and the clergy had a severe negative impact on the growth of the church in Chicago, where one student has determined that approximately seventy percent of the Czech population were indifferent to both Catholicism and Protestant denominations.[10]

Admittedly, the list of determinants accounting for intragroup feuding can hardly be exhausted here. Nevertheless, the combination of forces presented thus far does serve as a backdrop for the fratricidal struggle between the *Gmina Polska* (Polish Commune) and the St. Stanislaus Society in Chicago during the 1866–1880 period. In addition, all successors of these two competing parent organizations in Polonia were strongly influenced by the war between nationals and clericals in the late nineteenth century. The repercussions of this basic division lasted even beyond World War II, when the Polish American Congress came into being (1952) in order to serve as an umbrella organization through which the Polish National Alliance and the Polish Roman Catholic Union could mediate their differences. In order to show the origins of both the clerical and national parties in Chicago Polonia it is necessary to summarize events in the *ojczyzna* with the collapse of the 1863 Insurrection.

A most dramatic social upheaval was underway in Poland following the outbreak of the January Insurrection. On 6 March 1863 Nicholas Miliutin, speaking for Czar Alexander II, stood in a Warsaw street amidst great pomp and ceremony to announce his now famous land reform proclamations. The so-called Miliutin Decrees ordered that lands now in the possession of peasants, irrespective of size of holdings or title ownership, be declared freeholds; in addition, peasants now emancipated from field service to their former landlords, the *szlachta*, would no longer be required to make redemption payments for any lands received (the *chłopi* were said to have received a settlement four times as generous as that received by Russian peasants in the Emancipation of 1861); finally, in a move designed by the Czar and Miliutin to forever seal the emnity between the landless *chłopi* who, on the whole, had never supported the insurrections, and the *szlachta* who were in the forefront of each insurrection, it was decreed that the government pay the gentry for their former lands from taxes originally levied on these same gentry. In effect, as one historian of the period has concluded, "the Polish landlord was taxed to pay bonds to himself."[11] To add further insult to the perpetrators of the insurrections, Miliutin called for the organization of *gmina*, local government units which were now to include the new landholding peasants. Since these newly created *gmina* made provisions for equal suffrage, it was now possible for the peasants, who invariably outnumbered the gentry in the locals, to gain control of the political machinery and affairs of their respective *gmina*. In effect, Miliutin and the Czar were counting on this new democratization of the peasantry in the *gmina* network to once and for all wipe out the power of the gentry, which of course would put an end to the insurrectionist fever.[12]

In Prussian Poland, the political, economic, and social influence of the *szlachta* was likewise severely diminished. Revolts, poor harvests, and declining farm prices resulted in the widespread sale of gentry-owned lands, property which was quickly bought up by eager German landlords. One study shows that, during 1846–1855, nearly 1,250,000 acres of land transferred from Polish to German ownership in Poznania and West Prussia. And as the German-owned estates increased in size and number, there was a greater reliance on cheaper Polish seasonal labor, manpower which was supplied by Galicia and Russian Poland. Consequently, the rapid population movement out of these areas and into Poznania and West Prussia brought about the displacement of Prussian Poles already settled there, who could not compete with the cheap labor onslaught.[13] Bitter over the sudden manipulation of their economic futures by Poles from the other sectors, the Prussian Poles eventually emigrated to the United States, where many would remain hostile to their Austrian and Russian compatriots for the remainder of their lives. In this fashion then did the element of regionalism become a significant factor in the Polish emigration.

The appearance of the peasant-dominated *gmina* in Russian Poland was a bitter pill for the gentry-aristocracy to swallow. Numerous *szlachta* despaired or swore revenge over what they felt was a traitorous sellout of their rights; most accused the *chłopi* of having bartered away the last remnants of Polish independence to a foreign despot for a few acres of land. Some of these gentry-aristocrats were so thoroughly devastated by the impact of the Miliutin settlement that they made the final decision to escape Poland and attempt to build a new life in other parts of Europe. But many others also vowed to one day return to the mother country and even the score with the *chłopi* class. These sentiments of revenge, bitterness, and downright stubbornness, when allowed to fester in foreign lands, served as a catalyst for a solemn, sacred, and undying crusade to restore Polish independence and the Polish nation. At the same time, each of these emotional elements also served to create a mighty social chasm between gentry and peasant in such faraway places as the northwest side of Chicago.

Prominent aristocrats-in-exile such as Agaton Giller, soon to assume the mantle of leadership as spiritual founder of the Polish National Alliance in the United States, now assisted in the organization of the National Polish Government (N.P.G.) in exile. Choosing Rapperswil, Switzerland, as their headquarters, the N.P.G. decided on an overall strategy: alliances between Polish émigrés in the United States and those in scattered pockets of Europe would have to be established in order to keep alive the idea of Polish national self-determination. Since theirs was a cause which would one day be in need of international support, it was felt that world opinion would have to be made to see the righteousness of the exile philosophy. But the key to success, from the very outset of the National Polish Government, was thought to be in the hands of American Polonia. As Giller put it:

> When the masses of Poles in America is [*sic*] morally and nationally raised by the fact of being unified and is economically prosperous . . . it will render great services to Poland, even by the mere fact of representing the Polish name well in America. These services can gradually become very considerable when the Poles begin to exercise an influence upon the public life of the United States, when they spread among Americans adequate conceptions about the Polish cause and information about the history, literature and art of our nation, when finally they become intermediaries between Poland and the powerful republic so as to foster sympathy with our efforts for liberation and develop it into an enthusiasm which will express itself in action.[14]

The N.P.G. leadership—Giller, Mikolaj Michalski, and General Bosak-Hauke—likewise issued the call for an international network of *gmina*-in-exile, which presumably at some future date would carry the fight for Polish independence back to the homeland, and which, for the meantime, would at least serve as an effective propaganda vehicle. Via its newspaper, *The Independent*, the N.P.G. boldly proclaimed that it would establish the *gmina* wherever Poles were colonizing so that exiles would have a focal point for present political activities and a springboard perhaps for later military action. In essence, the N.P.G. would fight the Miliutin-instituted *gmina* in Poland with *gmina* of its own. In the highly charged romantic climate of the day, each *gmina* member truly believed that Czarist oppression was destined by the God of Poland to be overthrown.

The *Gmina* movement was activated in the New York City area by the renowned Henryk Kalussowski, father of the 1831 emigration. Kalussowski warned his compatriots to "never accept the greatest of liberty in exchange for the Fatherland." He exhorted them to "steadily resist the violence, scoff at the superior force and bid defiance to the enemy," as well as to value the "alien friendship" of America during the fight. But most of all, Kalussowski stated, "Let us rely on ourselves."[15] Kalussowski's position, of course, was based on the notion of permanent resistance to Russian occupation. Not only that, he was convinced that the *gmina* seed would best be nurtured on the soil of American Polonia where most of the inhabitants viewed their colonies as no more than temporary havens on the way to national restoration. He and Giller also recognized the potential in American *gmina* as a financial base for further insurrectionary programs; after all, it was American Polonia which contributed $16,000 to the insurrectionist cause in 1863. In any event, the establishment of a viable *gmina* in every major American Polonia now became a paramount project. In Chicago the task of establishing a functioning *gmina* fell on the shoulders of a twenty-three-year-old greenhorn of high aspirations—a certain Ladislaus Dyniewicz.[16]

Born in Chwałkow in the Prussian sector of Poland on 13 June 1843, Ladislaus Dyniewicz, by virtue of his youth, could hardly have taken on any decisive commitment in the Insurrection of 1863. Only a teenager when the Czar announced the Russian Emancipation and still only an impressionable youth during the Insurrection itself, Dyniewicz was not affected by the Miliutin decrees, which applied only to Poles in the Russian sector. Whether or not the subsequent Galician and Russian Polish migration to the Prussian side had any effect on the young Dyniewicz is not known. But he did leave the homeland, presumably for economic betterment, and arrived in the United States on 18 May 1866. Shortly after his arrival, and at about the same time that Peter Kiolbassa made his return to the St. Stanislaus Society, Dyniewicz moved to Chicago. He first found employment at the International Harvester Company, but not finding a promising future there he quit and took a job with the Chicago and Northwestern Railroad. After a few years of that proverbial immigrant thrift at which many historians marvel, Dyniewicz accumulated enough capital to purchase from Peter Kiolbassa a small bookstore located at 532 Noble Street, a concern which he opened for business in 1872. Whether or not the transaction between Kiolbassa and Dyniewicz was cause for the bitter personal feud between the two in later years is not known, but a year later Dyniewicz is said to have realized his dream of becoming a publisher when he expanded his bookstore operation into a printshop. From this Noble Street base only two doors away from where Holy Trinity parish would be built, Dyniewicz initiated a long and prosperous career in the publishing field that would one day catapult him and his family into Chicago's high society; there he would rub elbows with prominent merchants and such well-known publisher-editors as Victor Lawson of the Chicago *Daily News*. Dyniewicz was a classic example of how a thrifty, hard-working, immigrant could gain respectability and success in American life. When a special volume on high society homes in Chicago was published by the University of Chicago at the beginning of World War II, the Dyniewicz mansion at 5917 West Diversey was prominently featured as a "Polish American Landmark," perhaps calling attention to the fact that the Polish "radicals" of 1870 Chicago could be as easily seduced by the trappings of American life as any of their immigrant counterparts.

Dyniewicz's publishing house eventually printed a wide variety of Polish-language materials for an immigrant market always hungry for Old World novels, short stories, religious hymnals, textbooks, and dictionaries. Thousands of Dyniewicz house items found their way into the homes of Chicago's Polish immigrants. But along with such stock items, Ladislaus Dyniewicz, by October 1873, with able assistance from his son Casimir, began publication of the *Gazeta Polska*

(*Polish Gazette*), reputed to be Chicago's first Polish-language newspaper. It was through the editorial pages of the *Gazeta Polska* that Dyniewicz began stirring up the passions of nationalism lying dormant in the fledgling Chicago Polonia. It was a mission which absorbed the better part of his energies for more than a decade, as Dyniewicz was now head of the *Gmina Polska* (Polish Commune) in Chicago.[17]

The origins of the *Gmina Polska* in Chicago remain obscure due to the absence of any hard, primary evidence. Nevertheless, some secondary accounts written at the turn of the century, when Dyniewicz was in his sixties, offer a composite though still hazy picture of the early days of the Chicago *Gmina*. Stanley Osada, the historian of the Polish National Alliance, sets the birthdate of the *Gmina Polska* in Chicago in 1866, thus coinciding with Dyniewicz's arrival in Chicago; he also states that the *raison d'être* of the organization was strongly tied to the aspirations for a free and independent Poland maintained by the National Polish Government in Switzerland. Osada implies that the *Gmina* was probably a hastily conceived attempt by Dyniewicz and a small core of ardent laypeople to counter the potential strength of the more religiously oriented St. Stanislaus Kostka Society, which had been suddenly and inexplicably reactivated on 1 June 1866 by Kiolbassa. Since the reappearance of the St. Stanislaus Society was only two weeks removed from Dyniewicz's entrance into the United States, it might be hypothesized (again without solid evidence) that Dyniewicz's coming to Chicago, as well as his intentions for coming, may have been a matter of public knowledge and concern to inhabitants already living there. But the link between these two coincidental dates has never been positively established. Then, too, as Helen Busyn has suggested in her study of Kiolbassa's career, the subsequent and heated competition between the St. Stanislaus Society and the *Gmina Polska* became inextricably linked to an intense personal rivalry between Kiolbassa and Dyniewicz. We now know that both men were extremely ambitious and success-oriented, that both were well aware of the potential for personal financial gain in early Polonia, and that both were attempting throughout to seize and hold the reins of leadership in the community with the demise of Smarzewski-Schermann. Regional differences between the *Poznanskie* (Poznanians), *Kaszubi* (Pomeranians), and *Ślązaki* (Silesians) likewise contributed to further misunderstandings and ideological quarrels, although the majority of the population in *Stanisławowo* would, right up to the 1900 census, trace their ancestry to German Poland. And if the *Gmina* membership included sufficient numbers of dispossessed *szlachta* (memoirs, parish albums, and census reports are inconclusive on this point), whose bitterness toward resident *chłopi* in the settlement would have been quite understandable given the historic backdrop of the Miliutin decrees, one might even conclude that the *Gmina*-St. Stanislaus Society conflict had all the makings of a potent class conflict.[18] After all, in the *ojczyzna* these *szlachta* had always been protected by law, custom, and solid manor walls, at least until 1863; but in the streets of Chicago the deference accorded the gentry was not more than a figment of the romantic imagination. Force of circumstance now required gentry and peasant to live next door to each other in this new urban village. Under the daily pressures and routines of nineteenth-century urban life—filthy tenements, marital squabbling within earshot of nosy neighbors, rebellious children, the daily struggle for bread in the factories—one can easily understand how the traditional social deference accorded the gentry broke down. But Dyniewicz was well aware of these social, regional, political, and religious differences in Polonia. Anxious to increase the strength of the Chicago *Gmina*, Dyniewicz went about his business of recruiting in the fashion of any respectable democrat: in the preface to the *Gmina* constitution, which he drafted, he made it clear that the commune in Chicago was open "to all Poles . . . without discrimination toward any religion or place of birth."[19]

Meanwhile the Kiolbassa group, which still included the contingent loyal to Smarzewski-Schermann, involved itself in reconstituting the St. Stanislaus Society. Not caring to be outdone in any way by the *Gmina*, the Kiolbassa people also drafted a constitution. (These and later Poles were inordinately fond of drafting constitutions, as if the whole business somehow proved that they were in earnest about the idea and practice of democracy.) The rejuvenated Stanislawians pledged themselves to carrying out various spiritual and corporate works of mercy—comforting widows, taking care of the orphaned and the aged, visiting the sick, burying the dead—all of which were highly prized services in any immigrant community. The Society also assumed the responsibility of protecting the high moral standing of the community and of maintaining community peace, a formidable task as later events would show. In order to provide such services—in particular death benefits for widows, widowers, and their children—the Society, which by Kiolbassa's own account totalled 60 members in the year 1869, began to charge dues. The initiation fee was between five and ten dollars, depending on one's financial standing in the community; monthly dues were levied at fifty cents per member; and a special assessment of one dollar was collected whenever someone died. Anyone paying his or her dues was considered a full member in good standing.

All told, the initial outlay for a newcomer to the Society could total as high as seventeen dollars, a sizeable investment at a time when unskilled laborers were earning no more than $1.50 for each twelve-hour day. Tabulating all dues and expenses for the first five-year period, one might, depending on the mortality rate, contribute as much as fifty dollars, or the equivalent of approximately ten weeks wages according to wage standards for manufacturing workers in the 1865–1870 period. Fortunately, the death rate was extremely low in early Chicago Polonia; St. Stanislaus Kostka Church, for example, recorded only three funerals for 1871 (the year of the Great Chicago Fire). The upshot of all this is that the St. Stanislaus Society, with its solid 60 members, may have collected as much as $3,000

Peter Kiolbassa, undated (Chicago Historical Society)

prior to 1871, a considerable sum for a lower-class community. It is for this reason that the election of officers to the Society became such a political event (the early Polish settlers, besides writing constitutions, also cherished participation in their internal elections, for this too gave them an exaggerated sense of participatory democracy). Any elected official to the Society was automatically accorded prestige, respect, and the opportunity to make social contacts outside the community. After all, no one in Chicago Polonia, outside of the Stanislawian officers, could boast of overseeing so large a monetary sum. When the first elections were held in June 1866, the Kiolbassa party was victorious over *Gmina* candidates, who had attempted to infiltrate the ranks of the St. Stanislaus Society and who had hoped to siphon off funds for their political purposes. Kiolbassa, as expected, was elected president; Marcel Ziomkowski was chosen secretary; and five "counselors" were appointed to assist the elected officers—Joseph Dziewior (Kiolbassa's father-in-law), Lawrence Stas, Thomas Nowicki, Anthony Bok, and Anthony Matysiak. The fact that Smarzewski-Schermann was not part of Polonia's first elite group indicates that his influence by this time had already waned.[20]

The next public clash between the St. Stanislaus Society and the *Gmina Polska* arose when the northwest side Polonia began making plans to erect a parish church in 1867. Despite the need for a community parish, all group aspirations were set aside as Kiolbassa and Dyniewicz engaged in a long feud over the site of the projected structure. Kiolbassa, now a police officer in the Chicago Avenue district, argued that the church be built on the corner of Oak and Wesson streets; and since Kiolbassa owned the land there, he most probably hoped to make some sort of financial profit from the transaction. But the Stanislawian president was immediately opposed by Dyniewicz, who felt that the church should be built on Noble and Bradley, near the Smarzewski-Schermann grocery store and only two blocks away from the eventual location of Dyniewicz's printshop. Dyniewicz, perhaps with the private support of Smarzewski-Schermann, hoped to turn popular Stanislawian support away from Kiolbassa on the grounds that their president was "a tool of the saloonkeepers," who were pushing for the Oak and Wesson site for business reasons. Thus, aside from the philosophical differences between the St. Stanislaus Society and the *Gmina*, Chicago Polonia's first *cause célèbre* was initiated to some extent by a fight over the temperance issue.[21]

In order to crack the stalemate, the matter of the church site was arbitrated in the diocesan chancery by Bishop Thomas Foley, himself a newcomer to the diocese, who according to Kiolbassa selected the Noble and Bradley site because it was thought to be "a beautiful place." In the same account, the bishop described the Kiolbassa site as "a dirty place." Foley's assessment aside, there was something to be said for the aesthetics of the church's ultimate location. When the commemorative parish album of St. Stanislaus Kostka was issued during the golden jubilee of 1917, the contributing editors went out of their way to praise lavishly the church's site, an area densely covered with handsome stands of poplars which were said to have contrasted nicely with the grayish-white exterior of the church. Further substantiation of the Dyniewicz version came from the editors of the *Chicago Tribune*. When discussing the issue of slum locations in its editorial pages on 6 September 1874, the *Tribune* made note of the fact that the Oak and Wesson area was "the most dangerous section in the North Division" and was "packed with wooden dwellings, barns, sheds and warehouses. . . ." Not only was the Oak and Wesson neighborhood a fire trap due to inadequate water supplies for firefighters (a major crusade for the *Tribune* after the Chicago Fire), but, according to the editors, "Wesson Street is utterly impassable at night [because of] numerous potholes." Furthermore, conditions there were made especially dangerous for the young, since the likelihood of accidents was much greater in an area where, the *Tribune* claimed, "children are as numerous as blackberries in a Virginia field."[22]

Peter Kiolbassa never forgot the St. Stanislaus Kostka church site controversy of 1867–1869, nor did he ever forgive Dyniewicz for having embarrassed him before the bishop in the chancery office. The issue still rankled deep in Kiolbassa's soul some thirty years later. When *The New World*, official weekly of the Roman Catholic Archdiocese of Chicago, published a special issue devoted to the history of Catholicism in Chicago on 14 April 1900, it carried a piece submitted by Kiolbassa on the origins of *Stanisławowo*; in the article, Kiolbassa snidely referred to the Noble and Bradley site as fit territory for "Indians," and as a place "swarmed over by flocks of wild chickens."[23]

After Bishop Foley's intervention, which more or less set a precedent for diocesan intervention into Polish parish affairs, a modest church building was constructed on the corner of Noble and Bradley. Four adjacent city lots were also purchased for the then princely sum of $1700. Space inside the 40′ × 85′ multipurpose two-story building allowed for a chapel, a school, and a meeting hall. All of the construction work, done by a local Polish contractor named Pietruszek, totalled $6,685, excluding the cost of the land. If any prestige was salvaged by the St. Stanislaus Kostka Society, it was in the decision to name the church after the Society's patron saint. Dyniewicz and the *Gmina Polska* may have scored a minor victory in the selection of the church site, but the St. Stanislaus Society would always have the advantage of encouraging newcomers in the community to identify the parish church with the Society, and this enabled the Society to boost its membership dramatically in the early 1870s.[24]

Had the conflict over the establishment of St. Stanislaus Kostka parish ended in 1869, one might be justified in assessing the disagreement as no more than a minor episode wherein two groups of disgruntled immigrants were merely attempting to adjust to changing conditions and to each other. But later events surrounding the conflict demonstrate that the church site controversy was only the first shot fired in a long, bitter, and often bizarre struggle which was to persist between the emerging clerical party headed by Kiolbassa and the nationalist party championed by Dyniewicz and the *Gmina* during the 1870–1893 period. The clerical faction would, for the next quarter-century, work to maintain a highly controversial alliance among: the Congregation of the Resurrection, a missionary society soon to be invited by diocesan authorities to manage the Polonia mission;

dozens of parish societies at St. Stanislaus Kostka's, spawned by the parent Society; and the Irish Catholic hierarchy. This clerical party would over and over again demonstrate its vested interest in publicly emphasizing the religious over the political heritage of the Polish Catholic immigrant. This is not to say that the clerical party would ignore the powerful nationalistic sentiments and elements in Chicago Polonia; instead it would attempt to manipulate that nationalism for purposes of strengthening the parish church. On the other hand, the *Gmina Polska*, and eventually its many adopted sons and daughters, continued to feature the martyrdom of Partitioned Poland on center stage; and in order to achieve its basically political ends, the *Gmina*, rather than secularize the strong elements of religiosity in Polonia, would in like fashion attempt to capitalize on the strong Catholic base initiated by the clericals. In the ensuing and tangled process of divisive interaction between the two protagonists, the *Gmina Polska* would relentlessly attack the Congregation of the Resurrection for its alleged laxity on the issue of national self-determination and for its complicity in the "conspiracy" by the Polish clergy and the Irish Catholic hierarchy regarding the administration of Polish Catholic parishes. But in attacking the Congregation of the Resurrection, the *Gmina Polska* left itself wide open to charges of anticlericalism and Freemasonry—charges which the clerical party successfully exploited in order to win over the hearts and minds of thousands of simple and pious Polish Catholics who considered such criticism of their priests a sacrilegious act.

Neither side, of course, remained unscathed in this generation-long conflict. There were simply too many problems calling for resolution, too many tensions calling for balance, and too many souls to look after. Seldom was there sufficient manpower (the Resurrectionists experienced a severe shortage of priests throughout the late nineteenth century) to keep up with the tremendous waves of immigration; rarely were there any tested precedents to guide the leadership on both sides; there was not even enough room in the lodges and churches to handle the several hundred thousand Poles who flocked to this northwest side Polonia prior to World War I. Throughout this period the clerical party wrestled with a fundamental dilemma that had broken the spirits and wills of churchmen in other ethnic communities, churchmen who no doubt were as headstrong as the Resurrectionists: that is, to build a viable and lasting community parish system in any urban area in America required a commitment to *permanent* residency in the United States. Were Polonia's clergy expected to coax the faithful into embracing an American way of life, with its Gilded Age emphasis on economic mobility, under the guise of protecting a Polish Catholic tradition which would surely shed much of its essential national character in the process? Or to put the matter another way, would the Polish clergy dare manipulate the national consciousness of the immigrants in order to preserve the Catholic side of their character, even if in the end such actions would transform the flock into *American* Catholics? Is this why powerful pastors such as the Reverend Barzynski of St. Stanislaus Kostka implored their flocks to choose God *and* Country? And did God and Country mean God and Poland *or* God and America?

The *Gmina Polska* also was forced to undergo the torments associated with a crisis of conscience. How was it possible, for instance, to rise up from the grave-yard of Partition and national crucifixion, as Mickiewicz had prophesied, if every-one stayed in Chicago? And could the idea of Polishness even survive in the immigrant mind and soul in the wake of a devastated Catholicity? Polish Catho-lics or Catholic Poles? The debate inevitably continued.

Other than the naming of the parish church, the entire project at St. Stanislaus Kostka appeared to have gone according to terms laid down by the *Gmina Pol-ska*—the land, building, and title were all in the possession of the nationalist faction. Given the anticlerical elements the *Gmina* by now was absorbing, what could account for Dyniewicz's rather impressive victory over at the chancery? On the face of it, the element of chance was significant. Bishop Foley's hasty arrival in Chicago, brought on by Bishop Duggan's mental illness and abrupt departure from the diocese, did not permit the chancery sufficient time or offer satisfactory conditions for a thorough study of the situation in *Stanisławowo*; and regardless of how conjectural it may seem, it is unlikely that an administrator of Foley's capabilities and sense of priorities would have ever considered the matter of a church site a critical item on the chancery agenda, given the confusion in the chancery over the sudden Duggan-to-Foley transition. Yet, viewing the Polish situation from within, one can only conclude that no *Gmina* victory would have resulted had there not been at least some measure of support for the nationalist party position inside the parish itself. There is no decisive evidence as to the numerical strength of the contending parties in the late 1860s, but it is quite possible that Kiolbassa and the St. Stanislaus Society underestimated the strength and appeal of the *Gmina*. In correspondence to the Congregation of the Resurrec-tion at the time, Kiolbassa placed the Stanislawian membership at sixty (out of four hundred families), whereas he claimed the *Gmina* group numbered only ten members.[25] Kiolbassa's letter was an obvious exaggeration, perhaps calculated to convince the Resurrectionists that the Chicago Polonia mission was a secure one. For despite Kiolbassa's continued harrassment of the *Gmina*, the commune began to exercise a commanding authority shortly after the church structure was com-pleted.

In a startling communiqué submitted to the chancery, the *Gmina*'s position was made crystal clear. The nationalists now demanded that the diocese accept a controversial ethnocentric clause in the church deed: "This church is to be for the use of Poles." The implication of the *Gmina* demand was that the Poles would exclude all other nationality groups from their house of worship, a position which was certainly an insult to such neighboring ethnic groups as the Bohemians at St. Wenceslaus who had graciously accepted Poles in their church when the latter were without a church of their own. In light of this extreme position, Bishop Foley, perhaps realizing that he had make a mistake in backing the Dyniewicz group in the site controversy, now reversed his stance and refused to consecrate the church. Several attempts were made to arrive at some sort of compromise, but none evidently was satisfactory to Dyniewicz and the *Gmina* who held steadfastly to their "For Poles Only" position. When the chancery publicly announced that no consecration would take place until the wording of the deed to the property was changed authorizing diocesan ownership, the *Gmina* retaliated by refusing to transmit the deed to the diocese, a position which was clearly in violation of the recent (1866) Plenary Council canons which reaffirmed the abolition of trusteeship and the prohibition of lay ownership of church property. Dyniewicz, however, justified the commune's hard line by insisting that since Poles had made all the necessary financial sacrifices to build the church they ought not to be forced to share the church facilities with other ethnic groups.[26]

Kiolbassa, now sensing an opportunity to gain chancery approval for his group, called attention to the arrogance displayed by Dyniewicz and the *Gmina*. In correspondence to Superior-General Jerome Kajsiewicz of the Resurrectionists, Kiolbassa reacted to allegations made by the *Gmina* to the effect that the St. Stanislaus Kostka Society was unpatriotic toward the *ojczyzna*. He also went on to affirm that "the Silesians were the most devoted to the faith" (Kiolbassa was from Silesia), "whereas those from Poznan, West Prussia and *Wielko Polska* [Greater Poland] who called themselves *Szlachta Polska* [Polish Aristocrats] did not care about the Catholic religion and called other Poles foolish and bigoted *chłopi*."[27] Needless to say, Dyniewicz came from West Prussia.

The conflict between the clerical and national parties moved into a second phase when Kiolbassa requested that the Congregation of the Resurrection come to Chicago Polonia and administer the mission. Swallowing his initial defeat with the Irish-based chancery, Kiolbassa was determined to reverse the favorable attitudes toward the *Gmina* in the community; if the *Gmina* held the deed to the church property, Kiolbassa figured that the best way to wrest away that control would be to staff the parish church with priests favorable to the goals of the St. Stanislaus Kostka Society. The first order of business then would be to secure the services of a full-time Polish pastor at *Stanisławowo*, a task that involved all kinds of complications as the number of Polish missions in the United States had increased considerably with the downfall of the Insurrection. The steadily increasing numbers of Polish Catholics in Texas, Missouri, Wisconsin, Michigan, Pennsylvania, and Canada resulted in a brisk competition for the handful of available Polish or Polish-speaking priests. Between 1867 and 1869 the Poles in Chicago had considered themselves fortunate to obtain the services of an itinerant Jesuit, the Reverend Szulak, and a visiting priest from St. Wenceslaus parish, the Reverend Molitor, who was called upon occasionally to assist Szulak. But since Szulak's assignment in Chicago was only temporary and because Molitor was needed at his home parish (Polish priests were able to negotiate for better positions due to the shortage), neither was able to accept the full-time pastorate at St. Stanislaus Kostka.

In the autumn of 1869, however, the clerical party's position improved. When Kiolbassa's formal request for a Resurrectionist pastor was favorably received by Superior-General Kajsiewicz of the Congregation, Kajsiewicz dispatched Reverend Eugene Funcken, his North American Chapter Provincial, to Chicago to assess the overall potential of the Chicago mission. After a brief study, Funcken made out a positive report to Kajsiewicz suggesting that the Resurrectionists give Chicago "serious consideration." Funcken also mentioned that "the administrator of the diocese is very pleased that we shall serve the destitute Poles."[28] The Reverend Funcken then returned to Resurrectionist headquarters in Canada, apparently with at least preliminary diocesan approval for the Resurrectionists to assume administration of St. Stanislaus Kostka. Based on the Funcken report, Kajsiewicz, over some stiff opposition from his own staff who were arguing that the Congregation's European missions be given higher priority, authorized Reverend John Wollowski and Reverend Louis Elena to go to Chicago—Wollowski as pastor and Elena as his assistant. With the decision to receive the two Resurrectionists made known, the Kiolbassa party appeared to have once again gained the initiative in *Stanisławowo*; but a bureaucratic mix-up on the chancery's part inadvertently foiled Kiolbassa's well-laid plans.

It so happened that chancery officials under the direction of Reverend John Halligan, the interim administrator of the Chicago diocese during the Duggan-to-Foley transition, were likewise involved in negotiating for the services of a Polish priest. On the personal recommendation of the Jesuit Szulak, a diocesan priest by the name of Joseph Juszkiewicz was appointed pastor instead. The already confused bureaucratic mess was further complicated when the two Resurrectionists, Wollowski and Elena, arrived in Chicago on 1 November 1869 to assume their pastoral duties. When informed of the appointment of Juszkiewicz, Wollowski went to the chancery to inquire about the misunderstanding, and it was here that administrator Halligan informed the already exasperated Wollowski of a letter which he had sent to Superior-General Kajsiewicz on 21 October 1869:

> My Rev. Father: Whilst expecting a Polish priest from your V. Rev., meanwhile Kind Providence has sent us one, which circumstances relieves us now from want hitherto felt.
>
> > Your ob. serv.
> > John Halligan, Adm.[29]

Having read this curt notice, Halligan then gave the perplexed Resurrectionist thirty-five dollars for traveling expenses and suggested that he and Elena return to Canada. But despite this setback dealt to Kiolbassa and his supporters, events in the following months would demonstrate that neither he nor the Congregation of the Resurrection was going to be denied.[30]

A Parish album tells us that, at the outset of Juszkiewicz's pastorate, "the growth of the parish promised to be quite good," and that the congregation and the new bishop were quite happy with the new pastor. But such euphoria proved to be short-lived, as the entire Polish community was shaken to its core by a tragic and rather mysterious event. One night six masked men approached the residence of Polonia's sixty-nine-year-old pastor, gained entrance by feigning a sick call, and severely beat the helpless priest. The assailants further threatened to take Juszkiewicz's life if he did not immediately resign his pastorate and leave the diocese. The brutal and sacrilegious nature of the assault, so uncharacteristic of an Old World immigrant village mentality which traditionally held a great sense of respect and awe for clergymen, attested to the hardening of relations between clericals and nationalists.[31] And a new round of heightened tensions permeated Chicago Polonia when, after having attempted to bring the case before the civil courts and having it summarily dismissed for lack of hard evidence, the frightened and discouraged Father Juszkiewicz, probably never realizing that he had played the role of pawn, resigned his position at St. Stanislaus Kostka and retreated to the hills of Mount Carmel, Pennsylvania.[32]

By no means was the Juszkiewicz incident an isolated assault case, for it was fraught with numerous implications. At the time of the assault, it is known that a Resurrectionist priest named Father Adolph Bakanowski was in temporary residence at the home of the Stasch family, all of whom were members of St. Stanislaus Kostka parish. Bakanowski had come there in a most roundabout way. After the Wollowski debacle, Peter Kiolbassa is known to have left Chicago "to find some peace in Panna Marya," the original Polish settlement in Texas where Bakanowski was pastor.[33] While Kiolbassa and Bakanowski were visiting, Superior-General Kajsiewicz wrote to his subordinate asking him to return to the Resurrectionist Central House in Rome where he was presumably to receive a new assignment. Instead of immediately complying with his superior's request, Bakanowski complained to Kajsiewicz that the imminence of a Franco-Prussian war might make the trip too dangerous. He closed his letter by telling Kajsiewicz he would simply await new instructions. In the meantime, Bakanowski, according to his own testimony, journeyed to Chicago: "I presented myself to the local bishop," he said, "from whom I had received permission to say Mass for a month's time." Bakanowski also admitted that he had arrived "in Chicago at a most critical time as certain controversies had arisen between the pastor and his people."[34] The St. Stanislaus Kostka jubilee album (*Album Pamiątkowe*) substantiates the Bakanowski account somewhat with the declaration that "the parishioners began reproaching Father Juszkiewicz with insufficient care for the parish which was poor and underdeveloped," and that the parishioners "finally approached Father Bakanowski eagerly petitioning him to become pastor to replace Father Juszkiewicz."[35] Nevertheless, when this harassment of the Reverend Juszkiewicz began, Bakanowski in his memoirs claims that he (Bakanowski) refused the petition submitted by parishioners at St. Stanislaus and instead "took up residence at the opposite end of the city."[36] Bakanowski further offers the hypothesis that the *Gmina Polska* was behind the assault: "All of us were incensed," he writes, "by this atrocious crime, and we took steps to discover who the culprits were. . . . The people maintained that their pastor was assaulted by a secret society of Masons. He [Juszkiewicz] even admitted that during the assault, the assailants tried to force him to join their lodge."[37]

This *burza* (storm) over *Stanisławowo* was, to use the description of the historian Kruszka, most bizarre. From the few scraps of historical evidence available, it appears as if both the clerical and nationalist parties were involved in separate machinations and therefore shared, however directly or indirectly, some responsibility for the Juszkiewicz assault. But in the absence of a court trial, the innocence or guilt of either faction was never made known. The Juszkiewicz incident remains shrouded to the present day, calling attention to the fact that Chicago Polonia was capable of and would resort to violence whenever the balance between the clerical and nationalist factions was affected. Father Juszkiewicz was the first of several priests in Chicago Polonia who would encounter violence whenever the identity question of Catholic Polonia reached crisis proportions—witness the street riots involving the rise of the Polish National Church in the late 1890s and early 1900s. In any event, the overall significance of this first *burza* over *Stanisławowo* is that the contorted sequence of events in the 1866–1870 period enabled the Congregation of the Resurrection to establish an important beachhead in Chicago. And the mighty fortress built on this Stanislawian perimeter, which was to be the largest in all of American Polonia, would one day be used by dedicated soldiers of Christ, Polish-style, who would subsequently fan out through this still secular midwest metropolis in search of Polish Catholics and Catholic Poles who had lost their way while in search of their God and their Country. In a move designed to bring back peace to the beleaguered Polish enclave on Chicago's near northwest side, Bishop Foley appointed the Resurrectionist Bakanowski as temporary pastor of St. Stanislaus Kostka parish. The temporary status of the Resurrectionists in Chicago would become permanent once Jerome Kajsiewicz, several thousand miles away from stormy Chicago Polonia, had the opportunity to accept formally the Polish mission. After having thoroughly studied the Chicago situation, and after having made a special trip to Chicago in 1871 to discuss details of a Chicago diocese-Resurrectionist alliance, Kajsiewicz personally placed his stamp of approval on a pact which would enable the Resurrectionists to begin their Polish Catholic "empire" the likes of which no Polonia anywhere would ever match.[38]

3

The Coming of the Resurrectionists

> The Polish people, just as the Irish, were loyal to God and the Faith,
> and never became discouraged.
>> Superior-General Jerome Kajsiewicz, C.R.,
>> on his visit to Chicago Polonia in 1871.

Despite its brief thirty-five-year history, the Congregation of the Resurrection of Our Lord Jesus Christ was by 1871 in many ways well suited for the Chicago Polonia mission. Founded in 1836 by an ambitious group of soldier-scholars— Bogdan Janski, Peter Semenenko, and Jerome Kajsiewicz—each of whom had received a university education and each of whom had been a participant in the 1831 Insurrection, the Congregation seemed to possess the same qualities of intellect, devotion to duty and organization, and spiritual militancy which had enabled the Society of Jesus to become a major force in world Catholicism. Official histories of the Congregation of the Resurrection agree that Bogdan Janski (1807–1840), a brilliant and saintly man, was the prime spiritual mover who could draw into the religious society men of like talent and commitment. An economist of considerable stature at the University of Paris in the late 1820s, Janski for a short period fell away from the Catholic faith when he came under the spell of the socialist-prophet Saint-Simon. But this venture into radical French socialism ended when such figures as Lacordaire and Montalembert of the French Catholic liberal movement and the Polish Romantic poet Mickiewicz convinced Janski that the wave of the émigré future would be determined by Poland's historic Catholic ties and not by the alien gospel of Saint-Simon. Back in the Catholic fold both intellectually and spiritually, Janski became a strong and influential opponent of Saint-Simon and socialism.

Janski's spiritual colleague, Peter Semenenko (1814–1886), likewise came to the religious life in a most circuitous fashion. Semenenko, like Janski, stumbled away from the Catholic faith when disillusionment and a spirit of defeatism set in with the downfall of the 1831 Insurrection. Joining fellow émigrés in Paris, Semenenko came in contact with Janski who guided him back to the faith. The third

co-founder of the Resurrectionists, Jerome Kajsiewicz (1812–1873), like his compatriots in the Congregation, initially suffered the humiliation of defeat in the
Insurrection, fell from the Church, and did not regain his spiritual bearings until
his meeting with Janski in Paris. The Congregation, which eventually professed
its first vows under Pope Gregory XVI on Resurrection Sunday in 1842, derived
its name from this most celebrated feastday in the Polish liturgical calendar.[1]

Because Janski was already dead when the Resurrectionists professed their
vows, the difficult administrative role of Superior-General was first assumed by
Semenenko, who committed the Congregation to battling the excesses of Polish
Messianism then coming into prominence via the literary circles of Andrew To-
wianski. By concentrating on "the organization of secular priests leading the religious life . . . and on religious having the calling of secular priests," Semenenko
hoped to channel the energies of experienced clergymen in an all-out fight against
socialism, modernism, and materialism. This nineteenth-century secular trinity
was to be met head-on by a network of community-parishes that would form the
bulwark of the Resurrectionist counterattack. But the establishment and maintenance of churches was not enough. Echoing the ideas of Janski, Semenenko believed that any community where the Socialist threat was present would have to
be saturated with religious and social institutions of all types which might cater
to the needs of an emerging industrial working class. The primary goal then in
each community was to establish a religious presence, an effectively coordinated
cradle-to-grave chain of services from which no working-class community could
turn away. This religious presence would be made known not only by the parish
churches but also by elementary, secondary, and higher institutions of learning;
by the establishment of rectories, seminaries, novitiates, and convents; by hospitals, welfare agencies, and homes for the aged, the infirm and the orphaned; and
by a wide selection of religious fraternal organizations and parish societies cater-
ing to all age groups and interests and all intimately interwoven into the community structure and its culture. In effect, the community-parish system was to touch
in some way every aspect of human life; and because of the plan's peculiar adapt-
ability to densely settled urban areas, one can readily understand why the Chicago
Polonia mission appealed to a goodly number of Resurrectionists.[2]

Most Polish Catholic parishioners today, whose lives were enriched by the
saturation techniques adopted by the Congregation of the Resurrection in the
elaborate community-parish network in Chicago, have come to appreciate the organizational genius of the Resurrectionists. Their fascination with and compe-
tence in the mundane details of daily parish life enabled the Resurrectionists to
build over and over again a community-parish model which, in turn, was meticulously copied and applied by later generations. But still one must keep in mind
another factor of major significance which enabled the Resurrectionists to establish themselves in Chicago: despite the fact that the Congregation's Central House
was located in Rome, it was still a Polish-based religious society and only the

second ever born in Poland (the Piarists were the first). As the Reverend John Iwicki tells us in his history of the Congregation, the Resurrectionists always displayed their distinctly Polish stamp wherever they established themselves: in the Catholic areas of Paris the community was known as "Pretres Polonais" or "Mission Polonais"; in Rome, it was referred to as the "Collegio Polacco," the "Preti Polachi," or the "Congregazione Polacca." This inherent Polish character or "presence" was to be a decided advantage when the Congregation had to deal with non-Polish members of the American hierarchy, who ordinarily deferred to the Resurrectionists whenever certain Polish questions called for solution. On the other hand, the location of the Congregation's Central House in Rome was advantageous when dealing with the Holy See. In any case, until Eugene Funcken, a Westphalian, entered the Congregation in 1853, the Resurrectionists had accepted only Polish candidates; but when this policy had proven to restrict severely the missionary potential of the Congregation in non-Polish areas, the General Chapter in 1857 adopted a policy of recruiting non-Polish candidates. Thus, by 1860, the Resurrectionists were granted the *Decretum Laudis* by the Holy See; consequently they opened missions in Turkey, Bulgaria, Canada, and the United States. The first mission in the United States was founded at Parisville, Michigan, in 1865, where a small contingent of Poles established a colony in Sanilac County, in the "thumb" area in the northeastern part of that state.[3]

When the Reverend Bakanowski came to Chicago in 1870, the Resurrectionists were already engaged in a vigorous internal debate over the issue of ministering to souls outside the boundaries of Partitioned Poland. The debate, which was to continue well into the twentieth century, came about when the Congregation's "internalists" began arguing that the society's manpower and financial resources were being wasted on a far-flung mission empire.[4]

But the "internationalist" position of Superior-General Kajsiewicz prevailed. Kajsiewicz contended that the Congregation simply could not abandon the thousands of Poles who were moving abroad, for without a sympathetic Polish-speaking clergy these souls would surely be lost to the Church. Kajsiewicz also knew from first-hand experience in the United States the dangers a Polish family was exposed to when it tried to cope simultaneously with a foreign environment, the struggle to earn a living, and the desire to remain spiritually united. Even Semenenko, who would again assume the position of Superior-General after Kajsiewicz's death and who would be strongly tempted to give in to the internalists, steadfastly held to the idea that the Polish family was the heart of the community-parish system. Accordingly, in July of 1871 Kajsiewicz journeyed to the United States, went to Chicago, and formally acknowledged the Congregation's intention to accept the Chicago Polonia mission on a permanent basis. During his stay in the diocese, Kajsiewicz and Bishop Foley successfully negotiated and concluded a historic pact giving the Resurrectionists rights to administer all non-diocesan Polish parishes in the Chicago diocese for a ninety-nine-year period, an agreement which first included rights to administer the parish of St. Stanislaus Kostka. In return for these rights it was assumed that the deed to the parish would be turned over to the diocese, thus allowing for Foley to consecrate the church.[5]

The Foley-Kajsiewicz pact was, of course, a great victory for Kiolbassa's clerical party. With the Irish hierarchy-Resurrectionist alliance sealed, the clerical party was now party to any communications taking place between the diocese and the parish. Furthermore, the Resurrectionists would not hesitate to use the pact to strengthen or even exploit their favored position in times of turmoil, when chancery support was especially called for. Then, too, the Polish community at large stood to gain from the alliance because the Resurrectionists, more so than any other religious house in Chicago at the time, were thoroughly familiar with the Old World religious customs and mores which the transplanted *chłopi* wished to revitalize in their new urban environment. Consequently, the Resurrectionists were able to assist in the process of making less painful the countless social and cultural adjustments which so often baffled, and then broke, many newcomers. As the future unfolded, the organization-minded Congregation constantly strived, often against tremendous odds, to keep the Polish immigrant "in the fold" by exposing that immigrant to a wide variety of religious, social, and cultural activities maintained by dozens of church societies working within the community-parish system. And despite their periods of apathy to some of the more radical political causes espoused by the *Gmina Polska*, the Resurrectionists were still committed to assisting their parishioners in maintaining strong ties with the Polish past. Finally, the Foley-Kajsiewicz pact brought to Chicago Polonia a religious society whose priests exerted a form of leadership for which a sizeable segment of the community yearned. The coalition of parish groups which was first attracted to the goals outlined by the rejuvenated St. Stanislaus Society, in turn, lent their support to the Resurrectionists by founding a community-parish system which would one day become one of the largest such immigrant networks ever instituted in the United States. *Stanisławowo*, by virtue of the 1871 pact, spawned an intricate combination of parish societies and fraternal organizations which astounded and bewildered Catholics and non-Catholics alike.

But the pact also had its drawbacks. The prospect of a long-term alliance between the downtown Irish hierarchy and the clerical party certainly alienated the nationalist faction. Dyniewicz and his supporters took this opportunity to accuse the Resurrectionists of conspiring with the Irish in order to exploit the Polish working class. Embittered by the alliance, Dyniewicz then moved out to the Lower West side parish of St. Adalbert (*Wojciechowo*), where he established another *Gmina* base. But in no way did he abandon the Stanislawian *Gmina*; instead he advised his membership there to worm its way into the existing parish society network and again press the attack should another opportunity arise.[6]

A second weakness in the Resurrectionist-diocesan pact was evident even to the Resurrectionists themselves; that is, the pact made no allowance for the resolution of the Resurrectionist's inner struggle regarding "foreign" missions. As opponents of Kajsiewicz's brand of expansionism had feared, the Congregation was not always able to supply the Chicago mission with sufficient numbers of priests. Until local postulants were accepted into the Chicago branch of the North American Chapter in 1885, and until the Congregation founded a local novitiate in 1901, the shortage of priests continued to plague the Chicago Polonia parishes. Consequently, most of the Resurrectionist parishes in Chicago grew to unmanageable proportions, especially at the parent parish of St. Stanislaus Kostka, which experienced dimensions of growth never before witnessed in American Catholicism—a phenomenon we shall later examine.[7]

By 1871 the parish of St. Stanislaus Kostka was already showing signs of considerable vitality. Parish records for that year tell us that the Resurrectionists had by this time enrolled approximately 1,500 families, married 39 couples, and baptized 174 infants. In order to handle the steady influx of parishioners, Adolph Bakanowski, now the pastor, recalled John Wollowski to Chicago to assume the duties of assistant pasor. The numerical increase in the parish also dictated the creation of a new parish society, the St. Joseph Society, which was rushed into operation in order to assist the St. Stanislaus Society in gathering and managing financial support for the parish. Women in the parish also organized the Society of the Living Rosary, an organization that handled housekeeping duties in the altar and sacristy areas of the church. Later the Living Rosary women undertook a variety of spiritual and corporeal tasks related to the good order of any urban parish—organizing fund-raising activities, visiting the sick, taking care of children with working mothers, and conducting religious services centered around the community praying of the "living rosary."[8]

The steady growth of *Stanisƚawowo* was largely unplanned. In the aftermath of the Great Chicago Fire (which brought only scattered and somewhat minor damage to the surrounding parish neighborhoods) there was an unprecedented need for both skilled and unskilled labor in the building trades. This need was conveyed to the Old Country many times over via letters, photographs, and newspaper clippings. At the same time, Bismarck's innocuous "culture struggle" with the Catholic Church in Germany forced thousands of Poles out of Posen and Pomerania, a migration which played a significant role in the development of St. Stanislaus Kostka, which at the time was the only Polish Catholic parish in Chicago.[9]

This new immigration had an immediate impact on the earlier settlers, many of whom soon realized that the existing parish facilities were inadequate. With rumors of the proposed establishment of another parish circulating freely throughout the community, it became apparent to all the old-timers that another confrontation between the clericals and nationalists was in the offing. The Resurrectionists and the St. Stanislaus Society immediately took the position that an expansion of existing church facilities was the proper course of action. Since the Resurrectionists were in the process of centralizing their authority at St. Stanislaus, this position, of course, was to their advantage. But the St. Joseph Society, which Dyniewicz and the *Gmina* had by now thoroughly infiltrated, argued for the establishment of a new parish, since it would be used as a springboard for further nationalist activities and control. Working unilaterally, the *Gmina*-dominated St. Joseph Society purchased a large tract of land, three blocks south of St. Stanislaus, for $10,000. The *Gmina* timetable for action on the matter was cause for great alarm in the clerical camp, since the establishment of a parish nearby would undoubtedly bring about a renewal of the ideological war which the Resurrectionists so far had been able to hold off. Unhealthy (from a Resurrectionist standpoint) financial competition between the two parishes was also certain to tear apart the social fabric of the community, and intense competition for parish members was all but conceded by Father Bakanowski. Kiolbassa, of course, fumed at this resurgence of *Gmina* activity in the Stanislawian stronghold: "Alongside the good grain," he remarked, "the cockle began to sprout out." [10]

There was good reason for Dyniewicz to move in such haste, for the clericals were now beginning to telegraph various distress signals from far outside the Stanislawian village. In Union, Missouri, a newly established newspaper named *Pielgrzym ("The Pilgrim")*, under the editorship of Mr. John Barzynski and the Reverend Alexander Matuszek, was setting out "to champion the matters of religion and fly the banners of Catholicism" in all Polish-American settlements in the United States. The editorial emphasis on Catholicity rather than Polishness was disturbing enough to Dyniewicz, but what served to rankle him even more was the fact that John Barzynski was the brother of a Resurrectionist priest and that Matuszek was a Jesuit. The threat of a Resurrectionist-Jesuit alliance spreading a clerical umbrella over American Polonia, while a Resurrectionist-Irish hierarchy alliance was doing likewise on a local level, was more than Dyniewicz could stomach. Dyniewicz and the *Gmina* were also concerned that *Pielgrzym* was favoring a policy of assimilation into American life which was totally at odds with the *Gmina* position calling for Poles to return to the homeland after the day of liberation. John Barzynski, after all, stated categorically that *Pielgrzym* would always be "working for the Poles, but [that] every Pole born on American soil will never be a European Pole." The aim of *Pielgrzym* then was to convince "each Pole [to] *retain his Catholic faith, learn the language and history of Poland, but be given a chance to become a good Yankee.*" [11]

The Reverend Vincent Barzynski, whose mark on the history of *Stanisławowo* was yet to be impressed, not only championed this policy of assimilation articulated by his brother but also used the pages of *Pielgrzym* to declare war on the *Gmina Polska* and organizations of its kind. In a letter to Semenenko, Reverend Barzynski stated that *Pielgrzym* would always battle those "Masonic clements" who were attempting "to create an indifference among Poles by leveling all classes in society." These Masons, Barzynski thundered, "recognize neither the aristocrat [nor] the slave, the Catholic nor the non-Catholic etc., but reduce all men and all things to the very dust of the earth." But since "the Resurrectionists and the Jesuits are now able to unite their efforts in the field of Polish-American journalism," via *Pielgrzym*, the Church would have at its disposal a reliable tool which might be used in the battle to save souls in American Polonia.[12]

The policy of assimilation advocated by the brothers Barzynski and *Pielgrzym* won over numerous urban villagers within American Polonia who were coming to realize that the migration to *Nowy Świat* was indeed permanent and that it was foolish to labor in the streets of *anomie* in anticipation of some far-off day of liberation. Besides, many of the recent settlers were drawn to the Catholic emphasis of their Polish heritage. Noting wide pockets of support for their position, the Barzynski brothers and a prominent Detroit clergyman, Reverend Theodore Gieryk, began making plans for a consolidation of all Polish Catholic parish societies in the United States under one central organization controlled by the clergy. The plan closely paralleled the structure of the Roman Catholic First Central Union set up in Czech-American quarters and that of the Central-Verein in German-American society. The Gieryk-Barzynski proposal would unite the efforts of all religious, social, and charitable organizations that were growing helter-skelter in each local Polonia. In effect, Gieryk and the Barzynskis, via an open letter to Poles in America, were advocating the formation of what Thomas and Znaniecki later called a "supra-territorial organization." From the clerical side this supraterritorial would come to be called the "Polish Roman Catholic Union" in the United States (to which the nationalists would counter with a supraterritorial of their own making—the Polish National Alliance). An organizational meeting of all interested parties took place in Detroit on 3 October 1873. At this convention, John Barzynski, who had earlier established the *Organizacja Polska w Ameryce* ("Organization of Poles in America"), moved that the Detroit and Union, Missouri, locals consolidate their membership with the understanding that another meeting, to be held after an extensive joint membership drive, be held in Chicago during the following year. The motion accepted, the participants selected a subcommittee made up of Gieryk, John Barzynski, and Peter Kiolbassa to be responsible for arranging a national convention of all Polish-Americans in the United States. In this fashion then did the call go out for the formation of the Polish Roman Catholic Union in America, which would come to *Stanisławowo* on 14–16 October 1874.[13]

The brothers Barzynski were most optimistic about the prospects for such a national fraternal organization. In another letter to the Reverend Semenenko, Vincent Barzynski stated outright that the coming convention was "the will of Providence and of Mary, Queen of Poland." John Barzynski, caught up in the enthusiasm of the moment, even renamed his newspaper. Anticipating that *Piel-*

grzym would become the official organ of the forthcoming supraterritorial, Barzynski changed the masthead to read *GAZETA POLSKA KATOLICKA*, or *The Polish Catholic Gazette.*[14]

The first convention of the Polish Roman Catholic Union (PRCU) met, just as planned, in Kiolbassa's bastion, the parish hall of St. Stanislaus Kostka. From the outset of the meeting there was never any doubt about the general objectives of the national organization. First, it was agreed that the fundamental goal of the PRCU would be the preservation of Catholicism among future generations of Poles in America; at the same time, the founders wished to preserve the Polish identity in American life. Next, the PRCU committed itself to the education of Polish-American youth via an elaborate Catholic parochial school system, both elementary and secondary; to this end, it was thought necessary to firmly establish seminaries and convents which would train priests and nuns for work in American Polonia. Lastly, the PRCU delegates gave priority to the establishment of hospitals and libraries and the creation of a network of "immigrant parish" banks.[15]

The arrival of the PRCU in Chicago, the selection of Chicago as a national headquarters, and the broad-based institutional framework elaborated upon called for some sort of response from the nationalist party. A vigorous counterattack launched by the *Gmina* was all but guaranteed when Dyniewicz pored over the contents of the PRCU Constitution (entitled *Constitution of the Polish Catholic Societies of Mutual Aid in the United States of North America*). In the Constitution's introduction, the clerical party drafters made it clear that PRCU members were "to serve God and Country with pure Catholic heart, and with the customary integrity of our Polish ancestry, independently of those wicked men who seek exclusive possession of our souls and bodies." The reference was obviously made in regard to the "Masonic elements" in the Chicago *Gmina*. In Article Two, Dyniewicz noted that "the Union certainly desires to become, within a short time, one of the principle causes enabling Poles in America to achieve a condition free of foreign influence. . . ." Did the statement mean to imply that the *Gmina* was that "foreign influence"? Did the statement mean that the cause of *ojczyzna* was to be abandoned in favor of some ill-defined policy of Americanization? The vague wording of the Article appeared to single out the *Gmina*, but still Dyniewicz was not sure. But the crux of the clerical party position and its intended influence was precisely spelled out in Article Three, entitled "The Religion and Morality of the Union." It was here that Dyniewicz detected the long shadow of the Foley-Kajsiewicz pact: "It [the PRCU] promises absolute clerical obedience to the bishops, and the pastors appointed by them, as the custodians of faith and morality"; furthermore, "if any society belonging to the Union shall keep . . . an excommunicated member, e.g., all those enrolled in secret societies, this society, as a penalty for breach of faith, shall lose all rights of union. . . ." The PRCU would never harbor "men of doubtful character, uncertain morals, and little knowledge of the Catholic religion." Finally, any local fraternal organization requesting membership into the Union would need "a testimonial letter from the local pastor stating that this society is in communion with the Holy Roman Catholic Church."[16]

No piece of evidence coming out of this Chicago Polonia battleground of one hundred years ago focuses more sharply on the clear-cut divisions between the clericals and the nationals than does the PRCU Constitution. The events leading up to the October 1874 convention also account for the corresponding moves taken by the St. Joseph Society to establish a parish free of Resurrectionist control. With the *burza* of "union" looming on the Polonia horizon, the nationalists became all the more convinced that the fight over the new parish was in effect a fight for survival.

As could be expected, the St. Stanislaus Society strongly objected to the proximity of the site selected by the rival St. Joseph Society. Numerous negotiation sessions, headed by the Reverend Bakanowski, between the two parish societies always ended in failure, and occasional if one-sided pleas by Bakanowski for peace and understanding in the community were also to no avail. Frustrated by the intransigence of the *Gmina*-run St. Joseph Society, which held all the chips in the bargaining process because it possessed the capital for the church site and building, Bakanowski eschewed his role of neutral negotiator for that of clerical partisan. On every occasion now, Bakanowski used the pulpit to attack the Mason influence in the St. Joseph Society. Thus it came as no surprise to any of the clericals when Bakanowski began receiving anonymous letters instructing him to stop his public attacks on the Masons. When the pastor ignored such attempts at intimidation, he began to receive a series of death threats which somehow made their way into the rectory. Bakanowski, aware of the seriousness of these threats, armed himself with a revolver, which he could be seen carrying whenever his priestly duties took him away from the rectory or church areas. The sight of an armed pastor dramatically illustrated how deep and swift the currents of hate had now become inside Chicago Polonia.

Given Bakanowski's intransigence, and having no viable alternative, the St. Joseph Society seceded from St. Stanislaus Kostka. That the secession move could succeed strongly indicated that the *Gmina Polska* was a dominant force within the Josephite organization; it was also an indication of the growing appeal of the nationalist position. Now out on their own, the Josephites funded the construction of another parish church—the parish village of Holy Trinity, or *Trójcowo* as it was called by Dyniewicz and his contemporaries, where the nationalists decided to make their stand. Here they would erect a bastion for the nationalist party which would be defended against all comers—the Irish hierarchy, the Resurrectionist Congregation, and the parishioners at *Stanisławowo*. The building of *Trójcowo* began a twenty-year war.[17]

The *Gmina* conquest at Holy Trinity was not gained without a price. As in their previous machinations at *Stanisławowo*, the *Gmina* arranged to have the title to Holy Trinity parish made out in the name of the St. Joseph Society. Applying the European custom of *jus patronatus* (right of patronage) in a collective sense so as to apply to all members of the St. Joseph Society, the lay leaders in the *Gmina* claimed ownership of "their" church without ever feeling that the Church canons regarding trusteeship had been breached. Of course, Bishop Foley could not agree with the Josephite claim. He saw the entire matter in the light of previous plenary decrees emanating from Baltimore, which opposed trusteeship in any form. So it came as no surprise to the *Gmina* when Foley, as he had done at St. Stanislaus two years previous, refused to consecrate the church of Holy Trinity. But this time Foley went one step further: he invoked the diocesan-Resurrectionist pact and insisted that the Josephites at Holy Trinity accept the administration of the Congregation of the Resurrection at the parish. Only then, Foley stated, could the process of negotiations between the chancery and the Josephites even begin. Based on the commitment he had made with Kajsiewicz, Bishop Foley was only carrying out diocesan policy. But what Foley had never taken into consideration was the possibility that the Resurrectionists might not be able to maintain a permanent pastor at the Polonia mission. After all, the tinderbox quality of the mission there, as well as the personal dangers confronted on a daily basis by Bakanowski, were beginning to wear down the patience of the Resurrectionist fathers. Father Bakanowski, totally exhausted by his strenuous schedule and the abuse showered upon him by the nationalists, suddenly resigned his post and departed for Panna Marya. His assistant, the Reverend Wollowski, then tried his hand at deflating community tensions. But Wollowski could not bring about a reconciliation between the contending parties either, and by autumn of 1873 he too was on his way back to Texas. Shortly after the departure of Wollowski, the Resurrectionist North American Chapter assigned the vigorous and healthy Reverend Felix Zwiardowski to the pastorship in *Stanisławowo*. Zwiardowski on his arrival immediately proposed that Holy Trinity retain its identity but that it be made a branch of St. Stanislaus Kostka. In a public gesture of reconciliation, Zwiardowski marched down Noble Street to Holy Trinity where he conducted a blessing of the church bell in open ceremony. He even confidently predicted, in a letter to Bishop Foley dated 12 November 1873, that "the church will be ready for consecration by summer." But the Zwiardowski peace initiatives were given a severe jolt when a delegation of parishioners at Holy Trinity voted to oust the Resurrectionist pastor and any of his associates. Then, in a move designed to seal the fate of Zwiardowski, the Trinitarian delegation in revolutionary fashion appointed a "committee of public safety" to guard their church from Resurrectionist intrusions.[18]

Such displays of open hostility, along with the brutal Chicago winters—which in 1872–1873 were the worst in Chicago's history—took the fight out of Zwiardowski. The *Jubilee Album* of St. Stanislaus Kostka tells us that Father Zwiardowski began "having difficulties with the Chicago climate [so that] his health was being jeopardized."[19] The grueling schedule which required that he and his assistant administer to several thousand souls also proved to be too taxing for the normally robust Resurrectionists. The assistant pastor, the Reverend Francis Lange, complained to Superior-General Semenenko (the replacement for Kajsiewicz who had died in 1873) that "we have as much work to do here in one day as you have back in Rome for a whole month."[20] Thus, spirited away by events far beyond his control, Zwiardowski followed his predecessors to their clerical haven in sunny Panna Marya. Peter Kiolbassa, in a tone of resignation, could only remark that "Father Felix was revered and loved by all."[21] Next in the litany-like procession of unsuccessful Resurrectionists was Reverend Simon Wieczorek. But Wieczorek could stand turbulent Chicago Polonia for only eight weeks and then he too was gone.

In the brief span of four years, the clerical-nationalist conflict had ground up the bodies and souls of five successive pastors. The ninety-nine-year pact between the still living Foley and the now deceased Kajsiewicz was ironically wavering between life and death. The Congregation of the Resurrection simply could not raise back to life the faraway urban village of *Stanisławowo* on which it was staking its missionary reputation. Instead of guiding a unified and dynamic community-parish as envisioned by the saintly Janski, the Congregation now found itself embroiled in the most serious intraethnic dispute taking place anywhere in Catholic America during the 1870s. The situation was so depressing to Resurrectionist observers on the other side of the Atlantic that serious consideration was again being given to abandoning the Chicago mission altogether. With the *Gmina Polska* already in frantic pursuit of a separate supraterritorial organization of its own, one aimed at galvanizing the nationalist sentiments cropping up elsewhere and one which could conceivably provide a formidable challenge to the PRCU, all the ingredients for a full-scale war between clericals and nationalists were already present, in miniature, on the Chicago scene. And as the *Gmina* moved more and more closely to its lofty and long sought after goal of a Polish National Alliance, the polarization between the "Catholic" party and the "Polish" party in Chicago came to take on greater significance in the wider arena of American Polonia. It is for this reason that we have troubled ourselves with examining what on first sight appear to have been nothing more than obscure and unimportant events dealing with the formation of two Polish Catholic parishes in Chicago; the fratricide engaged in by the Catholic and Polish parties would evolve into a Unionist (PRCU) versus Alliancist (PNA) battleground which would occupy the center stage of Polish American history in the pre–World War I period.

These, then, are the larger outlines of the central issues and problems hanging like a pall over the Resurrectionist Central House in Rome more than a century ago. But for better or for worse, Superior-General Semenenko, the sole survivor of the three Resurrectionist founders, was still going about quieting the doubters in his own house; he was still exhorting his fellow priests to come forth with a supreme effort for the Chicago Polonia mission that was the will of the Lord and the wave of the future of the Resurrectionist Congregation. Semenenko was still waiting to see if Father Vincent Barzynski, already on his way to Chicago in this dark autumn of 1874, might not by the grace of God bring this Resurrectionist mission back to life.[22]

4

The Barzynski Era:
From Strife to Schism

For some time neither Catholics nor Poles existed in America, but only Unionists (PRCU) or Alliancists (PNA); he who was not a member of the Alliance, the PNA did not regard as a Pole; while whoever was not a member of the Polish Roman Catholic Union, the PRCU did not regard as a Catholic.

Wenceslaus Kruszka, *Historya Polska w Ameryce*

Father Vincent Michael Barzynski arrived in Chicago on 6 September 1874. From that day on, for the next quarter-century, Father Barzynski's dynamic presence would bring about historic changes having a significant impact not only on *Stanisławowo* but on the rest of American Polonia as well. The historian Kruszka once described him to be "like Pope Gregory VII, a man of iron strength of will."[1] Judging by the handsome thirty-six-year-old Resurrectionist's future accomplishments, this remark was most appropriate. Adept at the intricate organization of human and material resources, Barzynski channeled the energies of his flock into the building of a gigantic community-parish system—churches, schools, religious societies, newspapers, fraternal organizations, welfare agencies, and hospitals— far exceeding the expectations of Superior-General Semenenko, Bishop Foley, the St. Stanislaus Kostka Society, and, to its dismay, the *Gmina Polska*. In the person of Father Barzynski, Chicago Polonia gained a "brick and mortar" pastor *par excellence*; no contemporary immigrant clergyman in the Chicago Roman Catholic Archdiocese even came close to matching his monumental building feats. These many Barzynski-directed institutions were to have an immediate effect on his own generation as well as far-reaching influences on future ones. Barzynski's motto—"For God and Country"—permeated these institutions to such an extent that coming generations were not always able, or even willing, to escape from their solid, Polish Catholic, first generation immigrant foundation. As for Polonia's future children who did occasionally slip away from the bark of Barzynski, they did so at the risk of paying Polonia's supreme penalty, ostracism

The Reverend Vincent Barzynski, pastor of St. Stanislaus Kostka Parish, 1874–1899

from the community-parish—a penalty Barzynski did not hesitate to impose when parish unity was threatened.[2]

Father Barzynski often spoke of unity during his long pastoral tenure at St. Stanislaus Kostka Parish—unity of family, of parish, and of religious faith. Being a fiercely loyal individual himself, he expected his flock to be the same. According to Barzynski, a true Catholic owed his allegiance to the Holy Father, to his bishop, and to his pastor. And this hierarchical order was not to be questioned, as God's authority came down to His children in only this sequence; it was this authority that provided the communion of faithful with a stable and all-powerful weapon against what Barzynski felt were the Church's most powerful enemies in the nineteenth century—socialism, Masonry, and anarchy—each of which if left unchecked would tear into the unified fabric of the community-parish.[3]

But as history has often taught men in different places and times, leaders manifesting an "iron strength of will" have usually evoked emotions of either strong admiration or deep resentment, thereby coaxing the forces of moderation, diplomacy, and tolerance to search elsewhere for fertile ground. Barzynski's fellow Resurrectionists even attested to this strong side of his character. Father Bakanowski, for example, once remarked to Superior-General Kajsiewicz that Father Vincent was a "zealous Priest [who] has worked like an ox from morning to eleven at night. . . . he thinks of a thousand tasks and after that he wants to do all of them diligently . . . [yet] he doesn't want to listen to any advice . . . [as] prudence and moderation are found in him rarely."[4] Bakanowski also made mention of Barzynski's quickness to anger, but he tempered the criticism by adding that Father Vincent was equally quick to forgive.[5]

If Barzynski was able to create institutional bridges made for crossing in later times—a generational cohesion of sorts—he was not always up to the task of defusing the explosive factionalism in *Stanisławowo* and *Trójcowo* which faced him upon his arrival and which would continue to torment him for nearly two decades. One can summarize the Barzynski era by pointing out its fundamental paradox: because the energetic Stanislawian pastor was so diligent in his attempts at "unification," he inadvertently prolonged the Unionist-versus-Alliancist struggle far beyond its normal life expectancy. Due to Barzynski's "iron strength of will," Unionists and Alliancists both found themselves clinging tenaciously and obstinately to outmoded ideologies, rarely pausing along the way to contemplate what the effects of their actions might be on their children. Because this fraternal enmity was allowed to persist over the entire first generation, Polonia's children born long after this period would come to absorb the awesome consequences of American Catholicism's only major schism. This schism, brought on by the rise of the Polish National Catholic Church in America, served to exacerbate Polonia's already severe and bitter "identity crisis." Long after so many other ethnic groups had been swallowed up by the seductive processes of Americanization which enabled them to enter the garden of material affluence, Polonia was still only beginning to emerge, ever so slowly, from her bloodied, misunderstood, and contorted past. Shaking her head in dismay at those endless fraternal conventions where the ugly scars of schism still embarrassed all, Polonia and her children would invariably step out into the streets, after countless and futile debates, still in a state of frustrated bewilderment. Not having found the peace and self-assurance which inevitably comes to those who have come to grips with their histories, Polonia was not able to meet head-on newer and more pressing social emergencies which were radically different from her older internal problems. And as the fathers of Chicago Polonia became grandfathers and great-grandfathers, this absence of internal peace was to become more and more painful, especially when the children began moving away to new lands on the suburban horizon in search of new and perhaps false gods to worship.

Vincent Michael Barzynski was born on 20 September 1838, to Joseph and Maryanna (Seroczynska) Bara in Sulislawice, a village located midway between Cracow and Lublin in Russian Poland. Vincent's hard-working father, who later changed the family name to Barzynski, was known to have held down several jobs simultaneously; he was town publicist, part-time watchmaker, and organist at the local church. Shortly after Vincent's younger brother, Joseph Jr., was born, the elder Barzynski moved his family to Tomaszów-Lubelski where he accepted a position as organist. Here, in Austrian Poland, Vincent received his elementary school education. When the time came for Vincent to attend secondary school, his parents reluctantly decided against sending him to Lublin because they feared that his frequent illnesses would not permit regular attendance. Fortunately, the Barzynski family befriended a retired inspector of the district high schools, a certain Narcyz Klembowski, who offered to devote his last years to tutoring Vincent and his younger brother Joseph. When Vincent was eighteen years old he decided to enter the diocesan seminary at Lublin in order to study for the priesthood. Completing the philosophy curriculum in 1858 and the theology courses three years later, he was ordained a diocesan priest on 28 October 1861.

Immediately after his ordination, Father Barzynski, suffering from an acute bronchial condition which incapacitated him for the next few months, was forced to return home. The illness brought on a chronic lung condition which would flare up occasionally and inopportunely for the remainder of his life. After recovering, Barzynski was appointed vicar of the parish church at Horodło, located on the Bug river, and from there he was transferred in the summer of 1862 to the Zamość Collegiate Church, where he was appointed to the position of canon by Suffragan Bishop W. Baranowski. Here Barzynski witnessed the execution of known and suspected Polish insurrectionists by Russian troops. As the Insurrection gained momentum, Barzynski returned once again to his hometown of Tomaszów, which had by now become a seedbed of Polish insurgency. In fact, several days prior to Barzynski's arrival there, Russians had executed twenty-two civilians who had been accused of military rebellion. Stung by these atrocities, Barzynski offered his services to the Polish provisional government and was assigned by one of the regional organizers to the dangerous task of gun-runner. But his subversive activities were soon discovered by the Russians, who then placed him under "special supervision" for six months.

After his release, Barzynski fled to Austrian Poland, where the political climate was said to be more friendly to the insurgents. Yet, having crossed the border without proper authorization and not having the necessary passport papers, Father Barzynski once again became a fugitive. During the autumn of 1863 he escaped to Cracow, where he stayed with the Reformed Dominicans while negotiating for an Austrian passport. In March 1864 the Austrian police discovered Barzynski's hiding place, apprehended him, and placed him under arrest. They jailed him at Olmutz for two weeks prior to transferring him to prisons at Iglau and Koniggratz. While at Koniggratz, Barzynski enjoyed a brief reunion with his father, just prior to his release. Granted a passport to leave Austria, Barzynski went to Paris, where he made acquaintances with numerous other emigrant priests from Poland, among whom were the Reverends Kajsiewicz, Semenenko, and Jelowicki of the Congregation of the Resurrection. Impressed by the missionary challenge of the Resurrectionists, Barzynski entered their novitiate in Rome and eventually took final vows on 18 September 1866. With Pius IX's blessing, Barzynski made the voyage to America where he was assigned to Polish missions in the Galveston, Texas, diocese under Bishop Claude-Marie Dubuis. When the Resurrectionists turned over their Galveston mission to the diocese in 1874, Father Barzynski requested and was granted the assignment at *Stanisławowo* in Chicago.[6]

The nationalist party at *Trójcowo* soon discovered that the Reverend Barzynski's policies would cause more problems for the *Gmina Polska* than had those of the previous five pastors combined. From the outset of his pastorship at *Stanisławowo*, Barzynski showed little patience with the Trinitarians. Instead of pursuing a policy of appeasement, as had most of his predecessors, he attempted instead "to cure the illness by killing the patient."[7] In a variety of moves designed to completely eliminate the *Gmina* presence, Barzynski almost singlehandedly triggered a twenty-year struggle between the clericals and the nationals for supreme control of Chicago Polonia. The first phase (1874–1877) of the conflict centered on the trusteeship question and the administration of church funds, as one of Barzynski's first ambitions was to build a gigantic church structure at St. Stanislaus; after a brief interim period, the conflict entered a second stage during 1881–1889 over the issue of legitimate ownership of church property at Holy Trinity, a phase which was highlighted by the entrance of the Polish Roman Catholic Union on the side of the clerical party and the Polish National Alliance on the side of the nationalist party; the third and final phase took place in 1889–1893 when the Resurrectionists attempted to gain administrative control over both the rival parishes, in effect, a final test of the Foley-Kajsiewicz pact.[8]

Shortly after his arrival, Father Barzynski began devising a long-range strategy for dealing with recalcitrant Trinitarians. Aware of the potent nationalistic responses Dyniewicz and the *Gmina* could generate whenever the cause of *ojczyzna* was invoked, Barzynski decided to abandon the past practice of fighting on the enemy's terrain. The fertile soil of the Foley-Kajsiewicz pact, he thought, would be the most conducive over the long run for nurturing the ideals of the clerical party. If the Trinitarians could be maneuvered into opposition to the chancery on practical and critical issues such as church management and funding, then certainly Bishop Foley would opt to come down hard on the *Gmina Polska*. The astute Barzynski recognized that an Irish-American bishop was not likely to concern himself with new immigrant debates regarding the pros and cons of Poland's international situation. But questions dealing with the bishop's authority and power of the purse? These any Chicago bishop would handle in the most diligent, efficient, and attentive fashion.

Having made this assessment (which was most accurate), Barzynski began to experiment with tactics designed to achieve what *he* felt should be Chicago Polonia's first priority—the raising of funds for a mammoth church building designed to house all Polish Catholics on the northwest side, a superparish of which he would be pastor. It was a position he knew the diocese would have to support. He also knew, however, that this financial burden could not be shouldered by the Stanislawians alone. For this he would need Trinitarian support. Boldly moving into the nationalist party's headquarters down the street, Barzynski commanded the Trinitarians to relinquish their autonomy over Holy Trinity church and to immediately take steps to remodel the structure, making it either into a school or a parish hall. He then informed the Trinitarians of his plans to construct the gigantic church building at St. Stanislaus which, he said, was to be used by *both* groups and which would remain under Resurrectionist jurisdiction (up to this time Holy Trinity did not have its own pastor). The Barzynski proposal was tantamount to an ultimatum, and seeing it in this light, the Trinitarians proceeded to argue their case for a separate parish before the chancery all the more vigorously. To this Barzynski responded by attempting to assimilate the St. Joseph Society funds into the Stanislawian treasury. When so brazen a move was successfully resisted by the St. Joseph Society, Barzynski compromised by granting Holy Trinity separate status—as long as he was pastor of both parishes. When the Trinitarian delegation refused this compromise measure, Barzynski informed Bishop Foley of its stubbornness, and together they decided that Holy Trinity Parish (still unconsecrated at this point) be closed down until further notice. Rather than submit to this diocesan intervention, the angry Trinitarians joined the German parish of St. Boniface and began a long series of negotiations with the Vatican to settle the dispute.[9]

In no way did the Trinitarian counterattack deter Barzynski's fierce desire to build his church. Complaining that the original structure was "too cramped, hot, dangerous, and not conducive to the divine service" (it was built during the Kiolbassa-Dyniewicz fiasco of 1869),[10] Father Barzynski engaged the P.C. Keely firm of Chicago to design and build a 200′ × 80′ structure with a seating capacity of 1,500. With twin steeples reaching 200 feet in the air, in the middle of which would stand a seventeen-foot statue of Saint Stanislaus Kostka, the church would assuredly dominate the Polonia skyline, a testament to the dominance of the clerical party. Barzynski drew up plans for a three-story rectory, totalling 9,450 square feet, to be connected to the new parish church. The entire cost of the two buildings would run close to $20,000, an enormous expense for Barzynski's predominantly lower working class parishioners, but an expense he felt was justified considering that his parish serviced over 400 families at the time of his arrival.[11]

What concerned Barzynski the most was the possibility that the community's scarce funds could be siphoned off by the equally aggressive nationalists. He claimed that the *Gmina* membership was made up of "troublemakers, visionaries, and lazy socialistic-minded idealists, all of whom were immensely cunning with their greasy palms, and all of whom were bent on destroying the bond between the common folk and their zealous and honest priests."[12] In a sermon delivered to a packed church in November of 1876 (probably on the feast of St. Stanislaus, 13 November), the Reverend Barzynski saw the opportunity to gather support from his parishioners for the building project, explain his own personal convictions and rather controversial positions, and attack any dissenters in the *Gmina*-St. Joseph Society-Trinitarian camp who might be within hearing distance. He began the sermon by reminding his listeners that the St. Stanislaus Society had been duly authorized by Bishop Foley to act as official spokesman for the parish, and that parishioners were not to lend their support to any other group which might be tempted to meddle in parish affairs. With God's help, the flock would have to assist the shepherd who, when acting alone, could do nothing. He then thanked his supporters in the audience for their wonderful financial support. But Barzynski did not stop here. Instead he chose to meet head-on some of the charges that had been leveled at him by his opponents, employing a simple but vigorous style of rhetoric that not only revealed the intensity of Polonia's internal strife but also his own personal character:

> But one thing hurts me more than anything else, and that is when I see your cold hearts, dear brothers, hearts I would work for until my death. For the past twenty-two months I have labored for you and your children, and still some of you cannot sincerely say, "May God bless you."
>
> Others complain that "We pay the priest's salary so that we should not have to thank him in any other way!" But listen to me, dearly beloved: Do you think I work for a salary like a farm hand or a clerk? Yet if matters came to that, I would; afterall, I have only accepted two months salary for the many months I have worked here. In any event, the salary is not the main issue here, and that isn't what keeps the priests going, for it is only God's will that we continue. . . .[13]

St. Stanislaus Kostka Church (Chicago Historical Society)

Interior of St. Stanislaus Kostka (Chicago Historical Society)

Barzynski then reminded the congregation of the many duties he and his assistants were required to carry out in order that the community-parish might function properly: he spoke of the priests' deep involvement in the parish, the schools, the hospitals, and the church societies; of their hearing confessions, preparing first communicants, and organizing religious processions; and of, most time consuming of all, their handling of parish finances. Finally, he returned to his favorite themes of authority, parish unity, and the building of a church that would last for generations:

> And still there are tongues without conscience, lacking in charity, continually speaking with malice. May God forgive them for they know not what they do. . . .
>
> Their various complaints in the end result really don't help anyone, and it is high time that unity begins to predominate in the Polish Catholic Parish of Saint Stanislaus Kostka, such as is the case in every other loyal Catholic parish in Chicago. The Christ Jesus wants it this way, the Bishop expects it this way, and that is the way you and I must want it.
>
> We must cling together, even if despondent and in tears, and lift our hearts to God in heaven as brothers in one. Let us work together. Everyone! Everyone! Everyone who believes in the Triune God, in Jesus Christ's Redemption, in the Real Presence. Everyone, the young and the old, the married and single, the rich and the poor, everyone with the spirit of good will—Let us all mutually love each

other; let us refrain from judging each other; let us not take advantage of anyone; instead let us confide in God Our Father who will hear our pleas and come to our assistance. Let us all do something constructive—as a group—and begin to build a church for the honor and glory of God and for the nourishment of our souls. This church will be a testimony not only to these unbelievers, but also an everlasting heritage to your beloved children, grandchildren, and great grandchildren.[14]

Barzynski's sermon is a classic example of the simple and direct style of rhetoric he and later generations of Polish-American clergymen used in their fundraising ventures. Even if by today's standards the rhetoric does not appear to be forceful (printed speeches read in one's living room never do justice to the real thing), Barzynski's style was nonetheless effective and successful. Transplanted peasants, many of whom retained the medieval notion of equating eternal salvation with monetary donations to the Church,[15] would give and give and continue to give to the support of Chicago Polonia's community-parish system. And for this reason Barzynski's "iron will" prevailed in this first major test. On the Christmas feast of 1877, the Reverend Barzynski celebrated a solemn high midnight mass before a tightly packed congregation which must have been deeply thrilled and awe-struck by its newly built, twin-spired house of worship—one of the largest in the city. The triumphal Christmas scene was only a beginning for the energetic and ambitious Stanislawian pastor who was destined to open new parishes thirteen more times in Chicago Polonia. And true to Barzynski's prediction, the hardy but aesthetically pleasing church of Saint Stanislaus Kostka still services Polonia's great-grandchildren on the near northwest side.[16]

This show of strength on the part of Barzynski and the clerical party did not come about without a price, as it did little to deter the influence or lower the morale of the *Gmina*. Shortly before the occasion of Barzynski's sermon, Henryk Sienkiewicz, the noted Positivist School novelist who wrote *Quo Vadis*, visited Chicago Polonia. In his *Letters of Travels in America*, Sienkiewicz refers to the fierce factional warfare brewing in *Stanisławowo* with the arrival of Barzynski. By 1876, Sienkiewicz claims, the clerical party was composed of seven different religious societies, whereas the nationalist party claimed two organizations—the Polish Village (Dyniewicz's *Gmina Polska*) and the recently formed Kosciuszko Society. Sienkiewicz tells us that both sides at the time were busily engaged in extending their influence beyond the confines of Chicago Polonia by supporting colonization projects in other states. The *Polish Gazette*, published by Dyniewicz, advertised prominently a *Gmina*-sponsored colony at Warren Hoino, Arkansas. The *Polish Catholic Gazette*, headed by Barzynski, printed glowing accounts of the clerical party-sponsored colony in New Posen, Nebraska. Before long, each newspaper was attacking the efforts of the opposite faction, pouncing on any issue, regardless of substance, to convince and win over its readers. Barzynski wrote that the Warren Hoino settlement was cluttered "with too many trees," thus hampering attempts to farm the area; any inhabitants there would most assuredly "starve to death." Dyniewicz counterattacked with the charge that "New Posen had no trees . . . [and] lacked materials for home-building"; the site was simply "too desolate."[17]

Sienkiewicz himself had mixed reactions to the dominant role of the clergy in Polonia's public affairs. On the positive side, Sienkiewicz admitted that the priests "maintained some degree of moral unity among the Poles." He also spoke highly of the clergy as teachers and as dispensers of the sacraments; the clergy and the churches provided "a refuge for new arrivals," and prevented Poles from disappearing "unnoticed among foreign elements." On the other hand, the same functions enabled the clergy "to wield political influence" and "to control the votes of [their] flock." Thus, Sienkiewicz argued, the Catholic clergy tended to perpetuate "community exclusiveness" by not encouraging contacts with Polish Protestants, especially those from Silesia and Mazuria.[18]

While all this was taking place, the Dyniewicz faction, chafing under recent setbacks dealt by both Barzynski and the diocese, began negotiating for the services of a non-Resurrectionist priest to take over pastoral duties at Holy Trinity. The move was in clear violation of the Foley-Kajsiewicz pact. It is quite possible that the St. Joseph Society never knew of the pact's existence let along the pact's contents; it is not known whether Foley or Kajsiewicz ever made public their agreement. In any event, the Trinitarians convinced a certain Reverend Adalbert Mielcuszny, who was not a Resurrectionist, to become their pastor. It is clear that the Trinitarians simply could not reconcile themselves to ever being led by a Resurrectionist.

Father Mielcuszny was ordained in the historic Polish diocese of Gniezno in 1860. After serving in several small Polish villages, he was given permission by his superior, Bishop Brodziszewski, to emigrate to New York so as to work in Polish colonies there. In 1874 he was installed as pastor of St. Stanislaus Parish in New York City, where he served for two years before becoming engaged in an irreconcilable conflict with his parishioners. He was then dismissed from his pastoral duties by Archbishop McCloskey. After his release, Mielcuszny came to Chicago where he had many friends, one of whom was Ladislaus Dyniewicz. The nationalist leader, after explaining the current situation at Holy Trinity, convinced Mielcuszny that he would have a bright future as pastor of the parish. However, according to Canon Law a visiting priest was not permitted to function until granted that permission by the local bishop. Accordingly, a Trinitarian delegation confronted Bishop Foley about Mielcuszny's permanent installation as pastor. Such daring was hardly appreciated by Foley, who by now was probably becoming most exasperated with Polonia's never-ending internal governance difficulties.

Holy Trinity Church in the late 19th century

Interior of Holy Trinity Church in the late 19th century

Foley, as could be expected, reiterated his earlier stance requiring a Resurrectionist to head the parish. To this the delegation is said to have chorused: "We don't want Resurrectionists; we want saintly priests!"[19]

Having reached another stalemate, which should hardly have come as a surprise to the Trinitarians, the delegation decided to press its case further by going to the Vatican, a strategy which had previously been used during the Reverend Zwiardowski's tenure at St. Stanislaus Kostka. Writing to Cardinal Franchi, then the Prefect of the Propagation of the Faith in the Vatican, the delegation went on to describe how a large urban parish of several thousand souls was being held in check by diocesan authorities in Chicago, how this parish was in desperate need of reopening, and how a capable priest to handle its affairs had been procured. After three such written attempts, the delegation succeeded; this is quite surprising when one considers that the Vatican at the time was seldom concerned about the plight of urban immigrant parishes in the United States (not until the Plenary Council of 1884 was the issue even addressed satisfactorily in the United States). On 24 April 1877, Father Adalbert Mielcuszny, much to the satisfaction of the nationalist faction who felt that they had in Mielcuszny a champion of Polish liberation, was installed as pastor of Holy Trinity Parish. Barzynski was infuriated by this sudden turn of events. He must have been somewhat embarrassed by the fact that the Trinitarians, who were technically his own parishioners, went all the way to the Vatican in their attempt to oust him. He also must have known that Cardinal Franchi's negative opinion of his leadership could easily be transmitted across the city of Rome to the Resurrectionist Central House, thus embarrassing him even further. The parishioners at St. Stanislaus Kostka were equally upset by the Vatican's decision because the financial burden for the construction of the new church would now fall solely on their shoulders. Barzynski continued to attack Mielcuszny verbally, insisting that the new Trinitarian pastor was a "schismatic." Mielcuszny was even physically assaulted on one occasion, although guilt for this incident was never pinned on the Stanislawians.[20]

The harassment of the Reverend Mielcuszny was to continue throughout his tenure at Holy Trinity. The *Chicago Tribune* reported that he was "frequently . . . insulted in the street, and [that] several persons of local prominence had threatened him, and repeated time and again that he must get out of the place [Holy Trinity]."[21] Mielcuszny further complicated and aggravated this difficult situation by making out the deeds to the parish church and property not only in the name of the bishop, but also to the parish and to himself. Bishop Patrick Feehan, in line with the policies of his predecessor (Foley died on 19 February 1879), retaliated by suspending Mielcuszny from his priestly duties, first by forbidding him to hear confessions, and then by removing him from the pastorate. Feehan's declaration apparently countermanded Cardinal Franchi's decision—a classic example of how one legal canon of ecclesiastical authority could be used to negate the effects of another canon. Feehan was strongly influenced in his decision by Barzynski, who bent over backwards to provide the newly appointed bishop with all the sordid details of previous nationalist party maneuvers to gain control over all property at Holy Trinity. Yet, despite the bishop's formal suspension, the undaunted Mielcuszny refused to leave his parish or to change the beneficiaries in the church deed, arguing throughout that he was serving at Holy Trinity's at the pleasure of the Vatican and that he had personally contributed to Holy Trinity's financial support out of his own pocket—a fragmentary piece of evidence which points to the fact that Polonia's priests may have had outside economic interests (diocesan priests took vows of obedience and chastity only, whereas religious orders usually took vows of obedience, chastity, and poverty). When Mielcuszny persisted in his disobedience to the chancery Feehan decided to close down Holy Trinity Parish. This only resulted in further street riots in front of Holy Trinity and down the block at St. Stanislaus Kostka.[22]

The eruptions on Noble Street took their toll, both physically and psychologically, on the normally robust and feisty Mielcuszny, who was now only a shadow of his former self. Mrs. Englemann, his housekeeper, reported that on the sultry morning of 2 June 1881 the 51-year-old pastor could be seen pacing back and forth across his basement apartment in the Holy Trinity School, muttering over and over again, "They are making me lots of trouble. It is too bad, too bad." Attempting to calm himself, Mielcuszny sat down to a light early lunch of his favorite radish salad. Meanwhile he sent Mrs. Englemann over to the home of another parishioner to handle some parish business. When she returned at 11:30

A.M., she found the pastor lying face down in a pool of blood. He was dead. Suspecting foul play (the priest's watch and gold chain were missing, and there were bruises on his forehead), Mrs. Englemann called the police. Rumors quickly circulated throughout the neighborhood that Pastor Mielcuszny had been murdered, and hundreds of angry parishioners began milling around the church. But no violence occurred, and an autopsy report by two physicians stated the cause of death as apoplexy. Despite the medical evidence, few parishioners believed the autopsy report; many felt that Mielcuszny had indeed been murdered by Stanislawian henchmen.[23]

The death of Mielcuszny, the circumstances of which paralleled those of the Juszkiewicz incident, robbed the Trinitarians of their parish leadership. In the meantime, Father Barzynski journeyed to Rome to discuss the overall Chicago Polonia situation with his superiors. Perhaps he simply made the trip in order to formulate future plans of action for the Chicago mission, but he may also have come at the behest of his superiors who wanted more information on the death of Mielcuszny and some of the recent street fighting in *Stanisławowo* and *Trójcowo*. In any event, Barzynski's work in Rome led to another victory for the clerical party. On 5 October 1881, four months after Mielcuszny's burial, a committee headed by Barzynski met with Archbishop Feehan to discuss the future of Holy Trinity. As a result of this meeting with the archbishop (Chicago was elevated to the rank of archdiocese on 10 September 1880, and Feehan was appointed its first archbishop), Barzynski was given control once again over both St. Stanislaus Kostka and Holy Trinity parishes; this was in effect a reaffirmation of the Foley-Kajsiewicz pact. Holy Trinity's independent status was now dissolved with the stroke of a pen. But the Trinitarians had no intention of surrendering to what they considered a Resurrectionist-Archdiocesan conspiracy. During the next three years they continually brought pressures to bear on Feehan to have Cardinal Franchi's decision of 1877 reinstated; and since the parish had grown to over 6,000, Rome once again began to take notice.[24]

While Feehan was discussing these and other matters in the Vatican in 1884, he dispatched his Vicar-General, Father Conway, to the troubled Polonian parishes. Conway was under instructions to conduct an open parish meeting that both Stanislawians and Trinitarians were to attend. At this supposedly open meeting of 23 April 1884, Conway suggested that Holy Trinity parish be reinstated as a branch of St. Stanislaus Kostka, a condition which Barzynski had insisted upon ever since his arrival in Chicago. But Conway gave the Trinitarians an opportunity to vote on his proposal. At this point in the meeting, bedlam broke out in the church as angry Trinitarians began shouting Conway down. The aroused national party delegation then began singing the nationalist version of the Polish national anthem, *Jeszcze Polska Nie Zginęla* ("Poland Is Not Yet Lost"), openly rejecting the clerical version of the anthem, *Boże Coś Polskę* ("God Bless Poland"). With parliamentary order broken down, Conway left the meeting. The Trinitarians, in response to the archdiocese's one-sided stance, communicated their position to James Cardinal Gibbons, the ranking U.S. prelate. Already widely known for his opposition to ethnic pluralism, Gibbons refused to side with the Trinitarians; "Take the matter up with your bishop," was his curt reply. And when the Trinitarians approached Feehan as instructed, the disgusted archbishop closed Holy Trinity parish once more, this time for five years. The parish was closed on five separate occasions between 1873 and 1893, forcing Trinitarians to seek accommodations in neighboring parishes.[25]

With the Holy Trinity issue again on the back burner, Barzynski was able to devote his every physical, mental, and spiritual effort to expanding the community-parish system in Chicago Polonia. In what must rank as one of the more significant "brick and mortar" achievements in nineteenth-century American Catholicism, the Chicago Resurrectionists, with Barzynski at the throttle, moved swiftly throughout the city in attempts to realize the dreams and aspirations of the saintly Janski. Wherever a Polish colony settled, there Barzynski would build a church; and for each new church the Resurrectionists either supplied a pastor from their own congregation or made personal recommendations to the archdiocese for Polish-speaking diocesan priests. From archival materials and authorized histories it is possible to plot the growth and development of this phenomenal community-parish system—a system in which the Resurrectionists and/or Barzynski were either directly or indirectly involved on twenty-three separate occasions. When one takes into account that each church was surrounded by a host of adjunct institutions, the full impact of Resurrectionist achievement unfolds.

For example, by the turn of the century in the West Town/Logan Square area, the nucleus of which was formed by St. Stanislaus Kostka and Holy Trinity parishes, the community-parish system encompassed six parochial grammar schools, two parish high schools (one at St. Stanislaus Kostka and one at Holy Trinity), one college (St. Stanislaus College), several orphanages, two newspapers (the *Dziennik Chicagoski* initiated by Barzynski, and the *Naród Polski*, official organ of the Polish Roman Catholic Union), the headquarters of the PRCU, hundreds of parish societies, several social welfare and cultural organizations and even one Polish-run hospital (St. Mary's of Nazareth on West Division Street). All these institutions, needless to say, were administered and operated on a predominantly Polish Catholic basis. The nationalist party, on the other hand, was simultaneously involved in the process of building corresponding agencies of all types to match the clerical party's institutional strength, a phenomenon we will discuss later. This highly compact cultural center of Chicago Polonia became a powerful magnet for drawing unto itself large numbers of new immigrants. St. Stanislaus numbered 40,000 parishioners by 1900, and in the same year Holy Trinity was approaching 25,000, making these two of the largest Roman Catholic parishes in the United States at the time. There was considerable speculation that St. Stanislaus was indeed *the* largest Catholic parish in the world at the turn of the century.

The Stanislawian-Trinitarian settlements became a model for later Polish Catholic settlements in Chicago, a model so powerful and attractive that, despite the clerical-nationalist struggle, no Polish Catholic parish was able to break away from the model until after Vatican II.

The Stanislawian-Trinitarian features in the West Town/Logan Square neighborhoods were quickly adopted by the three other major Polish complexes in Chicago: in the Lower West Side and South Lawndale communities, of which St. Adalbert's (*Wojciechowo*) was the heart; in the Bridgeport/New City (now known as the Back of the Yards) areas on the mid-south side, of which St. Mary of Perpetual Help and St. Joseph's were the nuclei (prior to 1900, anyway); and in the South Chicago settlement surrounding the U.S. Steel district along Lake Michigan on the far southeast side, of which Immaculate Conception and St. Michael's were the centers. During and immediately following World War I, the West Town/Logan Square sector, then known as the "Polish Downtown," advanced westward down North Avenue and northwestward along both sides of Milwaukee Avenue, creating a "Polish Corridor" which would soon tie the Polish Downtown with such contiguous areas as Norwood Park, Jefferson Park, Avondale, Portage Park, and Belmont-Cragin. The same sort of advance began from original, or primary, Polish settlements on the south and southwest sides. The primary communities on the Lower West Side and in the Back of the Yards eventually moved down both sides of Archer Avenue, giving rise along the way to sizeable Polish settlements in the southwest sector of the city—notably, McKinley Park, Brighton Park, Archer Heights, and Garfield Ridge. On the far southeast side, the South Chicago "steel mill settlement" spilled over into Pullman, Hegewisch, and Calumet City, and into Lake County in northwest Indiana, where thriving Polish communities could be found in North Hammond, Whiting, the Indiana Harbor section of East Chicago, and several neighborhoods in the newly built industrial city of Gary.[26]

Such expansion by a single ethnic group had been unprecedented in the history of the Chicago archdiocese and necessitated policy adjustments on the part of the Irish hierarchy in the downtown chancery. But, unfortunately, such policy changes were slow in coming; most were not fully implemented until the episcopacy of Cardinal Mundelein, when most of Polish Catholic Chicago was already rigidly institutionalized. This rapid expansion in Polonia, however, was also at the root of many of Barzynski's difficulties throughout the 1880s and 1890s; it was his untiring and sometimes fanatical zeal in keeping pace with this immigration explosion, especially the financial end of the pastor's "business," that prolonged the clerical-nationalist controversy and extended it far beyond the primary parish settlements. So when Barzynski's never-ending quest for funds moved into the nationalist's terrain (and when one studies the evidence presented in Map Three carefully, one can understand why Barzynski's quest was never-ending), it was inevitable that the nationalists would come to center their attack on the Con-

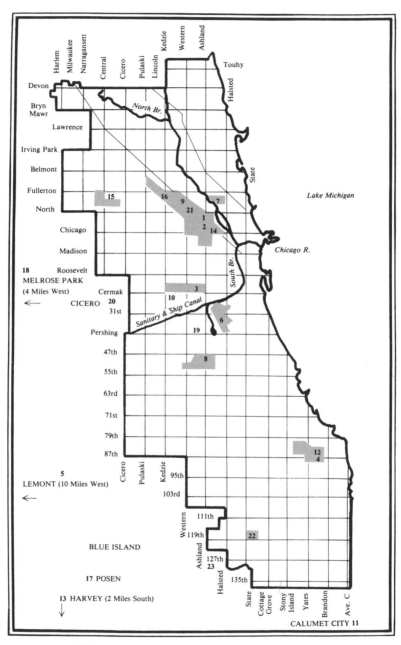

Map Three: Polish Parishes in Chicago, 1867–1900

MAP NO.	NAME OF PARISH	DATE	ADDRESS/ COMMUNITY AREA	ADMINISTRATION
1	St. Stanislaus Kostka	1867	Noble & Evergreen/West Town	C.R. 1867–present
2	Holy Trinity	1872	1118 N. Noble/West Town	C.R. 1872–1893
3	St. Adalbert	1873	1615 West 17th/Lower West Side	Diocesan priests approved by Rev. Barzynski and C.R.
4	Immaculate Conception of the B.V.M.	1882	2944 E. 88th/South Chicago	Diocesan priests approved by Rev. Barzynski and C.R.
5	Sts. Cyril & Methodius	1883	Suburb of Lemont	C.R. 1883–1910; Diocesan 1910–present
6	St. Mary of Perpetual Help	1883	1039 W. 32nd/Bridgeport	C.R. 1884–1886; Diocesan 1886–present
7	St. Josaphat	1884	Belden & Southport/ Lincoln Park	C.R. 1884–1889; Diocesan 1889–present
8	St. Joseph	1886	W. 48th & Hermitage/ Back of the Yards	C.R. 1886–1889; Diocesan 1889–present
9	St. Hedwig	1888	Webster & Hoyne/Logan Square	C.R. 1888–present
10	St. Casimir	1890	W. Cermak & S. Whipple/ South Lawndale	Diocesan 1890–present
11	St. Andrew the Apostle	1891	Suburb of West Hammond (Calumet City)	Diocesan 1891–present
12	St. Michael	1892	83rd & South Shore Dr./ South Chicago	Diocesan 1892–1897; C.R. 1897; Diocesan 1897–present
13	Ascension (Mixed Nationalities)	1892	Suburb of Harvey	Diocesan 1892–1898; C.R. 1898–1902; Diocesan 1902–present
14	St. John Cantius	1893	Carpenter & W. Chicago/ West Town	C.R. 1893–present
15	St. Stanislaus Bishop and Martyr	1893	5352 W. Belden/Belmont Cragin	C.R. 1893–present
16	St. Hyacinth	1894	3636 W. Wolfram/ Avondale	C.R. 1894–present

MAP NO.	NAME OF PARISH	DATE	ADDRESS/ COMMUNITY AREA	ADMINISTRATION
17	St. Stanislaus Bishop and Martyr	1894	Suburb of Posen	Diocesan 1894–1898; C.R. 1898–1902; Diocesan 1902– present
18	Sacred Heart	1895	Suburb of Melrose Park	C.R. 1895–1901; Diocesan 1901– present
19	Sts. Peter and Paul	1895	38th & S. Paulina/ McKinley Park	Diocesan 1895–present
20	Our Lady of Czestochowa	1895	Suburb of Cicero	Diocesan 1895–present
21	St. Mary of the Angels	1897	Hermitage & Cortland/ Logan Square	C.R. 1897–present
22	St. Salomea	1897	11824 S. Indiana/Pullman	Diocesan 1897–present
23	St. Isidore	1900	Suburb of Blue Island	C.R. 1900; Diocesan 1900–present

The list excludes three parishes: St. Boniface (1864) on Noble & Chestnut in West Town to which some Poles belonged prior to the building of St. Stanislaus Kostka; St. Wenceslaus (1863) on DeKoven & Des Plaines in the Near West Side to which Poles also belonged; St. Mary of Mount Carmel (1892), an Italian parish which was administered by the Resurrectionists during the 1897–1906 period.
The abbreviation C.R. refers to the Congregation of the Resurrection.
Map Numbers correspond to locations on Map Three.
Addresses are 1976 locations.

gregation of the Resurrection and Barzynski in particular. After all, Barzynski had gained the undesired reputation of ruthlessness in parish financial matters; he was generally attacked by the nationalists as a money-hungry priest. Yet, aside from the inevitable financial worries, one can still come to appreciate the efforts of Barzynski or any other "immigrant pastor" to provide for a spiritually starved immigrant flock like the Poles in Chicago. The spiritual stakes in the Resurrectionist venture into Chicago, when viewed by contemporaries in the 1880s, went far beyond worldly criteria. The Polonia mission had been established primarily to prevent "leakage" and to save souls. This was indeed an era in American Catholicism, or to put the matter in a better way, an era in European immigrant Catholicism in America, when most observers felt that immigrants would certainly lose the faith in alien, congested, urban ghettoes if abandoned by the church. Thus, the horrible spectre of losing immigrants not only to secularism but also for all eternity plagued many an immigrant pastor of lesser devotion to duty than Barzynski. After all, in this pre-ecumenical era, losing one's Catholic faith was tantamount to eternal damnation, or so many immigrants believed.[27]

From Barzynski's correspondence we know that this issue constantly plagued him. On the other hand, the researcher looks in vain for a Barzynski "theology" of the community-parish or for a systematic philosophy that may have guided him through these difficult and trying years. Instead, one reads dozens of pieces of correspondence of a man totally dedicated to highly practical affairs such as estimating the cost of a new school building, staffing a school with a sufficient number of teaching nuns, pouring over account ledgers for the purpose of shifting funds to a less financially stable parish, organizing a new women's parish sodality, or purchasing an empty lot for a new parish on the northwest side. These were the kinds of unspectacular but nevertheless essential day-to-day details which engaged the mind of a man who by all accounts was incredibly pragmatic for an immigrant pastor; in fact, this was a man who rarely even found the time to become involved in any contemplative pursuit (one wonders how or when he even found the time to pray). Barzynski was certainly no Janski, who would have transcended his surroundings through prayer and meditation. Nor was he a Kajsiewicz, who would have diplomatically guided the Congregation's younger priests through these stormy secular waters. Nor was he like St. Francis, who surely would have charmed opponents into blissful surrender. Barzynski was not even a Loyola, who would have synthesized sword and mind into a potent weapon to smite the unbeliever. Instead, he was more like a Chicago ward alderman (to pardon so unholy a comparison): he was a dispenser of favors who saw no problem in naming his brother Joseph as pastor of St. Hedwig's, despite heavy opposition from the nationalists; he was one who could remember (with relish) details which most other men would just as soon have forgotten, such as total square feet of an empty lot in Belmont-Cragin; he was a persistent cajoler of men ("this convent ought and must be built"); and he was a man who knew his enemies, and who, despite his vocation, found it most difficult to forgive or forget those who— like the "schismatic" Mielcuszny—had betrayed him.

In hundreds of unsubtle ways Barzynski came to influence dozens of contemporary Polish clergy in Chicago, most of whom sensed his power even in his absence. At the risk of over-simplification, it can be said that Barzynski's power and influence rested on the bedrock of organization. He was indeed an organizational genius, a builder. Any Polish Roman Catholic in Chicago, or in any other Polonia in Buffalo, Pittsburgh, Detroit, Milwaukee, or Cleveland, who was raised in the second or third generation, can easily recall the Barzynski type—those ageless Polish-American monsignors (only a handful were ever consecrated bishop), who incessantly went about organizing bingo parties, smokers, and bazaars in a never-ending quest to raise funds for more churches, and more schools, and more convents, and more orphanages—never questioning the cycle of "brick and mortar" Catholicism. Just like those faithful ward lieutenants in the political arena who always marched to the tune of the endless stream of Irish mayors in twentieth-century Chicago, these Polish-American pastors marched to the beat of Irish bishops, who also seemed to be ever-present.

This then was the Barzynski legacy to Polish-American Catholicism in the

United States: when the immigrants needed their churches, Barzynski always built them.

A small sample of the Barzynski mind at work will illustrate the point. In a letter to the Resurrectionist Superior-General Valerian Przewlocki in 1887, Father Barzynski claimed that "we have 3500 families and 20,000 souls [at St. Stanislaus Kostka]" and that the school enrollment had risen to "1150 boys and close to 2000 girls." Student needs were handled by "only 20 teaching nuns" (a student-teacher ratio in excess of 150 to 1 on a full-day schedule, and 75 to 1 on a split-day basis). The value of the Stanislawian real estate complex was appraised at "approximately $200,000" but funds were still desperately needed to build a school "for at least 5,000 pupils" (an estimate which proved to be most accurate by the 1890s). Thus, and as always, Barzynski ended his letter with a plea "for more assistants and more money."[28]

This expansion in Polonia severely strained not only Resurrectionist resources but also the Foley-Kajsiewicz pact. Barzynski, as we have indicated, was constantly plagued with staffing the new parishes with priests, a demand the Central House was never able to keep up with. Out of desperation, Barzynski even persuaded Fathers Zwiardowski and Moczygemba to come back to Chicago on a temporary basis, and when this move proved insufficient, he finally resorted to using the services of Polish-speaking diocesan priests—a practice he would soon come to regret. Even though Barzynski personally authorized the selection of each pastor and assistant for Polonia's churches, it was usually more difficult for him to screen all candidates thoroughly because writing for academic credentials to various institutions was most time-consuming, and obtaining letters of recommendation from Polish dioceses was troublesome and unproductive, especially since it was virtually impossible to verify all the personal information submitted. Then, too, since Barzynski had been making the selections (Foley and Feehan invariably approved of his chocies), he was ultimately responsible to the archbishop for each selection. It was a practice he would later come to regret, as bad personnel decisions came to reflect negatively on his personal reputation and on the reputation of the Congregation of the Resurrection.[29]

But despite all this, there are still some critical questions demanding further scrutiny: in light of this expansion, why had Barzynski fought the Trinitarians so long and so hard? After all, some of his adversaries were indeed capable of assuming some of his administrative burdens. And why had he been so opposed to Father Mielcuszny or to other Polish-speaking priests the Trinitarians invited? The nationalist ideology notwithstanding (Barzynski at times seemed willing to exchange ideological differences for practical gains), was there some other hidden element that persistently brought out the nationalist's fierce hatred for Barzynski and the Resurrectionists? Events surrounding the 1889 reopening of Holy Trinity supply us with some of the answers to these questions.

In the early autumn of 1888, an incident occurred at St. Adalbert's Parish

(*Wojciechowo*)—that other nationalist party stronghold occasionally serving as a refuge for disgruntled Trinitarians on the Lower West Side—which would have an immediate impact on the Holy Trinity stalemate. A diocesan priest named John Radziejewski was pastor at *Wojciechowo*. A close friend of Vincent Barzynski, Radziejewski was one of those non-Resurrectionist Polish clergymen who, by virtue of the Foley-Kajsiewicz pact, had been handpicked to safeguard the clerical party's interests in an era of growing nationalist strength. In order to assure complete clerical control over the dissidents, Radziejewski in September of 1888 issued from his pulpit an edict which was intended to serve as the basis for a governance document for the growing number of religious societies, some already dominated by nationalists, within the parish's jurisdiction. The main provision expounded by Radziejewski was that each society immediately place itself under the direct control of the Archbishop of Chicago and the pastor of the parish; furthermore, the pastor was to preside over all meetings at which he was present. The second provision was that the parish pastor and his assistants were to be present at all elections of any of the societies, and that the priests were to have the authority to reject all candidates deemed unsuitable for office. Third, no constitutional or by-law changes were to be made without the pastor's authorization. Finally, any society not accepting all the provisions was no longer to consider itself a Catholic society. When six church societies, totalling approximately 700 members, refused to accept the Radziejewski ultimatum, they were immediately ostracized, a move most likely engineered by Barzynski himself. The evicted societies then held mass meetings to plan some sort of rebuttal, for most feared that the Radziejewski proposals would eventually be applied to all Polish Catholic societies in the Chicago archdiocese. The groups decided to petition both Radziejewski and Archbishop Feehan on the matter, but their efforts were disregarded and came to nothing.[30]

With the nationalist's safety valve at *Wojciechowo* temporarily shut off, a delegation of Trinitarians decided that an attempt would have to be made to reopen Holy Trinity Parish, which had now been closed for the past eight years. So bitter and stubborn were the two sides regarding the nomination of a pastor that no candidate since Miecuszny's death was found to be acceptable to either Barzynski or the *Gmina*. Therefore, in an apparent spirit of reconciliation, the Trinitarians in early 1889 agreed to submit to Feehan and Barzynski by turning the deed to the church over to the archdiocese and by accepting the services of a Resurrectionist. Having conceded these two major points, the Trinitarians expected no further problems. The sudden about-face by the Trinitarians was probably due to the fact that 10,000 nationalist parishioners were without a parish outlet, especially now that the Radziejewski decrees at *Wojciechowo* had been supported by the archdiocese. So on Sunday morning, 3 March 1889, the nationalist party found itself passively standing by when a Resurrectionist, the Reverend Simon Kobrzynski, marched down Noble Street to celebrate a solemn high mass at Holy

Trinity church. After seventeen long years, peace appeared to have come to *Stanisławowo-Trójcowo*. But the peace lasted only one hour. Having finished celebrating the mass, Kobrzynski now began transferring the receipts of the Sunday collection to the rectory at St. Stanislaus. This action of course brought the angry Trinitarians out into the streets once again. Kobrzynski explained to the crowds that he was within his rights to make the transfer, as the archbishop had clearly stipulated that Holy Trinity had been designated as a *branch* of St. Stanislaus Kostka and, therefore, was not an independent parish. But Kobrzynski's pleas were to no avail as rioting broke out on Noble Street between Stanislawian and Trinitarian parishioners.

An uneasy truce reigned for the remainder of the summer. But a Trinitarian group led by Joseph Grajczyk, Peter Binkowski, and a certain parishioner named Wajtalewicz planned a counterstrategy. By August, they had arrived at a plan to test again the rights of trusteeship. When the fire insurance policy to Holy Trinity church reached its expiration date, the group had a new policy drawn up in the names of the trustees rather than in the name of the archbishop, as was standard procedure for the time. Furthermore, after each Sunday collection was taken (Wajtalewicz and Binkowski were parish ushers whose duty it was to take up the collection), the trustees would offer Father Kobrzynski only a stipend, rather than turning over the entire collection to him. When Kobrzynski informed the archbishop of these machinations, the archbishop issued an edict to the Trinitarians which was read at one of the Sunday masses on 1 September 1889 by Kobrzynski himself. The high-strung Resurrectionist told his congregation that the trustees were to resign their trusts, change over the policy to the name of Archbishop Feehan, and turn over the entire collection to their pastor. Until this was done, the parish of Holy Trinity would have all solemn high Sunday masses and all weekday masses cancelled; the only masses offered were to be Sunday low masses (where there was no singing by the celebrant or the choir and no participation by the congregation). This rather mild form of rebuke, however, was cause for a wild demonstration within the sanctuary itself. Worshippers began stamping their feet and throwing their hymnals about the church; women groaned hysterically; children were sent running up and down the church aisles, while other adults climbed over the pews in an effort to leave the church as a sign of protest. The shaken Kobrzynski, who believed that Trinitarians in particular were prone to such forms of anarchy, returned to the altar in an attempt to finish the mass. During the Offertory, Binkowski and Wajtalewicz moved to the front of the church to take up the usual collection. Whether they did so in a particularly aggressive or threatening fashion is not known; however, when Kobrzynski saw them coming toward the altar he took their approach as a threat and fled. The *Chicago Tribune* reported that Kobrzynski "was then secreted for several hours by personal friends, who feared the excited people would use him roughly if they laid hands on him." Upon hearing of the unruly demonstration, Archbishop Feehan instructed Kobrzynski to set up a new parish committee (a good indication of the archbishop's deference to Barzynski) in an attempt to once again resolve the differences. This the committee could not do. Feehan then ordered Holy Trinity closed once more. This was the last time that the Feehan-Barzynski alliance was able to bring such power to bear on their beleaguered nationalist adversaries. By 1891, the Trinitarians reappeared on the scene with powerful allies equal to the task of inducing a final showdown.[31]

From a supraterritorial standpoint, the clerical-nationalist struggle had been gaining momentum throughout the 1880s in American Polonia. A counterpart to the clergy-dominated Polish Roman Catholic Union had arisen in Philadelphia in 1880; known as the Polish National Alliance (*Związek Narodowy Polski*), this was a polyglot organization of various like-minded nationalist groups, including the old *Gmina Polska*. Basically, the PNA was the culmination, in American dress, of European forces devoted to the cause of Polish independence. From his headquarters-in-exile in Switzerland, Agaton Giller, in an open letter to American Polonia (published in all major Polish newspapers in the United States), put forth the major philosophy of the coming PNA in 1879. Giller argued that "since emigration exists and constitutes a great power . . . it should be the task of a well understood patriotism to make it as useful as possible for the national cause," which could only be accomplished by an organization "which will unify the scattered members and control them in such a way that they will not be wasted but will be preserved for the fatherland." Giller appealed to "the national consciousness" of "every Polish peasant," realizing all the while that the time spent away from the fatherland had been central to developing a national consciousness. Giller also stated that "if a national intellectual class [could be] formed in America the numerous masses [would] be changed into an active human group useful for the national cause. . . ." Binding "these isolated individuals into more or less numerous associations and communities" would prevent loss of nationality and identity. Giller's hope was that a national organization (such as the PNA) would allow for individual members to prosper both morally and economically, and when this prosperity had reached the optimum level, Poles would be ready "to return to the fatherland to be useful citizens."[32]

With these sentiments to guide delegates at the Philadelphia convention of 1881, Ladislaus Dyniewicz enthusiastically pledged the support of the Chicago *Gmina* for the fledgling Polish National Alliance. Through the advertising efforts of Dyniewicz's *Polish Gazette* and the newly founded PNA weekly, *Zgoda* ("Harmony"), the PNA encouraged Poles to become active in American politics so as to become a viable force in changing the direction of America's foreign policy toward Partitioned Poland. But the chief obstacle to national self-determination was the clergy in Polonia "who for centuries have kept the people blind," preventing them from "rising above the Irish in this country," so much so that the "Polish name will never shine with any light in this land." The *Zgoda* editors also required that "all existing Polish organizations form this one great national entity [the PNA] . . . [and] use the power of its organization to maintain a progressive periodical, which will enlighten and instruct the emigrant" so that Polish emigrants "would rise above the level of the uneducated masses . . . [and] be better able to fulfill their mission with regard to Poland."[33] The rhetoric used by Giller, Dyniewicz, the Trinitarian trustees, and the editors of *Zgoda* went a long way toward convincing thousands of Polish immigrants to side with the Polish National Alliance. And when clergymen saw their flocks streaming in the direction of the Alliance, in order to retain credibility with their parishioners, they too joined the Alliance.

By the late 1880s, the original clerical-nationalist struggle had evolved into a nationwide struggle between the Alliancists, belonging to the PNA, and the Unionists, from the PRCU. Thus, by the time of the incidents at *Wojciechowo* and *Trójcowo*, Chicago Polonia was already caught up in a nationwide Unionist-versus-Alliancist struggle. The nationwide turmoil, then, provided the backdrop for Radziejewski and his edicts at St. Adalbert's. And because Barzynski and Kobrzynski were staunch Unionists, both refused to budge one iota at St. Stanislaus or at Holy Trinity.[34]

By 1890 Barzynski was, without question, the most powerful Unionist in all of American Polonia. He had observed with some dismay and apprehension the events leading to the formation of the Polish National Alliance. In Chicago he had seen how the ultrapatriotism brandished by Dyniewicz's *Gmina Polska* had come to envelop some of the most intelligent, articulate, and influential parishioners at Holy Trinity, and worst of all, how this influence was beginning to infect the previously uninvolved masses. As the Chicago *Gmina* was absorbed into the PNA, and as the process of transformation from local nationalist party constituency to supraterritoriality was completed, Dyniewicz was no longer even the main spokesman for *Trójcowo*. Instead, newer and more sophisticated leaders came to represent the interests of the Trinitarian Alliancists—individuals like Joseph Gillmeister, who attended the famed "Founders meeting" at the Philadelphia Convention of 1881, Francis Jablonski, editor of the *Zgoda*, and Anthony Mallek, the popular organist at Holy Trinity church who did much of the PNA's door-to-door canvassing and who represented *Trójcowo* at the PNA's national conventions from 1886 through 1888. Working closely with Grajczyk, Binkowski, Wajtalewicz, and the other Trinitarian "trustees," this leadership core continued to exert various pressures on the Unionist stronghold at *Stanisławowo*, especially via a series of explanatory letters to the Vatican. Although the rabid anticlericalism of Dyniewicz's heyday was slowly passing (the PNA admitted members of the clergy into its organization, but without any special privileges), Barzynski would not lower his guard, for he knew that the Alliancists were still focusing their sights on him and the Congregation of the Resurrection.[35]

In an effort to compensate for the ever more powerful influence exerted by the PNA, Barzynski devoted considerable time to conducting a journalistic war with the Alliancists. Basing his campaign on an attempt to sway newly arrived Polish immigrants in Chicago, which Peter Kiolbassa claimed in a *Chicago Tribune* article in 1886 to number 40,000–45,000, the Stanislawian pastor began making plans for establishing a Resurrectionist-operated publishing company. When Father Vincent's brother, John, became seriously ill, the old clerical party warhorse journal, *Gazeta Polska Katolicka*, was sold to John Smulski, who would one day use his publishing interests himself to run for mayor of Chicago. When John Barzynski died in 1886, the money from the Smulski transaction was used by Father Vincent to organize the Polish Publishing Company, which opened in 1887. All the while, Barzynski was closely supported in this journalistic endeavor by his old friend at *Wojciechowo*, Pastor John Radziejewski, who was issuing all those notorious edicts in his parish. Hoping to steal some of the nationalist's thunder, Barzynski and Radziejewski named the first organ of the PRCU *Wiara I Ojczyzna* ("Faith and Fatherland"), an extension of Barzynski's old "For God and Country" trademark. Barzynski also issued a highly polemical weekly entitled *Kropidło* ("Sprinkler"), which from its inception was nothing more than an Alliance-baiter. *Kropidło* failed after one year, but *Wiara I Ojczyzna* survived, under the capable editorship of Stanislaus Szwajkart. In 1899 it became the *Naród Polski* the still-surviving official weekly of the PRCU. But Barzynski's most successful journalistic venture was the *Dziennik Chicagoski* (loosely translated as *"The Polish Daily News"*), a paper which published its first issue on 15 December 1890 and remained in the field until its closing in 1971. Through the editorial pages of *Dziennik Chicagoski*, the community-parish complex of the Resurrectionists was given its fullest expression, the antisocialism of Janski was reinterpreted for a new generation of readers, and the principles of a new Catholic social order in the city were outlined in the highest moral terms. The *Dziennik* also prided itself on its firm allegiance to the Constitution of the United States and asked its readers to become politically active in the democratic process.[36]

This journalistic onslaught did nothing to constrain the Trinitarian resolve. Feehan's decision to close down Holy Trinity in 1889 spurred Gillmeister and Mallek to appeal to the Vatican for a final settlement. As a result of their efforts, the lines of communication between *Trójcowo* and the new Prefect of Propaganda, Cardinal Simeoni, were reopened.[37] The Mallek-Gillmeister letter was followed by another lengthy appeal to Cardinal Simeoni, this one signed by Joseph X. Grajczyk, Peter Binkowski, and Dominik Bartoszewicz. This letter, written entirely in Latin and dated 2 April 1891, brought the Trinitarian position clearly into focus. After thanking Cardinal Simeoni for his reply to the previous communiqué, Grajczyk, who drafted the letter, got to specifics, which, because of their critical nature, are included here in their entirety:

The note of the Sacred Congregation for the Propagation of Faith refers to the dissension in the Congregation of the Resurrection, which has been going on for some years, but which by no means was ever desired and which now must end. On the contrary, because the rebellious Resurrectionist clergy have returned to our parish church, an unhappy state of affairs has resulted whereby the pastor of our church, who by carelessness in temporal affairs, has lost our funds. I am in charge of temporal matters in the parish now and am forced by these circumstances to consider going to a secular judge in order to get him to move against the clergy. However, I hesitate to do this if a canonical process can be gotten underway to solve this affair.

The parish of Holy Trinity was founded nineteen years ago by these same Fathers of the Resurrectionist Congregation with the permission of Bishop Foley. The pastor was independent, the deed for the church property was in the hands of the Bishop, and all were living in peace with the neighboring parish of St. Stanislaus Kostka. But then Vincent Barzynski was made pastor of St. Stanislaus Kostka Parish, and the status of our parish was completely changed. For this priest, coveting money and power, and always hoping for a Bishop's seat himself, was determined to undermine our parish both in legal and illegal fashion so that his power would grow and so that his funds would be increased. But since neither of his attempts to pursuade the people succeeded, and since he was unable to sway the will of the Bishop for his own purposes, he stole the parish deed from the Bishop's archives on the pretext of augmenting church property so as to pursuade a creditor, who had not yet been paid, to have the building and assets of Holy Trinity auctioned off in a public sale. But the parishioners paid the creditor. So then Barzynski tried other things: he declared that all the religious societies of the parish were schismatic and "masonic," proceeded to carry off the Holy Eucharist, closed the church and persuaded the Archbishop [Feehan] that no more pastors were to be installed at the parish. For many years the parishioners sought justice in vain, but because the English Archbishop could not speak Polish, he either sent them back to Barzynski or else asserted that without the permission of the Congregation of the Faith the bond by which all Poles in Chicago were under the authority of the Fathers of the Resurrectionist Congregation could not be broken; Vincent Barzynski, leaning upon the authority of the Superior-General of the Resurrectionist Congregation in Rome, hence refused consent for our having a pastor independent of St. Stanislaus Kostka parish. This state of affairs continued until 1889 when Simon Kobrzynski was named pastor of Holy Trinity. In the beginning of his pastorship, he thought he understood some of our just complaints, but after a few months compelled us to: a) transfer our financial contributions to St. Stanislaus Kostka; b) hold divine services at St. Stanislaus Kostka; and when the parishioners refused, he closed the church.

New attempts to open the church failed, and since then our present delegate, charged with the responsibility of investigating the affair, hopes to prove that not all are friends of Barzynski and that he [Barzynski] is not victorious.

Having set forth these matters, we humbly pray that your Eminence grant that—

I–The parish of Holy Trinity not be suppressed but be restored to its original state. For it was indeed created canonically and also because the parish of St. Stanislaus Kostka, to which approximately 50,000 parishioners belong, is utterly incapable of containing so great a multitude on Feast days, and even sometimes on regular days.

II–The pastor of the said parish be instituted independent of the Fathers of the Resurrectionist Congregation, for the Fathers of this Congregation do not care for us in temporal affairs, but instead continually contract debts, borrowing at high rates of interest, thus taking money from the public treasury with great detriment to the Church and the faithful, the sweat of whose foreheads and labor of whose hands it would seem should go to their own bankers for safekeeping.[38]

When Grajczyk admitted to the Vatican that Barzynski and the Resurrectionists were "taking money from the public treasury with great detriment to the Church and the faithful," he was registering what had become the central complaint of Holy Trinity parishioners. Grajczyk was obviously referring to the alleged Resurrectionist mismanagement of the *Bank Parafialny* (Parish Bank), which had been a creation of Father Barzynski in 1875. Rather than deposit funds with alien bankers who could not be trusted and who might be tempted to invest Polonia's savings elsewhere (the current practice of red-lining), Barzynski encouraged parishioners to save at his Parish Bank on the theory that funds would remain in the neighborhood. Immigrants, of course, were told that it was much safer to leave their money with a priest than with a banker. Barzynski offered the depositors a small interest on their savings, but often this interest was waived by the depositors for any number of reasons: the parish might use these interest payments to improve the community-parish; the token payments often were accepted in lieu of school tuition; and the deposits were under direct control of the community-parish. In essence, then, the *Bank Parafialny* thrived on an immigrant sense of security. The Parish Bank operation also met the approval of Bishop Foley and Archbishop Feehan, both of whom were aware of the Bank's existence and encouraged its continuance. By 1889 the assets of the Parish Bank reached $135,000, an amazingly healthy figure when one considers that *Stanisławowo* was an extremely poor and economically underdeveloped area. Added to parish deposits of $115,000, which were (curiously) placed in a local bank, the financial state of St. Stanislaus Kostka, on the surface at least, appeared to be most prosperous. However, difficulties arose when Barzynski began using the Parish Bank's capital to finance construction of churches and schools throughout Chicago—i.e., outside the boundaries of *Stanisławowo*. One Resurrectionist financial report made shortly after the Kobrzynski incident showed that Parish Bank funds were being loaned out in amounts dangerously close to the Bank's total assets:

St. Hedwig's Parish	$6,500
St. Josaphat's Parish	5,000
Holy Trinity Parish	5,000
St. John Cantius Parish	15,000
Printery	30,000
St. Hedwig's lots	15,000
Land in Nebraska	5,000
Shares in Printery	20,000
Small outstanding loans	4,000
Total amount loaned	$105,500

The same report also showed that annual income at St. Stanislaus Kostka Parish, most of which was derived from mass stipends and Sunday collections, was in excess of $52,000 per annum (approximately $1,000 per week), whereas expenditures totalled approximately $44,000 per annum.[39]

In any event, the first signals of real financial distress at the Parish Bank were not transmitted to the Resurrectionist Central House in Rome until the late 1880s, at which time Barzynski was facing considerable pressure to finance the parish of St. Hedwig's. Barzynski may also at this time have been guilty of overdrawing funds from the Bank. He must have communicated these difficulties to Superior-General Valerian Przewłocki by autumn or winter of 1888–1889, for this was when the Congregation decided to send its master accountant, Reverend Simon Kobrzynski, to *Stanisławowo* in order to smooth over Barzynski's difficulties at the Parish Bank (which also may account for why Kobrzynski and Barzynski decided to transfer funds from Holy Trinity to St. Stanislaus Kostka). Yet neither was able to alleviate the Parish Bank's already desperate situation; by this time it was in arrears to depositors to the awesome total of $404,000 (the debt eventually reached $550,475). On 15 January 1896, the Congregation's new Superior-General, Paul Smolikowski, wrote to Archbishop Feehan asking how the Resurrectionists and the archdiocese might arrive at "a definite settlement" to the Parish Bank situation. As a consequence of this debacle—the solution to which was to evade and embarrass General Chapter meetings of the Congregation for another two decades—Smolikowski issued three orders regarding the Parish Bank, all of which were adopted at the Resurrectionist's General Chapter meeting of 1901:

first, no further loans for buildings or other land purchases were to be made from the Parish Bank's capital (a clue which leads one to believe that Barzynski was still overdrawing funds in the 1890s); next, each pastor in the Chicago Province was instructed to file an annual financial statement with the Province's Procurator (a position established because of the Parish Bank's collapse), indicating total income and outstanding debts for the previous year so that any excess income could be used by the Procurator to amortize the debt of the Bank; last, all funds derived from mass offerings and collections and not spent during a given fiscal year were to be sent directly to the Congregation's Central House in Rome. With these General Chapter regulations put into effect, the Reverend John Kasprzycki, who was then head of the Chicago Province and who was to succeed Smolikowski as Superior-General of the Congregation in 1905, was asked to file a complete financial statement of the Chicago mission.

Kasprzycki's report—"Rendiconto della missione d'e Chicago"—dated 10 June 1901, put the Bank's total assets at $505,731 and its deficit at $8,014. The report revealed that by the turn of the century the Resurrectionist province of Chicago was at least beginning to stabilize its shaky economic status; yet, even though the deficit of $8,014 was a small one, it was none the less a deficit, and consequently the Resurrectionists were still in no position to amortize the debt of the Parish Bank. The report also clearly demonstrated that the Resurrectionists were willing to speculate ($41,000 in gold mine stock) in order to extricate themselves from their financial morass, a highly controversial undertaking considering that the Bank's depositors were still awaiting redress. In any event, with the 1901 General Chapter guidelines in effect, the Congregation was able to lower the Bank's debt by about $20,000 per year during the 1904–1911 period, and about $30,000 per year thereafter until the debt was cleared in the early 1920s.[40]

In retrospect, then, Grajczyk's argument regarding Barzynski's mismanagement of parish funds certainly rested on solid ground, although nobody in the clerical camp would have admitted this in the spring of 1891. The hundreds of families who were either horribly inconvenienced or even financially ruined offered living testimony to the overorganization and overexpansion of the community-parish system advocated by Barzynski and the Chicago province of the Resurrectionist Congregation. The reputation for efficiency and able management established by Barzynski and the Congregation in matters other than the Parish Bank—the splendid church societies, the parish school system, the Resurrectionist press, and numerous social and cultural organizations—would be tarnished for a long time to come. And many later Resurrectionists to the Chicago mission, most of whom were extremely talented, dedicated, well-educated, and highly moral men, would suffer the torments and frustrations of a tremendous credibility gap foisted upon them by Barzynski's mismanagement of the *Bank Parafialny*.

Yet, in all fairness to Barzynski, one must keep in mind that when Polonia's people began to disperse to other areas of the city in the 1880s, a move prompted by the increased population density in *Stanisławowo*, they demanded that the church move with them. Barzynski complied with the wishes of his expanding flock in the only way he knew how—by using the resources of the *Bank Parafialny*. This is not to say that Barzynski was blameless in taking this approach, but when one views the options open to Barzynski at the time one can conclude that his resources were severely limited. The Polish Roman Catholic Union and the Polish National Alliance had by no means in the late 1880s and early 1890s attained the prosperity they were to enjoy during World War I, when both were capable of generating millions of dollars for Polish War Relief. Accordingly, Barzynski could not, as later pastors did, request funds from the major supraterritorial fraternals. The total stock and personal property of the PRCU, for example, did not reach $500,000—or the equivalent of the *Bank Parafialny's* debt—until 1909. The Chicago archdiocese, faced with heavy financial burdens of its own in coming to the aid of a dozen other nationality groups in the city, was in no position to ease the Polonian Parish Bank situation. Chicago Polonia was simply too economically underdeveloped during Barzynski's lifetime. In light of this fact, the community-parish concept, which Barzynski taught his flock to accept, was most probably misconstrued by the Trinitarians to mean *neighborhood-parish*. Judging from his frenetic parish building activity in the 1880s and 1890s, Barzynski no doubt applied the concept of community-parish to *all* of Chicago Polonia, and that is probably why he failed. Another development took place at the Third Plenary Council that also forced Barzynski to overexpand. In Title Six of the Council's decrees, a provision was passed that required all existing parishes to erect and maintain parocial schools within two years. Thus, by 1886, any "pastor who failed to supply the means for erecting such a school was to be reprimanded by the Bishop and induced to comply," and any "pastor who failed to build this school would merit removal."[41]

Grajczyk's other major contention in the Cardinal Simeoni letter—that Barzynski harbored an overwhelming desire to become a bishop—also merits consideration. As we have already seen, Barzynski was without question one of the Chicago archdiocese's most dynamic and aggressive priests. As ranking Resurrectionist in Chicago and titular head of Polonia's 90,000 Roman Catholics (in 1890), Barzynski was in many ways a *de facto* bishop. After all, the souls under Barzynski's care surpassed the total number of Catholics in many small dioceses in the United States. But the piece of evidence that most seems to corroborate the Grajczyk charge is a letter written by James Cardinal Gibbons to Archbishop George Mundelein of Chicago some thirty years later. Gibbons, the top-ranking U.S. Catholic prelate at the time, admitted to Mundelein that he had received a request to consecrate a Polish-American bishop in 1890. Despite the fact that Gibbons gave no other particulars regarding this request, one can probably assume that Father Barzynski was the Polish-American priest the petitioner had in mind.[42]

Grajczyk's final contention—that St. Stanislaus Kostka Parish with its 50,000 souls was just too large a parish in which to conduct meaningful religious services—was likewise justified. The Catholic population of *Stanisławowo* was larger in 1890 than the entire population of such Illinois cities as Rockford, Peoria, Quincy, Springfield, East St. Louis, and Aurora; *Stanisławowo* was the second largest "city" in Illinois, next to Chicago. One can readily understand why parishioners in such crowded circumstances became terribly annoyed when direct communications between individual worshippers and their pastor became more and more strained, and why communications between Trinitarians and Stanislawians often broke down, even during the periods of compromise and reconciliation in 1884 and 1889.[43]

The Grajczyk correspondence resulted in a thorough investigation of the Trinitarian situation by Cardinal Simeoni. Grajczyk and Frances Jablonski even made a personal appearance before the Office of the Propagation of the Faith in the Vatican, at which time they detailed the Trinitarian complaints. The Grajczyk-Jablonski testimony eventually led to another hearing, this one conducted by the Apostolic Delegate to the United States, Monsignor Francis Satolli, held in Chicago during early June 1893. All parties concerned were given an opportunity to testify—Archbishop Feehan, Father Barzynski, and delegations from both St. Stanislaus Kostka and Holy Trinity. This historic conference arrived at several decisions of importance regarding Polonia's future spiritual growth: first, the Resurrectionists were ordered by Satolli to relinquish their authority over Holy Trinity parish, in effect an abrogation of the Foley-Kajsiewicz pact; next, Satolli selected another religious congregation—the Holy Cross Fathers from the University of Notre Dame in South Bend, Indiana—to take over the administration of Holy Trinity Parish. As a result, the Holy Cross Fathers sent a newly ordained, 26-year-old priest to *Trójcowo*, the Reverend Casimir Sztuczko, who was immediately named pastor there; and Barzynski's subsequent complaints and verbal attack on Satolli notwithstanding (the Stanislawian pastor accused the Apostolic Delegate of being "high-handed"), the twenty-year struggle between *Stanisławowo* and *Trójcowo* appeared to have come to an end.

The Reverend Sztuczko moved quickly to accommodate the PNA, formally accepting the local Alliancist societies into Holy Trinity on 4 September 1893, and as a result Holy Trinity became a center of PNA activities in Chicago Polonia. Sztuczko, demonstrating his good faith in the PNA, joined the organization himself. He frequently attended the organization's national conventions, and became so prominent and illustrious a member that he was invited to be the keynote speaker at the PNA's national convention in Toledo in 1901. Thus Sztuczko, almost single-handedly, was able to silence some of the harsher anticlerical elements in the nationalist party. His positive attitude toward the PNA over the years also led to greater cooperation between Polonia's clergy and the Alliance, and, in addition, led to the acceptance of some badly needed reforms within the Alliance

Early Holy Trinity settlers—the Nawrot family

regarding its support of religious activities. The Trinitarian's twenty-year vigil, however taxing, was amply rewarded, because no one knew in the summer of 1893 that Sztuczko would spend his remaining 55 years as pastor of Holy Trinity.[44]

Barzynski's immediate reaction to the events of 1891–1893 was a complete reassessment of priorities concerning the relationship of Roman Catholicism to these ultranationalistic tendencies in his community-parish system. After 1893 he gradually came to accept the hard fact that in order to maintain clerical control of the flock, the shepherds would find it necessary to place a much greater emphasis on Country, on *ojczyzna*; for up to now almost all had gone for God, and this emphasis on God had not worked out too well. This decided change in Barzynski's conceptual framework was most significant. After 1893, the clerical party would cautiously remove obstacles to greater nationalistic participation. The change was not sudden, but the seeds were sown. And the harvest of this planting—which was not to be gathered in until the Mundelein era—would, ironically, have a negative impact on American Polonia's involvement in the mainstream of American Catholicism during the 1920s and thereafter, right up to the advent of the Second Vatican Council.

Barzynski's first major attempt to corral his share of Polonia's ultrapatriots came in his decision to initiate another supraterritorial organization—the *Liga Polska* ("Polish League"). Barzynski and his supporters had first raised the idea of the League during the centennial celebration of Poland's Constitution and during "Kosciuszko's Year," festivities which commemorated Poland's baptism into

Holy Trinity Parish Committee, 1893: Fran-   *The Reverend Casimir Sztuczko in his early*
cis Jablonski, Peter Binkowski, Joseph   *years as pastor of Holy Trinity Parish*
Grajczyk

democracy. But nothing of immediate importance was accomplished at the time. Now, in the light of the recent Trinitarian victories, Barzynski and the Resurrectionist-owned *Dziennik Chicagoski* worked to bring together various interested parties. This newly forged alliance of clericals and nationalists outlined the basic principles and primary goals of the *Liga Polska* in 1896. They included: 1) nurturing the development of Polish people in America; 2) extending greater efforts in education through more schools, libraries, and publications; 3) upholding Polonia's moral union through brotherhood and by a mutual spiritual influence; 4) improving Polonia's material condition by extensive cooperation among her many organizations; 5) making a special effort to befriend the poor by making available public charities; 6) and organizing a national treasury. Essentially, then, the *Liga Polska* was intended to be a halfway house between the PRCU and the PNA. In an attempt to incorporate a fundamentally religious approach into a national social-welfare organization, the League's adherents hoped to reach newcomers still uncommitted to the PRCU or the PNA, and, after this was accomplished, to pressure the newcomers into holding joint memberships in the *Liga Polska* and the PRCU. Yet Barzynski's strategy was all too obvious to the PNA membership, many of whom saw the *Liga* as merely another attempt on the part of the clericals to take away the life of the Alliance. But despite the blatant pseudo-nationalist appeal of the *Liga*, the PNA, strictly observing a policy of toleration toward the clerical crowd during Polonia's first brief "era of good feelings" in the summer of 1893, made no organized move to drive the *Liga* off.

Perhaps by this time the nationalists had already become supremely confident in the intrinsic social value and power of their basic philosophic positions and hence found no need to mount another anti-Barzynski drive. Then, too, with the advent of the Columbian World Exposition in Chicago in 1893—an event which brought Cardinal Gibbons, Archbishop Ireland, Archbishop Ryan, and Apostolic Delegate Satolli to Chicago—both the clericals and nationalists found it necessary to observe a low profile. Each attempted to outdo the other in demonstrating to the hierarchy that Chicago Polonia was a unified and peaceful place. This "unity" theme was capped by a Polish Day celebration at the Exposition on 7 October, a gala event in which 50,000 marchers closed ranks for the audience of nearly 100,000 visitors. The historian of the PRCU, Miecislaus Haiman, claimed that the clerical party viewed the event as a "Pax Dei," a "peace of God descending on the Polish people in America that would last forever." But in Chicago Polonia, the Pax Dei lasted exactly one year. Trouble was already brewing at the community-parish of St. Hedwig's (*Jadwigowo*), trouble which would culminate in the most prominent schism in the history of American Catholicism.[45]

5

A Dark Passage:
The Chicago Independents and the Rise
of the Polish National Catholic Church

Those who try to undermine our Church harbor an ominous design against the essence of our national, religious, and social life. To be exact, we will state that the history of the development of the Polish Catholic Church in America is not without a dark passage here and there. Such is the world. There have been sharp disturbances in Polish parishes (in Winona, Baltimore, Philadelphia) now and then— disturbances which have brought disgrace to our nationality.

Dziennik Chicagoski, 2 January 1894

If the "settlement" imposed by the Apostolic Delegate in 1893 brought an uneasy calm to *Stanisławowo* and *Trójcowo*, it did little to solve or even alleviate problems associated with the ever-sharpening clerical-nationalist debate over God and Country which was sweeping through all corners of American Polonia during the last decade of the nineteenth century. Urban parishes inhabited by Poles were destined to witness a re-creation of the classic Stanislawian-Trinitarian battle many times over, but now with a greater degree and a higher incidence of spiritual, psychological, and physical violence. Polish Catholic priests assaulted in their churches made for banner headlines in the *Chicago Tribune* and the *New York Times*. Mobs of angry Polish housewives took to the streets, demanding a voice in parish affairs. Most were able to frustrate every effort of Chicago's finest, as hundreds of local Irish-American gendarmes appeared totally bewildered by pots-and-pans brigades invading Polish churches. In such fashion, then, was the general populace alerted to Polonia's strange inner quarrels. And within Polonia, journalistic attacks and counterattacks launched in rapid succession by the Resurrectionist *Dziennik Chicagoski* and the nationalist weekly *Zgoda*, regarding the respective ideologies of each camp, soon degenerated into vicious character assaults, bruising the senses and egos of die-hard participants for decades to come.

By the time Polonia's clergy were able to examine the rubble of their crumbled houses of God and Country during the Polish Catholic Congresses—belatedly convened in 1896 and 1901 to stem the upsurge of thousands of "Independents" then defying episcopal and pastoral authority—they were forced to acknowledge the origins and establishment of American Catholicism's only major schismatic group, the Polish National Catholic Church in America.

As we have demonstrated earlier, every immigrant group in the United States experienced some sort of crucial watershed period highlighted by severe internal conflict. These years of "dark passage" often shaped a given immigrant group's collective identity during the so-called process of "Americanization." Defenders of the "Melting Pot" hypothesis (a most durable and resilient concept in American historiography and in the American political arena) have proudly and consistently pointed to the American milieu as a magnificent crucible in the complex interactive process of forming "new" Americans, who somehow were mysteriously purged of their foreign influences. The thrust of this chapter is to demonstrate that Polonia fashioned its own crucible, one capable of melting its own unique tensions, and one that forged a collective identity which was to retain elements of Polishness and Catholicism far into the twentieth century. On the other hand, evidence from this 1893–1907 watershed period clearly indicates that the failure of Polonia's leadership to resolve fundamental tensions involving religiosity and nationalism was a major factor in bringing about schism. When the individual torment surrounding the elementary decision as to whether one was to identify himself as a Polish Catholic or a Catholic Pole spread, collectively speaking, throughout the lay community, the permanency of the schism was all but guaranteed.

Polonia's inner torment was seldom understood by outsiders, most of whom cared little about Polish-Catholic identity problems. Yet, in fairness to these other nationality groups, one must keep in mind that each was undergoing a peculiar identity crisis of its own. And as for the indifference manifested by native Americans—this was to be expected, especially in those Anglo-Saxon quarters generally regarded as thoroughly assimilated. But still the indifference was painful. After all the vicious debates, the ugly parish riots, the insidious journalistic warfare, the excommunications, the rise of a schismatic church and its unhappy harvest of spiritual suicide and social fratricide, after all this painful and shameful embarrassment (what other ethnic group in American Catholicism had cut itself off from the Church?)—who even noticed or cared? Most Catholic Americans, even many *Polish* Catholic Americans, know little of the origins of the Polish National Catholic Church, or why 250,000 Polish National Catholics persist in schism. How could American Catholicism's most significant schism have occurred in such isolation? Was the Polish ethnic group so isolated that even its watershed years escaped the attention of so many outside of Polonia? To summarize these discomforting questions: if the rise of the Polish National Catholic

Church did indeed result in Polonia's acute schizophrenia (Polish Catholic or Catholic Pole); if indeed the schism was responsible for Polonia's subsequent, enormous sense of self-guilt and exaggerated self-consciousness (the Irish, German, Italian, and Lithuanian immigrant Catholics were never schismatic); if the schism indeed had shattered the unity of the Polish-American soul; and if all of this still made little or no difference within the mainstream of American Catholicism—can we say that the work of the schismatics was all in vain? Do we even dare suggest that the schism of Polish National Catholics was a useless schism?

Or, from the vantage point of the late 1970s, can we suggest that this relatively unknown schism occasionally flowers in the fading sunlight of post–Vatican II ecumenism, reminding all religious men in America of a time when the God and Country of one's native land was a burning, timely, and most meaningful issue? Of a time when language, nationality, and religion were all solidly welded into the social fabric of one's community? Of a time when one's ethnic roots and culture, even at the expense of periodic conflicts and "schisms," played a significant role in forming one's spiritual outlook? And can we not say that the religious schisms of one era often provide bountiful harvests of spiritual harmony in later times by dramatically drawing attention to differences which orthodox believers would otherwise have chosen to ignore?

The American Catholic Church may never again witness as spectacular a period of expansion as that brought on by the massive immigrant implosion occurring between the Third Plenary Council of Baltimore and the beginning of World War I. Between 1884 and 1914 the United States found itself host to approximately 20 million immigrants. Because this "new immigration" was largely composed of peoples coming from the predominantly Catholic countries of Eastern and Southern Europe, the American Catholic Church was able to double its numerical strength within one generation—from 8 million to 16 million communicants. This rapid immigrant implosion changed forever the character of the American Catholic Church. The Church's hierarchy, to be sure, would remain a preserve of upward-bound Irish-American clergymen, with but a few notable exceptions who happened to be of French or German origin. But the rank-and-file Church, those millions of unknown laypersons who in the historiographical lexicon are labelled the "inarticulate faithful," was then predominantly first generation, new-immigrant, Catholic. This rapid transformation in the composition of the lay Church was cause for much consternation and no little confusion in the hierarchical ranks. One of the most vexing problems facing the hierarchy was the status of national parishes (those organized on an ethnic group basis) as opposed to territorial parishes (those organized on a geographical basis, irrespective of nationality or ethnicity). On the eve of the Third Plenary Council, for example, the Bishop of St. Louis moved that all national parishes be denied regular status within his diocese; henceforth each national parish was to be "succursal" to territorial parishes. The upshot of this rule was to discourage the formation of any more single-nationality parishes, as well as to break up some of the more established ones (which in St. Louis were predominantly German). Yet when the bishops gathered for the Third Plenary Council in 1884, the "immigrant problem," despite its growing severity, was mysteriously relegated to the background. Only in Title Eight of the Council's decrees was any attention paid the immigrant. Brief discussions took place regarding the reception of immigrants at the various ports of entry. Other talks centered on the problems of Irish, German, and Italian immigrants (the Vatican, not too surprisingly, viewed any immigrant problem as an *Italian* immigrant problem). Proclamations were issued forbidding Catholics, especially immigrant Catholics, from joining secret societies. But outside of recommending special missions to American Indians and Negroes, no other ethnic groups were singled out for special treatment, or even discussed.[1]

The territorial-versus-national parish issue was to remain a highly sensitive one until 1918, when national parishes for the most part were legislated out of existence via reforms in Canon Law—much to the relief of Americanizers within the hierarchy. But until then, intense campaigns, first by the Germans, then by the Poles, and finally by Lithuanians, Ruthenians, and Slovaks, were conducted on behalf of retaining national parishes. In turn, it was hoped by some militant nationals that these nationality parishes would then be administered by auxiliary bishops representing a given nationality within a single-nationality diocese. Faced with the request for a nationwide Polish-American diocese administered by a Polish-American bishop, it was to be expected that elements of the American hierarchy would offer resistance to the concept of "episcopal nationalism," especially after various nationality groups such as the Poles and Germans began exerting greater degrees of militance in the mid-1880s.

The most severe challenge to the preeminence of the Irish-American hierarchy came from the fastest growing segment of the immigrant Catholic population of the last quarter of the nineteenth century, the German Catholics. From their densely populated base in the Cincinnati-St. Louis-Milwaukee "German triangle," German-American Catholics began agitating for equal rights for their numerous urban parishes. In October 1886 the Reverend Peter M. Abbelen, Vicar-General of the Milwaukee Archdiocese and personal theologian and adviser to Archbishop Heiss, sailed to Rome with a petition signed by numerous German-American clergy representing the "triangle." The Abbelen Memorial charged that the Irish-American hierarchy was being overly zealous in its attempts to Americanize German-language parishes, especially those in the dioceses of New Orleans and Baltimore. The Memorial also demanded full parochial status for German parishes, concluding that any program designed to rapidly assimilate the German element would be culturally disastrous.

The Abbelen Memorial served to further polarize the liberal and conservative members of the hierarchy. Proponents of the liberal ideology, including Cardinal

Gibbons of Baltimore, Archbishop Ireland of St. Paul, Bishop Spalding of Peoria, and Bishop Keane of Richmond, advised the Vatican to disregard the Abbelen petition. They argued that the Catholic faith and the American way of life were compatible; that American Catholicism could flourish alongside the positive contributions of Protestantism; that Protestantism contained many innate virtues; that Catholicism was not the only road to salvation; and that non-Catholics, therefore, did indeed belong to the "soul" of the Church. The liberals' position was obviously one of religious tolerance; thus they became markedly annoyed when national parishes displayed a fanatical loyalty to Old World ways, a devotion they felt was misguided, as it worked counter to amicable Protestant-Catholic relations and counter to Catholic assimilation into the American mainstream. Many of these liberal sentiments were given national exposure by James Cardinal Gibbons. In his 20 August 1891 installation address in honor of Milwaukee's newly appointed Archbishop, the Reverend Frederick Katzer (a German-American), Gibbons summarized the assimilationist stance for his German-speaking audience: "Let us glory in the title of American citizen. We owe our allegiance to one country, and that country is America."[2]

Gibbons's Milwaukee statement was intended as a direct rebuttal to the conservative (and anti-assimilationist) positions held by other members of the American hierarchy—notably Archbishop Corrigan of New York, Archbishop Ryan of Philadelphia, and Bishops McQuaid of Rochester, Horstmann of Cleveland, and Wigger of Newark. Oddly enough, shortly after the installation address, Archbishop Katzer and Bishop Messmer of Milwaukee joined the anti-assimilationists. These conservatives, although not always hostile to the American environment, were still deeply suspicious of native Protestants, who, they claimed, were bent on destroying the Church. Pointing to the rise of such organizations as the American Protective Association in the late 1880s as evidence of anti-Catholic hatred, the conservatives argued that the Church's first line of defense was the family and the parochial school. If Catholic families wished to retain ethnic values, they were to be encouraged by their clergymen. And if the parochial schools, which these families supported, became seedbeds of Old World nationalism and cultural traits, the Church, according to the conservatives, was obligated to assist rather than hinder the process. If the national parishes became shelters for the preservation of Old World languages, the hierarchy, rather than lamenting the practice, was to encourage it, for language retention on the parish level was a powerful antidote to immigrant "leakage." It was precisely the issue of leakage which so alarmed the conservative members of the American hierarchy and such laypersons as Peter Cahensly.[3]

Cahensly, a wealthy German merchant, was greatly concerned about the welfare of newly arrived German Catholic immigrants in the United States. Under Cahensly's leadership and guidance, the St. Raphael Society was begun in order to preserve the German Catholic heritage of the immigrants, who, according to

Cahensly, were falling away from the Church at an alarming rate. Accordingly, Cahensly and the Society conducted a study of the problem of leakage in order to determine just how severe it was. Using statistical devices that were quite unrefined even for that time, Cahensly charged, in *St. Raphaels Blatt*, the Society's periodical, that the American hierarchy was responsible for the loss to the church of at least 16 million immigrants (a figure which he subsequently lowered to 10 million). Cahensly and the St. Raphael Society, in its famed Lucerne Memorial, laid their charges before the Vatican in 1891. When the liberal assimilationists learned of the Lucerne Memorial, they of course worked to have the petition flatly rejected. Eventually, the liberal efforts proved successful, for on 28 June 1891, just weeks prior to Gibbons's Milwaukee address, Pope Leo XIII announced, via the offices of Cardinal Rampolla, that the Vatican would take no action regarding the Lucerne petition on the grounds that the charges were "neither opportune nor necessary."[4]

Despite Leo XIII's rejection of the Memorial, he still remained quite concerned about the problem of ethnic dissension in the American Church. He knew, or at least he was told by his advisers, that the ethnic question was related to any number of controversial issues in the American Church, one of which was the problem of financial support for parochial schools. The national parishes had already given the parochial school system considerable financial backing, and Leo did not wish to offend this traditional generosity. On the other hand, Leo wished to avoid open conflict over a project strongly favored by Archbishop Ireland and other liberals—the proposed establishment of Catholic University in Washington, D.C.

In order to stabilize the ethnic situation, and hoping to defuse some of the explosive ethnic outbreaks occurring with great regularity in the early 1890s, Leo decided that the time had come to send a personal envoy to the American Church, a Papal Ablegate (later to become Apostolic Delegate) who was to have extraordinary powers transcending those of the bishops. If Leo's decision was not particularly controversial in the eyes of the American hierarchy, it was still somewhat annoying. Since the American Church was still officially a "mission" Church (the mission status was not removed until 1908), American bishops possessed absolute power in their dioceses, a practice which was sanctioned under the then current Code of Canon Law. Since the authority of bishops in mission areas was final, the liberal assimilationists were able at times to make unilateral decisions which were to the detriment of the national parishes. But now with the Ablegate on the scene, in the person of Archbishop Francis Satolli, a mood of apprehension swept through the hierarchical ranks, especially since the Vatican, perhaps intentionally, had not spelled out precisely the powers of the Ablegate. Liberals like Archbishop Ireland expected Satolli to put down the sporadic ethnic uprisings and support a policy of Americanization; conservatives like Corrigan, McQuaid, and Katzer, on the other hand, publicly made it known that they would oppose greater centralization of power in the American Church under the Cardinal Archbishop of Baltimore, whom they viewed as an arch-Americanizer. Neither side, however, really knew how Satolli would view the development of ethnic pluralism, which by the 1890s was already becoming a hallmark of the American Catholic Church. No one, not even Satolli's close friend Ireland, could predict whether the Ablegate would support assimilationism. Would Satolli demand that such growing nationality groups as the Germans and Poles surrender to the policies of Gibbons and render their loyalties "to one country—America"?[5]

These were some of the central issues and questions facing the American Catholic Church when Satolli rendered his verdict at *Stanisławowo* and *Trójcowo* in the summer of 1893. Satolli's decision in favor of the nationalist faction at Holy Trinity, and his reprimand of the Resurrectionists at St. Stanislaus Kostka, could not have been anticipated by either the liberal or conservative parties in the hierarchy since both had traditionally viewed the entire immigrant question within an assimilationist/non-assimilationist framework. Intraethnic group conflict, such as had been taking place in Chicago Polonia, befuddled the thinking of both parties. Neither side was able to comprehend the fact that these intraethnic uprisings had little or nothing to do with the issue of assimilation, or that these conflicts were invariably caused by a host of local issues and conditions which were, at least in the initial stages, only vaguely related to the question of Americanization.

The immigrant implosion of the early 1890s was not only bringing worry to the hierarchy but was also cause for great concern in the Resurrectionist camp in Chicago. With changing economic conditions in *kraju* (the "Old Country")—an agricultural crisis in Congress Poland, the Germanization of former Polish estates in Pomerania, and a sluggish economy in Galicia—poverty was a fact of life in each sector of Partitioned Poland. These economic factors were nearly always responsible for the rapid upswings in the rate of emigration. Between 1870 and 1914, 1.3 million people emigrated from Russian Poland, 1.2 million from Prussian Poland, and nearly 1.1 million from Galicia.

With the rate of emigration undergoing another sharp increase in the 1890–1894 period, Chicago Polonia once again was forced to accept thousands of newcomers, most of whom were no longer able to eke out a living in *kraju*. Since an immigrant pipeline, operated by the Polish press, was now functioning efficiently between *Stanisławowo/Trójcowo* and Partitioned Poland, it was not at all surprising that a majority of the new settlers made the northwest side Polonia their permanent home. In many respects the new settlers helped transform the neighborhood into a "Polish Capital," even "a second Warsaw." The Polish Downtown—the area in the vicinity of the Milwaukee-Division-Ashland triangle—soon became one of the busiest commercial areas in the city, providing an economic support system for a population which skyrocketed to 50,000 per square mile. With a population density in excess of 450 per acre in the city blocks surrounding

St. Stanislaus Parish, housing conditions rapidly deteriorated, and the slums of *Stanisławowo* soon gained notoriety both locally and nationally. The Congregation of the Resurrection, always running an exhausting and desperate race to establish more community parishes, could barely keep pace with such staggering numbers. Barzynski experienced chronic staffing shortages and continually badgered dioceses in Poland for suitable seminary candidates to assume positions of responsibility in his extensive network. The shortage of teaching nuns was even more critical, at least until the School Sisters of Notre Dame, the Felicians, and the Franciscans of Blessed Kunegunda were able to train postulants on a local level.[6]

Despite the severity of the economic depression of the early 1890s the clergy were either unable or unwilling to divert parish resources into social welfare programs. Thus the Resurrectionist Fathers were faced with an embarrassing anomaly: on the east side of Noble Street, passersby viewed a spectacular, immaculately whitewashed church with towering twin steeples (St. Stanislaus had even undergone some extensive renovation in 1892); on the west side of the street, and for several blocks beyond, all one could see were some of the most dilapidated tenements in all of Chicago. But any substantial welfare effort on the part of the community-parish would have been complicated by the severe "cash flow" problem which faced the Resurrectionists ever since the demise of the *Bank Parafialny*. Since numerous parishioners faced the prospect of losing their life savings, and since this loss coincided with the depression, many began openly rebelling against the Resurrectionists. By the autumn of 1894, most of the Polonia community's anticlerical sentiment was focused upon the Congregation of the Resurrection, and in particular on Father Vincent Barzynski and his brother Joseph, then serving as pastor of St. Hedwig's. And it was at St. Hedwig's that the Independent Movement first gained a foothold in Chicago.[7]

St. Hedwig's Parish, located approximately one mile northwest of *Stanisławowo*, was founded by Vincent Barzynski in 1887. Wishing to keep abreast of the population movement in that direction, he purchased a square block of property bounded by Hamilton, Webster, Hoyne, and Lyndale avenues, and loaned money to prospective parish groups who then constructed a church-school. After the building's completion in December 1888, Father Vincent requested that Archbishop Feehan install his younger brother Joseph as pastor of St. Hedwig's, and Feehan agreed. Under Joseph Barzynski's pastorship, and with the aid of three successive assistant pastors—Francis Breitkopf, C.R., Joseph Snigurski, and Matthew Gronchowski—St. Hedwig's had grown to 1,300 families by 1894. After Gronchowski was transferred that summer, Vincent Barzynski accepted the services of the Reverend Anthony Kozlowski, a highly personable, energetic, and handsome thirty-seven-year-old priest.

Of the hundreds of personnel decisions Vincent Barzynski had ruled on, his selection of Kozlowski was by far the most controversial. His brother Joseph vehemently opposed the selection of Kozlowski, for reasons unknown, though later events show evidence of a strong personality clash. The two clergymen seem to have been natural combatants in the often stereotyped struggle between an older, more experienced, and earthy pastor and a younger, more idealistic, and innovative assistant. As spiritual father of nearly 5,000 souls at St. Hedwig's, Joseph Barzynski invariably and unavoidably got bogged down in the daily administrative routines required of him. And when such pastoral pressures got the better of him, he was prone to long periods of sullenness during which he was unapproachable. Only after long and heated discussions, Father Vincent later candidly admitted, during which he "begged [his] brother to accept Father Kozlowski as assistant at St. Hedwig's," did Father Joseph grudgingly relent.[8] But the two never got along. Kozlowski, dynamic extrovert that he was, immediately won the loyalty of several hundred parishioners, especially ladies, many of whom were attracted to Kozlowski's charming ways. Pastor Joseph, in a foolish attempt to compete with his assistant's personal magnetism, often went to extremes, and was soon accused of "handling himself too clownishly among his parishioners."[9]

But personality differences alone did not account for the growing polarization of St. Hedwig's Parish into pro-Barzynski and pro-Kozlowski factions. Pastor Joseph's alleged ineptitude in parish fiscal matters and his heavy-handed, authoritarian approach to parish problems raised the spectre of another *Stanisławowo* in the minds of some nationalists. The clerical party at St. Hedwig's, on the other hand, was somewhat troubled by Kozlowski's theological background, particularly his ideological ties to the Old Catholic movement in Europe. When the Old Catholic Bishop of Green Bay, Rene Vilatte, visited Chicago to proselytize among Roman Catholics in Polonia, encouraging them to establish an "independent Polish National Church," there was considerable cause for alarm in the clerical camp, especially after Kozlowski began sympathizing with the Old Catholic cause.[10]

No adequate biographical account of Reverend Anthony Kozlowski yet exists, but from a number of contemporary observations and later scholarly studies of the Independent movement in Polonia, it is possible to trace the Kozlowski-Old Catholic-Independent connection.[11]

Anthony Stanislaus Kozlowski was born on 13 January 1857 to a family of Polish nobility. Interested in the subject of religion throughout his youth, Kozlowski eventually took up theological studies in various Polish schools. His eclectic tastes drew him to Bulgaria where he studied the Orthodox faith for a short time. He then joined the Trappist monks, but this experience too was cut short because of the physical demands placed on him by the monastic life. Kozlowski then went to Italy for a time, where he came under the influence of the theologians Ignaz von Dollinger and Joseph Reinkens. Both Dollinger and Reinkens were outspoken opponents of the Vatican I decree on papal infallibility, and both were instrumental in organizing a September 1871 meeting of 300 like-minded protesters in Munich; this meeting led to the formation of the Old Catholic Church.

Although Dollinger eventually broke with the Old Catholic movement, Reinkens remained a staunch supporter and was eventually elected by a synod to serve as first bishop of the Old Catholics (bishops in the Old Catholic Church were elected by both clerical and lay members of a synod and were directly responsible to that synod). Reinkens was consecrated by Bishop Heykamp of the Little Church of Utrecht in Deventer, the Netherlands.

In substance, the Old Catholic movement accepted the decrees of the first eight ecumenical councils, while repudiating the teachings of Trent and Vatican I. Old Catholics recognized the primacy of the Bishop of Rome, but could not accept the doctrine of papal infallibility; they accepted all seven sacraments, but denied Transubstantiation in the Eucharist (while still believing in the Real Presence); they rejected the notion of indulgences, veneration of the saints, relics, auricular confession (preferring group absolution instead), and the dogma of the Immaculate Conception. Old Catholics likewise refused to continue such devotional practices as the praying of the rosary, wearing scapulars, and conducting religious processions. Finally, the Old Catholic Church adopted the practice of using the language of the vernacular instead of Latin at the celebration of the Mass and other religious services, a change which goes far in explaining why the Old Catholic Church appealed to any number of intense nationalist groups in the late nineteenth century.[12]

Kozlowski's later priestly career clearly shows how the theology of Old Catholicism influenced him in the direction of Independentism. A burning devotion to the maintenance of nationalism in religious affairs and a firm commitment to the language of the vernacular in religious services were but two such beliefs Kozlowski transported to St. Hedwig's parish upon his emigration to the United States. But he gave no indication of his Old Catholic ties when he was ordained by Archbishop Peter Jorio in Taranto in 1885.

The period from September through December 1894, spanning Kozlowski's brief but stormy tenure as assistant pastor of St. Hedwig's, is obscured by a thick fog of intrigue. Clericalists, nationalists, and the slowly evolving third party of Independents were engaged in exchanging charges and countercharges. The bitter Barzynski-Kozlowski feud quickly became known throughout *Jadwigowo* (the "village of St. Hedwig"), and Bishop Vilatte's Old Catholic Church made a determined bid to infiltrate nationalist organizations at St. Hedwig's. In the meantime, a group of Independents began conducting an anti-Barzynski campaign (against both Vincent and Joseph), which nearly always took on the character of a vicious personal assault. Finally, a petition was circulated in *Jadwigowo* to either oust Joseph Barzynski or at least nominate Kozlowski as pastor of the parish. In order to reconstruct and understand the composite narrative of these perplexing and confusing events, it is necessary to isolate them, and then to examine the separate phenomena associated with the rise of the Independent schism.

An examination of the Satolli settlement of June 1893 in *Stanisławowo-*

Trójcowo[13] reveals that, despite the alleged nationalist party victory in ousting the Resurrectionists from *Trójcowo*, the archdiocese of Chicago and its archbishop still remained in control. Not wishing to stoke up the smoldering remains of the trusteeship question which had plagued American Catholicism throughout the nineteenth century, Satolli made no allowances or concessions whatsoever on the issue of lay control of church property. Yet, inadvertently, Satolli's decision brought about a major split in the nationalist party ranks; while some Polish National Alliance members chose to remain loyal to Holy Trinity parish and accepted all of Satolli's conditions, a growing number of malcontents became increasingly bitter over Satolli's handling of the property issue. So when the Stanislawian-Trinitarian settlement was made public, the battle cry of "Independentism" was raised in numerous urban quarters throughout American Polonia. Thus, despite an apparent dilution of nationalist strength brought on by the Satolli conditions, the increased ferociousness manifested by the radical Independent wing made up for any lost ground. By the time the *Dziennik Chicagoski* was able to sound its "dark passage" alarm on 2 January 1894, new battle lines along the old clericalist-nationalist front were already being formed. More informed and more politically astute clergy, like Casimir Sztuczko at Holy Trinity, were able to distinguish between "loyal nationalists," who remained behind at *Trójcowo* and adopted a policy of cooperation between the PNA and the clergy, and the more dangerous "independent nationalists," who were now viewed as the real threat to parish stability in Polonia. Consequently, several prominent pastors in American Polonia—Vincent Barzynski in Chicago, Jan Pitass in Buffalo, and Benevenuto Gramliewicz in Scranton—moved swiftly to put down this new rebellion.[14]

With hopes of crushing the Independent movement in Chicago, Vincent Barzynski decided on a somewhat different strategy: he hoped to form a new coalition of old-time clericals and loyal nationalists, without, however, relinquishing any control. To this end he worked feverishly, in the spring of 1894, at organizing the first national meeting of the *Liga Polska*. In an outline draft of the proposed League constitution, Barzynski stipulated that the League was to be "a fraternal alliance standing above all factions." Riding the crest of a new wave of harmony brought on by Polish Day celebrations at the Columbian Exposition of 1893, Barzynski appeared to offer the loyal nationalist constituency solid clerical support for nationalist aims and ideals, as the League was pledged "to defend, support and foster the Polish national cause by open and legal means." Yet Barzynski had no intention of having the clerical viewpoint overshadowed; he indicated that the League "would never engage . . . in any activity against the Holy Roman Catholic Faith or the principles of Christian morality set forth by the Church." But in order to insure the Polish League's devotion to the Church, Barzynski attempted, perhaps foolishly, to pack the League convention with trustworthy clericals, a move which alienated many of the loyal nationalists he was attempting to win over. Accordingly, Article V, Section 4 of the proposed Constitution declared that "delegates shall be chosen from among pastors of Polish parishes or their assistants, and also from editors of Polish newspapers in America who worked in the spirit of the League."[15]

When the first national convention of the Polish League took place in May 1894, the issue of clerical dominance was hotly debated by the 230 delegates who were representing some 34 Polish settlements in the United States. The Polish National Alliance delegation, of course, was adamantly opposed to Article V, Section 4. And when the convention finally resolved that "Pastors of Polish parishes, or their assistants . . . are by virtue of their office automatically made delegates of the League," the "progressive" delegation (those opposing clerical domination) of the PNA walked out of the convention, leaving behind more conservative PNA colleagues who still hailed the Polish League as "beautiful and noble" in its aims. Due to the PNA split at the convention, the Stanislawian slate backed by Barzynski easily gained all the major offices, with Kiolbassa capturing the presidency, Victor Bardonski, a local pharmacist and parishioner at St. Stanislaus Kostka, gaining the vice-presidency, and Stanislaus Szwajkart, editor of the *Dziennik Chicagoski*, winning the post of secretary. Based on the election results, there was now little doubt that Barzynski's intended coalition of clericalists and nationalists had been only a ruse. The clerical coup at the League convention was directly related to the rise of Independentism in Chicago; many of the progressives in the PNA now joined the Independent group. Thus the rise of the Polish League, which was begun as a reaction to the Independent movement, in effect contributed to swelling the ranks of the Independents.[16]

One of the most outspoken opponents of Vincent Barzynski in this rapidly evolving Independent party was an individual named Jacob Tamillo. Tamillo's attacks, usually leveled at both Vincent Barzynski and the Resurrectionist Congregation, first gained wide public attention on New Year's Day 1892 at St. Stanislaus Kostka Parish Hall, where a mass demonstration regarding Czarist oppression in Congress Poland was taking place. Peter Kiolbassa, the meeting's chairman that day, invited various speakers to the parish rostrum, all of whom attempted to enlighten the audience of 2,500 as to the political and social evils then prevalent in Russian Poland. When Tamillo's turn came to address the group, rather than speaking on the subject of the day, he instead said that he would discuss the issue of oppression in *Stanisławowo*! And when the unflappable Tamillo demanded of Kiolbassa thirty minutes in which to tell the Stanislawians how badly off they really were, bedlam ensued in the parish hall. Clerical loyalists hoping to put down this "agitator" immediately began taunting Tamillo; other clericalists, amused by Tamillo's temerity, began laughing uncontrollably, while the hapless Tamillo tried to regain their attention; and others used a variety of gestures to humiliate this representative of Independentism from *Jadwigowo*, all the while threatening Tamillo with physical harm if he did not leave the rostrum. Tamillo's supporters, who were strategically situated throughout the audience but who were too few in number to stem the Stanislawian tide, began chanting "Let him speak!" But despite their efforts, Tamillo was heckled off the stand. In retaliation for this public humiliation at St. Stanislaus Kostka, Tamillo, nine days later, circulated throughout the northwest side Polonia an inflammatory pamphlet entitled, "The Great Protest of Jacob Tamillo Against Father Vincent Barzynski," the introduction to which reads as follows:

> My friends: you are protesting against the actions of the Tsar of Russia in Europe. Why do you not protest against a greater tsar and despot who resides at Ingraham street, near the Northwestern railroad? You do not know him, but I, Jacob Tamillo, do. I have seen him, and conversed with him on the speaker's stand at the large Polish hall of St. Stanislaus Parish in the presence of 2,500 people gathered there on January 1. I have seen him between three and four o'clock in the afternoon when he had taken off his mask of Catholicism, and presented himself barren to the teachings of the Church.
>
> I can truthfully say that . . . it is our duty to take action.[17]

Barzynski retaliated with the charge that "Jacob Tamillo attended the gathering filled with the sayings of false prophets . . . [and that] he failed to convince the people because of his lies." Barzynski also published a list of questions, personally addressed to Tamillo, which appeared in the *Dziennik Chicagoski*:

1. Did I wear any kind of a mask of Catholicism?
2. How did I take off this mask?
3. In what barrenness did he see me?
4. What and how are the 2500 people, who were present at the mass meeting, going to prove and side for me?
5. For what reason is Mr. Tamillo publicly attacking me in his articles?[18]

Coming on the heels of the collapse of the *Bank Parafialny*, Tamillo's feud with Barzynski hardly came as a surprise to depositors whose funds had suddenly vanished. Consequently, Tamillo's complaint reached many a sympathetic ear, especially outside of Barzynski's Stanislawian stronghold. Several weeks after the publication of Tamillo's pamphlet, the nationalist weekly *Zgoda* joined with Tamillo in registering concern over escalating salaries received by priests in Polish parishes. *Zgoda* claimed that most of Polonia's clergymen were receiving approximately $800 per annum in 1892, and this on top of "suitable lodging and board." Barzynski's salary, in particular, came under close scrutiny, as he was alleged to have received $100 per week in the late 1890s. In an attempt to correct these supposed abuses, *Zgoda* outlined a program for reform of parish administration that seemed to add fuel to the fires of Independentism: first, the editors demanded the immediate institution of parish finance committees as well as the establishment of parish treasuries supervised by lay cashiers; next, they asked that each parish maintain a dual accounting system, one maintained by the pastor and the other by the parish treasurer; they also demanded that parishes give a public disclosure of parish finances at least twice a year and that the current practice of transferring funds from one parish to another be abolished.[19]

In retaliation for what they considered an undue intrusion into religious affairs, the clericalist forces bombarded Chicago Polonia with editorial salvos of their own, attacking "secret societies" (the PNA) and threatening those who joined them with excommunication; the *Dziennik Chicagoski* likewise chastised the "Alliance theologists" who were bent on "jeopardizing the position of bishops and priests" and who, consequently, were "dangerous to our people." The journalistic warfare conducted by the clericalists continued throughout the 1892–1895 period. Each week the *Dziennik Chicagoski* devoted considerable editorial space to explaining the efficacy of the traditional spiritual and moral authority of the pope, the bishop, the pastor, and the Polish Catholic family, while branding progressive or liberal elements in the Independent ranks as "religiously indifferent" at times, and in more extreme instances as "satanic" in origin.[20]

One of the sharpest defenses of the clericalist philosophy as well as one of the most bitter attacks on the liberal-progressive Independent camp came on 20 August 1892, during the final days of the *Bank Parafialny*. Opening a lengthy editorial, the *Dziennik Chicagoski* hailed "the very distinguished Fathers of the Resurrectionist Congregation, who, at the request of, and through the efforts of, the Saint Stanislaus Kostka parishioners, came and took charge of the greatest parish in the world." Having made this gratuitous observation, the *Dziennik* editors complained bitterly about the growing ranks of Independents, who were being led by "anti-Catholic directors—agitators, outcasts, anarchists, and other people of socialist beliefs."[21] But in continuing its editorial broadside against the Independents, the editors, while attempting to defend Vincent Barzynski and the Resurrectionists against their many critics, inadvertently let slip that the clericalists were in the process of losing control of their extensive community-parish network:

> The liberals . . . directed a series of violent attacks against them [the Resurrectionists], especially against their principle representative, the pastor of the parish. Any infraction, or whatever the liberals found objectionable in the conservative camp, was attributed to one person. Various pretenses were utilized in an effort to slander him; if these proved unsuccessful, his foes did not hesitate to employ the most vulgar forms of defamation and calumny. To make matters worse, some of the unworthy members of the clergy, envious of the prestige gained by this clergyman, joined the ranks of the attackers and began a vulgar polemic. When peaceful answers were not effective, when the weight of the facts was ridiculed, and when virulence had increased (beyond endurance), a great indignation arose in the

conservative camp. Those who did not understand these peaceful answers were dealt with in a more adequate manner, with a certain
violence. Then was born the famous but shortly lived newspaper,
Kropidlo (Aspergillum), and since then the nickname of "Clerical
sprinklers" has been applied to the representatives of the conservative
camp, who reciprocated by calling all members of the opposing
camp, Masons.

The fight drags on—in alternating periods of violence and calm.
The only difference now is that some of the priests who were forced
to leave the liberal camp will not, because of pride or prospects, enter
the conservative camp. They secretly, or under pseudonyms, carry
on this conflict with the Resurrectionist Fathers, fortifying newspapers with ugly articles.[22]

The *Dziennik* editorial also implied that the cohesiveness of the clerical party
had surely deteriorated, and may even have been near a state of collapse, long
before Kozlowski came on the scene at St. Hedwig's. The editorial also offered
strong evidence that the initial strength of the Independent movement was derived
basically from two sources—disillusioned nationalists and anti-Barzynski or anti-
Resurrectionist clergy.[23]

By 1894, the Independent movement was the predominant issue in American
Polonia; it was clearly associated with such reforms as gaining lay ownership
of church property, combatting excessive spending on the part of clergymen, exposing the autocracy of parish pastors, and winning independence from Resurrectionist and/or diocesan control. In Cleveland, an Independent group under the
leadership of Reverend Francis Kolaszewski broke away from the diocese over
the issue of fiscal mismanagement. When Kolaszewski applied to Bishop Vilatte
to consecrate his church and ordain him in the Old Catholic Church, rioting took
place between Kolazewski's Independent supporters and Roman Catholics. In
Omaha, another Old Catholic priest named Stephan Kaminski, with considerable
lay support, managed to gain control of St. Paul's Church. When Roman Catholic
parishioners there counterattacked in attempts to regain their church, the Reverend Kaminski shot two of the infiltrators in a pitched gun battle. In Buffalo,
Independents under the Reverend Anthony Klawiter also began their own parish
after raising charges of fiscal mismanagement at St. Adalbert's Parish and after
challenging (unsuccessfully) the alleged autocratic rule of Reverend Jan Pitass,
the newly named Dean of all Polish Roman Catholic parishes in the Buffalo diocese. Further outbreaks also took place in Winona, Detroit, Pittsburgh, Scranton,
and Milwaukee. When Independent missionaries like Kolaszewski and a certain
Reverend Radziszewski (Rademacher) came to Chicago in the autumn of 1894 to
work out plans with Jacob Tamillo regarding the founding of an Independent
branch at St. Hedwig's, the *Dziennik Chicagoski* once again sounded the alarm.
Under a banner headline—"Schismatics Invade Chicago!"—the *Dziennik* advised

the "honest public to turn away this gang from Cleveland," as the schismatics "are fortified with the power of an evil spirit—that is, with lies, slander, sacrilege and blasphemies . . . [and] are all set to wage war against the Holy Spirit." The infamous Tamillo, according to the editorial, would only lead good Catholics "into the mire," while "taking advantage of the imprudent and the ignorant in Godly matters." Kolaszewski was portrayed as "a perverted schismatic and excommunicated blasphemer." The *Dziennik* then closed its piece by advising all Roman Catholics to remain faithful to the local bishop.[24]

Journalistic rebuttals by the *Dziennik Chicagoski* notwithstanding, the dramatic surge of strength and growing appeal of the Independents was already having a telling effect on Chicago Polonia, and at St. Hedwig's Parish in particular. Joseph Barzynski, visibly upset by Kozlowski's enormous popularity with the liberal-progressive faction, was continuously at odds with his younger assistant regarding the latter's public contacts. Tensions between the two reached the breaking point when a mysterious petition was circulated in the community, either by Kozlowski's supporters or possibly by Kozlowski himself. A copy of the petition has not survived, but we do know that it contained one, or perhaps both, of the following points: that Kozlowski be retained as assistant pastor of St. Hedwig's; or that Joseph Barzynski be removed as pastor of St. Hedwig's and be replaced by Kozlowski. Hundreds of parishioners signed the statement, most probably thinking that their signatures were intended to support Kozlowski's retention. However, when the petition was submitted to Archbishop Feehan as a *bona fide* request to oust Barzynski, Kozlowski was eventually implicated. On 18 December 1894, Feehan dismissed Kozlowski from his priestly duties, an action that was jointly decided upon by the archbishop and Joseph Barzynski. But Kozlowski's dismissal did not deter the resolution of his supporters in the Avondale area. On 3 January 1895, an Independent committee once again approached the archbishop with new evidence. This time the committee pointed to a $500 discrepancy in the parish account ledger, and it requested that Barzynski be removed for fiscal mismanagement. But after a chancery investigation into the matter, Barzynski was cleared of the charge.[25]

The pro-Kozlowski forces, however, now holding a clear majority at St. Hedwig's, remained undaunted in their bid to remove the Resurrectionist pastor. A newly organized Independent committee headed by President John Skaja and Secretary Peter Bloch announced their intention to place the Kozlowski case before the Apostolic Delegate. Accordingly, Skaja, Bloch, and Kozlowski made plans to journey to Baltimore, where they were to join with another Independent contingent headed by a certain Reverend Stefanowicz, Stefanowicz's brother, and a cleric named Rosicki. Judging it imprudent to confront Satolli directly, the Reverends Kozlowski and Stefanowicz chose to remain in a Washington, D.C. hotel room while the other four members approached Satolli. Granted an audience with Satolli in early February, the Independents proceeded to relate their grievances against the Resurrectionists and the Barzynski brothers. The committee then suggested that Kozlowski be named pastor at St. Hedwig's in place of Joseph Barzynski. Satolli, apparently anxious to avoid a repetition of the Stanislawian-Trinitarian fiasco, acceded to the demands of the Independent group and promised to make the trip to *Jadwigowo* during the coming May when he would formally approve the transfer. Having received this verbal pledge from the Apostolic Delegate, the Skaja-Bloch committee wired back to Chicago announcing the favorable verdict. [26]

Given the circumstances, Satolli's decision was indeed a surprising one, leading one to the conclusion that the Independent case contained numerous legitimate points far and above any mere personality clash between Barzynski and Kozlowski. It is highly doubtful that Satolli would have committed himself to a pro-Independent position if such issues as parish disorganization, financial mismanagement, overly harsh treatment of PNA members, and autocratic administration had not all combined in such a way as to create an intolerable situation for Kozlowski and his supporters. Then, too, Satolli must have been greatly concerned over the numerous Independent outbreaks occurring throughout Polonia in 1894, and perhaps he reached the conclusion that some compromise was in order if a major schism was to be avoided. If Satolli's action at Holy Trinity in June 1893 can be taken as any sort of precedent, it is reasonable to conclude that Satolli was attempting to defuse other potentially explosive situations in Polonia simply by incorporating nationalist party strength into the normal administrative channels of parish organization. On the other hand, one still wonders whether Satolli was fully aware of the extremes to which the Independents were willing to go in order to extricate themselves from Resurrectionist and diocesan bondage. Finally, one can always speculate on the effectiveness of communications between the Apostolic Delegate and the Archbishop of Chicago. From all outward appearances, Feehan may not have known of Satolli's decision to support the Skaja-Bloch committee. For Feehan had already decided to remove Joseph Barzynski, at least temporarily, in favor of the Reverend Joseph Gieburowski, who, to the chagrin of the Independents, was another Resurrectionist.

Why had Feehan made this sudden change? In all probability he came to fear for Joseph Barzynski's life. On Sunday, 13 January, as Barzynski entered his church vestry, he was confronted by seven adult males who refused to allow him to celebrate the usual children's mass. Rather than challenge the group, Father Joseph returned to the rectory. That afternoon, Barzynski's supporters, approximately 300 in number (Kozlowski claimed 800 supporters), met in the church hall, deciding to keep their church open at all costs. With the threat of another street riot in Polonia, the local police were called to the scene and Barzynski swore out warrants for the arrest of the early morning intruders. [27]

The 13 January church incident at *Jadwigowo* brought forth a dramatic eleventh-hour appeal from Vincent Barzynski. In an open letter published on Saturday, 19 January, in the *Dziennik Chicagoski*, a perplexed and contrite Vincent Barzynski came to the defense of his brother:

> Dear brothers and sisters in Christ! First of all, before I begin to discuss the matter of Reverend Anthony Kozlowski and St. Hedwig Parish, I feel obligated to admit that I am at fault and to beg your forgiveness, for, truthfully speaking, it was I who started all this trouble. I begged my brother, Reverend Joseph Barzynski, to accept Reverend Kozlowski as an assistant at St. Hedwig's Parish.
>
> Therefore, I beg your forgiveness, dear brothers and sisters, because it was inconsiderate of me to send an unknown priest to your parish. I trust God that I will be forgiven by all of you for my lack of foresight, for whatever damage has been unintentionally done.
>
> As for me, I promise earnestly to pray for you and your parish, for I do not wish to absolve myself of even a part of this great sorrow which has fallen upon you. It is my desire, therefore, by this letter to voluntarily right the wrong that was done and to make the entire affair clear to the public eye, according to the holy truth of God and the holy spirit of the love of Christ.
>
> As I look upon the crafty execution of the affair in your parish, for which every Catholic and Christian heart suffers great pain, for which every honorable Pole is ashamed, I see the foes of Poland are joyous and that the enemies of the Church have cause to ridicule. Therefore, I am crushed with anxiety before God and consciously feel that I am obligated to make a sincere effort to correct the wrong. Because of this, I wish again to announce publicly by this letter that to a large extent, the fault was mine dear fellow workers, brothers and sisters.
>
> Some say that my brother is at times rude in his expressions and is easily aroused to anger. But on the other hand, no one can accuse him ever of being a flatterer, hypocrite, cheat or conspirator. No such accusations were made by any layman or clergyman.
>
> Some claim that the pastor did not select any parish committee. This, however, is not an established fact, for Reverend Joseph Barzynski has a large number of important parishioners assisting him in keeping accounts and order in the church.
>
> As to accounts, who has charge of them now? You all know that everyone has charge of them. Whoever desires to examine them may do so at any time; nothing is hidden. Income and expenses are not kept secret; the account books are always open.
>
> Finally, a parish committee may be elected each year and changed each year. The same system applies to the care of the parish books. As long as the individuals concerned are honest and sincere, serving the cause of God and the good of the parish.
>
> My dear friends, there is nothing debatable in the matter concerning Reverend A. Kozlowski and Reverend J. Barzynski. The entire

affair is an express and indisputable disregard not only for the priests and the church of God, but also for the authority of the bishop. "Those who hear you, hear me—and whosoever despises you despises me, and whosoever despises me despises the One who has appointed me."

Do you think, my brothers, that you are permitted to manage the House of God as you please? What would you say if someone entered your home and told you how to manage it? Do you think, perhaps, that your home is better than the House of God? Would you permit just anyone to take over the management of your home in your stead? The parish and the parish church must receive as much respect and consideration as your home and family!

My dearest brothers, I realize that I have unfortunately presented the priest in question as an assistant of St. Hedwig Parish. Because of this, I have involuntarily become the cause of these great sins, which are weighing heavily upon my heart.

Therefore, I beseech you, not to jeopardize your eternal life! Remember my twenty years of labor among you and your children and grandchildren. Heed my pleas to you! Return to the path of righteousness, to the way of peace and respect for the laws of the Church.

Your obedient servant and brother,
Father Vincent Barzynski, C. R.[28]

But the Independents, buoyed by the prospects of the Skaja-Bloch committee negotiations that were taking place at the time, openly displayed their contempt for Father Vincent's appeal. On the night of 3 February, mobs of Kozlowski supporters marched around St. Hedwig's rectory, some taunting Father Joseph, others shouting death threats. A contingent of local police was sent over to the rectory from the nearby Attrill Street station with orders to guard Joseph Barzynski around the clock; but the pastor instead chose to move his belongings to St. Stanislaus Kostka, leaving the parish of St. Hedwig's to his two assistants, the Reverends Gieburowski and Paboski. Barzynski's retreat to *Stanisławowo* did nothing to quell the Independent mob. Learning that Feehan was simply going to substitute one Resurrectionist for another, the Independents decided to storm the church. On the morning of 8 February, in subzero temperatures, several hundred men and women, armed with all types of household weapons, broke through the police cordon around the rectory, smashed through the front door of the priest's residence, and went about their wild search for Resurrectionists inside. "Get the priest and lynch him!" someone shrieked. Officer Hamill, who was in charge of the police watch, was blinded by pepper tossed about freely by squads of outraged women parishioners. Seeing this, Patrolman Wendt waded into the crowd, swinging his club at the attackers, who now came from every direction, but a club-wielding fanatic smashed him in the back of the head, knocking him unconscious. Calls for reinforcements to the Attrill Street station brought numerous police wag-

St. Hedwig's Church (Chicago Historical Society, photo by Stella Jenks)

ons to the scene, but the mob regrouped and attacked the police lines once again. Finally, with weapons drawn, the police were able to subdue the rioters, who were then cordoned off at gunpoint while the priests at the rectory (both un-harmed) were brought to safety. Numerous arrests were made. As a result of the 8 February riot, Archbishop Feehan closed St. Hedwig's Parish.[29]

The senseless behavior of the mob at *Jadwigowo* seemed to remove whatever options the Independents still had at their disposal in order to arrive at some amicable compromise. When news of the tumult reached Apostolic Delegate Sa-tolli, he reversed his original pledge to the Skaja-Bloch committee. In a telegram sent to Bloch shortly after the riot, Satolli explained his position:

> Dear Sir: I am grieved more than I can tell you at the scandalous performance which took place in the church of St. Hedwig last Sun-day [February 3]. It is too bad that your people cannot control them-selves sufficiently at least to respect the sanctity of the House of God, and the celebration of the Divine Liturgy. You must understand that

St. Hedwig's Church and school, scene of the 1895 riots

the government of the diocese and the right of removing or changing pastors and other priests belongs to the bishop. If the parishioners have any valid reason for objecting to the priests assigned to them, they should present those reasons to the bishop, and he is bound to give them his careful consideration. When he has done so, the people are bound, if they wish to remain good Catholics, to abide by his decision. I beg you and the others who are discontented with the priests you have to be patient, and I assure you that proper consideration will be given to the matter, and such provision made as will secure peace and harmony. It is hoped that there will never be a repetition of the scandal of last Sunday.[30]

Upon receipt of the telegram, a delegation led by Bloch once again approached Satolli, this time in a more subdued frame of mind. The Independent committee once again asked that Barzynski be removed, but this time simply requested that a diocesan (non-Resurrectionist) priest be appointed pastor of St. Hedwig's instead of Kozlowski. The committee also requested that it be allowed to manage the parish's fiscal affairs. Since neither proposal was at all radical, Satolli promised that a satisfactory solution with Archbishop Feehan would soon be reached. When the Apostolic Delegate received the news that Father Gieburowski and other members of the Barzynski party had been arrested for assaulting an Independent named Petta (the incident took place during the second Satolli-Bloch negotiation sessions), he decided that both Barzynski and Gieburowski should be removed permanently from St. Hedwig's. Naturally, the Independents were jubilant, for they were certain a diocesan priest, even perhaps Kozlowski, would be selected as pastor. Several Independents, to show their good faith, even went back to Feehan, asking his forgiveness regarding the February riots, and requesting that the archbishop reopen their church. Feehan, apparently moved by such conciliatory gestures, told the Independents that the entire matter would be resolved that coming Sunday.[31]

On the morning of 25 February, at a time when the usual Sunday high mass would have been celebrated, Reverend Peter Muldoon, Chancellor of the Archdiocese (and later to become the Bishop of Rockford), appeared before the entire congregation of *Jadwigowo*. Introduced to the parishioners by Skaja and Bloch, Muldoon made the announcement concerning the archbishop's selection of a pastor for St. Hedwig's: he was the Reverend Eugene Sedlaczek of the Congregation of the Resurrection! The Independent delegation was speechless, while the Barzynski contingent greeted the decision with a round of applause. The stung Independent delegation then began questioning Muldoon, asking for an explanation of the archbishop's decision. When none was forthcoming, the angry Independents first began demonstrating inside the church before marching out into the street. Muldoon was somehow able to regain the group's attention and summoned them to return. Then in a terse, authoritarian fashion, Muldoon reminded his audience that he was speaking for the bishop, who in turn spoke for the Apostolic Delegate, who in turn spoke for the Holy Father in Rome; if the parishioners of St. Hedwig's could not accept the authority of Holy Mother the Church, then he, Muldoon, would order the church closed. Having made his point, Muldoon watched as the congregation quietly filed out of St. Hedwig's. Approximately one thousand never returned.[32]

With the departure of the Independents, a new rival committee of loyalists— the St. Hedwig's Parish Committee (SHPC)—now moved to solidify the hold of the pro-Resurrectionist forces. On 1 March the SHPC issued a public declaration defending the choice of Sedlaczek, while condemning the "opposing group for having brought down the wrath of God and the contempt of humanity" on their parish. Having "twisted the words of the Archbishop," and having "disregarded his orders," the Independents had involved themselves "in the kind of activity that leads to schism." Branded as "Successors of Judas . . . who impart the hypocrisies of Pharisees," the Independents, according to the SHPC, were neither Christian, nor Catholic, nor Polish, nor patriotic.[33]

Incited by this public statement, and still bristling over the appointment of Sedlaczek, the Independents made yet another attempt to recapture their old stronghold and oust Sedlaczek. On the night of 14 March, under the direction of the original parish trustees, a meeting of 1,200 Independents was conducted at Dziewior's Hall, at which time a plan of action was hotly debated. One spokesman at the meeting insisted that the Independents were not anti-Catholic, but were simply anti-Resurrectionist. He argued that any action taken be directed solely at the Congregation. "We are tired of them," he said. "They propose to own us entirely—our money, our thoughts, our political beliefs, our bodies and souls— we will have no more of it. . . . We Poles have recognized that the Resurrectionists are dangerous enemies we must crush. And we will."[34]

Having heard such inflammatory rhetoric, and knowing that the Independent pastor Kaminski in Omaha had that very day been involved in a gun battle while fighting for his parish church, the crowd at Dziewior's Hall called for immediate action. The decision was made to attack St. Hedwig's the following morning.

Shortly after dawn on the 15th, approximately 200 Independents under the leadership of John Lewandowski began their march, four abreast, toward the church building. Gaining access through the rear of the church, the Independents moved quickly into the basement area where they easily subdued five very surprised police officers. Another 150 marchers went up into the sanctuary and occupied it, not really sure of what to do next. Shortly thereafter, police reinforcements, all fully armed, appeared on the scene. Intimidated by this show of force, the Independents surrendered without much disturbance. Some rock throwing occurred outside the church, but there were no injuries and there was no further violence as the police began making their arrests. That evening, Father Sedlaczek, anxious to prevent any further disturbances, bravely addressed a large group of Independents in Khalup Hall. In a tense atmosphere, Sedlaczek stated that

> I have nothing to do with Father Anton, Barzynski, nor his brother Father Vincent. It is certainly not my fault that he [Joseph Barzynski] has displeased you. It is true that I am a member of the Order of the Resurrection, but I ask you as thinking men, can I help it that I am a Resurrectionist? But I am willing to do all you ask. If you let me continue in the parish, there shall be no cause for complaint. I shall do nothing without your committee. . . . If any of the members of the parish at any time wish to know how the money is spent, I shall show them the books.[35]

When Sedlaczek finished his speech, a vote was taken on his retention, and all 700 present shouted "nie" ("no") in unison. Stung by this setback, Sedlaczek left the hall in tears. When news of the meeting reached the archbishop, who was fearing for Sedlaczek's life, it was decided to close the church again.[36] The situation at St. Hedwig's had by now deteriorated into a state even worse than that at Holy Trinity during the 1870s.

Ten days after the Khalup Hall incident, another meeting was called, this time by the clericalists on their home grounds. All thirty-four parish societies at St. Stanislaus Kostka convened for the purpose of supporting the Resurrectionist position and to counter the Khalup Hall resolution against Sedlaczek. The officers of the thirty-four societies issued a resolution of their own, published in the *Dziennik Chicagoski*, calling for loyalists at St. Hedwig's to support Sedlaczek. The resolution also condemned the outrageous press coverage of events at *Jadwigowo* by the anti-Resurrectionist newspapers *Katolik* ("Catholic"; formerly *Wiarus*) of Winona. In defense of Vincent Barzynski, the societies claimed that there was "complete unity between the pastor and our parish, and [we] accord this pastor, the Reverend Vincent Barzynski, our deepest gratitude and recognition for his noble, faithful, and untiring work for our souls, hearts and thoughts, enveloped with evangelical abstinence and love of man."[37] Oddly enough, the Stanislawian resolution made no mention of Joseph Barzynski's pastoral activity, an omission which may have been intentional. But by this time, however, the effectiveness of any such resolutions was long past. On 24 May the *Dziennik Chicagoski* sadly announced that the Independents had already begun construction of their own parish church and were "on the road to schism."[38]

Meanwhile Kozlowski was busy organizing his forces. During May of 1895, in a dramatic show of strength which clearly indicated how far-reaching his support really was, Kozlowski registered more than 1,000 of the 1,300 family heads at *Jadwigowo* into the forthcoming Independent parish of All Saints. Yet, to prove to all concerned that the Independents were in no way to be construed as a schismatic body, Kozlowski applied for regular status for his "Independent Polish Catholic Church of America" within the Chicago Roman Catholic Archdiocese; but his petition was rejected.[39]

Kozlowski's application notwithstanding, the clericalists considered Kozlowski's defection final. Almost daily, the *Dziennik Chicagoski* would issue some omenous warning concerning All Saints: all Catholics daring to attend services conducted by Kozlowski did so under the pain of committing sacrilege; "and for the benefit of those who are thinking of following this path," the *Dziennik* warned, "we wish to inform them that they are heading toward perpetual damnation."[40]

Vincent Barzynski responded to the announcement about All Saints in his usual style. He warned all the faithful to render obedience to the archbishop, who "clearly spoke as the Apostle of all nationalities." Then Barzynski solemnly asked: "Who has ever heard of the Catholic Church ever allowing a parish to be founded without a bishop or a priest? Without a House of God or the Sacraments? Without a preacher or the Sacrifice of the Mass? What could be more immoral than degrading the Catholic clergy and tearing away thousands of people from the faith of their fathers?"[41]

Archbishop Feehan in the meantime was exerting his influence to reopen St. Hedwig's, hopefully under more normal conditions. After meeting with Sedlaczek and several Barzynski loyalists, Feehan decided on a 16 June 1895 reopening date. His plans, however, were interrupted a day before the proposed ceremonies when the Independents obtained a court order preventing the archdiocese from carrying out its scheduled activities, on the grounds that the original trustees, all of whom were Kozlowski supporters, still owned the church property at St. Hedwig's. As a result, on 20 June, the case of *Jacob Dziewior et al.* vs. *Catholic Bishop of Chicago* was heard by Judge Payne in the Superior Court. During the legal proceedings, the attorney for the Independents, Max Kaczmarek, concentrated solely on the issue of property ownership. After hearing all the arguments from the complainants, Judge Payne several days later ruled in favor of the archdiocese: "If you question the legal right of the Archbishop to the property," he stated, "here is the place to determine it; but if you admit his legal right and question his ecclesiastical right, you have brought your case to the wrong court, for the civil court cannot and will not interfere with the ecclesiastical policy of the Church."[42]

With the reopening of St. Hedwig's, a new pastor was appointed in place of Sedlaczek. He was another Resurrectionist, Reverend John Piechowski, a most conciliatory individual who during his next fourteen years at St. Hedwig's devoted a great deal of time to welcoming back any "lost souls" from the Independent Movement.[43]

Having lost their legal battle, the Independents channeled all their remaining resources into completing construction of their church. On 12 August, after Feehan refused to conduct the consecration ceremony, Kozlowski performed the rite himself. Addressing his congregation that day, Kozlowski for the first time indicated that All Saints would sever its connection with the archdiocese, claiming that ties with the Old Catholic Church under Bishop Vilatte would prove to be more fruitful in the long run.[44] No sooner was All Saints consecrated than the Independents began proselytizing on Chicago's south side at St. Joseph's Parish, where Michael Pypłatz, a diocesan priest, was pastor. The issue at St. Joseph's once again revolved around property. Permission was needed from Pypłatz in order to purchase a lot for construction of a new church, a move which Pypłatz overruled, since he feared the establishment of another Independent church.[45]

With the threat of Independent expansion on the south side, Archbishop Feehan, taking the strongest course of action available to him, excommunicated Kozlowski on 27 September 1895. The excommunication order was then read from the pulpit two days later at all Sunday masses at all Polish and Bohemian parishes in the archdiocese:

> Whereas, the Rev. Anthony Kozlowski, a Polish priest, not belonging to the Archdiocese of Chicago, and having no jurisdiction in it, has grievously violated the laws and the discipline of the Catholic Church and of the Archdiocese of Chicago; and
>
> Whereas, he persists contumaciously in his unlawful and schismatical conduct;
>
> Therefore, after due process of ecclesiastical law, the Reverend Anthony Kozlowski is hereby publicly and solemnly excommunicated.

The effects of this most grave censure of the Church are:
First—He is cut off from the communion and the society of the faithful.
Second—The faithful are forbidden, under severe penalty, to hold communion or any intercourse with him.
Third—He cannot receive or administer any sacraments. If he should attempt to give absolution in the tribunal of penance, the absolution is invalid.
Fourth—He cannot be present or assist at any of the public exercises or offices of religion. He cannot be present at mass, vespers, or any other public services.
Fifth—He cannot receive or fill any office in the church.
Sixth—If he should die in that ecclesiastical state he should be deprived of Christian burial.[46]

Commenting on the excommunication, the archdiocesan newspaper, *The New World*, viewed Kozlowski as "tainted and blemished . . . [and] one to be shunned and avoided"; for it was Kozlowski who "leads into deeper disgrace and disobedience a body of Polish people, who foolishly promise to follow him. . . . What a sorry spectacle to behold him who promised to bring tidings of great joy, inculcating by word and example, contempt, anarchy and schism."[47]

Of course, the excommunication order and *The New World* editorial raise several significant questions. If Kozlowski had initially served as assistant pastor of St. Hedwig's without permission of the archdiocese, why had Vincent Barzynski selected him in the first place? And had Barzynski even informed the Chancery of his selection?

Chancellor Muldoon's explanation of Kozlowski's status, carried on the front page of the Sunday edition of the *Chicago Tribune* on 29 September 1895, sheds some light on these issues. Muldoon claimed that when the Bishop of Taranto had ordained Kozlowski in 1885, he did so on an *admissam* basis only—that is, Kozlowski was only empowered to celebrate the mass, but he did not possess the right to preach, baptize, unite in marriage, or absolve in the confessional. Muldoon also went to great lengths to explain that no action had been taken on the Kozlowski excommunication until the Bishop of Taranto had first revoked Kozlowski's *admissam* status—an interpretation Kozlowski immediately denied, contending that he had never received any official notification from the Bishop of Taranto on the matter.[48]

As for Barzynski, we have already seen that he assumed much of the blame for Kozlowski's appointment. Yet there is little doubt that the Stanislawian pastor was a victim of an exceedingly porous and faulty personnel system then operative between European dioceses and U.S. missions. H. J. Heuser, prominent editor of *The Ecclesiastical Review*, and one who had long fought the battle to close "abundant loopholes" in the transference of priests from European to American dioceses, made the following observations: European bishops were using American dioceses as a dumping ground for unsuccessful priests. Hoping that the new environment would somehow transform these failures into "useful and edifying priests," European bishops were allowed to make these transfers without regard for the integrity of the American Church. According to Heuser, whose editorials were read with great attention by the hierarchy, such European experiments were proving to be harmful to the vitality of the American Church, especially in immigrant areas. As a result, "complaints frequently reached Rome to the effect that America was being made a refuge for disgruntled and unqualified clerics" who, if they were already "a scandal to the public," became "a burden to the dioceses which had to provide them with a livelihood according to their *titulis missionis.*"[49]

Heuser's observation was indeed penetrating, but there were other causes for the funneling of poorly qualified priests into Polonia. For one, the screening processes used by both the archdiocese and the Resurrectionists in bringing in outside candidates left much to be desired. Perhaps both were merely acting out of desperation in response to the chronic shortage of Polish-speaking priests when they introduced clergymen of questionable vocation, yet the Chancery invariably supported Barzynski's judgments in personnel decisions. There is no record of a public veto of any candidates selected by Barzynski for any of the Resurrectionist parishes.[50] This, of course, does not mean that the Chancery did not object behind closed doors. But if it had, Barzynski probably would have made such personnel vetoes a public issue. In any event, if the Archdiocese of Chicago was forced to admit in the pages of *The New World* that Kozlowski had been administering without proper authorization, it only did so after the fact, and only after having been the first American diocese to suffer the impact of a major schism.[51]

With Kozlowski excommunicated, the Independents were immediately faced with the problem of establishing legitimate ecclesiastical succession. Accordingly, Kozlowski set out to have himself consecrated a bishop in the Old Catholic Church. After having received a positive recommendation from Vilatte (who later was to become a competitor of Kozlowski), and after having been notified of its formal approval by the Old Catholic Council in Berne, Switzerland, Kozlowski was consecrated a bishop there on 13 November 1897. Oddly enough, the consecration ceremony, conducted by Bishop Herzog of Berne, Archbishop Gul of Utrecht, and Bishop Weber of Bonn, came on the feast of St. Stanislaus Kostka.

During the next ten years Bishop Kozlowski multiplied his earlier efforts at St. Hedwig's many times over, founding 23 parishes stretching from New Jersey to Manitoba. Kozlowski's organization, which housed 17,000 communicants by 1900, was called the "Polish Old Catholic Church" during his lifetime. After his death in 1907, the Chicago Independents, not having a validly consecrated bishop of their own (Kozlowski never consecrated any new bishops himself), joined the Polish National Catholic Church in America under Bishop Francis Hodur, a phase of Independentism which falls outside the scope of this study.[52]

The Chicago archdiocese, through *The New World*, maintained a vigorous attack on Kozlowski between 1895 and 1907. Shortly after Kozlowski's consecration as bishop, for example, the archdiocesan weekly published an editorial entitled "Bishop Kozlowski and His Dupes." The archdiocesan stance was quite predictable: the Polish Old Catholic Church was nothing more than "a small body of turbulent and malcontent Poles" who were affiliated with "a schismatical church in Europe, distinguished mainly for the insignificance of its members and the untenableness of its position." *The New World* regretted "that this so-called Bishop should have been able to seduce from their allegience even so comparatively small a section of a nationality which in bygone times has given so many and such devoted proofs of its loyalty to the Church."[53]

On 29 June 1898, when Pope Leo XIII pronounced the major excommunication "Apostolicae Sedis," which named Kozlowski as having been responsible for the schism, *The New World* published the entire text along with Cardinal Ledochowski's transmittal of the proceedings.[54] Even when Kozlowski suffered through a period of severe illness in the summer of 1899, *The New World* could not find a word of sympathy: "Bishop Anthony Kozlowski professes himself in danger of death. A case of plain old-fashioned notoriety seeking, the outcome of the principle that conscience makes cowards of us all."[55] And when Kozlowski died on 14 January 1907 at St. Anthony's Hospital in Chicago, *The New World* closed its bitter feud with mixed emotions—the archdiocesan weekly found the circumstances surrounding his death "tragic and depressing" (referring to rumors then circulating that Kozlowski had been poisoned), yet the editors still instructed all Roman Catholics in the future "to give pestiferous ex-priests a wide berth."[56]

The Independent presence at nearby All Saints Parish was likewise a visible reminder to the clerical party of its recurring policy failures, although few admitted such at the time. Instead, the *Dziennik Chicagoski*—like its archdiocesan counterpart *The New World*—rather than analyzing the origins of Independentism, simply chose to use every available opportunity to mock the Independents. When All Saints was solemnly consecrated on 11 November 1895, amidst great fanfare, the *Dziennik Chicagoski* was unable to resist the opportunity to remind its readers that the event coincided "with the anniversary of the hanging of the Chicago anarchists" (the Haymarket Square rioters); the newspaper further claimed that the ceremony was highlighted by the attendance of "saloonkeepers, and followers of Coxey's army [who] hung out German flags, revolutionary French flags, or banners of 'red' Socialists"; the *Dziennik* mockingly reported that by noon "all the saloons . . . were crowded," and that a majority of the guests were in a "tipsy" state; lastly, the *Dziennik* poked fun at the attending Independent priests, like Kolaszewski of Cleveland, Kaminski of Omaha, Klawiter of Buffalo, and an "unknown priest of Irish descent," who took part in a "consecration ceremony" attended "by a handful of befuddled persons . . . and a crowd of inquisitive individuals who wanted to see the comedy."[57]

But such self-amused accounts were hardly typical. More often than not the *Dziennik Chicagoski* reflected the intense bitterness within the Resurrectionist camp over the rise of Independentism. The ordeal of 1895 had, among other things, contributed to the ruin of Vincent Barzynski's health. Two days after the consecration ceremony at All Saints, Barzynski wrote an open letter to Chicago Polonia, carried in the *Dziennik Chicagoski*, which revealed that his iron will had finally met the test. On the recommendation of the archbishop, leading Stanisla-wians, and his physician, Barzynski stated that he would take a leave of absence in order "to recuperate in the sunny clime of California." Apologizing for using the *Dziennik* rather than addressing the faithful in person—"my health does not permit me to speak to you in person"—Barzynski warned Chicago Polonia that "the number of godless people is continually increasing." He also expressed alarm at "the rise in drunkenness, divorce, family desertion and blasphemy . . . among Poles in America," evils he felt were attributed to the rise of the Independents and their journalistic propaganda:

> The cause of all this to a large extent falls upon the writings in loathsome newspapers which tend to poison the hearts of weak-minded persons, and first of all the hearts of the youth. Upon such foundations the devil builds independent temples (churches not connected with the pope) and makes those who have been excommunicated his dignitaries. These individuals then garner all the evil into one sacrilegious flock in order that not one may escape the claws of the devil.
>
> Because of these circumstances I wish to warn you, my dear brothers and sisters in Christ, against coming in contact with such persons, and to advise you to keep a more careful eye on your children. Precautions should also be taken against reading godless literature, for he who swallows this poison becomes lost forever. All kinds of schism, history shows, becomes established in lies; it thrives on these poisons These lies are spread as decayed matter is spread by bugs.
>
> Only the "truth of the Lord lasts forever," and in it life and salvation!
>
> The various forms of schism sin against the Holy Spirit. They not only contradict the recognized Christian truths but at the same time kill in the individual's heart the love of man and God. You all know that sins against the Holy Spirit will not be forgiven in this world or in the next. That is why all schismatics become lost without penance.[58]

Barzynski's retreat into the wilderness gave him the time and presumably the peace of mind to analyze the Independent movement in a sober fashion. Writing from Yuma, Arizona, that Christmas, Barzynski continued to caution his flock about the temptations and dangers of "liberal materialism," a phrase which he felt aptly described the intense property consciousness of the Independents.[59] And he never failed to challenge the lay leadership principle of Independentism:

> If you desire to work in the name of God, pay heed to the words of Christ, because God the Father gave us only one Christ; if you wish to labor for Christ, then listen to Peter, for Christ gave us only one Peter; if you want to work in Peter's name, obey the Pope, because he is the only true successor to the first Pope; if you wish to work in the Pope's name, obey the Bishop, because only the Bishop rules the diocese; if you wish to obey the Bishop, then you must obey your pastor, for the Bishop gave you only one pastor.[60]

Barzynski's oration was a classic statement on the hierarchical model of governance in the Catholic Church, a principle of authority with which any transplanted Polish peasant could readily identify. The lay church in the Old World village as in the New World immigrant ghettoes was expected to accept its place at the bottom of the pyramid, or at least so Barzynski thought. Lay people were given "only one pastor" and therefore were to obey him. But these Independents? They had violated the Church's treasured principle of authority, and Barzynski was certain that they were like any other Protestant group which might attempt to stand the pyramid on its point; with a ceiling so top-heavy with assertive lay people, the pyramid would surely topple over and collapse.[61]

Some of the blame for the existing Independent movement was likewise shifted in the direction of the Polish National Alliance. Although the Alliance vigorously denied any responsibility for the rise of Independentism, the clerical faction found such denials unconvincing. A letter to *The New World* written by "A Polish Priest of the Archdiocese" argued that there had been a conspiracy between the PNA and the Independents:

> The Polish National Alliance, which develops itself from day to day . . . becomes more anti-Catholic. . . . The head officers of this organization are men who not only have no faith, but who turn other Poles against the faith of their ancestors, and their priests. In their official organ "Zgoda," they try to weaken the faith in the hearts of our faithful people, inciting them to disobedience to our priests, who are blamed for rebellions which occur in Polish congregations. Their editor, an ex-cleric, said at the anniversary celebration of the Polish Insurrection in Pulaski Hall, South Ashland Avenue, November 29: "There will come a time when the oppressed masses will throw out the priests." He further stated that the only place where people will find salvation like those in the Ark of Noah will be the Polish National Alliance (and therefore not the Catholic Church). Such and similar are the ideas of these men who publicly support and receive

into their organization schismatics that are excommunicated either by the Holy Father or their respective Bishops. It is high time that the Catholic Hierarchy in the United States who do not know what is going on among the Poles, should condemn such an organization which is trying to do the same work Martin Luther did in Germany. If there will be no severe interference and penalty we may fear that after a few years there will be few Poles keeping the faith of their ancestors.[62]

Rebuttals by the PNA to these charges notwithstanding, there is some evidence of cooperation between the PNA and the Independents. As Victor Greene has pointed out, the Polish National Alliance gave the Independents a "formal, organizational sanction" by not enforcing its 1895 provision barring membership to Independents. When the Alliance admitted a branch from Cleveland under the schismatic Reverend Kolaszewski, it invited such charges as those raised by the "Polish Priest" and the *Dziennik Chicagoski*.[63]

If the rise of the Independents in Chicago Polonia during the mid-nineties gave rise to much soul searching within the Polish community, it likewise spurred a number of outside analyses, some of which were written by perplexed observers of Polonia who found the Polish ethnic group most difficult to comprehend. In an article entitled "Recent Schismatical Movements Among Catholics of the United States" published in the *American Ecclesiastical Review* in July 1899, "A Close Observer" (again anonymous), after analyzing the relationship of the Old Catholic Movement to Independentism, concluded that the Kozlowski break occurred because the "misguided but strong-headed" Poles were clamoring for "a Polish bishop and Polish priests for Polish people!" "Close Observer" did not feel the Kozlowski Independents were in any way schismatic, as they "did not reject, either openly or secretly, the *Vaticanum* [the First Vatican Council]"; in fact, the writer claimed that the First Synod of the Independents of Chicago had "reemphasized the primacy of the Holy See, and added its *explicit* declaration of assent to the dogma of the Immaculate Conception . . . and adhered strictly to the Roman rite in all things." Consequently, the anonymous writer came to the conclusion that the Chicago Independents formed an "avowedly orthodox, though utterly contumacious" movement which had the sole aim of realizing "the false ideal of a true 'American-Polish-Catholic diocese'"; thus Kozlowski's movement, rather than being schismatic, was no more than a "secessionist faction"—an interpretation which has persisted to our times in Polish-American historiography.[64]

Responding to "Close Observer," Reverend Wenceslaus Kruszka, a Ripon, Wisconsin, pastor who would someday rival Father Barzynski in his impact on American Polonia, focused on one central fact which he felt adequately explained the rise of Independentism. Kruszka's observation, which must have been known to Barzynski, Feehan, and Kozlowski long before it was published, was remarkably simple, but had largely been ignored:

> . . .the true cause of the present unhappy movement among the Poles
> in this country is that their congregations are too large. . . . As long
> as the parishes were kept within proper proportions, there was no
> thought of independence. But as soon as healthy divisions were
> stopped, and large congregations began to develop—of about 1,300
> families say—the result was another Independent church.[65]

After drawing the line at "1,300 families" (the precise count at *Jadwigowo* on the
eve of the break), Kruszka went on to pinpoint the growing "identity crisis" in the
Resurrectionist parishes in Chicago:

> For it is well understood that to govern a parish properly, the pastor
> must control the members, must "know his sheep"—that is to say,
> *the pastor* must know them personally, and not leave them to his
> assistants altogether. This necessary knowledge is impossible if his
> congregation counts some 10,000 souls, or perhaps 20,000 souls, or
> even 40,000 as is the case of one congregation in Chicago. No one
> shepherd can look after so large a flock. Even a pastor of a small
> parish will have difficulty to satisfy every member of his congrega-
> tion; for a pastor whose flock runs into the thousands it is quite im-
> possible to influence the discontented members and make them keep
> peace or submission.
>
> The need then is for smaller congregations, for more pastors, and
> fewer assistants. This is not my opinion only. I understand that the
> Apostolic Delegate has declared himself in favor of smaller parishes.
> Nationality need not enter at all into the question of the appointment
> of bishops, and our present hierarchy will be able to control and rule
> the Polish element, if we have due regard for the old Roman maxim:
> *Divide et impera.*[66]

Kruszka's argument was not directed at the heart of Barzynski's community-
parish concept. He agreed that the religious, by their sheer physical and moral
presence, would have a lasting spiritual and social impact on the surrounding
community. But Kruska did indict Barzynski for his failure to extend this most
cherished Resurrectionist principle to a Chicago Polonia now supersaturated with
newly arrived immigrants. According to Kruszka, even a man of "iron strength
of will" was no match for 250,000 souls.

Barzynski never got the opportunity to challenge Kruszka's thesis. He died
three months prior to the publication of the article. But before his death, he still
was able to make one last attempt to put Polonia's house back in order, via the
First Polish Catholic Congress of 1896, a national meeting of American Polonia's
numerous religious and fraternal organizations. In this eleventh-hour attempt at
reconciling ethnic nationalism and ethnic religiosity, the Buffalo Congress addressed itself to the problem of episcopal representation in the American hierarchy. The *Dziennik Chicagoski*, rather than favoring "a Polish bishop exclusively

for Poles [because] anarchy would result from it [and] because other nationalities would demand the same consideration," instead called for the appointment of "a Polish assistant Papal Delegate [who] would be the best judge of our affairs."[67] In addition, the *Dziennik* presented a comprehensive program for consideration: 1) the organization of the Polish Catholic Clergy in America into a formal body; 2) condemnation of the Independent movement; 3) support for an Immigration Home for Poles; 4) the establishment of a religious seminary; 5) formation of an all-embracing Polish Catholic labor organization in America.[68]

Despite the good intentions of the Buffalo Congress and its call for unity between clericalists and nationalists, the First Polish Catholic Congress floundered because of several inherent weaknesses. First, the Congress was still controlled by the clergy, especially by Barzynski and Pitass, and since the Independent movement was a predominantly lay-oriented force, the exclusion of a viable lay voice at the Congress eliminated the possibility for reform regarding any supposedly legitimate Independent concerns. Next, the selection of delegates, although designed to consider parish delegations on the basis of numerical strength, led to the breakdown of the Congress. Since it was agreed that one delegate be admitted for each 1,000 parishioners in Polonia, and since parishes with less than 1,000 parishioners received only one delegate, it was obvious from the outset that the large parishes, especially the Resurrectionist bloc from Chicago and the Pitass bloc from Buffalo, would control the proceedings. Hence when the convention degenerated into making vicious attacks on the PNA, the clerical party lost support from such moderates as Reverend Casimir Sztuczko from Holy Trinity.[69]

If the First Polish Catholic Congress failed to stem the Independent tide in 1896, it did succeed at least in drawing together for the first time the disparate elements of American Polonia, and it did set the stage for future Congresses in the twentieth century (the Second Congress was held in Chicago in 1901). But by that time Barzynski was gone. His death from pneumonia on 2 May 1899 at the Alexian Brothers Hospital in Chicago naturally came as a great shock to Polonia. At age sixty-one, after thirty-eight years in the priesthood, the Reverend Vincent Barzynski, in his multiple role as Provincial of the Resurrectionists in Chicago, as pastor of the largest Catholic parish in the United States, and as administrator or coordinator of dozens of parishes, schools, fraternal organizations, newspapers, orphanages, and hospitals, was one of the most prominent figures—if not *the* most significant figure—in the history of nineteenth-century Polonia. His style of leadership, however controversial, left its imprint on Polish American Catholicism. Many a future pastor in Polish Catholic Chicago, and elsewhere, would adopt his ambitious and aggressive ways. His loss to American Polonia was felt by friend and foe alike. Supporters of Barzynski frantically searched for another leader to step into his national role; some unsuccessfully assumed the role themselves. Although a handful were to surpass some of Barzynski's achievements, none was ever again as dominant in Polonia as the Stanislawian pastor. Barzynski's enemies were likewise faced with a dilemma—no longer would they have a convenient scapegoat on which to hang the ills of Polonia; instead, they would now be forced to solve problems and make adjustments in a more sober fashion.

Barzynski's funeral was a most dramatic and spectacular affair. More than 500 funeral carriages, with 10,000 marchers alongside, made up the funeral procession alone; in addition, hundreds of clergymen and thousands of laypeople from throughout the United States lined the funeral route from St. Stanislaus Parish to St. Adalbert's cemetery. Each parish society from each Polish parish in Chicago sent representatives, even the Polish National Alliance. The *Dziennik Chicagoski* closed its editorial for the day with the words: "Dead is a patriot, who after his first love of God, always had his eyes fixed on the Fatherland."[70]

It has not been all that difficult to isolate the phenomena which contributed to the rise of the Independent movement in Chicago Polonia. A number of factors were significant: the obvious and open disillusionment shown by fanatical nationalists over the Satolli settlement; the eleventh-hour attempt by Barzynski to capitalize on the growing strength of the nationalist party via the institution of the Polish League; the demise of the *Bank Parafialny* and the resulting clamor over inept Resurrectionist parish management; the uncompromising stance of numerous nationalists over the issue of church property ownership; the proselytizing activity of the Old Catholic Church under Bishop Rene Vilatte in the Chicago area; the personal differences and ambitions of Joseph Barzynski and Anthony Kozlowski at St. Hedwig's; the public attacks on the policies of Vincent Barzynski by such outspoken parishioners as Jacob Tamillo; the long and bitter journalistic war between the clerical *Dziennik Chicagoski* and several nationalist organs; the mysterious breakdown of communications between Apostolic Delegate Satolli and Archbishop Feehan of Chicago; the street riots at *Jadwigowo*; the legal battles over church property at St. Hedwig's. All these contributed to or later solidified the Independent movement. But a number of significant questions remain and will probably continue to invite debate.

For instance, was the Chicago Independent movement a truly schismatic movement at the time of the archdiocesan pronouncement of Kozlowski's excommunication in September of 1895? Up to that point, the Independents had clearly *not* challenged any doctrinal features of Roman Catholicism. And until the Vatican pronouncement of excommunication in May 1898—a nearly three-year interim during which some type of reconciliation might still have been worked out by either side—Independents unquestionably accepted the doctrines of the Primacy and Infallibility of the Pope. Even after May 1898, it is questionable why the Independent movement was labelled "schismatic." It is true that the Vatican excommunication had been based on the charge that Kozlowski "had contumaciously rebelled against legitimate authority," and that he had called himself

"Bishop of the Catholic Independent Diocese of Chicago."[71] These were serious charges, to be sure. Nevertheless, the lay membership in the Independent movement had by no means challenged, even as late as May 1898, any doctrinal teachings of the Church. In substance then, the Chicago Independents broke from Roman Catholicism over *jurisdictional* differences rather than *doctrinal* ones. The Independent movement was really a jurisdictional schism rather than a doctrinal schism. To put the matter another way, the central issue insofar as the Independents were concerned was that the Chicago archdiocese should have taken the initiative in developing a national diocese for Poles within the territorial diocese of Chicago. Had canonical arrangements been forthcoming which would have synthesized or integrated territoriality and nationality within the Chicago archdiocese—and given the immigrant character of the American Church it might have appeared logical and wise to do so—it is quite likely that no schism would have occurred in Polonia. But from an Independent standpoint, unfortunately, this symbiosis of territory and nationality was never to come. With the triumph of the Americanist Crusade during World War I, and the subsequent impact of Americanism on the revised Code of Canon Law drawn up in 1918, national parishes, with very few exceptions, were practically eliminated. And without national parishes there could be no national diocese. After 1918, the territorial parish, regardless of the numbers or strengths of the nationality groups it was intended to serve, reigned supreme. And with this reform in the canon code, it followed that the establishment of a single nationality diocese like the one created by Kozlowski was destined never to gain acceptance. Thus despite the many gratuities thrown in the direction of "the solid Immigrant Catholic Church" by the Americanized hierarchy, it was all too clear, especially after the formation of the Polish National Catholic Church, that the idea of ethnic pluralism on both the hierarchical and lay levels of the American Catholic Church was not widely favored.

Another phenomenon—that of the return of numerous Independents to the Roman Catholic Church after the consecration of Polonia's first Roman Catholic bishop in 1908—reinforced the notion that the Independent movement was largely a jurisdictional rather than a doctrinal schism. *The New World*, for example, rejoiced when it could announce that "Independent Poles Rapidly Return" and that "Schismatic Bodies The Country Over Are Growing Repentant And Obediently Returning To Their Ancient Allegiance."[72] And when the Independent parish of The Immaculate Heart of the Blessed Virgin Mary in Cleveland returned to the fold along with the Reverend Kolaszewski, preparations were made to formally readmit the "schismatics."[73] But if the return of Independents did not reach the levels expected, it was most probably due to the fact that the American Catholic Church was no longer willing by World War I to support the growing national consciousness of the "New Immigration" on any level. By such sins of omission, the American hierarchy in effect offered clear proof that it had never really understood that the Independent movement was fundamentally a lay movement. The excommunication of Kozlowski had solved nothing, and it had really missed the whole point of the Independent protest.

This raises another issue regarding the Independent movement in general and the Polish National Catholic Church in particular. That is, did the rise of Independentism heighten or did it diminish the ethnic consciousness of Poles in the United States?[74] Although research into this question in some ways transcends the scope of this study, the question is in many ways directly related to the identity crisis suffered by the forces of Kiolbassa and Dyniewicz in the urban village of *Stanisławowo*. Perhaps the rise of Independentism was one response to the burning question of whether or not the Polish immigrant's proper role was that of a Catholic Pole or a Polish Catholic. In Poland, such an identity crisis would probably not have taken place, as the hierarchical establishment there was thoroughly Polish. Conflict between Church and State and between Church and Culture was thus kept to a minimum. The Church in Catholic Poland simply was the majority group. But in the United States not only were Poles a minority group within the Catholic Church but Catholics as a whole also constituted a minority group within the pluralistic religious structure of the country. Hence there was a good deal of competition *within* American Catholicism, as various ethnic groups at times tried to "out-Americanize" each other. When an Irish Catholic gave vigorous support to Gibbons's Americanization campaign, that Irish Catholic was in effect stating that he was a loyal and assimilated American. Polish Catholics in the United States, on the other hand, at least prior to World War I, found such gestures of loyalty unnecessary and even distasteful. Having their own problems in resolving the issues of Catholicity and Polishness in an American environment taxing enough, many Poles (witness the later rhetoric of Kruszka) refused to pay homage to an Irish-American Catholic hierarchy. When powerful pastors like Vincent Barzynski made "arrangements" with the Irish-American hierarchy, arrangements which brought them power in the first place in addition to augmenting that power later, nationalist party Poles took strong exception. And when their efforts at reform were continually frustrated by the hierarchy, the battle cry of Independence was taken up with a vengeance. Thus, as the Independent movement and later the Polish National Catholic Church gained momentum, especially in the 1900–1920 period, Polish Roman Catholics, in order to maintain support in their own community, were consistently called upon to display boldly, and sometimes exaggerate boldly, their Polish heritage. In this way, then, did the Independent schism contribute to a heightened ethnic consciousness in Polonia, sometimes even long after the historic hair-splitting over Polishness and Catholicity had come to be taken for granted or even forgotten.

But one issue was not easily forgotten. It was one which would continue to smoulder in the minds and hearts of thousands of *za chlebem* urban peasants in the Independent ranks. That is, many went to their graves convinced that they had been exploited by Vincent Barzynski and the Congregation of the Resurrection. Each time these Independents or their children or their grandchildren passed by one of the monumental parish complexes administered by the Congregation but legally owned by the archbishop of Chicago, the old wounds would fester. Scurrilous attacks by the muckraking *Dziennik Ludowy* ("The People's Daily") and *Bicz Boży* ("The Whip of God") reminded the Polish masses of "How Churches Are Built." The *Dziennik Ludowy*, on 20 May 1907, lamented that "the people have contributed their last cent . . . for the revelry of these soul healers." The *Ludowy* screamed even louder when it discovered that two Polish Catholic priests and a young lady had skipped town with a Sunday collection. "And so we go on, endlessly," the editors remarked, "with the poor Polish people being swindled, robbed and kept in the dark as to who swindles or breaks them."[75] In another editorial, the same daily charged that a Polish Catholic priest in South Chicago was "inhuman and unapproachable," that he behaved like "some despotic prince in the old country."[76] Relentlessly pursuing "The Black Locust" who allegedly were "conducting orgies of new exploitation . . . when thousands of people are starving, and when hundreds of Polish workingmen have no roofs over their heads," the *Dziennik Ludowy* remarked satirically that "the Roman Catholic Union should be proud of such Polish culture in America."[77]

These editorial salvoes fired at the clericalist party despite their minority Polish socialist origins continued with ever greater intensity well into the 1920s. If the *Dziennik Ludowy* and *Bicz Boży* persisted in their harrassment of the Resurrectionists and the surviving Barzynski institutions, the press of the Polish National Catholic Church—via *Straż* ("The Sentinel") and *Rola Boża* ("The Field of God")—later extended that attack to include the entire Roman Catholic Church and the papacy as well. Hence the divisive and bitter climate created by the savage journalistic warfare of the Independent period continued to confound scholars as late as the mid-1960s. Even during a brief ecumenical respite, scholars assessing the roles of Barzynski, the Resurrectionists, and the American Catholic and Polish National Catholic hierarchies appeared to have the same difficulties encountered by Kruszka at the turn of the century.[78]

Yet, despite the heavy involvement of the clergy in the Independent movement (Kozlowski in Chicago, Kaminski in Omaha, Klawiter in Buffalo, Kolaszewski in Cleveland, and Hodur in Scranton) and despite the efforts by these priests to infiltrate Resurrectionist institutions (the press, the fraternal organizations, the parish societies, the well-established immigrant school system), the evidence overwhelmingly supports the hypothesis that Independentism was dominated throughout by the laity.[79] Without the active support of thousands of parishioners who were demonstrating their concerns in the urban parish riots of the 1890s, it is doubtful that the ambitions of such nationalistic clergy as Hodur or Kozlowski would ever have been realized. As we have seen, the enormous influence exercised by Barzynski and the Resurrectionists during the last quarter of the nineteenth century was responsible for the creation of a personnel system that prevented many an outstanding candidate from becoming pastor of his own parish. Robbed of upward mobility in an immigrant church that accorded priests, especially parish pastors, unusually high status (compared to those in other ethnic groups like the Italians or Czechs), and not given the opportunities to institute more humane reforms to bring about greater and more meaningful contacts between pastor and parishioner, energetic young priests like Kozlowski soon found themselves supporting the positions of their exploited congregations.

In conclusion, the evidence strongly suggests that the Foley-Kajsiewicz pact of 1871 gradually gave rise to a cozy alliance between the Irish hierarchy and the Congregation of the Resurrection in Chicago. This arrangement enabled Vincent Barzynski to build a power base at *Stanisławowo* which was subsequently used as a model for a splendid community-parish network that assisted in the assimilation of tens of thousands of Polish Catholic immigrants in the Chicago area. At the same time, the pact also allowed for the rise of a Barzynski-dominated pastoral appointee system that often bordered on the dictatorial. When this system created financial ruin for numerous lay parishioners, those exploited quite understandably tried to recoup their losses inside the system, turning to sympathetic assistant pastors for further advice, understanding, and reforms. When these assistant pastors, like Kozlowski, were unable to gain redress for lay parishioners inside the community-parish system, the struggle was then moved to higher levels of authority—to the Archbishop of Chicago and to the Apostolic Delegate. Only after lengthy and repeated attempts *within* the hierarchical chain of command had failed did the Independents bolt from St. Hedwig's. And even after declaring their "independence," these so-called "schismatics," at least in the initial stages, made it clear that they had no intentions of leaving the Church.

Finally, the Barzynski legacy to Polish Catholicism in America is still highly visible in two major regards: it demonstrates its viability through a community-parish system which, quite remarkably, has persisted into our times and which continues to serve the spiritual, moral, cultural, and social needs of thousands of Polish Americans; it also demonstrates its influence in the persistence of a highly controversial schism, one responsible for the formation of a separate national church, offering living testimony to the fact that American Polonia would continue spiritually, morally, culturally, and socially divided well into the twentieth century.

6

A Bishop for Polonia

Annuncio vobis gaudium magnum. Habemus papam, eminentissi-
mum ac reverendissimum Dominum Carolum, sanctae Romanae ec-
clesiae cardinalem Wojtyla, qui sibi nomen imposuit Joannem Pau-
lum Secundum.

> Cardinal Felici on the central balcony of St.
> Peter's in Rome, 6:44 P.M., 16 October 1978.

The man to whom they naturally look as their authoritative leader is
the priest. He has practically absolute power over them. The only
thing that will deprive him of that power is the flagrant and evident
abuse of it. That there has been such abuse, through imprudence and
indiscretion on the one hand, and through unscrupulous and unworthy conduct on the part of some of our Polish brother priests, will not
be denied. . . .

> The Editor of the *American Ecclesiastical Review*,
> October 1903.

Cardinal Felici's announcement of 16 October 1978 electrified the entire
Christian world: Karol Wojtyla, Archbishop of Cracow, was now Pope John Paul
II. The first non-Italian pope in four-and-one-half centuries was Polish. The man
"they called from a far distant country" was now Bishop of Rome. Only seventy-
five years earlier—the life span of the average Polish-American—another eminent
clergyman, the Reverend H. J. Heuser, editor of the American hierarchy's most
prestigious journal, was gathering evidence intended to demonstrate precisely
why Polish candidates were unsuitable to become bishops in *any* diocese.[1]

Polish-American Catholics today have witnessed the elevation of priests "of
their own kind" to every level of the hierarchy from the papacy to the College of
Cardinals to any number of diocesan sees, including Chicago. Thus it may come
as a surprise to Polish Catholics to learn that, at the turn of the century, most of
the Americanist hierarchy were putting Polish and other Slavic immigrant priests
at the very bottom of their lists of candidates for bishops of American dioceses.

In fact, so alarming were reports of scandal in Polish parishes in the United States—fiscal mismanagement; alleged misconduct in the personal lives of the clergy; riot-torn parishes in Omaha, Buffalo, Cleveland, Scranton, and Chicago—that even Miecislaus Cardinal Ledochowski, the highest-ranking Polish prelate in the Vatican, began issuing a series of reports that questioned the overall spiritual quality of Polonia's priests. In his position as Prefect of the Propaganda Office, it was one of Ledochowski's primary responsibilities to scrutinize "the qualities requisite for election to the episcopate."[2] Judging from Ledochowski's personal reservations on the matter, the Polish drive for ecclesiastical parity or equality, known as *równouprawnienie*, looked dark indeed.[3] If a Barzynski in Chicago or a Pitass in Buffalo had been unacceptable to a Polish Cardinal in the Vatican, then certainly the chances of gaining acceptance in the American hierarchy were practically nil.

Ever since the Emigration of 1863, many Polish priests had attacked what they felt was an "Irish Catholic Church" in America. Yet, in many dioceses throughout the United States, Irish bishops had actually deferred to the judgment of leading Polish pastors. Such was indeed the case in Chicago where the Resurrectionists, by virtue of the Foley-Kajsiewicz pact, were guaranteed special powers and privileges in the archdiocese. Aware of the fact that the Polish Catholic population in the late 1890s was already larger than many entire dioceses in Illinois, the Irish chancery therefore treated the Reverend Vincent Barzynski as a *de facto* bishop of Polonia. Fully cognizant of such preferential treatment, Barzynski, in order to maintain his power-broker position within Polonia, wielded his authority in such a way as to prevent the emergence of any rivals. No strong, upwardly mobile pastors were tolerated for long. Barzynski's policy of *realpolitik* in church affairs can be traced back to 1875, when he was completing his first full year at St. Stanislaus Kostka. From the beginning of his tenure as pastor, Barzynski had remained open to compromise and negotiation with the downtown Irish hierarchy. Whenever sensitive negotiations were called for, both Bishop Foley and Archbishop Feehan, out of sheer necessity, permitted Barzynski to assume the role of chief mediator between the chancery and Polonia. And for the remainder of his priestly life, outside of a single attempt in 1890 to move up himself, Barzynski faithfully pursued this policy of accommodation. While he lived, the policy of accommodation was strictly enforced, despite several serious and well-orchestrated challenges to this arrangement by clergy outside the Congregation of the Resurrection or outside the Chicago archdiocese. But with Barzynski's death in 1899, this policy of accommodation gradually gave way to a national call for equality.[4]

The first step taken by Barzynski toward instituting the policy of accommodation came during the Third Annual Convention of the Polish Roman Catholic Union in 1875. It was here that Barzynski organized the Association of Polish

Catholic Priests in the United States of America, the forerunner of numerous "unionizing" efforts by Polonia's clergy. The Constitution of the Association, largely drafted by the Stanislawian pastor himself, clearly spelled out the spirit and policy of accommodation. A major objective of the Association of Polish Catholic Priests was to be "the more perfect preservation of the unity and harmony among Polish Catholic priests serving as missionaries in the United States of America." In order to arrive at this ideal of harmony, Polish priests were called upon to deliver "a more prompt and efficacious assistance and support . . . [for] our most reverend bishops, who heretofore were accustomed to experience no small troubles and anxieties with reference to the Polish mission." Furthermore, the Association's membership was warned about the dangers of "secret societies" which might lead to "the corruption of morals" and even to "unbelief." By this it was meant that priests were to avoid ultranationalistic Polish organizations such as the *Gmina Polska*. Barzynski also condemned any "pernicious rivalry among priests," already anticipating the corrosive effects which could be brought on by a rival organization of priests.[5]

The statutes of the Association's constitution reemphasized the principle of hierarchical authority as well as the policy of accommodation: "sincere obedience to the proper ecclesiastical authority" was demanded of all members, as was the call for "reverence and love for the most reverend bishops, as befits upright priests"; the formation "of the strongest union with the infallible Head of the Catholic Church, the Center of Unity" was pretty much taken for granted. Then, in a move designed to cement the coming Irish-Polish clerical alliance, the Association opened its membership only to those Polish Catholic priests who had actually been accepted into the diocese by Bishop Foley. Members were also pledged to adhere strictly to the Baltimore Ceremonial (1866) in regard to the performance of ecclesiastical obligations, and innovations in the liturgy were promptly discouraged unless permission had otherwise been granted by the local ordinary. Finally, members of the Association of Polish Catholic Priests were not even permitted to attend annual meetings of the organization unless given that permission by the bishop. This move more or less bonded the loyalists to the hierarchy and at the same time shut out the malcontents.[6]

In exchange for their loyalty and fealty to the Irish bishops, the Association's membership was free to establish a wide range of institutions on the parish level set exclusively on a Polish Catholic base. These could include parish sodalities and fraternal organizations, if they were "in accord with the injunctions of the Council of Baltimore"; "Polish-English parochial schools"; printshops set up to publish "at least a few Polish Catholic periodicals"; and parish libraries. But if members were found guilty of any transgressions outlined by the Constitution or by-laws, they would stand to lose their voting privileges and even invite possible expulsion altogether, if two-thirds of the Association's membership indeed voted to expel. Overall, the Constitution of the Association of Polish Catholic Priests proved to be something of a showcase for Barzynski's organizational genius. Here he managed to balance the already existing tensions between a strongly nationalistic clergy and those who saw fit to pledge their loyalty to the Irish hierarchy. He well knew that without widespread consensus on this issue, there could be no ecclesiastical discipline, for in matters of the Church, all ecclesiastical discipline was tied to the vow of obedience. In any event, the fact that the Association was dominated by Barzynski gave the Resurrectionists the opportunity to strengthen their position of influence in the "Irish Catholic Church" in America.[7]

The Association of Polish Catholic Priests, largely due to its close ties with the Polish Roman Catholic Union, met no serious challenge over its first decade of life. However, as the Polish National Alliance gained greater influence in Catholic Polonia during the 1880s, some of the more nationalistic clergy, already upset by the subordination of Polonia to the Irish-American hierarchy, began the search for a more militant base. On 24 October 1886, shortly after the Sixth National Convention of the Polish National Alliance, which numerous priests had attended, a certain Reverend Dominic Majer, a St. Paul clergyman, issued the call for a rival organization. Eleven priests in American Polonia responded affirmatively to Majer's suggestion that a new union of Polish priests throw its support behind the PNA. This small group was of the opinion that neither the PRCU nor the Association of Polish Catholic Priests was adequately supporting programs which tied the spirit of Catholicism to Polish nationalism. Using the language of the ultranationalist PNA, this handful of priests, none of whom was from the Chicago archdiocese, organized the Allied Priests.[8]

Sensing that the Allied Priests might be able to destroy the fabric of the Resurrectionist-Irish bishop alliance, Barzynski reacted by attempting to enroll the entire membership of the Association into the PRCU, which, in effect, would make the Association a puppet of the powerful supraterritorial fraternal. When some of the Association's own membership objected to Barzynski's ploy on the grounds that the Association would lose its autonomy if swallowed up by the PRCU, Barzynski dismissed the plea of the dissidents and formally approved a motion linking the Association to the PRCU, which was by now involved in a life-and-death struggle for membership with the PNA. As a result of Barzynski's action, some of the malcontents quit the Association for membership in Majer's Allied Priests.[9]

Faced with a crisis in his loyalist camp, Barzynski now decided to test the strength of his own personal support within the American hierarchy. At a meeting held at St. Stanislaus Kostka Hall on 2 March 1887, the iron-willed Stanislawian pastor made every attempt to stave off the invasion begun by the Allied Priests. Barzynski assisted his stalwarts in drafting the first "memorial" to the American hierarchy on record; entitled "The Memorial of the Polish Catholic Clergy in the United States of America," the document addressed "all bishops in the United

States." The document, of course, solely expressed the views of Barzynski's "Unionists," a term used to describe all Polish Catholic priests maintaining joint membership in the PRCU and Barzynski's Association. The Memorial went on to brand the PNA, the parent organization of Majer's Alliancists, "an irreligious organization" which had conspired to dupe clergymen into preaching "the falsehoods" of the nationalist party in Polonia.[10] In a counterattack to the Unionist Memorial, the Allied Priests then drafted another document, subsequently delivered to Cardinal Ledochowski, which denied all charges of "irreligiosity" set forth in the Memorial. The Alliancist letter pleaded with Ledochowski "to use his influence in putting a stop to these malicious lies spread in the matters of religion and the faith and utilize the power of the crozier to bring back peace, union and love amongst the Polish nationality in America."[11] But the letter to Ledochowski only served to heighten the tempo of the journalistic war then being conducted by both sides: *Kropidło*, owned and operated by the Resurrectionists, used every opportunity to respond editorially to attacks on Unionists made in *Zgoda*, the Alliancist weekly, which was also published in Chicago; and each time *Kropidło* unleashed another editorial barrage, it was in turn met by another salvo in *Zgoda*. Not until Casimir Sztuczko of Holy Trinity parish brought parishioners into the PNA in 1896 did the feud even begin to subside.[12]

The struggle between the Unionist and Alliancist clergymen in Polonia was certainly a most significant phase in the wider clerical-national war already discussed. Yet, how does all of this relate to the issue before us—the quest for equality in the selection of Polish candidates for bishops in the United States? The entire Unionist-Alliancist episode appeared to have convinced prominent and influential Americanizers in the hierarchy, Archbishop Ireland in particular, that the ever-feuding Polish clergy were simply incapable of assuming leadership roles in the American Church.[13] Thus when James Cardinal Gibbons received a formal request in 1890 to install a Polish candidate in a particular diocesan see, the request was denied.[14] Numerous sporadic requests for an all Polish diocese in the United States were received by the hierarchy throughout the 1890s; each petition was denied. The hierarchy had only to point to the Unionist-Alliancist rift and to the ongoing Independent outbreaks to show that Polonia's clergy were simply unable to maintain order in their own ethnic houses. Furthermore, the hierarchy—Gibbons, Ireland, and Keane—felt that the creation of a national diocese would undercut the territorial sovereignty of bishops in those locales where dense Polish populations were in strong evidence. But it was the growing popularity of the idea of a national diocese for Polonia which again prompted a rebuttal from a rather unexpected source—Cardinal Ledochowski, now the Prefect of the Sacred Congregation of the Propaganda of Faith. Ledochowski's powers were considerable. Since the United States was still a "missionary church" in the 1890s (a status it was to maintain until 1908), all jurisdictional powers in the American Church resided in Ledochowski's Propaganda Office. In other words, had Cardinal Ledochowski seen fit to acknowledge the organization of an all-Polish diocese or to appoint a Polish candidate to head a given diocese, such would certainly have transpired. And the Polish clergy knew this. Hoping to capitalize on Ledochowski's recent appointment and spurred on by the boldness of the Cahensly movement on behalf of German-American Catholics (which resulted in the consecration of German bishops in Cleveland and Milwaukee), the Polish priests pressed their case. The Association of Polish Clergy expected, at the very least, parity in Chicago, Buffalo, and Scranton.[15]

The response to Polonia's drive for equality was published first in *The Ecclesiastical Review* in July 1892. In an article entitled "The Cardinal Prefect on the Election of American Bishops," Ledochowski took the position that the American Church could never "substitute for the approved methods of ecclesiastical rule those which approach more closely to popular suffrage." On the other hand, while showing his disdain for any democratic procedures for the selection of bishops, the Cardinal-Prefect admitted that "abuses have obtained here and there in the election of Bishops which destroy the right order of things and create strife and scandal." Accordingly, Ledochowski reminded the clergy that they must employ "a well understood and safe norm" for electing bishops, one that was based on the method proscribed by the Propaganda Office in 1834 and which had since been revised three times during the 1850s. This "safe norm" outlined the following points: first, every three years each bishop was to submit to the Holy See the names of those priests in his diocese deemed "worthy of the Episcopal dignity"; next, when a vacancy materialized in a given diocese, a synod of bishops was to be called which was then to screen the names "of those most worthy," whose names would then be submitted to the archbishop or senior bishop in an ecclesiastical Province; third; the qualities of the candidates on that list were to be discussed "publicly" at a convention of bishops and the minutes of those deliberations were to be sent to the Office of Propaganda. Ledochowski then called attention to other provisions which had been passed on favorably by the Plenary Council of Baltimore in 1866, provisions which were supposed to give "the lower clergy" a voice in the selection of their bishops. Under the Baltimore guidelines, "regular Consultors and irremovable Rectors of the Diocese" were permitted to assemble for the purpose of submitting three names to the Metropolitan See; furthermore, each member of this rather select group was to be given one vote to be cast in secret ballot in order to determine the list of three candidates to then be submitted to a synod of bishops; finally, if the synod for any reason did not include at least one of the three names submitted by the Consultors and Rectors in its final list to the Office of Propaganda, the reasons for the omission of certain names were also to be submitted to the Propaganda Office in writing. In concluding his explanation of procedures, Ledochowski added a section of fourteen "Qualities Requisite for Election to the Episcopate":

I. Name, surname, age, native country of candidate.
II. To what diocese and Ecclesiastical Province did he belong?
III. Where did he make his studies—and with what success?
IV. Has he any academical degrees? What are they?
V. Has he been professor at any time? and in what branch?
VI. Has he done any missionary service, and has he gained any experience in the same?
VII. How many languages does he understand? What are they?
VIII. What offices has he held, and with what success?
IX. What degree of prudence has he shown in counsel and in action?
X. Does he enjoy health of body? Is he frugal, patient, practical?
XI. Is he firm of purpose, or of a changeable disposition?
XII. Does he enjoy a good reputation, or has there ever been a stain on his moral conduct?
XIII. Is he attentive in the performance of his priestly functions, edifying in his outward demeanor, carefully observing the rubrics?
XIV. Does his dress, his manner, his speech and his entire conduct betoken gravity and religious respect?[16]

In a uniquely quaint, medieval fashion, the questions posed by Cardinal Ledochowski gave every indication of being a search for the man of perfection, in mind, body, and spirit. The prefatory explanation of the Propaganda regulations, at least on the surface, was impressive enough, and when added to the Baltimore reforms gave the appearance of comprehensiveness and thoroughness. For the proponents of Polonia's equality thesis, however, the Polish Cardinal's response was nothing more than a stout defense of the status quo. Most immigrant pastors in America suspected all along that the superficial democratic process involving the diocesan consultors and rectors could easily be subverted at the synod of bishops. In most of the metropolitan sees, the synods were headed by the Irish—in Chicago by Archbishop Feehan, in Buffalo by Bishop Quigley, in New York by the McCloskey-Corrigan-Farley faction that dominated the archdiocese there from 1864 to 1919 (only to be succeeded by more "progressive" Irish archbishops). Only in Milwaukee, as a result of recent and hard-fought-for changes, was the diocese headed by a German-American, Frederick Katzer, who happened to be sympathetic with the Polish equality drive. Then, too, most rectors of parishes were removable and replaceable, especially where powerful clergy like Barzynski

did the bidding for their Irish superiors. Hence, the chances for gaining irremovable rector status and/or diocesan consultor status were slim indeed, especially
for those choosing not to support the Polish immigrant-Irish alliances like those
existing in Chicago. Even in Chicago, with all of Barzynski's muscle and Father
Gordon's influence, only two Polish pastors gained irremovable rector status and
diocesan consultorships as late as 1915. In effect, each diocesan synod appeared
to be managed by those clergymen whose fealty to the Irish was above reproach
and without question.[17]

Cardinal-Prefect Ledochowski was probably well aware of the political ramifications of his positions and of the effects the intricate mechanism devised for the
selection of bishops would have on the Polish clergy in America. The obvious
question, which calls for treatment here, is why the Polish Cardinal never offered
even one note of encouragement to his compatriots on this side of the Atlantic.
Why did Ledochowski insist on a menial state for Polish priests in America? In
answer to these, it must be kept in mind that Ledochowski had on occasion been
an outspoken opponent of Polish nationalism. After all, it was Ledochowski who
had participated in the Germanization of the Polish Church after the Insurrection
of 1863, a process which eased the way for *Kulturkampf* in Poland during the
Bismarck era. And it was Ledochowski who was bitterly opposed to using the
Polish language in the liturgy (he was said to have forgotten all but the basic
rudiments of the Polish language), preferring German. One prominent authority
on the period states that on one occasion Ledochowski, in justification of Germanization, compared the Poles to Burgundians who had not lost a thing by becoming Frenchmen.[18] Another authority describes him as *civis Romanus*, the true
churchman who placed the standards of Rome high above those of national interests.[19] There is much truth in both these assessments, for it is highly unlikely that
he would have been appointed Prefect of the Propaganda Office had he been more
Polish than Roman; and his policies appear, all along, to have favored the Irish-
American hierarchy, who, by every significant indicator, were always more Roman than Irish. In the 1890s then, as Wakin and Scheuer have reminded us, the
grass-roots nationalism prevailing at the parish level in immigrant America was
being de-emphasized in favor of the policies of "catholicity" or "Romanization"
espoused at the chancery level of the American Church.[20] In 1892, Cardinal Ledochowski was only doing his best to assure his "Roman" brethren on the other
side of the Atlantic that the flames of Polish nationalism should always be doused
by waters coming from the Irish Sea.

In his fascinating study of Irish and German immigrant Catholics in New York
City, Professor Jay Dolan quotes a nineteenth-century priest who found it necessary to complain of autocratic rule in his particular diocese. The anonymous priest
lamented the fact that "the will of the bishop is the only law."[21] Concluding that
this situation was indeed widespread in the New York archdiocese, Dolan goes on

to build a strong case for his thesis that "the emergence of boss rule in the church was a phenomenon fostered by the urbanization of Catholicism."[22] The flood tide of immigration and its subsequent impact on the explosive population growth in numerous archdiocesan and diocesan sees indeed paralleled the powerful centripetal forces which ended in the eventual centralization of chancery offices everywhere in immigrant Catholic America. In New York, according to Dolan, the sceptre of hierarchical authority passed from one Irish chieftain to another. In Chicago, the situation was no different. Here Irish bossism in the church passed from Duggan to Foley to Feehan to Quigley. But in Chicago, as we have maintained throughout, Irish "bossism" in the church was supported by the Congregation of the Resurrection, at least until World War I. As we have seen in previous chapters, the Resurrectionists, backed by Irish power in Chicago, adopted this same style of authoritarian rule in their administration of the community-parish network. But this authoritarian style, largely promulgated by Barzynski in his lifetime, was also a powerful stimulant to the forces of Independentism, forces which were fully up to the task of doing battle with the Resurrectionists within Polonia and the Irish hierarchy outside Polonia. When this Independent movement blossomed in other Polish areas, leading to the formation of the Polish National Catholic Church and the subsequent consecration of Francis Hodur as a "schismatic" bishop, everyone down the hierarchical line from Leo XIII to Ledochowski to Feehan must have known that the "Polish Question" in America was more volatile than Cahenslyism in German-American quarters, or similar movements for ethnic parity in some of the other Slavic parishes, for instance, the Ruthenian ones.

To most members of the American hierarchy, these elements of Polish radical populism in the American church were somehow different from those of comparable nationality groups. For who else would be willing to wield the club of schism over so long a period as the Polish Independents? None of the traditional autocratic tactics for dealing with dissidents seemed to work, not the excommunication of Kozlowski and his followers at *Jadwigowo*; not the official Vatican condemnation of Hodur's group in Scranton; not the repeated warnings and threats issued by chancery offices in such Polish cities as Chicago, Buffalo, Cleveland, Detroit, and Milwaukee; and not a continuous stream of antinationalist denunciations emanating from the Resurrectionist publications network. None of these autocratic ways seemed to make any difference. What was even more puzzling to the standard-bearers of "legitimate" hierarchical authority was how to approach a schismatic movement which was bent on lay control of all phases and aspects of parish life. As Professor Victor Greene has demonstrated, there was a direct correlation between the rise of the Polish National Catholic Church and the sharpened demands for equality, and this correlation clearly demonstrates that Cardinal Ledochowski's procedures and tactics were outdated.[23] Then, too, the death of Vincent Barzynski in 1899 created a leadership vacuum in Chicago and American

Polonia. With no successors of Barzynski's stature in the Congregation's Chicago mission, the vitality of the archdiocesan-Resurrectionist pact was threatened, even though Reverend Jan Kasprzycki and Reverend Francis Gordon would do their best to maintain Resurrectionist interests. Consequently, Polonia's clergy came to look outside the Congregation of the Resurrection for leadership. Two clergymen in particular now assumed Barzynski's mantle and, in the process, stepped into national prominence in Polonia: one was a persistent critic of the Resurrectionists, the Reverend Wenceslaus Kruszka, a maverick in Polish clerical circles because of his frequent, and often outrageous, positions on a wide variety of topics relating to Catholic Polonia; the other was the indomitable pastor of Holy Trinity parish in Chicago, who lived three short blocks from Barzynski's old rectory, the Reverend Casimir Sztuczko. Each in his own unique style had a powerful influence on the course of Polish-American history; each assisted in breaking down anti-Polish resistance in the American hierarchy and in the Vatican; and each did his share in breaching the wall of boss rule which had been built by the Irish hierarchy. But where Sztuczko consolidated and utilized existing institutional forces in Polonia, especially those organizations devoted to balancing the positions and sentiments then held by both the PRCU and the PNA, Kruszka attempted to harness anti-Irish feelings then prevalent in Polonia, and do battle with the Irish hierarchy in the field of journalism, in education, and generally in the world of ideas.

Wenceslaus Kruszka has aptly been described as the nestor of Polish historians in America. Author of numerous works in history, theology, and philosophy, among which is the celebrated *Historya Polska w Ameryce*, Kruszka was also in many ways a nestor of Polonia's history. Trained in theology and philosophy at the Gregorianum in Rome and at the Jagiellonian University in Cracow, Kruszka was certainly the most prolific spokesman in American Polonia in the early twentieth century. Emigrating to the United States in 1893, he headed for Wisconsin, where, two years later, he received Holy Orders at St. Francis Seminary. After his ordination, he was appointed assistant pastor of St. Adalbert's parish, in Milwaukee's rapidly growing south side Polonia. He served here for one year and then moved to Ripon, Wisconsin, where he became pastor of St. Wenceslaus parish. He remained in Ripon until 1909, at which time he moved back to St. Adalbert's to accept the pastorship there. He remained at St. Adalbert's until his death in 1937. By all accounts, Father Kruszka was the catalyst in the drive for ecclesiastical equality in Polonia. Almost single-handedly, he unleashed a tremendous propaganda campaign aimed at forcing the Irish hierarchy to consecrate Polish auxiliary bishops in select Polish dioceses in America. He was certainly a catalyst in a movement which not only tore at the roots of American Catholicism but also at the core of Polonian Catholicism as well.[24]

The first shot in Kruszka's battle with the Irish hierarchy was fired in the little known but prestigious *The Freeman's Journal*, then published in the state of New

York. In July 1901, *The Freeman's Journal* agreed to publish Kruszka's highly controversial article, "Polyglot Bishops for Polyglot Dioceses." In this tract, Kruszka first advanced the thesis that since the American Catholic Church was in effect "a church in miniature of the Universal Church," it was imperative that bishops be selected to represent all of America's numerous nationality groups. Furthermore, since the American Catholic Church was a "multi-lingual" church and since communication of "the Word" had, historically speaking, been the most significant element in missionary work, it was necessary to select only those candidates for bishop who would be able to communicate with the nationality groups in a given diocese in their native tongues. Hence, for Kruszka, the most important qualification for bishop, aside from all the other priestly virtues, was that each candidate be a linguist. In the conclusion to his article, which would forever label the Ripon clergyman a feisty and unpredictable maverick, he boldly asserted that "Henceforward in the United States whoever (whatever candidate) knowingly accepts on his shoulders the burden of becoming bishop of a polyglot diocese, himself not being multilingual, in so doing commits a mortal sin."[25] Kruszka's message was crystal clear: Irish candidates accepting the bishopric in such heavily Polish dioceses as Chicago, Buffalo, Scranton, Milwaukee, or Cleveland, were doing so at the risk of eternal damnation if they were unable to speak Polish!

When Kruszka first submitted this radical ethnocentric piece for consideration by the *American Ecclesiastical Review*, he was flatly rejected. The editor, Heuser, no doubt suspicious of Kruszka's desire to expand the crusade for equality, replied to the Ripon pastor: "The one phrase . . . alone would be sufficient to defeat your proposition, for it ignores the fact that some bishops so constituted by the Holy See have no choice of refusing or accepting the charge, and the same charge may easily be misinterpreted in other respects. Hence, I feel it would not help the cause you justly defend, to publish your paper in its present form."[26] Heuser's refusal to publish was supported, of course, in various ecclesiastical quarters. Bishop James Trobec of St. Cloud, Minnesota, who knew several Slavic dialects and even a smattering of Polish, scolded Father Kruszka: "Then woe to the Holy Father who has charge of the whole world, and woe to all the bishops in missionary countries, especially America, for there no one understands the language of all his subjects."[27]

The Catholic Universe, official journal of the Cleveland diocese, then headed by Bishop Ignatius Horstmann (who, oddly enough, owed his position in many ways to the clamor over Cahenslyism), expressed the following editorial viewpoint:

> The claim for episcopal appointments on the plea that a bishop must be able to address all his people and that the Polish clergy are exceptionally qualified as linguists, if it proves anything it proves too much. It would prove that instead of a Polish bishop we ought to

have all Polish bishops. The Germans could make a similar case for
German bishops; the Bohemians for Bohemian bishops; the Italians
for Italian bishops; the Irish for Irish bishops.[28]

The reactions to Kruszka's extremism were hardly surprising given the enormous population explosion of several major immigrant groups in each of the metropolitan areas of the Northeast and Midwest. Perhaps, too, the hierarchy had
been startled by Kruszka's about-face on the matter of ethnic bishops. After all,
only two years before, in another article in the *American Ecclesiastical Review*,
Kruszka stated without reservation that "nationality need not enter at all into the
question of the appointment of bishops."[29] The question that calls for further
consideration here concerns developments in Polonia which may have encouraged
Kruszka to offer his "polyglot bishop or mortal sin" thesis. Was he playing the
role of an ecclesiastical con man, or were his deeply ethnocentric views really
shared by respectable clergy in Polonia? And was the laity at all concerned over
an issue which cynics might have viewed as involving only ecclesiastical mobility
and having little to do with the spiritual lives of the laity? The organization and
development of the Polish Catholic Congresses at the turn of the century provided
a forum from which Polonia could debate these and other related issues. Although
there has been no definitive study of the Polish Catholic Congresses, several
scholars have given the subject enough attention so that we can trace the paths
along which the Congresses moved.[30]
   The First Polish Catholic Congress convened in Buffalo on 22–25 September
1896, mainly to slow the inexorable advances made by Independentists. Dominated by Vincent Barzynski and Jan Pitass of Buffalo, the First Congress took a
decidedly "loyalist" stance when it supported a Barzynski-backed resolution
which thanked "the American bishops for their protection of the Polish clergy," a
resolution that was passed by acclamation. Barzynski and Pitass both paraded
staunch anti-PNA positions before the Congress delegates throughout; in fact, the
delegates were only seated in the first place after having been approved by a
clerical party subcommittee on membership. Throughout, the First Congress was
to be a showpiece for the PRCU; the only Alliance delegates seated were those
clergymen who held joint membership in the PRCU and the PNA (a move by
Barzynski and Pitass which infuriated Casimir Sztuczko). Hence, when the Independent revolts led by Hodur and Kozlowski were publicly villified as PNA-
sponsored and PNA-supported (which was not true), resolutions to this effect met
with loud demonstrations of approval. At the same time, study groups dominated
by clergymen introduced the issue of *równouprawnienie* in regard to the selection
of bishops, all the while recognizing that such unnegotiable demands for ecclesiastical parity were directly linked to Independent demands for a separate Polish
diocese in America. The First Polish Catholic Congress, by introducing the issue
of parity on the convention floor, thus was forced to face a dilemma of its own

making: the supporters of Barzynski and Pitass were calling for loyalty to the present hierarchy, while at the same time they were adopting a strong nationalist position on the bishop question. It appeared as if the First Congress wanted both to condemn the Alliance-Independent ties and to move toward greater independence from the Irish-American hierarchy. The Congress, in effect, was absorbing the nationalist fervor of the Alliance. Even more contradictory was the position taken by the clericals, who called for popular support on the bishop question while at the same time sneering at the "lay control" principle advocated by the Independents. As Professors Greene and Buczek have demonstrated, the First Polish Catholic Congress only served to deepen the divisions between Unionists and Alliancists, and, of even more tragic consequence, the division between the clergy and the laity. Conscious of these divisions, but adamantly refusing to relinquish clerical control, Barzynski finessed the passage of a resolution which called for the appointment of a Polish-American adviser to the Apostolic Delegate to the United States. The resolution may have surprised the Americanists, many of whom were totally opposed to the idea of having an Apostolic Delegate in the first place; but nothing of substance resulted from the Barzynski resolution, and the issue of *równouprawnienie* was temporarily dropped.[31]

By the time the Second Polish Catholic Congress met in September 1901, Barzynski was dead. And so was President William McKinley, who had been assassinated in Buffalo, two weeks before the Congress convened, by the Polish anarchist, Leon Czolgosz. The rampant public demonstrations of the First Congress were nowhere in evidence during the somber aftermath of the assassination. With McKinley's death, it simply was not wise to unleash the forces of Polish nationalism, and with Barzynski gone, the vehement anti-PNA planks were likewise buried. Proof that Barzynski's Unionist party strength had waned came in the selection of Casimir Sztuczko, the energetic Alliancist, to the position of National Secretary of the Executive Committee of the Second Congress. The main order of business was to agree on means to stave off further Independent revolts. Accordingly, the issue of ecclesiastical parity was reintroduced, and the Second Congress passed a resolution authorizing Jan Pitass and Wenceslaus Kruszka to take Polonia's case to the door of the Vatican; in conjunction with the Vatican mission, the Executive Committee decided to confront the American hierarchy once again.

In a landmark memorial dated 10 November 1901, addressed "To Their Graces, the Most Reverend Archbishops of the Roman Catholic Church in the United States," the Sztuczko Committee summarized what it felt were not only the general concerns of the Second Polish Catholic Congress but also those of Kruszka and hundreds of other Polish priests in America. Comparing Polonia to all other immigrant groups in the American Church, the Memorial stated unequivocally that "we Poles are the most distressed and unhappy [because] . . . many of our brethren, lead [*sic*] by some unworthy and fallen priests, have started in our midst a schism running in open revolt against the Roman Catholic Church." The Sztuczko Committee recognized that "this so-called Independent Movement . . . causes many scandalous broils and lawsuits; it degrades our community and inflicts irreparable religious, moral, social and economic ruin." In addition, the Independent Movement was said to be gaining momentum because its followers believed that "the Roman Catholic Archbishops and Bishops of America have no use whatever for the poor ignorant Poles; that they are bent on wiping out the Polish Nationality in this country; that they show neither charity nor justice in their dealings with Poles; that they have not the spirit of Our Lord Jesus Christ and that therefore no one is obliged to obey them." The Sztuczko Committee then pointed out that the Independents "denounce our good and loyal priests as contemptible traitors of the Polish Nationality, ignoble slaves of the foreign-born hierarchy, contemptible hypocrites who for a lucrative parish are ready at any moment to sell the Polish people as Judas betrayed his master. . . ." Claiming that 50,000 souls had already been "apostasized" in favor of the Polish National Church, the Committee concluded that "the schismatics have the popular side of the affair [because] they have so-called Polish bishops." Furthermore, these Independents "accuse the Polish Roman Catholic clergy of treason to their nation when holding allegiance to Irish and German bishops." In order "to wage successful war" against the Independents and "disarm them of their arguments" the Polish Catholic Congress was making the following recommendation:

> We are far from suggesting a national bishop for all the Poles of this country, or exclusively for them anywhere, but there are sees in which the Polish language could effectively be employed by their incumbents.
>
> Furthermore, the appointment of men, speaking Polish, to various auxiliaries would be very salutary. The advantages from such appointments would be numerous and grand.
>
> We are convinced that Auxiliary Bishops located throughout the country wherever there are large colonies of Poles would work wonders toward forestalling the movement of "Away from Rome." They would keep the Church acquainted with the needs and condition of their people. They elevate the tone of both the clergy and the laity, by establishing unanimity and uniformity where hitherto differences and discords prevail; in short, they would be the connecting link between the Poles and our Holy Mother the Church.[32]

The Polish Catholic Congress Executive Committee ended its lengthy memorial on a note of hope—"Polonia semper fidelis." Addressing the statement to the Apostolic Delegate, Sebastian Martinelli, and to his Eminence, James Cardinal Gibbons, and to all the archbishops and bishops in the United States, the Polish Catholic Congress was indeed hoping that the hierarchy, at its annual meeting to be held in another eleven days in Washington, D.C., would finally resolve the issue of *równouprawnienie* and come to understand that the issue of equality was directly related to *kościół narodowy*, that is, a separate national church for Poles.

However well thought out and planned this strategem may have been, it must have come as a great shock to the memorial's drafters when Sztuczko received a curt reply (dated 16 December 1901) from Archbishop John Keane of Dubuque, who was speaking for the Americanists: "The Archbishops have no authority in the selection of Assistant Bishops—a matter which belongs exclusively to such Diocese or Province as it may concern—it is not in our power to take any action in regard to it."[33]

Adhering to a strictly legalistic approach, Keane's response was a safe position for the Americanists. Although it could appeal directly to the consciences of diocesan consultors in dioceses where the Poles constituted a majority of the Catholic population, the annual meeting in itself could not, of course, circumvent regular diocesan procedures regarding selection of candidates. In fact, at the time Keane wrote Sztuczko, the Ledochowski guidelines were still largely intact. Yet Keane's reply to the Polish Catholic Congress did not mention the possibility that when acting as individuals within their own dioceses bishops might exert pressures on the consultors to include Polish candidates. Also, as Keane himself knew only too well, the final lists of candidates submitted by the consultors were always screened by the bishops themselves. Since the bishop's list was the one considered by the Vatican to be "official," and since each chancery office was the final point of departure for the Vatican, selections made by the bishops could conceivably be placed at the top of such an official list, and hence be given serious consideration by the Vatican—without the consultors even knowing whether *their* list had been altered in any way. The only canonical regulation governing circumstances of disagreement was that the bishop had to state in writing to the Vatican his reasons for disagreement with the consultors. Thus, the Vatican may have been fully informed about changes in the list of candidates, but the consultors themselves were not always aware of such changes, especially when the ordinary chose not to pass on such information to the consultors. Of course, any discrepancies were made public when the Vatican selected a particular candidate for consecration, but by then it was too late for the consultors to do anything about the selection, except of course to complain—which the Poles often did in their dioceses.[34]

Keane's indifference to the Polish Catholic Congress memorial provided Polonia's clergy, and Kruszka in particular, with a ready-made excuse for embarking on a policy of intrigue in the quest for *równouprawnienie*. Weaving together the many strands of this story in the post-Congress period is exceedingly difficult because so many conflicting pieces of evidence have in one form or another been handed down by Kruszka himself in his tangential autobiography. The first thread in the ravelled yarn of *równouprawnienie* which calls for separate treatment is the role of the laity. It is significant that the Congress memorial indicated that the desire to consecrate Polish-American priests as bishops was one universally accepted in Polonia, which was the Congress's way of saying that individual ambitions for upward mobility were of lesser significance. It was a position which the Polish press, even the nationalist press, supported. *Zgoda*, the PNA weekly, in an editorial published shortly before the Second Congress, argued that "the Polish people are on the verge of taking drastic steps if the bishops do not agree to have Polish priests hold higher offices such as vicar, bishop, or higher."[35] *Zgoda* was also greatly distressed over the fact that Archbishops Ireland and Keane were even attempting to implement a policy of anglicanization not only in the language of the liturgy but also in the use of English as a common language in the Catholic school system—programs which *Zgoda* was certain would stir the wrath of the Polish laity and serve to reinforce the rampant radical populist movements in Polonia.[36] Ironically, it was the Alliancist *Zgoda* which was continuing to beat the drums for the ecclesiastical party, while the clerical newspapers, especially *Wiarus* and *Dziennik Chicagoski*, remained silent on the equality and anglicanization issues. In this unusual set of circumstances (for Polonia), where outright propaganda for the Polish cause was thought to be critical, it was the secular Alliancists who were now unashamedly championing Barzynski's old theme of "For God and Country." Noting the Alliance's recent ploy, and not wishing to have its old adversary share the thunder of the moment, the Resurrectionists continued their attacks on Kruszka and his strategies designed to defeat the Americanizers.[37]

Due to the hard-line position taken by the bishops at the annual meeting of 1901, as expressed in the Keane memorandum, the joint mission to be undertaken by Kruszka and Pitass was cancelled.[38] Instead, Kruszka convinced a prominent member of the hierarchy, the German-American "sympathizer" in Milwaukee, Archbishop Frederick Katzer, to forward the Polish petition to the Vatican. By now the petition specifically requested Polish ordinaries or auxiliaries in twelve dioceses: Chicago, Buffalo, Scranton, Pittsburgh, Milwaukee, Green Bay, Detroit, Cleveland, Grand Rapids, St. Paul, Duluth, and Hartford. Kruszka's original "polyglot bishops in polyglot dioceses" proposal was now abandoned in favor of a call for a national all-Polish diocese in America.[39] Katzer's mission was three-fold: first, he was to emphasize the appropriateness of Polonia's requests for bishops before Cardinal Ledochowski; second, he was to educate the aging Prefect of the Propaganda Office as to the nature of Polonia's explosive population growth in the twelve dioceses mentioned; third, in his capacity as an objective (non-Polish) and non-partisan observer of the Polonia scene (though Katzer was hardly "non-partisan"), he was to explain the relationship of the Independent schism to the population explosion and to the demand for Polish bishops. With the Katzer mission set for the winter of 1901–1902, morale appeared to improve in the Polish Catholic Congress headquarters; and when Katzer wired back to Kruszka informing the latter of his upcoming appointment with Ledochowski, an air of excitement seemed to prevail, especially in Chicago and Milwaukee. But no sooner had these preliminary briefings between Katzer and Ledochowski taken place when the seventy-nine-year-old Cardinal-Prefect died suddenly. Katzer remained in the Vatican for a few months, hoping to arrange for a new set of negotiations with the incoming Prefect, but the negotiations and the anxiety of waiting proved too tiring for the Milwaukee archbishop, who complained now of poor health and requested a return to his home in Milwaukee. The following summer, Katzer too was dead.[40]

With Ledochowski and Katzer both gone, Kruszka went about the country gathering the fragments of the aborted mission. In doing this unpleasant task, he could not hide his emotions and frustrations from the Americanists and the Vatican diplomats. He even bitterly accused the Congregation of the Resurrection, which still maintained its Central House in Rome, of having deliberately sabotaged the Katzer mission. The Ripon whirlwind was certain that the Resurrectionists had somehow discovered a way to intervene at the highest levels of the Vatican to snuff out the Katzer mission, so as to maintain their supremacy in the archdiocese of Chicago.[41] In retaliation for such alleged machinations, Kruszka penned another emotionally charged letter to *The Freeman's Journal*, the title of which clearly expressed his personal view—"Polish Bishop Subject Not Dropped." In this piece, Kruszka publicly endorsed Bishop Muldoon of Chicago and Bishop Spalding of Peoria as well as "many others [who] are sympathizing with our movement." For good measure, he fired another salvo in the direction of the Americanists. He labelled any bishop "not knowing the Polish language . . . a stranger, a foreigner and a barbarian." Coming at a time when the Polish campaign was attempting to gain support within the hierarchy, Kruszka's second broadside in *The Freeman's Journal* indicated that the Ripon maverick had abandoned all hopes of working from within the hierarchical power structure.[42]

With the failure of the Katzer mission, the Executive Committee of the Polish Catholic Congress passed another motion, dated 18 May 1903, which authorized Kruszka and Pitass, now pastor of St. Stanislaus parish in Buffalo, to represent the Polish people in the United States before the Vatican. The purpose of the Kruszka-Pitass mission was to continue negotiations with the Vatican on the bishop question. Upon notification of this appointment, Kruszka began another national campaign aimed at collecting evidence to support Polonia's case. Kruszka's strategy, like his temperament, was simple and direct. He knew that the Office of Propaganda in the Vatican had been only vaguely aware of the rapid population growth in Polonia, especially in the cities, during the previous decade. Kruszka also showed his characteristic disdain for any population estimates made by the hierarchy in diocesan cities. Accordingly, he set himself to the task of collecting signed affidavits from large city mayors which were to "certify" how many Poles resided in each municipality. The response to Kruszka's request was, by his own account, most gratifying: Mayor Carter Harrison, for example, certified that Chicago had 250,000 Poles (in 1903); Mayor David Rose of Milwaukee certified 65,000 Poles in his city; Buffalo claimed 70,000 Poles; Detroit and Pittsburgh, 50,000 each; Cleveland, 30,000; and Toledo, 14,000. Armed with these mayoral affidavits as evidence of Polish Catholic strength and having the official Polish Catholic Congress petition in hand, Kruszka confidently sailed for Rome in June of 1903. He was accompanied by the Honorable Rowland Mahaney, a former Buffalo, N.Y., congressman who was a last minute replacement for Pitass, who decided not to make the trip.[43]

On 1 July 1903, Kruszka was granted an audience with Albin Cardinal Symon, who was of Polish ancestry himself and who happened to have been selected as the personal representative of Leo XIII, for the Pontiff was seriously ill. Cardinal Symon promised Kruszka that he would use his influence to expedite the matter of the petition, but he counseled patience due to the gravity of the pope's condition. On 13 July Kruszka and Mahaney were granted an audience with Cardinal Gotti, the recently appointed Prefect of the Propaganda Office, and on the next day the three discussed the petition with Cardinal Rampolla, the Vatican Secretary of State, amidst reports that Leo XIII was on his deathbed. Six days later Leo was dead, and hours after his passing came word that Archbishop Katzer too had died. Thus, in a matter of hours, the prospects for the formal acceptance of the Polish Congress petition appeared darker than ever. Kruszka was stunned by the news, but according to his memoirs his faith in Divine Providence was never for a moment allowed to waver.[44]

While Kruszka waited patiently in Rome, his activities as well as the decisions of the Polish Catholic Congress were carefully scrutinized in the Catholic press, by the hierarchy in particular. As was the case so often in the past, the pages of the *American Ecclesiastical Review* were used as a litmus test to gauge public reactions to Kruszka's controversial positions. In an article entitled "American Bishops and Polish Catholics," H. J. Heuser argued that the Polish Catholic Congress plea to the hierarchy had indeed been "well founded." Heuser did not believe for a moment, however, that the Vatican would ever establish separate and independent Polish dioceses like those already in existence in oriental churches or in parts of Austria (a point which Kruszka had duly noted). Heuser gave two reasons for his position: first, "in the United States there is a legitimate prospect of ultimate amalgamation of all the different nationalities." Arguing straight from the text of the Americanists, he was certain that the present ethnocentrism in Polish and other Slavic communities would not last "beyond the present century." Second, due to "the difference in local conditions which suggests union of religious interests rather than division, there is positive legislation of the Church against a system of double and independent administration in the same locality." In other words, Heuser (and no doubt the Americanists) opposed any juxtaposition of the territorial and national principles and practices of parish church organization. Heuser did, however, qualify his position when he conceded that the

Vatican was presently advising great caution when dealing with the complex issues and ramifications of the territorial and national principles of organization. He noted that it would probably be best to appoint bishops and vicars who might be "familiar with the language and peculiar customs of the people of separate nationality."[45]

Up to this point in his lengthy analysis, Heuser gave every indication of maintaining his role as the cool and detached observer-commentator. But inexplicably, in the remainder of his article, the editor of the prestigious *American Ecclesiastical Review* donned the robes of a partisan, and now appeared to be nothing more than a mouthpiece for the Americanists. Judging by the rhetoric he used, Heuser indeed appeared to be relishing his role as hatchetman. Deciding to take the fight to Kruszka and nationalists of his ilk, Heuser questioned "the absolute trustworthiness of the candidates" for the office of bishop now swelling the Polish clerical ranks. His verdict was a harsh one: vicars, yes; bishops, no. The Poles might indeed be "industrious, generous and courageous," but they were also "hot-tempered . . . and their lack of familiarity with the ways of Americans renders them often suspicious." Not only that, but Polish Catholics generally failed to understand that "freedom and the exercise of liberty" in America also required the upholding of "certain laws and restraints." According to Heuser, Polish priests, as a whole, had not yet matured to the point where they could be said to accept certain responsibilities and modes of conduct associated with the priesthood. In fact, Heuser was convinced that too many bad priests had emigrated from Poland, that America was getting only the riffraff. But he hoped "for the increase of that better element among the immigrant clergy" whose sole reason for selecting the American mission would not merely be "unfitness at home" in the mother country.[46]

Hoping to influence the final outcome of the Kruszka mission in the Vatican, the *American Ecclesiastical Review* continued its criticism of Poles in the very next issue. In "Slav Catholics in the United States," Heuser accused Slavic congregations of persistently practicing variations of the illicit trustee system, which he claimed was the basis of Independentism. Trustees, he stated, were even selling tickets to parishoners entitling the holders to receive the sacraments, and dues-paying systems in Slavic parishes were widespread. Pastors in many of these parishes were still being found guilty of fiscal mismanagement and of "hiding the true financial picture of their parishes from their bishops." The situation was further complicated by "the mutual opposition of certain elements" in parishes which made it nearly impossible for the sensible administrator to manage. Besides, Slavic Catholics were generally too "fiery" and "independent," and as a whole overly resentful "as a result of long oppression" in their partitioned homeland, which was why "they ignore or defy authority as represented by the ecclesiastical head, who, they think belongs to another race that never troubles itself about them and cannot understand them."[47]

The attack marshalled by Heuser on behalf of the Americanists was probably supported by a majority of Catholic priests and bishops whose ancestry was non-Slavic. The imprudent use of ethnic stereotypes by someone of Heuser's stature is also strong evidence that ethnic prejudice was indeed a significant factor in the final selection of candidates for bishop in any number of dioceses. This pair of articles, timed to coincide with the Kruszka mission, also demonstrates clearly just how far away the American Catholic hierarchy was from arriving at even some minimum form of accommodation with the idea and practice of ethnic pluralism. In a day when Catholicism itself was fretting over its "minority status" in American life, the hierarchy, at least when judged by the harsh assessment of national and ethnic minorities it made in its flagship journal, was placing itself in a position where it would be able to exert precious little influence in immigrant quarters in a later day when even greater social issues were at stake. Ironically, by rejecting the notion of ethnic pluralism during the bishop question, the hierarchy made it that much more difficult for ethnic institutions to assimilate into the wider and more powerful aspects of American social life. By shunting aside the clerical leadership in Polonia during a period when Polonia was suffering her greatest crisis—the agony of schism—the institutional Catholic Church was unknowingly determining its own status as a permanent minority in American life.[48]

With the election of Giuseppe Sarto as pope, Kruszka resumed the Polish campaign for equality. All documents originally addressed to Leo XIII were now made out to Pius X. In the period during which the College of Cardinals conducted their business, the Association of Polish Catholic Priests held its national meeting, called for the purpose of submitting a list of qualified candidates to Kruszka should he be successful in his meeting with the pope. On 16 October 1903, at the same time Heuser was writing his attacks on Polish clergymen, the Association telegrammed Kruszka its list of candidates. Heading the names of Polish candidates for bishop was Reverend Hyacinth Gulski, pastor of St. Hyacinth's parish in Milwaukee, who received 56 votes; next on the list, with 53 votes, was the Reverent Stanislaus Nawrocki, current president of the Association of Polish Catholic Priests, chaplain of the Polish National Alliance, and pastor of St. Mary of Perpetual Help parish in the Bridgeport area of Chicago; in third place, with 48 votes, was Reverend Francis Lange, pastor of St. Josaphat's parish in Chicago, member of the board of consultors for the Chicago archdiocese, and past chaplain of the PNA; fourth on the list, with 47 votes, was the Reverend Mitchell Barabasz, holder of S.T.D. and Ph.D. degrees, and vice-rector of St. Mary's Theological Seminary in Orchard Lake, Michigan. Barabasz was followed by: Jacob Pacholski, pastor of St. Stanislaus parish in Winona, Minnesota, and frequent contributor to *Wiarus* (44 votes); Edward Kozlowski (not to be confused with the Independent, Anthony Kozlowski), pastor of St. Stanislaus parish in Bay City, Michigan (40 votes); Francis Wojtalewicz, pastor of Immaculate Conception parish, who had devoted all his energies to tending to the spiritual needs of steel-workers and their families who resided in the nearby U.S. Steel area on Chicago's south side (34 votes); Witold Buchaczkowski, newly appointed rector of the Orchard Lake seminary (33 votes); John Szukalski (33 votes); and Paul Rhode, one of the first graduates of St. Stanislaus College, and the hard-working, 32-year-old assistant pastor of St. Michael's parish in South Chicago (31 votes).[49]

The national meeting of the Association of Polish Catholic Priests, despite its fundamental agreement with the Kruszka campaign for *równouprawnienie*, was simply unable to arrive at a consensus candidate. Even the frontrunner Gulski, was able to capture only 13 percent of the total vote (419 votes were cast). The final tabulations also clearly showed that a dramatic power shift had taken place in Catholic Polonia since Barzynski's death. Alliancist candidates were now popular and attractive candidates; Unionists were not. Outside of the Orchard Lake voting bloc, which was made up largely of academicians, all the candidates were heavily engaged in pastoral work, that is, each was highly visible and successful in urban parish work. The convention also demonstrated that regionalism was a significant factor in the balloting, as witnessed by the clustering of votes for Michigan, Wisconsin, and Illinois candidates. Finally, and perhaps most significant of all, not a single Resurrectionist made the Association's list of candidates.

Having received the results of the election, Kruszka next submitted three separate petitions to the Prefect of the Propaganda Office in order to gain an audience with the pope. The third in this series of appeals, an eight-paragraph note written in Latin and dated 28 March 1904, brought about the long-awaited meeting with Pius X.[50] The historic audience with the Pontiff was scheduled for 15 April. That morning Kruszka was greeted by Monsignor Bisleti, the papal secretary, who instructed Kruszka to remain in the papal visiting room until the pope was ready. Moments later, the Pontiff entered the visitor's room from behind two massive wooden doors, at which time Bisleti made the formal introduction and a request for the Polish Congress petition and all accompanying documents. Glancing over the materials, Pius X asked, "Do you plan on returning to America now?" To which Father Kruszka, his voice quivering, responded: "I will return, but what am I to tell the Poles in America? Before I go back I would like to hear from His Holiness as to his decision concerning the situation over Polish Bishops in America. I have sat in Rome for ten months, and still there is no such diocese." Then, in Kruszka's own account, the Pope is said to have quietly replied: "It will come in due time. Tell the Poles in America this: that the matter will be resolved according to their wishes." Kruszka was speechless. Monsignor Bisleti cut through the silence by asking of Kruszka, "Do you wish to say anything more?" Having completely forgotten a carefully prepared response in Latin for the occasion, Kruszka could only reply: "I thank you from the bottom of my heart, Your Holiness." The audience, fourteen years in the making, was over in minutes.[51]

An elated Kruszka cabled the Executive Committee of the Polish Catholic Congress announcing the triumphant papal decision. Polish clergy everywhere in America rejoiced over what they believed was a great victory over the forces of Americanization. But the buoyancy of the day was tempered by several troublesome and unanswered questions. For instance, why were no specific candidates on the Association's list even mentioned? And why no specific dioceses? And what remained of the matter of a national diocese for Poles in America, at the very moment the forces of Independentism were formally announcing their final break with Rome?

From his Scranton headquarters, Reverend Francis Hodur, perhaps the most radical populist in all Polonia, was already in the process of formulating a nationwide appeal for a permanent national church for Polish Independents everywhere in America. Irish domination was said to have killed all hopes for an amicable solution to the Polish question. It was time, Hodur announced, "to organize a Polish National Catholic Church in America . . . to which we are calling the first synod."[52] It was becoming obvious to most serious observers in Polonia that the work of Kruszka, Sztuczko, and the Polish Catholic Congress had been in vain. The audience with Pius X had come too late. The floodwaters of schism were unleashed. Yet, despite some of the rapid gains registered by the Polish National Catholic Church in 1904–1907, the wheels of the Vatican monolith moved ever so slowly toward implementation of the papal decision in favor of Polonia. Perhaps, as the Prefect of the Propaganda Office had once indicated, "the difficulty is on the American side."[53] Four years would pass before American Polonia would again come to bask in the triumphal spirit of the 15 April 1904 meeting between Pius X and the indomitable Father Kruszka.

Why was there such a long delay? First, there is evidence suggesting that the Congregation of the Resurrection consistently attempted to block the Kruszka mission. The *Dziennik Chicagoski*, under Barzynski's successor, Francis Gordon, had on any number of strategic occasions used its editorial space to attack Kruszka's "polyglot bishops" thesis. Now, in the wake of the "victory cable," the Resurrectionists, aware of the fact that no member of the Congregation had been included on the Association's list of candidates, engaged in a good deal of speculation on the possibility of a Polish bishop coming to Chicago from outside the Congregation itself. Accordingly, in 1904, the Resurrectionists speeded up their negotiations with the Vatican and with Archbishop Joseph Weber, suffragan bishop of the Lwów diocese, in order to bring Weber into the Congregation.

Resurrectionist accounts all agree that Weber had been a lifelong friend of the Congregation, a relationship that extended back to the "founder's generation." While still a young man, the future Archbishop of Lwów had spent time as a student at the Resurrectionist central house and seminary at Rome, then under the watchful eye of Peter Semenenko. While in Rome, Weber became seriously ill, and, according to Resurrectionist sources, pledged to take his final vows in the

Congregation. But upon regaining his health, he was recalled to Poland by his superior, Bishop Puzyna; his sickbed vow went unfulfilled. Weber was then ordained in Poland, where he moved rapidly up the hierarchical ladder, for Poland contained numerous historic dioceses which afforded talented pastors the opportunities and the outlets to make use of their administrative skills. Young pastors who caught the attention of their superiors were often carefully groomed for the responsibilities that came with the mitre and sceptre, and such was the fortune of Joseph Weber in the Polish church. By December 1895, now in his twenty-fifth year in the priesthood, Weber was not only the Rector of the Theology Seminary in Lwów but also the auxiliary bishop of that diocese. At age fifty, then, at the height of his hierarchical career, it was hardly expected that this talented Polish bishop, who had assumed every conceivable administrative burden in church affairs, would now walk away from it all in order to fulfill a boyhood vow. Yet, according to Resurrectionist accounts, this is precisely what Weber had in mind. Thus, when the idea of coming to Chicago was first raised by Superior-General Jan Kasprzycki in 1905, Weber, who the year before had been raised to the rank of archbishop, accepted. He was granted special permission to be relieved of all his duties in Lwów, whereupon he joined the Resurrectionist Congregation, professing his final vows on 2 February 1907.[54]

It was now assumed by any number of clergymen in Chicago that the transfer of the sixty-two-year-old archbishop to their archdiocese was the solution to the bishop question which Pius X and the Propaganda Office had in mind all along. After all, even the most ardent nationalist in the clergy would have agreed that Weber's credentials were impeccable. But before such fantasies were realized, another development unfolded which somewhat overshadowed the Weber profession into the Congregation of the Resurrection.

In the spring and summer of 1905, Archbishop Albin Symon was sent by the Vatican on a celebrated tour of American Polonia in order to make a firsthand study of the Polish situation. Since Symon was the Pope's personal representative it was also assumed in some quarters that he was making the trip so as to make positive recommendations on Polish-American candidates for the bishopric. It was also thought that Symon's personal recommendations would be sufficient to override recommendations to the contrary made by the Americanists. Beginning his tour in New York City on 18 May, Archbishop Symon, by his own account, visited 153 Polish parishes in 29 different dioceses, delivering more than 350 speeches to numerous groups along the way. On 24 June, before a packed house at St. Stanislaus Kostka Hall in Chicago, Symon devoted a good part of his remarks to extolling the virtues and accomplishments of the Resurrectionists in Chicago. Seated to his left that afternoon was the Honorable Leon Szopinski, a member of the national executive board of the Polish Roman Catholic Union. If ever a moment had come that called for some sort of dramatic announcement on the bishop question, this was it—right in the "Capital of American Polonia." But to the surprise of the guests, no announcement was forthcoming either on that afternoon or at any other time during the Symon tour of Polonia.[55]

Instead, the archbishop made two separate reports to the Vatican, one dated 5 October 1905 and the other 23 April 1906, neither of which was made public. In the first report, Symon emphasized the remarkable institutional development taking place in Polonia, praising throughout the sacrifices the Polish working class was making for the more than 500 parishes it had erected on American soil, "each with an elementary school attached to the parish church." He then called attention to the dedicated work performed by the Polish-based orders of teaching nuns, singling out for special commendation the efforts of the Resurrectionists, the Felicians, the Franciscans (of Blessed Kunegunda), and the Sisters of Nazareth. He was especially impressed by Polonia's social welfare contribution—the orphanages, homes for the aged, hospitals, and immigrant homes. He called attention to Polonia's influential newspaper network and to Polonia's institutions of higher learning, namely St. Stanislaus College in Chicago and St. Mary's Theological Seminary in Orchard Lake, reminding the Vatican that the Orchard Lake Seminary had already graduated some 350 Polish priests, almost all of whom were serving in missions throughout American Polonia. Symon even incorporated into his report a personal endorsement of Catholic Polonia submitted by President Theodore Roosevelt as well as commendations "of admiration and praise" submitted by James Cardinal Gibbons, the Apostolic Delegate, numerous archbishops and bishops, and several mayors of predominantly Polish cities.[56] It now appeared that the high tide of the Americanists "on the other side of the Atlantic" was rolling back. In his second report to the Vatican, Symon specifically called for the selection of "Polish suffragan bishops . . . in Buffalo, Pittsburgh, Chicago, Milwaukee, Detroit and Philadephia" who might "serve the one million Polish Catholics in these cities."[57]

All these efforts on the part of Archbishop Symon, however, were nearly torpedoed by another one of those embarrasing incidents which always seemed to be inappropriately timed and which seemed to lend substance to charges made by the *American Ecclesiastical Review* that Poles were irresponsible and hot-tempered. This latest in the endless sequence of detours standing in the way of *równouprawnienie* involved the celebrated tempest over the publication of Kruszka's *Historya Polska w Ameryce* (*"History of the Poles in America"*), a thirteen-volume work published by the *Kuryer Poliski*, a Milwaukee newspaper owned and operated by Kruszka's half brother, Michael. The release in 1905–1906 of the first few volumes of the *Historya*, some of which had already appeared in serial form in Polish newspapers, riveted Polonia's attention to the infamous *burza* over *Stanisławowo* in the 1871–1893 period. Concentrating primarily on the conflict between the Resurrectionists and the *Gmina Polska*, Kruszka portrayed the Resurrectionists in the role of villain, and in the process salted some of the still festering wounds caused by Barzynski's tenure as pastor.

All the hoopla over the publication of the *Historya* naturally brought a great deal of notoriety to Kruszka, whom the Resurrectionists immediately placed on the defensive. Oddly enough, the origins of this new Kruszka-Resurrectionist feud could be traced to Kruszka's Polish Catholic Congress-sponsored voyage to Rome.

During the long delay between his audiences with the Office of Propaganda and the pope, Kruszka continued his research for the *Historya*. The plucky "Nestor of Polish American History" was even able to gain unlimited access to the Resurrectionist's archives at the Congregation's central house. The permission to use the archives was granted by the unsuspecting Superior-General, Paul Smolikowski, who probably thought that Kruszka was only looking for more evidence for *równouprawnienie*. In any event, based on the documentary materials he located, Kruszka formulated his controversial thesis that the Resurrectionists had all along engaged in conspiracy in order to gain and then maintain control over Chicago Polonia. As could be expected, the Resurrectionist press retaliated swiftly when Kruszka's position was made public. Smolikowski himself submitted a lengthy article to the *Dziennik Chicagoski* which attacked "the Reverend Kruszka and his use of so-called documents." Reverend Francis Gordon, editor of the *Dziennik Chicagoski*, even charged that "Father Kruszka abused Smolikowski's confidence, and fraudulently copied, stole and published entirely private and secret matters," which made Kruszka "guilty of libel."[58] Despite these charges, however, Gordon implied that some of the materials which were taken illegally by Kruszka were indeed sensitive to the Congregation's reputation.

The controversy over the *Historya* spread into the neighboring archdiocese of Milwaukee as well. The Resurrectionists went so far as to question the judgment of Bishop Messmer, who was opposed to the Kruszka campaign for ecclesiastical equality, for having granted the *imprimatur* and the *nihil obstat* to the *Historya* (the *Historya* was published in Messmer's diocese). The situation became even further complicated by another separate conflict between the Kruszka brothers and Messmer over other unrelated issues. It so happened that the *Kuryer Polski*, which had published the *Historya*, was at the time supporting a campaign for a mandatory program for the teaching of Polish language courses in the Milwaukee public schools. If the Board of Education in Milwaukee had voted in favor of this program, it could have cut into the parochial school enrollment in Milwaukee and into the financial resources of the archdiocese, which Messmer was understandably distressed over. And since Messmer had earlier taken a public position against the idea of a national Polish diocese in America, the incidents having to do with the publication of the *Historya*, when viewed in conjunction with the Milwaukee school fight, lead one to believe that the Vatican purposely delayed action on the bishop question. On top of all this, Kruszka was accused by another Milwaukee pastor of having committed adultery with a woman from St. Casimir's parish, a charge Kruszka vehemently and repeatedly denied, although "conscience bound" he assisted the woman in question financially. In any event, this swirl of activity and charges and countercharges involving Kruszka and Messmer was scarcely conducive to a resolution of the issue of *równouprawnienie.*[59]

Fortunately for Polonia, cooler heads prevailed. The conclusions made by Archbishop Symon in his report to the Vatican were accepted by the Office of Propaganda, which, in turn, instructed Archbishop James Quigley to call for an election, at which time all Polish pastors in Chicago would be given the opportunity to select a candidate for the position of auxiliary bishop. Thus, it was a foregone conclusion that Chicago Polonia would gain one of the seats recommended by Symon (the other bishopric was to go to Milwaukee). In Quigley the Polish pastors had indeed found a champion for their cause. When he succeeded Feehan in 1902, he had been one of the few Irish bishops to speak out in favor of *równouprawnienie*, having had the opportunity to experience the Polish crisis firsthand while still Bishop of the heavily-Polish Buffalo diocese. Quigley scheduled the long-awaited election for 16 August 1907 at Holy Name Cathedral parish hall. The archbishop opened the meeting by laying down the ground rules for the day: first, he adopted a one man-one vote principle, thus removing any speculation that pastors of larger parishes would have a greater voice in the proceedings; next, he reminded the electors that the candidate selected was not going to head an all-Polish diocese in Chicago, but would instead be representing all nationalities in the archdiocese; finally, he pledged his support for the consensus choice of the electors—their man would become the first Polish bishop in Chicago and in the United States. Shortly after the election, Quigley left for Rome. In his briefcase were the votes indicating that 26 of the 32 Polish pastors in Chicago had selected Reverend Paul Rhode of St. Michael's parish, the same pastor who had finished dead last in the original canvass made by the Association of Polish Priests in 1904.[60] On 7 May 1908, Rhode was formally notified by the Vatican of his selection. On 28 July 1908, he was consecrated, and Polonia's quest for equality ended.

All of Chicago Polonia was jubilant. The *Dziennik Chicagoski* cheerfully acknowledged the selection of Rhode. "Habemus Episcopum" was the headline gracing the *Dziennik* editorial page. Success had come, the *Dziennik* argued, because Polonia had persistently "knocked at the door in Rome." Not acknowledging Kruszka even once, the Resurrectionist daily claimed that "all credit was due to Archbishop Quigley." The *Album Pamiątkowe*, the commemorative parish album of St. Stanislaus Kostka, boasted of the fact that "Bishop Rhode was a pupil in our school." Thus, after nearly forty years of rioting, bloodshed, deadly fratricidal warfare, and schism, Chicago Polonia now seemed at rest. All parishes, whether clerical or national in persuasion, joined hands and celebrated in the streets; nearly 200,000 Poles, according to *Chicago Tribune* estimates, participated in the consecration festivities. Another 20,000 uniformed men formed the largest honor guard ever to march Chicago's streets. Each of the 32 parishes in

Bishop Paul Rhode   *Father Wenceslaus Kruszka*

the archdiocese sent large delegations, many wearing the striking colors of the PRCU, the PNA, the Polish Alma Mater, the Polish Veterans, the Polish Women's Alliance, the Polish Singers Union and Choirs of America. One by one the groups marched past their newly consecrated bishop-hero. Seven hundred Polish priests, another 300 diocesan priests from other ethnic groups, hundreds of nuns, 20 bishops, and 3 archbishops joined the endless parade down Noble Street in the heart of the northwest side Polonia. And when the marching ended here, it was resumed again elsewhere—later in the day through the near west side Polonia of *Wojcie-chowo*, and still later, far into the night, in the Steeltown Polonia of South Chicago, where Rhode had earned the honor of being "a worker's priest." Thousands upon thousands of homes along the various parade routes were hidden behind rows and rows of bunting and flowers. Throughout, Rhode's sturdy smile assured a shaky Polonia that the Old World religious ways would still persist, that the religious structure was still intact, that the heart and soul of Polonia, despite the angry past, throbbed with life. At the banquet that night, the feisty Archbishop Quigley, in dramatic oratory, chastised the Partitioning Powers for "the crime of the centuries." With voice rising, Quigley exclaimed, "I have never despaired of the ultimate resurrection of Poland." Drawing a comparison between Poland and Ireland, "who stand side by side in suffering," he concluded that "the blending of nations in the United States" will make for "the noblest laughter of the Church." This no doubt was Quigley's response to hard-line Americanists. On the other hand, Rhode quietly acknowledged that he was no polyglot bishop. "I ask for no favor but to work," he said to the hushed crowd, "no privilege but the right to offer my services not only to my own reverend archbishop, but also to all the prelates who, having a contingent of my countrymen in charge, may choose to use my more intimate knowledge of them, the strength of common origin, to the end that the Polish people of this country may rise to the highest plane of religious and civic righteousness."[61]

When the cheering was over, the new auxiliary bishop of Chicago wrote a letter to Kruszka, thanking him for his efforts and reminding him that he would forever be remembered in the bishop's prayers. Neither the soft-spoken Rhode nor the battle-hardened Kruszka could know in the warm summer of 1908 that Polonia's fight in this American church had hardly begun.

The War for Poland:
The Americanization of Polonia

A Polish soldier in the American Army is fighting just as much for
the unity and future of Poland as the soldier in the Polish army is
fighting for the unity and greater future of the United States, although
one is fighting under the Stars and Stripes and the other under the
White Eagle.

> Editorial in the *Dziennik Związkowy*, 31 July 1918.

There is no question that the elevation of the Reverend Paul Rhode to auxiliary bishop of Chicago was a major triumph for the surviving elements of both
the clerical and national parties. The long hierarchical career of Rhode—spanning
the "War for Poland," the Great Depression, and World War II—bridged the first,
second, *and* third generation in American Polonia. Bishop Rhode was living
proof that a dedicated priest could also be as enthusiastic a national as the most
ardent PNA member. Throughout his tenure as bishop, Rhode would be considered by both the Polish Roman Catholic Union and the Polish National Alliance
as the "Primate of Catholic Polonia," at least outside of the Polish National
Church, which reserved this honor for Bishop Hodur.[1]

The deep ethnocentric concerns of Polish-American Catholicism would always remain the focal point of any Rhode administration, even when some of the
larger issues and questions of American Catholicism threatened to distort or even
blot out the interests of Polonia. The period ushering in the Rhode administration
in Chicago was one during which Polonia learned to overcome many of the obstacles surrounding the "God against Country" factionalism which had dominated
the first two generations of Polonian life. The so-called social solidarity of sec-
ond-generation Polonia, which at least one noted historian of Polonia claims was
the ground floor of Polonia's later upward political mobility in Chicago, can be
traced to what we might describe here as the "Rhode Era of Good Feelings."[2]
This brief respite, lasting only from the summer of 1908 until the early stages of
World War I, was the only period in the first two generations of Polonian life

during which there was some inner peace. Not only did the PRCU and PNA arrive at a *rapprochement* of sorts, but also peace was made with "the outside," that is, with the American and Irish-American hierarchy. The Irish-Polish clerical *detente*, to which both Archbishop Quigley and Bishop Rhode contributed greatly, also enabled Chicago Polonia to develop internally. At the parish level, Poles were experiencing a mild cultural and educational renaissance. Even working-class Poles were treated to a wide variety of theatre productions playing in any number of parish halls. Night school attendance, especially for English language instruction, increased sharply, although never rapidly enough for hard-nosed nativists. All this was accompanied by a tremendous increase in the readership (and circulation figures) of the Polish press—which meant that a good part of the second generation was becoming immersed in the bilingual ways of American city life. And the movement, however rudimentary, from the unskilled, lowest-level occupational categories to semiskilled, and even skilled, labor in working-class Polonia did indeed contribute to a widespread belief that this new American way of life was perhaps worth a lifelong commitment.[3]

But despite many of these social changes, there still lay deep within the recesses of the Polish immigrant consciousness the memory of those who had been left behind in *kraju*. It was true that conditions in the homeland were nowhere near as chaotic as during the period of the Insurrections. The economic strides made by "Organic" Poland, still being cracked onward by the whip of Positivism, had certainly improved the living conditions of Poles in the cities. But in the real *kraju*, out in the countryside, conditions were still relatively primitive. Nevertheless, by immersing itself in the processes of industrialization which had been ongoing in Prussian Poland for nearly thirty years, Organic Poland was creating new urban working classes in the manufacturing regions of Western Poland. Life was no longer the unbearable "vale of tears" which had sent thousands upon thousands of Polonia's forefathers to the shores of *Nowy Świat*. Now, in the 1900–1914 period, the vast Polish emigration was originating in the Russian and Galician sectors. Here life *always* had been bad, at least from an economic standpoint. And the stream of newcomers coming into Chicago from the Eastern and Southern sections of Partitioned Poland served as a constant reminder to the *za chlebem*, hell-bent on achieving success in America and then going back, that Poland was still not free. Chicago Polonia, like the Polonias in every corner of America, always was conscious of the Partitions. Patriots could sing endlessly at the PNA local chapters that "Poland will not perish," but most wondered whether the day would ever come when Poland would regain her historic freedom. In the widest sense of the term, the Romanticism of Mickiewicz had never died.[4]

News of the outbreak of the war in Europe was received in Chicago Polonia with mixed emotions; some Poles, especially the more nationalistic, were quite enthusiastic about the prospect of independence, while others received the news with a great sense of relief—similar to collective responses in Paris, Munich, Berlin, and London. Throughout Polonia, especially in nationalist quarters, news of the war was cause for community celebrations; many Poles even prayed in the churches for a World War. Poles everywhere were soon urged by the Polish press in America to join the military forces of the homeland, who were now engaged, as Mickiewicz had prophesied, "in raising from the dead our fatherland . . . in a universal war for the Freedom of peoples." The justice of Poland's crusade in this "day of liberation" would be recognized by *szlachta* and *chłopi* alike, who would throw aside their social differences and join together in the "War for Poland." When this conflict would end, Poland was supposed to rise Christ-like from the grave of Partition and resume her rightful place as Poland the nation-state. And then Poland was to teach all nations how to live in harmony.

But such exhilarating excursions into Romanticism aside, the War for Poland was destined to have another quite unintended and unpredicted impact on American and Chicago Polonia. No one in the Polish National Alliance in August 1914 could foresee the massive Americanization program Polonia would endure (or in many quarters, welcome) while fighting this war. Alliancists, especially, did not expect some of their most trusted colleagues to engage in efforts to out-Americanize even the most ardent of nativists (who stubbornly held to the isolationist position championed by William Jennings Bryan). The pent-up frustrations over a series of anti-immigrant crusades begun by these nativists in those mysterious Anglo-Saxon organizations—the American Protective Association, the Ku Klux Klan, and even the emerging country clubs—seemed to add fuel to the engine of Americanization in Polonia, the intensity of which first impressed and then startled some of America's most well known nativists, such as Henry Ford.[5]

But this was only the half of it. American Polonia also put forth a supreme effort during the war to convince Partitioned Poland that she was indeed Poland's "Fourth Part." With White Eagle organizations and Polish Legions sprouting here and there, Polonia in many ways attempted to even out-Polonize the homeland, almost as if she were guilty for having left everyone behind in the first place. This émigré guilt called for rendering to Poland as much as, or more than, the Poles themselves. The sense of uprootedness, on the other hand, is what probably contributed to Polonia's rendering to America even more than the Americans. In any event, it was this dual and simultaneous process of Americanization and Polonization that was ultimately to determine the real meaning and identity of the hyphenated Polish-American after the War for Poland had been won. The evidence on this point is indeed staggering. The war rhetoric of this entire period proves that American Polonia wished not only to go to the battlefield and save democracy for Poland but also to save Poland for world democracy. To be sure, this dual process of allegiance at first confused noted Polish spokesmen who travelled to America early in the war to gather support for the Polish cause. Roman Dmowski and Ignace Paderewski both found it difficult enough to explain the Polish situation before the diplomatic courts of Europe (and to President Wilson) without having to contend with pressures, however warranted, emanating from Poland's Fourth Part. But these two pro-Russian statesmen soon learned how to capitalize on Polonia's dual loyalties, and Chicago Polonia's political leadership, including the influential John Smulski, came around to support the Dmowski-Paderewski program as well as an incumbent Democratic president who began as a peace candidate and ended up by declaring his support for the "self-determination" of "historic nations" in Europe.

Unfortunately, when the smoke of war and of the subsequent peace conferences had cleared, all Poland's Fourth Part had to show for its multipurpose crusade was a Pilsudski-led socialist state in which the voice of democracy was effectively stifled. An ill-advised Polish offensive into Russian territory, led by Marshal Pilsudski, *after* the Great War, brought Poland even further humiliation at a time when Poland should have been basking in the sunlight of Versailles. The Pilsudski military coup followed shortly after, puzzling thousands of Poles in America who felt that the dream of Mickiewicz had been betrayed. With such unexpected events serving as a backdrop, Poles in the United States, except those who actually did return to Poland after the war, slowly came to the realization that America was to be their *permanent* homeland. Knowing they were never to return to *kraju*, the Fourth Part of Poland turned to more mundane matters, like erecting hundreds and hundreds of bungalows on the northwest and southwest sides of Chicago. In these bungalow-zone bastions, thousands of Polish-Americans would for a long time to come, right on up to another world war, suffer the ambivalence of neither being totally Polish nor totally American. But, then, one could say that this "aloneness" was the essence of Polonia.

Chicago Polonia during World War I certainly mirrored American Polonia when it came to reflecting those images of tangled and conflicting loyalties to both America and Poland which competed for the minds and hearts of all Polish-Americans. Cognizant of how old-line inner tensions between clericals and nationals had frustrated cooperative endeavors in previous years, leaders of the PNA and the PRCU closed ranks in order to communicate a new spirit of unity or solidarity. Despite persistent strife with Polish socialists in America who formed the Committee of National Defense—an organization which strongly supported the pro-Austrian, pro-Socialist position advocated by Pilsudski—the PNA and the PRCU worked long hours in order to effectively transmit the message of unification. The unification theme would find expression in church sermons, in religious ceremonies of a patriotic bent, in hundreds of newspaper editorials, and in the organizational meetings, both local and national, of the supraterritorial fraternals.

The War for Poland was only in its first few weeks when a "Polish Central Committee in America" organized itself around the theme "Separate but United." Recognizing the immediate need for a treasury and an army, the PNA, the PRCU, the Polish Women's Alliance, the Alliance of Polish Falcons in America, the Alliance of Polish Clergy, and the Polish National Council decided at their national meeting on 2 October 1914 to organize the Polish Central Committee. The newly formed organization was to serve as a rallying point for those elements in Polonia not already committed to the Committee of National Defense. It was the powerful Polish Central Committee that both Dmowski and Paderewski would attempt to win over to their "pro-Russian" position, and it was the Polish Central Committee which served as the forerunner of the gigantic *Wydział Narodowy Polski* ("Polish National Department"), organized two years later as an umbrella organization designed to centralize Polonia's massive fund-raising efforts on behalf of Poland. In practice, the "separate but united" watchword meant that the individual treasuries of each fraternal organization (with the exception of the socialist "Committee of National Defense," which went its own solitary way) were to be controlled by the respective organizations themselves; but once the funds were collected, they were to be pooled for common purposes. In this fashion, such prominent fund-raising efforts as the National Treasury of the Polish National Council, the Independence Fund of the Polish National Alliance, the Polish Treasury of the Polish Roman Catholic Union, the Kosciuszko Fund of the Polish Falcons and, the War Fund of the Polish Women's Alliance came to be centralized.[6]

But Polonia's early activism had little bearing in the 1914–1916 period on the American public, which was most hesitant to become involved in "Europe's wars." As long as such pervasive sentiments in favor of isolation held the public's favor, Polonia's press, so as not to appear "unpatriotic," was forced to maintain a lower profile. Readers of the *Dziennik Chicagoski* and *Dziennik Związkowy* had to remain content with stories tracing troop movements back and forth across Polish and French soil. Yet, despite the general American apathy, Polonia's organizations quietly stepped up their activities for war relief. The war relief efforts were no doubt stimulated by President Wilson's encouragement of such indigenous relief work, but the biggest boost for Polonia's war drives came in 1915, when Paderewski began his celebrated tour of the United States as an official representative of the Polish National Committee. And when President Wilson, largely due to the prodding of Colonel House, received Paderewski as a representative of not only Poland but also Poland's Fourth Part, Polonia's press went to work on a determined campaign to glorify its two newly discovered "war heroes," President Wilson and "Citizen" Paderewski. The *Dziennik Związkowy*, in particular, jumped on the Wilson bandwagon. Duly taking note of Wilson's opposition to literacy tests as a prerequisite for American citizenship and at the same time forgiving the President for anti-immigrant remarks made during his earlier academic career at Princeton, the *Związkowy* called for Polish-American support of Wilson in the election of 1916. Soon, every prominent Polish newspaper in Polonia was extolling the virtues of Wilson and Paderewski, as if to call attention to the dual war roles of Americanization and Polonization. Who could be more American than President Wilson himself, or more Polish than Paderewski?[7]

Encouraged by Wilson's support of Paderewski, Chicago Polonia rewarded the efforts of its first "hero-president" in the election of 1916. In the predominantly Polish Sixteenth Ward on Chicago's near northwest side, an area taking in the community parishes of *Stanisławowo, Trójcowo, Jadwigowo,* and *Marianowo,* among others, voters cast 6,903 votes for Wilson and only 2,373 for Charles Evans Hughes. This heavy pro-Wilson support was cleverly acknowledged by Colonel House, who bestowed on the Polish Sixteenth Ward the honorific title "Banner Ward of All Chicago." On a city-wide basis, the support for Wilson in the Polish wards was equally resounding, with nearly three out of every four Polish voters casting their ballots for the incumbent president.[8]

From 1916 on, Polonia's support for Wilson never wavered. The *Dziennik Chicagoski,* still under the control of the Resurrectionist Fathers, considered any political enemy of President Wilson to be an enemy of Polonia. The *Dziennik Związkowy* consistently protrayed Wilson as the loyal friend of the war-torn immigrant. Both newspapers cleverly utilized their editoral cartoons and sketches to vividly convey pro-Wilson sentiments. By the end of 1917, the Resurrectionist daily even designed a new masthead which incorporated the president's determination to create "a unified, independent and autonomous Poland."[9]

The adulation of Polonia's hero-president came from the highest levels of Polonia's fraternal organizations as well. Dr. Karol Wachtl, eminent Stanislawian, author of the parish history of St. Stanislaus Kostka and the history of the PRCU, and secretary of the Polish National Committee, invokcd perhaps better than most the acute sensitivity of Polonia to ultra-Americanization and ultra-Polonization. In a letter to President Wilson, Wachtl submitted for the president's consideration an English-to-Polish translation of the "Star Spangled Banner." In the dedication of that translation, Wachtl thanked the president for having awakened "in our hearts a permanent and unextinguishable gratitude toward the United States." Waxing patriotically eloquent, Wachtl addressed the president as "the first of world statesmen" and as "a worthy representative of the divine idea which created this country the home of liberty for all men near and far, for all the oppressed and for all striving for freedom and independence." Only the president had been "courageous enough to demonstrate these rights of political self-determination and liberty and absolute independence for Poland." In conclusion to his letter, Wachtl stated that he had translated the American anthem into Polish in order to demonstrate "how closely we unite and combine in our souls the American spirit of loyalty and patriotism with the loyalty and patriotism for Poland."[10] To Wachtl, Americanization and Polonization were interdependent.

Such eloquent rhetoric in support of Americanization and of President Wilson was purposely used by Polish-American spokesmen in support of Poland's self-determination. But the rhetoric still had to be backed by deeds. In order to deliver the vote for Wilson, it now became urgent for Chicago Polonia to hold voter registration drives. Polish politicans like Congressman Stanley Kunz had always lamented the fact that Chicago Polonia lagged far behind other New Immigration groups (with the exception of Lithuanians) in the matters of naturalization, citizenship, and voter registration. Chicago Polonia, in general, still smarted from criticism leveled at it by such Americanizing outsiders as Graham Taylor of Chicago Commons. Taylor had once testified before a federal investigating team that Chicago's Poles "have no comprehension of our political institutions."[11] To counter such criticism, voter registration and citizenship drives were begun by Anthony Czarnecki, who was a member of the powerful Board of Election Commissioners in Chicago at the beginning of World War I. Czarnecki set himself the task of convincing Polonia that the most efficient way to support the War for Poland was to take one's citizenship responsibilities seriously. Focusing his attention on the community-parish network in Chicago, Czarnecki preached the message of voter registration to hundreds of parish fraternals and religious sodalities. Because "the law makes it your duty," Czarnecki told his listeners, voting was an "indispensable" element in demonstrating one's patriotism. Besides, without a sizeable voting bloc in Chicago, Poles would never be able to exert political influence. Housewives in particular were exhorted to convince their "politically backward" husbands to undergo naturalization. Through Czarnecki's efforts and influence, naturalization and voter registration booths were made available in each Polish ward in the city. Polonia's first all-out campaign for "Polish Power" during World War I, however, was only moderately successful. By 1920, only a third (33.7 percent) of all adult males of Polish extraction were naturalized, and among Polish females the percentage was only slightly higher (35.4 percent). But Czarnecki's drive did establish within Polonia a solid voting core and a political consciousness that would enable Polonia by the 1930s to assume a share of the Democratic party's coalition style of politics during the New Deal.[12]

In addition to the citizenship and voter registration drives, Chicago Polonia, throughout the war, used the parish fraternal network to engage in any number of patriotic efforts. One of these concerned community-wide support for the registration of servicemen in the armed forces of both the United States and Poland. Since President Wilson and Paderewski had already agreed to allow for the recruitment of American Poles into the Polish army, there was no protest whatsoever when Polish-Americans were conscripted into the American Expeditionary Forces. The Polish press throughout the war expressed a wide range of emotional appeals directed at young men of fighting age. The *Dziennik Związkowy* worked to bolster the military ranks by constantly calling attention to feats accomplished by those already in active combat. In an editorial entitled "Stars," the *Związkowy* in 1918 boasted of "Polonia's young men who have gone to the battlefields of France to give the Germans a whipping." Calling attention to the current Polish-

American practice of placing service stars in the windows of homes of families who had sent their men off to combat, the *Związkowy* noted with great pride that "at least sixty service stars" were prominently displayed in the windows of homes on a single city block near the editorial offices of the *Związkowy* (Marshfield Avenue between Division and Chicago). The *Związkowy* editorial praised Polonia's "dearest sons, brothers and fathers" who were now fighting "for a holy cause" so that Poland might become "united, free and self-governing." The editors concluded that "it is worth giving one's blood and property, in the face of so sincere a promise for Polonia's future."[13]

The *Naród Polski*, in advertising the opening of a new recruitment station on North Milwaukee Avenue, made an emotional appeal surpassing that of the *Związkowy*. Shortly after the formal U.S. declaration of war in April 1917, the *Naród Polski* issued the following editorial blast:

> War! War!
> War in the defense of human rights, in the name of liberty, in the name of the people.
> War!
> And the Star Spangled Banner is our banner. And our Polish Roman Catholic Union is not only Catholic, but also patriotic, which always and everywhere manifested those dearest emotions and is still manifesting them.
> The time has come for the great trial. And what is happening?
> In the home of the Polish Roman Catholic Union, atop which wave Polish and American flags, a recruiting station has opened up. . . .
> And so, Poles, rouse your spirits! Let's harden our strength, let's not be cowards!
> Because the Star Spangled Banner is our banner! . . .
> Fellow countrymen! Are we to remain in the rear, behind others? Are we to wait until this country compels us to join the ranks of the army? . . .
> Do not wait until the Germans and the other foes of the United States come to your homes and dishonor your mothers and daughters, and lead off your aged fathers, burning your homes and robbing you of your property. . . .
> Let us revive among us the tradition of Kosciuszko and Pulaski, who fought for the freedom of this country.
> Now is the time to join the army. Do not wait and do not say, "Let the others go first." Your country calls, it is time to go and defend our new Fatherland.
> Long live the United States of America![14]

To supplement such lively war rhetoric, both the *Dziennik Chicagoski* and the *Dziennik Związkowy* regularly published "servicemen lists," rows and rows of names of those servicemen coming from the community-parishes. Published in long columns, page after page, the lists gave readers the impression that Polonia's contribution to the military effort was second to none. The servicemen lists also supported the twin themes of Polonization and Americanization, as they included names of soldiers in both the A.E.F. and the Polish army. After the formal declaration of war by the United States, the Polish press in Chicago carried in its news columns stories on other ceremonial functions which lauded the Polish-American soldier. One of the most prominent and emotional such community endeavors was the Service Flag Ceremony, a ritual which was conducted with greater frequency in all the Polish parishes in Chicago as the war continued. Since Polonia's bravest "are now fighting for the United States and for Poland," the *Dziennik Chicagoski* issued a call for the public flag ceremonies "in their honor."[15] Typical of such flag ceremonies was the one conducted at St. Michael's parish in September 1918. Before several thousand parishioners who packed their church to overflowing, honor guards bearing a service flag marched in solemn procession through and outside the church. Emblazoned on the bright blue flag was the number 388 and six gold stars. The number signified the number of servicemen from St. Michael's who had enlisted in the American and Polish armed forces; the six gold stars symbolized the number of servicemen from the parish who had sacrificed their lives. After blessing the flag, the pastor gave a patriotic homily speaking to the heroism of Polish youth. After the church portion of the ceremony, the guests moved to the parish hall, where more speeches were delivered and both the American and Polish anthems were sung. This was followed by a series of dramatic skits put on by the children of the parish school and by any number of solo singing performances. Next, a French general, who had directed Polish troops in France, gave a speech attesting to the bravery of Polonia's finest. The afternoon was concluded with the taking up of a collection for war widows and Polish war relief.[16]

Polonia's traditional fondness for collective ritual was also translated on numerous occasions into elaborate parades which were organized whenever Polish recruits left for boot camp or for the battlefront. The parades always began at the church and usually made their way to the local railroad station. Along the way, brass bands played, boy scouts marched, church choirs sang, and drum and bugle corps performed. Invariably the parades were preceded by long and lavish dinners for the recruits, who were made to listen to a stream of patriotic speeches delivered by community and church leaders.[17]

"Loyalty banquets" were also frequently held in Polonia in honor of its servicemen. Sometimes these banquets were held in conjunction with those given by other nationality groups in Chicago. One such loyalty banquet, held at the downtown LaSalle Hotel on 6 February 1918, was attended by representatives of at least seventy-five nationality groups, all of whom contributed in some way to the patriotic extravaganza of the day (American Indians were even invited to do their traditional war dances on stage). At the banquet, "at which the Poles were the most numerously represented" according to an account in the *Związkowy*, leaders of Polonia's major fraternals were paid special tribute by those attending. The program included a rousing rendition of *Jeszcze Polska Nie Zginęła*, the nationalist version of the Polish anthem, done by the St. Hedwig parish school choir; a "loyalty address" by Edmund K. Jarecki, who was to serve as Cook County judge from 1922 to 1954; speeches made by the presidents of Polonia's fraternals and by recruitment officials; and, finally, a religious version of the Polish national anthem—*Boże Coś Polskę*—struck up by the St. Hedwig School band.[18]

All these patriotic and propagandistic efforts, to be sure, were to have a tremendous bearing on Polonia's overall military recruitment program. By the end of the war, Polish Catholic parishes recorded a total of 10,369 men sent overseas. Of this total, 7,803 enlisted in the American armed forces, while 2,566 fought under the Polish flag. Leading the way with total number of recruits was the flagship parish, St. Stanislaus Kostka, which sent 840 men to battle (750 American/90 Polish). On the south side, the ratio of recruits sent to the Polish army was higher: St. Joseph's parish sent 680 men (390 American/290 Polish); St. John of God enlisted 450 (300 American/150 Polish); and Sacred Heart sent off 350 (250 American/100 Polish).[19]

Much of this military recruitment was directly attributable also to the power of the Polish press in Chicago. By 1919, the total circulation of the *Dziennik Chicagoski* hovered near the 27,000 mark, and the *Dziennik Związkowy* had already risen to 43,000 paid circulation. Both of these dailies were also supplemented by weeklies, which circulated well beyond the confines of Chicago Polonia. For example, by the war's end, the *Naród Polski*, published by the PRCU, reached 80,000 readers; its counterpart in the PNA, *Zgoda*, skyrocketed to 125,000 paid circulation, making it one of the largest foreign-language newspapers in the United States. If one includes the *Głos Polek* published by the Polish Women's Alliance, the combined circulation of the Polish press in Chicago at the end of World War I came to over 300,000, or an average of one paid circulation per person in Chicago Polonia. Much of this boost in circulation was most probably due to the numerous additional features having to do with war news. But propaganda gimmicks also played a significant part in building up readership. Patriotic sermons delivered by Polonia's pastors were carried on occasion, and the monthly minutes of the fraternal organizations, which carried up-to-date reports on war relief funding drives, were printed. The *Dziennik Chicagoski* in April 1918 also began publishing a monthly serial feature "The History of the United States," which was designed to win the attention of the second generation. The *Związkowy* during the same period was featuring the works of the Polish Romantics—Mickiewicz, Słowacki, and Krasiński—alongside some of the most skillfully done political cartoons and sketches seen anywhere in American Polonia. What reader could resist Polonization when the verses of Mickiewicz were carried alongside a sketch depicting a tortured, crucified Poland, lashed to the cross of Partition, with a sadistic looking Teuton nearby? And what reader could resist the notion of Americanization when he was daily peppered with parish tallies of total contributions made for the Liberty Loan drives and when political posters advised him to "Remember the Flag of Liberty and Support it."[20]

But none of the war efforts in Polonia could match the astounding success achieved by the organizers of the Polish Victim's War Relief Fund, or the even more massive Polish National Fund (*Fundusz Narodowy Polski*). It was precisely in this area—collecting money, pure and simple—that Polonia was not outdone by any other ethnic group in Chicago. The community-parishes, the fraternal organizations, and the Polish press all coordinated their efforts for that one final push which all believed would contribute to making Poland not only politically free but also economically strong after the war. Once again the *Dziennik Związkowy* and *Dziennik Chicagoski* served as vital catalysts for the monumental fund-raising operations, while the community-parishes and the fraternal organizations functioned in their roles as conduits for the money taken in. The principal sources of income for the Polish Victim's War Relief Fund were the voluntary contributions made by the fraternals, donations from private individuals, war relief committee "exigency" funds, "dime bank" collections, and "mite boxes." Stamp fund drives by school children supplemented these other sources. As of 30 June 1917, the total of $333,549.60 had been collected nationally for the Polish Victim's Fund. The *Związkowy* and *Chicagoski* made an additional contribution by offering free advertising space for the Fund as well as printing financial statements prepared by the Fund's auditors. Throughout, the most powerful argument used by the editors of Chicago's Polish dailies was that each dollar contributed to the Fund actually was used to support family members of those left behind in *kraju*.[21]

But throughout the war, Chicago Polonia and its numerous urban counterparts elsewhere in American Polonia had come to establish a number of overlapping fund-raising activities. Accordingly, a national *sejm* (convention) to address this alleged inefficiency was called for by the Chicago-based *Wydział Narodowy Polski*. The *sejm* was held in Detroit in September 1918, at which time the Polish National Department, a polyglot organization which Paderewski claimed was representative of ninety percent of American Polonia, moved to consolidate and gain control of the numerous and competitive local fund-raising operations. From the leadership of the Polish National Department came the plans to put into effect the massive Polish National Fund (*Fundusz Narodowy Polski*). Sparked by the personal appearances of Dmowski and Paderewski, both of whom journeyed to Detroit from their Polish National Committee headquarters in Paris, the convention of 700 lay and 300 clerical delegates voted unanimously for a resolution setting a goal of ten million dollars for the Polish National Fund. In another convention development that was to have a significant impact at the later Paris peace talks, the Polish National Department and the Polish National Fund were brought under the control of Dmowski and Paderewski. Both would later use the passage of this resolution in support of their position that they indeed were the official representatives for Poland's Fourth Part.[22]

Organized so as to blanket all of American Polonia, the Polish National Fund was administered on the local level of American Polonia by 800 Citizen's Committees and levy representatives numbering as many as 15,000 workers. Supported by the old-line stalwarts—the churches, the fraternals, and the press—the Fund was most successful in Chicago. Overall in American Polonia, the Fund raised a total of $5,187,065. Even though the ten million dollar target was never reached, the Fund was looked upon as an overwhelming success by the Polish National Department, for the total contributions amounted to more than one dollar for every man, woman, and child in American Polonia.[23]

Despite the fact that the Polish National Fund served as a central clearinghouse and bank for Polonia's war contributions, it had only indirect ties with direct loan transactions made by Polonia to the Polish government. These loan transactions were instead handled by the Polish Loan Central Committee, which, by the end of 1920, is reported to have transferred a total of $383,750 in direct loans to Warsaw. In Chicago, the Central Committee's work was administered largely by the Polish Women's Alliance, which at the time was directed on an *ad hoc* basis by the Reverend Stanislaus Siatka and Mr. Stephan Napieralski, a layman from St. John Cantius parish.[24]

By far the single most important stimulus to Chicago Polonia's wartime drives was that provided by the famed diplomat and concert pianist, Ignace Paderewski. Few of Paderewski's personal appearances in American Polonia matched his historic visit to Chicago in March 1918. In a speech delivered before an estimated crowd of 35,000 jam-packed into the Chicago Coliseum on the afternoon of 3 March, Paderewski spoke at length about his role in the organization of the Polish National Committee in Paris. He expressed his unshakable faith in the ability of Poland's Fourth Part to have a definite impact on President Wilson whenever peace negotiations were undertaken; he also made it clear that Polish-American support for Wilson would reaffirm the support of the United States for the Polish National Committee in Paris. Paderewski pleaded for the self-determination of "all Nationals" in Europe, whether Czech, Moravian, Slovak, Serb, or Croat. He closed his address by pointing out that the "war was not yet won [and] that even greater effort was needed." Taking note of Polonia's efforts to Americanize, Paderewski paid tribute "to the Spirit of Washington and Lincoln," asking the crowd to transfer that same spirit and support for liberty to President Wilson.[25]

The following evening at the Morrison Hotel, Paderewski delivered a stirring address which was to become a classic expression of Polonia's dual wartime loyalties. Admitting to fatigue brought on by the strain of his visit, and somewhat embarrassed by the accolades showered on him throughout the evening, Paderewski came forth with a rousing, spellbinding piece of oratory which skillfully blended Polish romanticism and American desires for democracy and liberty. After congratulating Bishop Rhode and John Smulski for their personal efforts on behalf of the Polish National Committee, Paderewski opened with a few lines taken from *The Book of Polish Pilgrims*:

> Oh God of Kosciuszko, have pity on our country and on us. Grant us to pray again to Thee as our Fathers prayed on the battlefield, with weapons in our hands before the altar made of guns and cannon beneath the canopy of eagles and our flag.

To a crescendo of applause Paderewski told his audience that the prayers of Mickiewicz had been answered and that his dreams were now materializing as "the great war has come." Poland may have been "tortured by the invader . . . and neglected throughout the most appalling tragedy in her history." Nobody seemed "to care for our country," he said, until a "miracle" had taken place. This miracle had been Wilson's "peace without victory" speech of 17 January 1917— "only a few words, but they shook the world." In thanksgiving, Paderewski invoked Divine Providence "to bless the President and his noble friend General House." For the remainder of his address, Paderewski swung back and forth between appeals for Americanization and Polonization:

> For anybody who has but a rudimentary knowledge of American history it is obvious that chivalry, disinterested unselfish purpose in collective actions are just as inborn with the American people as ruthlessness and cruelty and greed are inherent in the enemy. Liberty, equality and fraternity have not been made in Germany. They were born here in America, in Philadelphia, on the Fourth of July, 1776, thirteen years before receiving their magic name in the French Revolution.

It was this spirit and the courage of the "Polish knights [that] miraculously preserved . . . the lasting patriotic Polish National Mission" as foretold by Mickiewicz. This mission was now reaching fruition because clearly "the Wilson Doctrine is the Magna Carta of mankind." For the efforts of Wilson on Poland's behalf, "Polonia's grandchildren's grandchildren" would always hold dear the ideals of President Wilson.[26]

For the remainder of the war, Chicago Polonia rode the crest of Paderewski's triumphal 4 March address. Contributions for the *Fundusz Narodowy Polski* poured into Polish National Committee coffers, and more than 2,500 young men signed up to fight under the *Orzeł Biały* (White Eagle). Three months later, on 2 June 1918, Polonia joined in an even larger celebration of Poland's heritage when more than 100,000 people from every community parish and fraternal organization in the city crammed into Humboldt Park for the "Kosciuszko Manifestation" honoring the National Polish Army in France. After enjoying a lengthy patriotic program conducted on a warm, sunny afternoon, the participants passed by acclamation a resolution calling for the "full support of President Wilson, the United States Government, the Allies and Poland." It was during these brief moments in the sunshine of nationalistic fervor that the ideals of the Polish and American nations were thought to be one and the same. But this notion of indivisibility could not last.[27]

When the armistice was signed that November, all attention was drawn to *kraju*. Between 8 November and 16 November 1918, the headlines of the *Związkowy* and the *Chicagoski* read as follows:

> Poland Proclaims Itself A Republic!
> Paderewski Withdraws From Slovenian Union
> Poland is a Republic—Daszynski is President
> Wilson Announces Terms of Armistice
> Poland Gains Access to the Sea
> Poland Free From Germany
> Germans Rush to Evacuate Poland[28]

As could be expected, such headlines not only caught the attention of every Pole in Chicago but also resulted in any number of community-wide celebrations after the signing of the armistice: big parades made their way down Noble and Division streets, in the Back of the Yards, in *Wojciechowo* and in South Chicago; the bands played and the fraternal organizations marched; the Stanislawian Zouaves came out all bedecked, waving their *sztandary* ("banners") for the crowds; and the churches were filled to overflowing with those offering thanksgiving. On 26 January 1919, Governor Frank Lowden proclaimed *Dzień Polski* ("Polish Day") in Illinois; four days later the *Dziennik Chicagoski* editorialized in jubilant fashion over the recognition of Premier Paderewski's government by the United States; and the following summer the *Chicagoski* began the practice of printing long columns of names of families who could now stop at their respective parish churches to pick up mail sent by relatives during the war. In these months following the great War for Poland, Chicago gave every indication to outsiders of being a happy place in which to live.[29]

But these celebrations were tarnished by several developments which forced the Poles to tone down the festivities and even withdraw once again into a ghetto shell. The first of these developments concerned reports coming out of Germany that Poles had been guilty of committing atrocities against the Jewish community in Lemberg (Lwów), which, if proved, would have put Poland in violation of the Minorities Treaty guaranteeing the rights of ethnic minorities in newly created states in Eastern Europe. In an effort to put an end to the rumors of pogroms in Poland, John Smulski, now President of the Polish National Department, and Dr. K. A. Zurawski, President of the Polish National Defense Committee, wired

President Wilson who was then aboard the U.S. transport *George Washington*. Both Smulski and Zurawski denied the allegations. Their cable bluntly stated that "Jewish pogroms on an anti-racial or an anti-religious basis do not exist." Smulski and Zurawski charged that the rumors had been spread as a result of "German intrigue."[30]

On 18 December 1918, Smulski, speaking for the Polish National Department in America and the Polish National Defense Committee, issued a "Proclamation To All Poles In The United States," which was published in the *Dziennik Związkowy*. In the "Proclamation," Smulski asserted that "the Jewish press is replete with despicable attacks against Poles." He also charged that Jews were unfairly boycotting Polish workingmen. Restating his earlier assertions made to Wilson, Smulski went on to warn Poles "not to yield to provocation" and to "remain dignified" as "truth always wins." He also stated that "fellow Jews" would themselves put a stop to such "pernicious propaganda." He then promised that the Polish National Department in America and the Polish National Defense Committee would conduct a joint investigation of the Lemberg incidents, to which President Wilson responded by forming a government investigation team, headed by Henry Morganthau, Sr., to study the Lemberg events.[31]

The joint investigation team and the Morganthau commission both reached the same conclusion, that there was insufficient evidence to indict the Poles of Lemberg. But the commission findings were not favorably received by Jews in the United States, who pressed for further studies. The debate over Lemberg continued well into 1919. John Smulski engaged in a brisk exchange of letters on the issue with a certain Rabbi Strauss from New York which was carried in the *New York Times*. Both Smulski and Strauss outlined their previous positions on the Lemberg incidents.[32]

Even after guarantees for the rights of Jews were incorporated into the Minorities Treaty, tensions continued between Poles and Jews in Chicago. Street fights between Polish and Jewish youth gangs were fought in the shadows of *Stanisławowo*, and tensions between Polish garment workers and Jewish shop entrepreneurs along Division Street heightened considerably. Bitter exchanges took place in Polish newspapers in Chicago between disgruntled (and often anonymous) Poles on the one hand and anyone daring to raise charges of anti-Semitism. But despite Polish attempts to fend off such charges, the overreactions printed in the Polish press made even sober observers pause and wonder. On 3 February 1919, the *Dziennik Chicagoski* skirted the edges of discrimination when its editors tied anti-Jewish sentiments then prevailing in Polonia to the success of Jewish businesses in the community. The same paper went over the brink when its editorial pages associated Jews with anarchy and Trotskyism.[33] The *Naród Polski*, during the race riot of 1919, also created a storm when it associated Jews in Chicago with "the German-Bolshevik hand."[34] Despite such editorial embarrassments, the *Dziennik Chicagoski* was accused by citizens in Polonia of having lived off the receipts provided by "Jewish advertisements," which were carried almost daily in the paper.[35] In any event, the Polish-Jewish tensions in Chicago and American Polonia after World War I carried over into the second and third generations, all the while leaving Poles highly sensitive to the entire subject of anti-Semitism, alleged or real.

Another development which had much to do with deflating the triumphal mood of Polonia after the war was the rising tide of a new, anti-immigrant "Americanism" blowing across the land in the wake of the "Red Scare." All of this nativist activity, as John Higham has shown, led to feverish attempts to initiate and pass laws dealing with immigration restriction, a subject which easily aroused the ire of Poles everywhere. Poles became even more outraged when attacks were leveled at Poles questioning their patriotic activities during the war, especially attacks on the means used by Polonia to raise funds for war relief. In an article in the *American Journal of Sociology*, Edward C. Hill minced no words in denouncing Polonia's war efforts. In particular, he spoke out against "racial organizations" which existed solely "for the purpose of maintaining or securing the political unity and independence and perpetuation of their native land." As an example, Hill went on to cite the activities of the Polish Central Relief Committee which engaged "in propaganda and promotion of Polish liberty . . . and makes no effort to Americanize its adherents or to promote the welfare of America."[36]

Although never attacking Hill by name, the Polish press in Chicago made every effort to do battle with "the chauvinism of Americanization." Arguing that the "Constitution of the United States guarantees all of us freedom," the *Dziennik Chicagoski* took exception to chauvinists who "twisted" the Constitution to their own immoral purposes and who aimed at "harming, oppressing and persecuting" the immigrant. The editors of the *Dziennik Chicagoski* charged that such "chauvinists" were the least American of all.[37] On another occasion, an editorial simply blurted out that "we don't want to melt in the Melting Pot."[38] The *Dziennik Związkowy* also joined in such counterattacks by rising up to defend the principle of cultural pluralism in American history and life. The *Związkowy* was known to reserve its finest editorial rhetoric for attacks on Henry Ford, whom the newspaper considered the arch-Americanizer, and on the two Ford-run newspapers, the *Dearborn Independent* and *Ford's International Weekly*, which publicized his anti-immigrant stances.[39] The Polish press was more tolerant of those Americanizers who were willing to concede, and even foster, the idea of cultural pluralism. For example, the *Dziennik Chicagoski*, in May of 1919, wrote a lengthy editorial praising George Creel for his "tolerance and understanding" of immigrants during the war. Creel had headed the wartime Bureau of Public Information, a government propaganda office which had been initiated to gain public support for Wilson's policies. Throughout his tenure as the Bureau's director, Creel had supported such fund-raising drives as the *Fundusz Narowdowy Polski*. Thus when the

Bureau was closed in 1919, the *Dziennik Chicagoski* applauded Creel for his efforts.[40]

Nevertheless, the Americanizers on the political and social scene often raised issues critical of Polonia which were difficult, or even impossible, to defend against. One of these embarrassments concerned the steady stream of Polish immigrants who decided to leave the United States after the war and return to Poland. The *New York Times*, basing its estimates on port-of-departure statistics, concluded that at least 40,000 Poles had left for Poland by February 1920.[41] The *Dziennik Chicagoski*, despite the fact that the total departures amounted only to approximately one percent of Poles in the United States, still found it difficult to explain the phenomenon to Americanizers. The *Chicagoski* usually argued that the dispersion was due to a powerful generational factor within Polonia. It was only natural, the editors argued, for older people who had been born on Polish soil to wish to return, while "younger people born on this soil . . . will remain because they are Americans."[42] On another occasion, the *Chicagoski* argued that all Polish-Americans ought to have the freedom to choose their homeland without outside pressures or distractions: "Everyone must decide for himself what he wants to do . . . [whether] to return to Poland and remain a Polish citizen, or to live the remainder of his life on the soil of Washington."[43]

Thus Chicago Polonia, despite her remarkable overall contribution to both the Polish and American governments during the war, was to enter the 1920s still somewhat ambivalent about the entire complex of questions and issues dealing with Americanization and Polonization. This uncertainty and hesitance must have been fairly widespread. On 21 February 1920, *Zgoda*, Polonia's largest circulation newspaper, shrewdly announced a new editorial policy which was designed to appeal to the best of both worlds; *Zgoda* told its readers that henceforth it would carry certain news items and editorials in both Polish and English. What it did not make clear to its readers was that it would reserve the right to change the substantive content in each respective edition. For example, in its English-language editorial for the day, *Zgoda* stated that—

> It is not sufficient to make America, and all that concerns America, understood to people whom we lead. We must also make these people, their traditions, their past, and their present understood by America. Nothing short of mutual understanding can bring about the desired results hoped for by all lovers of America and Americanism.

But in the Polish-language editorial for the same day, *Zgoda* took the position that—

> The flow of Polish emigration from Europe in the future will almost cease entirely; therefore the aim of the Polish National Alliance will

be to develop on the American soil only, among the youth born and brought up in America, the American Poles. So it is desirable that they early become acquainted with the object of the Alliance through these informational articles, also become used to the *Zgoda*, and slowly become acquainted with its Polish contents. It is a very serious development which interests us all; to "Polonize" is the reason why the English section in the *Zgoda* is coming to life.[44]

This set of editorials—one calling for Americanization, the other for Polonization—reveals the significant changes that had taken place in Chicago and American Polonia during the War for Poland. To *Zgoda* and its readers, Poland as a homeland was now history; the idea of moving back had to be abandoned once and for all. Yet the American environment was not totally acceptable either, nor, for that matter, were Poles acceptable to the nativist Americanizers. In attempting to balance herself delicately on a tightwire which had been rigged by nativists of every kind in the "Tribal Twenties," Polonia came to realize that perhaps the second generation, too, would still be viewed as "strangers in the land." For this reason Polonia was instructing her youth to retain her Polish past and culture. As *Zgoda* wrestled with the issue of dual loyalties, so too would thousands of Polish youth for the remainder of their lives. The effects of being a "hyphenated American," or a second-class American (from the standpoint of nativists), would persist for some time to come.[45]

8

Mundelein and Polonia:
The War for Ethnic Survival

Your archbishop is the one man in this town who is constantly in the spotlight. Shield him as much as you can. Have consideration for him, and he is likely to have consideration for you.

> Installation Address of Archbishop
> George Mundelein, 9 February 1916

It is not the spirit of insubordination but the deplorable neglect of Polish Catholics that prompted their clergy to bring these things to your notice.

> Letter of the Polish Clergy Association
> of Chicago to Archbishop Mundelein,
> 9 July 1917.

From James Quigley to George Mundelein, from Mundelein to Samuel Stritch, from Stritch to Albert Meyer, from Meyer to John Cody—the pendulum of leadership in the archdiocese of Chicago, throughout the twentieth century, has swung back and forth between the Irish-American and German-American hierarchy. This despite the fact that the archdiocese of Chicago housed the largest Polish immigrant settlement anywhere in the United States in 1900; and despite the census tabulations which listed the Poles as Chicago's largest foreign-born contingent in 1920 as well as the largest foreign-stock contingent in 1930; and despite Chicago Polonia's frequent boast that by the end of World War II it was a "Second Warsaw," containing more national parishes than any other ethnic group in the archdiocese. Yet, despite such strength of numbers, no Polish clergyman had ever headed, or ever would come to head, this the most Polish of all Polish sees in the world outside Warsaw itself. In a democracy where sheer numbers were supposed to make a difference, they did not. In an immigrant diocese where it was expected that after two generations of apprenticeship immigrant pastors would be moving on to higher places in the vineyard of the Lord, these immigrant pastors stayed put, seldom moving beyond the rank of monsignor, or permanent rector, or diocesan consultor. From the standpoint of Polonia's clergy then, the American Catholic Church, by the end of World War I, was neither "immigrant" nor "democratic." And the Poles, who had just fought a Great War over the self-determination issue, now were coming to realize that the War for Poland had not been a War for Polonia. The "Fourth Part of Poland," so highly exalted during the war years, from the clerical point of view at least, was now being forced to fend for itself.

Population strength had always been a significant variable in the minds of diocesan consultors when selecting an ordinary for polyglot Chicago. In the late nineteenth century and the first decade of the twentieth, when the Germans and Irish were the first- and second-ranking groups, the overall population strength of these two groups was a key factor in the selection of a bishop or archbishop. But when the Polish group surpassed the Irish and German groups during World War I, the archdiocesan consultors, the majority of whom were still Irish or German, no longer appeared to take the population factor seriously—much to the chagrin of the Association of Polish Catholic Priests. The same lack of support for bringing Polish candidates into the hierarchy which had held back the Rhode nomination for so long now appeared to be preventing Rhode from becoming archbishop of Chicago. In the end, the alleged boycotting of Polish candidates would lead to an open revolt against the archdiocese of Chicago, a revolt initiated by most of Polonia's powerful pastors. Begun during the height of the War for Poland, the war against the archdiocese of Chicago would one day cut across the entire spectrum of Catholic life in this midwest metropolis. Not only that, the ethnic "divide" carved out in the 1915–1920 period would tend to snuff out any organized social gospel movement in the archdiocese in matters not directly related to the process of selecting candidates for archbishop of Chicago.

Since we have already established the primacy of the community-parish in the social life of Polonia, we must now examine and attempt to explain how Polonia went about safeguarding and perpetuating its awesome social and financial commitment to its thirty-eight community-parishes at the end of the First World War. There is little doubt that Chicago Polonia maintained a vested interest in holding the line against encroachment by any nationality group (and later, by any racial or minority group). It is our purpose in this chapter, therefore, to untangle one of the most bitter interethnic struggles ever fought in any diocese in the annals of American Catholic history. Ironically, while the national party in Polonia was giving its all in a great War for Poland which was to eventually lead to its Americanization, the clerical party, the original party of Americanization in Polish Catholic life, was engaging in a struggle for survival which was to result in its permanent Polonization in American life.

"After Ireland no other nation has made such sacrifices for religion as Poland"—such was the viewpoint expressed by the editors of *The New World* in December 1905 when discussing the issue of home rule for Ireland.[1] The observation made by the archdiocesan weekly neatly summarized the relationship of Poles in Chicago to their Irish "superiors" at the beginning of the twentieth century. The spiritual and religious heritage of the Poles, was, to be sure, gaining some recognition by *The New World*'s Irish editors, but, somehow, the Irish contribution counted for more in the minds of the editors, who, in all likelihood, felt the Lord would have agreed wholeheartedly with their position. Polonia, and the other nationality groups in Chicago, would simply have to contend with the idea that, in church affairs (and most probably in political affairs as well), everyone came "after Ireland."

The clerical party in Polonia, especially the Resurrectionists, had never really complained about such an arrangement. The Resurrectionists indeed had, going back to the Foley-Kajsiewicz pact, realistically accepted this "nationality order" of Catholic life. After all, the pact of 1871 had rested on the premise that the downtown Irish chancery was supposed to run the diocese while embattled Polish pastors, like Fathers Barzynski and Gordon, were supposed to run their own parishes. Even when the Holy Cross Fathers came to *Trójcowo* in 1893–1894, they had offered no real challenge to the administrative status quo. And when diocesan priests were ordained outside the Resurrectionist province, or were brought in from the outside to serve in Resurrectionist or other Polish parishes, they were expected to and usually did follow the paths of least resistance to Irish or Resurrectionist authority; most accommodated themselves to a hierarchical arrangement which they were in no position to change.[2]

The fact that Chicago Polonia had never seriously threatened Irish supremacy in the archdiocese was at least partially instrumental in bringing about a general era of good feelings between Poles and the Irish chancery during the Quigley administration (1902–1915). From all outward appearances, the Irish-Polish relationships were relatively smooth throughout the Quigley term. After all, it was Archbishop Quigley who had played a most significant role in arranging for the consecration of Paul Rhode, a show of support which made him an immediate favorite in the Polish community-parishes. Even prior to the consecration of Rhode, it was Quigley who on any number of occasions had expressed his personal concern for the outcome of social welfare projects of special interest to Polonia. For example, the archbishop "who lived poor and died poor"[3] had maintained a lifetime interest in the care for orphans, not only in Chicago, where he was deeply involved in programs designed to procure decent housing for orphans, but also in Buffalo where he had organized fund drives on behalf of diocesan orphanages. So when the Polish parishes of the northwest side began a full-scale fund-raising campaign for an orphanage to be built on North Avenue and 52nd

Street (West), Quigley not only endorsed the project but also issued a special pastoral message on the subject which was then read at all Polish parishes in the city. He also organized an archdiocesan committee, which made recommendations on the proposed orphanage that all Polish pastors later unanimously accepted. Finally, Quigley instituted a parish assessment plan for funding the orphanage, which was then judiciously kept under the control of a community of Polish nuns.[4]

Throughout his administration, Quigley likewise maintained a deep commitment to the overall development of the parochial school system. Between 1902 and 1915, the total number of parochial schools in the archdiocese rose from 166 to 256—a 64 percent increase; and the total number of students attending these parochial schools jumped from 67,321 to 109,162—a 63 percent rise. The Quigley educational program was intended to keep pace with the rising number of students in the Catholic system, and it was a well-known fact that the biggest proportion of the increase came from the immigrant quarters of the city of Chicago.[5]

Of course, whenever another school was being opened, the archbishop could be counted on to take part in the groundbreaking ceremonies, if for no other reason than to share in the community-wide accolades which usually accompanied such school dedications. Such was the case in May 1908 when, concurrent with the official announcement of the appointment of Paul Rhode as auxiliary bishop of Chicago, Quigley was asked to share the dedication platform at St. Stanislaus Kostka with the Vice-President of the United States, Charles Warren Fairbanks. After paying a sparkling tribute to the educational program offered at St. Stanislaus and after thanking the Vice-President for "indorsing the religious education of young people of the United States," Quigley centered his remarks on the containment of the traditional enemies of the community-parish system. In his typical no-nonsense and straightforward style, the archbishop endeared himself to the Resurrectionists in attendance when he stated that—

> Children educated in the environment of the church cannot be disturbed by the agitations of socialists and anarchists. Anarchy and socialism see their doom in Christianity and education, [and] the doctrine of the Socialists that this life ends all will not be accepted by Christianity. Pleasure for the body is not the aim of life. The compliment in life here is in eternity.

But Quigley was not to end his address on this note. He immediately swung his rhetoric around to a topic which had nothing to do with parochial school education, but one which he reckoned would win the hearts of his Polish audience:

> Why don't the nations of this world rise up and protest the oppression
> of Poland by Germany? Why doesn't the American Congress protest?
> Because a great power is the oppressor other nations are silent. Po-
> land will be oppressed, but the nation will not be wiped out. The
> heart of the supreme part of the church is with her in the struggle.[6]

Quigley's surprise oration was, of course, well received, judging from the "thunderous ovation" given by the thousands attending. No doubt his address was tailor-made to appeal to the still-persisting Resurrectionist-Irish chancery alliance, but coming at a time when the Vice-President and other political dignitaries were on hand, the call for action on behalf of Partitioned Poland was especially appreciated by the nationalists in Polonia. Furthermore, the archbishop saw to it that his remarks were carried *in toto* on the front page of *The New World*.[7]

Quigley also played a significant role in bringing about the return of Polish Independents to the Roman Catholic Church. Taking the matter directly to the Vatican between 1908 and 1911, he clarified the procedures for bringing the nationals back into full communion. A Quigley memorandum on the subject emphasized the centrality of forgiveness while eschewing whatever bureaucratic technicalities might interfere with the process of restoration. The archbishop's leniency regarding this volatile subject was probably related to his lifetime work in the Extension Society, a missionary endeavor of the Catholic Church which always stressed tolerance in its dealings with non-Catholics. In any event, Quigley must have found his "middleman" role in bringing back returning Polish nationals most satisfying, especially after *The New World* reported that hundreds of the "schismatics" were making their way back to the fold in Chicago.[8]

But the era of good feelings between the chancery and Polonia could never have materialized had it not been for Quigley's pivotal role in cooperating with the Congregation of the Resurrection to allow for the transfer of Archbishop Joseph Weber to Chicago. Despite the fact that Weber's position in the archdiocese, from a jurisdictional standpoint, was only a ceremonial one (he was appointed titular Archbishop of Derna, Africa, in 1904), he could still have been viewed as somewhat of a rival to Quigley by virtue of his position as Delegate General of the Resurrectionist's North American Province between the years 1909 and 1918. But it was to Quigley's credit that he never opposed, at least openly, any of the prerogatives assumed by Weber, despite the widespread belief that Weber was *de facto* "Polish Archbishop" in the Chicago archdiocese. Besides, Quigley must have known even prior to Weber's transfer to Chicago that Weber's presence alone could easily have resulted in a breakdown of authority in the Polish parishes if all the Polish pastors were to take up parish business with "their" archbishop rather than the Irish archbishop. But such hierarchical competition never materalized during the Quigley years. Quigley was especially gracious in his dealings with

Weber, and the gentlemanly Weber, a quiet, scholarly, and pious individual, was easily able to reciprocate in kind when working with Quigley.[9]

Archbishop Quigley presided over the archdiocese of Chicago during a period of phenomenal growth, one which surely benefited Polonia and other New Immigration settlements. During the Barzynski era, which closely spanned the Foley-Feehan administrations, sixteen Polish parishes had been founded; under Quigley, another seventeen community-parishes were built. But despite the growth, there was only minimal conflict in the Quigley administration as compared to some of the earthquakes shaking the foundations of the Foley-Feehan administrations. Then, too, until Quigley arrived in Chicago, there were no diocesan high schools (although some religious orders maintained high schools prior to 1902). Under Quigley, eighteen diocesan-run high schools were established. Yet there were no instances of any unhealthy competition between the new diocesan schools and those established by the Poles, either at St. Stanislaus or at Holy Trinity (Weber High was not founded until 1930, and Gordon Tech not until 1950). The archdiocese and the Poles were astute enough not to infringe on each other's territory. During the Quigley term also came the building of the Quigley Preparatory and Theological Seminary, which was badly needed to assist in the training of priests for the mushrooming archdiocese. With the total number of parishes having increased from 252 to 326 in Quigley's term, it was expected that the demand for priests would also have to be met. During the 1902–1915 period then, the number of diocesan priests rose from 417 to 496, and the number of religious priests in the archdiocese went up from 149 to 294.[10] Yet, even here, there was no outward manifestation of competition or ill feeling between the diocesan-run theology program or the one administered by the Resurrectionists at their novitiate.

In the final analysis, however, the era of good feelings between Polonia and the archdiocese proved to be without institutional substance; it appeared to rest on the compromising natures of Quigley and Weber. When Quigley grew seriously ill in the early part of 1915, there was naturally a good deal of speculation about his successor. Supporters of Rhode could, of course, be expected to view the succession with anticipation; Resurrectionists, for the most part, appeared hesitant; and the non-aligned priests, especially the newly ordained, were for the most part confused by the political implications and ramifications of the succession. The speculation over a successor, as could be expected, centered around the potential candidacies of Chicago's two auxiliaries—the Irish McGavick and the Polish Rhode. The Right Reverend Alexander J. McGavick had been the first auxiliary bishop ever named to the Chicago archdiocese, his consecration having taken place in 1899, nine full years before the consecration of Rhode. Accordingly, with his seniority in the archdiocese and his Irish heritage, McGavick probably rated ahead of Rhode. Then, too, there was considerable speculation over the possibility that the Right Reverend Peter Muldoon, who had been named (on Quigley's strong recommendation) to head the newly created Rockford, Illinois, diocese, would be brought back to Chicago; after all, Muldoon had been Quigley's right-hand man prior to his promotion, and he possessed an intimate knowledge of the chancery and archdiocesan bureaucracy. As for Weber, his chances were absolutely nil, as the Delegate General of the Resurrectionists was already seventy years old. In any event, the Polish League pastors were still pushing for Rhode's nomination, basing their hopes and considerations on the population factor. Most believed that the Polish immigrant stronghold in the Chicago archdiocese could no longer be ignored.[11]

But Polonia was in for a totally unexpected jolt. On 10 July 1915, after suffering from a variety of ills which began during Holy Week of that year, Archbishop James Edward Quigley succumbed to his bout with paralysis and died. On the same day, the Consistorial Congregation in the Vatican publicly announced that Rhode was being transferred to head the Green Bay diocese, and all Polish clergy in Chicago knew that the era of good feelings had come to an end.[12]

As might be expected, the funeral ceremonies in honor of Archbishop Quigley were most elaborate, equal to those of any chief of state. A special funeral train, carrying the remains of the archbishop, moved slowly from Rochester, New York, where the Archbishop had spent his last days at the home of his brother, to Chicago, where church and civic dignitaries awaited the train's arrival. Once in Chicago, the body lay in state at the Holy Name Cathedral, where for the next three days thousands of mourners paid their final respects.

The Quigley funeral ceremonies were spread over two days. A solemn high pontifical mass was offered on 14 July and a requiem mass was offered the following day. Prominent members of the hierarchy, numerous civil officials and members of at least eight hundred Catholic organizations were in attendance. The general public, hundreds of thousands, lined the streets outside Holy Name and all along the cemetery route. The ceremonies were orderly and majestic throughout, despite the large crowds. Mourners listened to a stream of accolades acknowledging the administrative and organizational genius of their archbishop. In a strange twist of irony, the funeral sermon at the pontifical mass of the 14th was delivered by Bishop Rhode, who was conducting himself with his usual quiet dignity during those last days in Chicago. Rhode's address, which sharply contrasted with the long ponderous oration delivered by Hanna the next day, was simple and brief: "Quigley belonged to no one but God," Rhode told the mourners, "and he became in the highest sense the people's bishop. As the true priest of God he looked upon all races and nationalities as children of God. His main concern was at all times to understand the intent of his flock."[13] With these words, Rhode dutifully went off to Green Bay, where he would serve until his death in 1945; and Quigley went to his grave without ever disclosing whether he had actually recommended the Rhode transfer. In all probability, neither Quigley nor Rhode ever suspected that Chicago would, for the next quarter-century, be headed by someone neither Irish nor Polish.

Even as the city's schoolchildren passed Quigley's coffin to pay their final respects, rumors about Quigley's successor continued to circulate throughout Chicago. Prominently mentioned now were Muldoon, Edmund M. Dunne, Bishop of Peoria, and Archbishop Edward J. Hanna of San Francisco, all of whom were Irish. Since Muldoon and Dunne, together with the Bishops of Alton and Belleville, were the suffragans of the Chicago archdiocese and hence were empowered to submit the final list of three names to the Vatican, the rumors were given credence in the press, by the *Chicago Tribune* in particular. Muldoon and Dunne were rated even, with Hanna not far behind. In fact, Hanna, who had been a boyhood chum of James Quigley, had been invited to Chicago to deliver Quigley's funeral oration. Of course, all of this speculation was still idle, as the diocesan consultors were not expected to meet until after the funeral. Then, too, Chicago had been exposed to surprise selections in the past. In 1902, before Quigley was appointed to head the Chicago archdiocese, the frontrunner had been John Lancaster Spalding, Bishop of Peoria. But Spalding's unorthodox stance on Americanization of immigrants—he favored a more relaxed pace than Archbishop John Ireland recommended—put him in quick disfavor with other Americanizers in the hierarchy,[14] and Quigley was brought in from Buffalo instead. Nevertheless, the point here is that at no time was Rhode mentioned as a potential successor to Quigley outside Polish circles. In fact, most of Polonia received the news of Rhode's transfer from a small "filler" article shoved to the side of page 11 of the *Chicago Tribune*'s July 11 edition. The article merely mentioned the fact that Pope Benedict had authorized the appointment of Rhode to Green Bay.[15] When the news hit the front pages of the *Dziennik Chicagoski*, all of Polonia was understandably taken aback not only by the swiftness of events, over which no one in Polonia, except two Polish diocesan consultors, had any control, but also by the transfer decision itself. With the loss of their beloved Paul Rhode, Polonia seemed to be enduring an even more tragic wake than that of Quigley and his Chicago.[16]

The diocesan consultors, all of whom were "irremovable rectors" in their parishes, convened one day after the burial services. While they were conferring, the Reverend M. J. Fitzsimmons, pastor of Holy Name Cathedral, assumed the position of interim director of the archdiocese. The chairperson of the consultors was none other than A. J. McGavick, the only remaining auxiliary in the archdiocese. The power of selection (the recommendation of three names to the suffragans) still remained in the hands of the Irish bloc. Of the thirteen consultors participating, seven, including McGavick, were Irish, two were English, two were Polish, one was French, and one was German.[17] Working swiftly, the consultors in a matter of days finished their work and passed on the list of candidates to the suffragans, who were then empowered to submit additional names to the Vatican; but the suffragans could not delete the three names submitted by the consultors unless they were willing to state in writing their reasons for doing so. Since the entire process entailed the highest degree of secrecy and confidentiality, it is not known whether the Vatican's final choice was that of the consultors, the suffragans, or a consensus of both bodies. But the matter was decided by 25 January 1916 when the pallium and bulls carrying his formal appointment were received by the Most Reverend George William Mundelein, auxiliary bishop of Brooklyn. Two weeks later, on 9 February the Apostolic Delegate to the United States, Archbishop John Bonzano, formally installed Mundelein as the metropolitan of the Chicago see.[18]

In the six-month period between Quigley's death and the selection of Mundelein, the Poles made what was tantamount to a last-ditch effort to influence the outcome of the selection process. Probably the most overt and most publicized action taken by Chicago Polonia came on 28 July 1915, while the consultors and suffragans were still deliberating. In their "Address to the Apostolic Delegate in Washington X. John Bonzano, D.D.," which was published in *Naród Polski*, the Polish clergy made the following appeal:

Your Excellency:

Availing themselves of the sojourn of Your Excellency in this city, the delegation of the Polish citizens of Chicago is paying you a visit, in these days of genuine sorrow caused by the demise of our never-to-be forgotten archbishop, the Most Rev. James Quigley, and at the same time greet you with hearts sympathetic and truly Polish, and as such, inflexibly attached to our Holy Faith.

At this moment which finds you sojourning in our city, at this hour of grief consequent upon the death of the late archpastor and steward of our diocese, we learn that a singular honor has befallen our Polish community, namely, he who was the late archbishop's right hand, his chosen collaborator and excellent assistant, the Right Reverend Paul Rhode, D.D. is to be transposed from his office to that of bishop of the diocese of Green Bay.

It is indeed a great favor and honor that has befallen the Polish Catholics of America and our Polish community lacks words to express its gratitude to the Holy Father for this signal mark of this paternal solicitude for the interest of our Holy Faith among us. We wish to state that without exception the entire Polish Catholic community is overjoyed because the honor has befallen Bishop Rhode. . . .

. . . while acknowledging our great debt to our Holy Father for the favor which He has so benignly conferred upon us, and while thanking him with all our heart for it, we cannot as loyal children of God's Holy Church permit the occasion to pass without voicing at the same time our fear that here in Chicago, deprived of the care of a bishop from among our own race, who would know us intimately, the interest of our holy religion may suffer.

We number about 350,000 faithful and devoted Catholics and our number is continually growing. Our churches and other institutions are increasing in number. We have 140 Polish priests, 45 parishes and about 35,000 children in our schools.

In general, our religious interests are becoming so complex and important from the standpoint of our present and future growth that we feel in conscience bound to humbly pray your Excellency to remember us in a special manner and we earnestly beseech your Excellency that we be not left without care and guidance of a bishop of our nationality, who will understand our needs and aspirations.[19]

The appeal to Bonzano was extremely moderate in tone as compared to some of the bombshells dropped on the American hierarchy by Kruszka at the turn of the century. There is little question also that the appeal had been a face-saving gesture on the part of Polonia, as the Rhode transposal was being viewed here as a "promotion." On the other hand, the point of the address was clear: the drafters made claim to Chicago Polonia's great numerical strength, which they knew could not be matched in institutional terms by any other ethnic group; and the selection of a Polish bishop, whether a metropolitan or auxiliary (the appeal left the door open on this matter), was still viewed as of vital importance to the future of Catholic Polonia. In effect, the appeal called for not only a recognition of cultural pluralism but also of structural pluralism in the archdiocese of Chicago.[20] The appeal to Bonzano failed, but it was only the first shot fired in a war against an archbishop who had not yet even arrived.

George William Mundelein's credentials for the position of archbishop of Chicago were superb. He possessed all the requisite educational qualifications for the post, and then some; his personality and nature exuded confidence and decisiveness; he had made all the key personal contacts and friendships, both within the American hierarchy and the Vatican, that were considered to be important for gaining high office in the Church, although Mundelein probably would have risen up the hierarchical ladder without benefit of these contacts anyway. Besides all this, Mundelein was energetic, and he was very young in comparison to his colleagues in the hierarchy. But then George Mundelein had always been very young when he accomplished anything of importance to himself or the Church. In fact he was the youngest bishop ever consecrated up to his time in American Catholic Church history: at age 37 he was made auxiliary bishop of Brooklyn, and he was only 43 when consecrated archbishop of Chicago. Born on 2 July 1872, Mundelein was one of nine children born into a poverty-stricken Lower East Side New York family. But he rose above the squalor of tenement life by throwing himself wholeheartedly into his studies. From the first day he set foot in St. Nicholas parochial school, Mundelein proved to his teachers that he was going to get an excellent education, and do so quickly. Finishing an accelerated program at St. Nicholas and at De LaSalle Institute, the latter a Christian Brothers school, he enrolled at Manhattan College, where he startled the faculty by cutting through the curriculum in record time. He graduated from Manhattan at the age of 17. Rejecting an opportunity to attend the U.S. Naval Academy at Annapolis, Mundelein instead chose to enter the Benedictine seminary of St. Vincent in Latrobe, Pennsylvania. At this point, the teenaged Mundelein was only eight years away from becoming the chancellor of the Brooklyn diocese! How he managed to accomplish this would be a story in itself. To summarize, however, the energetic Mundelein graduated from St. Vincent's at age 20, but because canon law prevented a seminarian from being ordained until age 24 he was forced to wait another four years before taking Holy Orders. In the meantime, because of his outstanding scholastic record, he was admitted to the Urban College of the Office of Propaganda in the Vatican to continue his studies. Here he came under the tutelage of Bishop Charles McDonnell of the diocese of Brooklyn. Ordained in 1896, Mundelein returned home to Brooklyn as McDonnell's personal secretary. The following year he was appointed chancellor of the diocese, an incredible accomplishment for a newly ordained priest. Possessor of the Doctorate in Sacred Theology, *honoris causa*, from the Propaganda of Faith, Mundelein was also the only American member of the Academy of Arcadia, a cultural society devoted to the study of ancient language and literature, of which he remained a lifelong member.[21]

In 1906, the fast-moving Mundelein was raised to the rank of domestic prelate, holding the titles of Right Reverend and Monsignor. Three years later he was named auxiliary bishop of Brooklyn and titular bishop of Lorima. Upon his appointment to Chicago, an editor of *World Magazine* acclaimed the new archbishop as a true renaissance figure: Mundelein was cited as an artist, a trained diplomat, an able financier, a profound scholar, and most importantly, a gentleman. On the other hand, his tightly drawn appearance and intense face suggested a sternness and a stubbornness which signalled to those nearby that the archbishop was a born fighter; *World Magazine* also commented that Chicago's archbishop was "a militant prelate, who never seeks a fight, but who never evades one, and who has never lost one."[22] Chicago's new archbishop also brimmed over with self-assurance. Upon hearing the news of his appointment, he told his friends: "I am going there [to Chicago] full of courage, full of hope, full of confidence. I am not going to fail. . . . I am just old-fashioned enough to believe that God can do what He wants to, as He wants to, and through whom He wants to; and I am just an instrument in His hands now to do what He wants to do."[23] These are certainly the words of a man of faith.

In his inaugural address to Chicago's clergy at the formal installation ceremonies on 9 February 1916, Mundelein clearly outlined the tone of his forthcoming administration. Quickly drawing a distinction between himself and Quigley,

George Cardinal Mundelein, first cardinal of the Chicago archdiocese, 1924 (Chicago Historical Society)

Mundelein stated that "I am different from the late archbishop—the Lord cast me in a different mould." Elaborating, he pointed out that "Perhaps I am quicker in grasping a thing; and I am likely to act more quickly . . . and if I seem to hurry you a little when you call, it is not that I am not interested in you, but perhaps because other things may be waiting, and waiting impatiently."[24] Judging from these remarks, it must have been clear to Mundelein's audience, many of whom were priests, that the archbishop was a man who always hurried. And judging from the rest of his speech, it must have been equally clear that the archbishop would have little patience with priests who were not going to be organization men. "I am going to make mistakes," he told his audience, "but I am your archbishop, and I look to my priests to cover up my mistakes, not to expose, discuss or criticize them. For to whom else can I look for such consideration?"[25] It was in such fashion, then, that Mundelein warned the clergy of the Chicago archdiocese that he was an extremely sensitive individual.

Mundelein's installation banquet was held the following evening at the University Club in Chicago. Attended by hundreds of civic and church notables—the Governor of Illinois; several university presidents; numerous judges, politicians, and corporation executives; church leaders of many denominations; as well as members of the American Catholic hierarchy—the banquet nearly turned into tragedy. Known as the "poisoned soup banquet," nearly one hundred guests were stricken with severe stomach cramps, vomiting, and diarrhea. After finishing with the opening course of bouillon, many were sent scurrying for the exits and nearby restrooms. Among those taken ill were Bishop Muldoon, the Reverend John Whelen, editor of the *Brooklyn Tablet*, and numerous other church and civic guests; but Mundelein and the guests at the head table were spared. A later investigation showed that arsenic had been placed in some of the food vats, supposedly by a disgruntled anarchist, who, in a series of letters to Chicago's newspapers, stated his intent to rid the state of Illinois of its corrupt political and religious leadership. The Chicago police department conducted a lengthy search for the criminal and made several arrests, but the case was never solved nor the culprit apprehended. But rumors of plots to rid the nation of its entire religious leadership and to blow up churches in Chicago circulated for weeks after the banquet.[26]

After such an auspicious beginning, Mundelein began the process of coming to terms with the ethnic pluralism in his diocese. In the early stages of his administration, perhaps borrowing a chapter from Quigley, he made several sustained efforts to pacify some of the discontented elements in smouldering Polonia. The archbishop's first opportunity to placate the Poles came during March 1916, when Polonia was still in the initial stages of organizing the *Fundusz Narodowy Polski*. The archbishop, just as his predecessor had done on many occasions, made use of *The New World* to advertise his concerns for Polonia. On 24 March, for example, the archdiocesan weekly carried Mundelein's pastoral letter on the subject of war relief under a page-one headline "Archbishop Appeals for Polish Race." Beneath the headline, Mundelein, in a highly emotional text, stated his appeal:

> To us, who are living in peace and comfort and security, it seems almost incredible that countless lives have been squandered, that hundreds of thousands of families have been made fatherless, rendered homeless, reduced to starvation and beggary. And more par-

ticularly the smaller and weaker nations, that lie in the path of contending armies, have suffered untold misery. None more so than poor
unfortunate Poland. . . . Stricken, crushed, bleeding from every
pore, literally dying from hunger and want for help. . . .[27]

Not only was *The New World* instructed to carry the archbishop's magnanimous plea, but also to print additional reports on the subject of war relief submitted by Cardinal Gasparri, papal secretary to Pope Bendict XV; finally, a "Letter
of the Polish Bishops to the Prelates of the Catholic World," signed by eighteen
members of the hierarchy in Poland, was featured prominently.[28] The response to
Mundelein's appeal was most generous: $50,335.93 was reported to have been
collected in the archdiocese for the Polish Relief fund.[29] Mundelein, to show his
personal concern, mailed two separate checks of an undisclosed amount to Reverend Ladislaus Zapala of the Congregation of the Resurrection for Polish war
relief.[30]

Continuing to foster better relationships with Polonia, Mundelein, again taking a page from the Quigley administration, aggressively sought support for child-
care institutions, a subject which always brought out the best of intentions and
effort in Polonia. The archbishop consistently took the position that the state had
a responsibility to adequately finance orphanages, even if they were not non-
sectarian, as all children were beneficiaries of such institutions. Even when the
state failed in that responsibility ("the cold soul-less care of the state"), he, the
archbishop, would "take the place of father and mother until they grow old
enough to take care of themselves." Even if "the great State of Illinois and the
rich city of Chicago do not contribute a penny" toward the support of orphans,
he, the archbishop, would "manage somehow." Mundelein's pastoral went as far
as to claim that the archbishop would even "beg from door to door" for the orphans, "for their little souls are on his conscience and for each of them he must
one day answer at the judgment seat."[31] Of course, such simply worded and moving pastorals resulted in enthusiastic support for child-care institutions throughout
the archdiocese, especially in Polonia where Mundelein's pastoral was issued in
specially printed leaflets published in the Polish language. Furthermore, his pastoral was read in Polish in all of Polonia's parishes on 9 February 1917. In the
Back of the Yards Polonia, which contributed heavily to the support of Angel
Guardian Orphanage, Mundelein's support was well received.

Mundelein likewise enthusiastically endorsed the Liberty Loan drive in the
archdiocese of Chicago during World War I, a drive which most Poles felt com-
plemented Polonia's other national aspirations. Mundelein stated in regard to the
Liberty Loan drive that "the Church feels it a positive duty at this time to aid the
nation in every way that it possibly can in return for the peace and liberty that
the Church has always enjoyed in these United States."[32] Polonia's parish system
of course took this drive as seriously as all the others it had set in motion: St.

Stanislaus Kostka, for example, sold 867 bond subscriptions totalling $114,450; St. Hedwig's surpassed even this, with 900 subscriptions for $230,000; Sacred Heart registered a total of $103,250; Holy Trinity, another $79,300; St. John Cantius, $57,800; St. Mary of the Angels, $45,000; and St. Stanislaus Bishop and Martyr, $36,550.[33] Many of the Polish parishes in poorer areas of the city could not match the total subscriptions or dollar amounts reached by the larger parishes, but, overall, the exceptional cooperation between the chancery and the Polish parishes during the Liberty Loan drive reflected a closer sense and spirit of accommodation between Mundelein and the Polish pastors.

The war in Europe also gave Mundelein other opportunities to strengthen his ties with the Polish pastors. When the head of the Navy Chaplain Bureau inquired about the patriotism of Polish pastors during the war, Mundelein replied that "I doubt if there is a single Pole, at least in this district, that is in the slightest pro-German." However, at the same time, while recommending Fathers Grembowicz and Koralewski to the War Department as chaplains, Mundelein let it slip that he was not always pleased with the patriotic efforts of the older pastors: "Grembowicz and Koralewski . . . are all [representative] of the younger clergy and, besides, knowing the Polish language well they are more strongly imbued with an American spirit than the older Polish pastors here."[34] Mundelein also made sure that these "younger clergy" were recognized for their bravery in the war. In a special issue devoted to Catholic chaplains from Chicago, *The New World* designed a highly decorative front page for its issue of 8 March 1918: photographs of honored chaplains were surrounded by strategically placed stars, giving the effect of unquestioned patriotism. Prominently displayed were pictures of Grembowicz and Koralewski, and alongside these two was a picture of the war-hero chaplain, Father Francis Kulinski, who later became pastor of St. Florian's parish in the Hegewisch Polonia. When Peter Wojtalewicz was killed in action on 7 December 1917, reportedly the first Polish-American soldier from Chicago Polonia to be mortally wounded, Mundelein sent a letter of condolence to the family and to the parish pastor of the Wojtalewicz family. Such personal gestures on Mundelein's part were intended, to be sure, not only as genuine recognition of Polonia's contribution to the war effort, but also to help instill a more humane and personable image of the archbishop on the local level.[35]

The archbishop was also gravely aware of the financial strain placed on the Polish community in Chicago during the war. When the General Secretary of the Catholic Extension Society, the Reverend E. B. Ledvina, complained to Mundelein about the alleged lack of support in Polish parishes for Extension Society work (which had been a pet project of Mundelein throughout his administration), the archbishop wrote Ledvina the following note: "The Polish parishes are collecting now, and have been for some time, for the difficult [sic] funds to aid the sufferers of the war in Poland. That is practically taking up all of the charitable endeavors of the people here in the various Polish colonies, and I believe the priests themselves have been very generous towards this good work." Yet, so as not totally to discourage Ledvina, Mundelein promised that he would approach the Polish pastors on the subject "to let the seed sink in and perhaps bring later fruit."[36]

Such gestures, some public and some private, indicated that the archbishop was genuinely sympathetic to the Old World aspirations of Polonia during the war. But despite all such work and pastoral cajoling on Mundelein's part, some of which may indeed have been oriented to public relations, he was simply unable to stave off every challenge, some of which were calculated and deliberate, thrown his way by the Polish pastors. No matter what, the archbishop was never able to live down the Rhode "transposal" to Green Bay. Throughout the War for Poland, there were numerous points of contact and cooperation between the chancery and the Polish parishes, some of which we have already pointed out. Yet, simultaneous with some of Mundelein's peace talks with Polonia, many of the older and more established pastors insisted on conducting a guerilla campaign all their own, designed to subvert the Mundelein administration. Oddly enough, these pastors took strength from the re-convocation of the Association of Polish Priests, which had been called into session by Rhode (just prior to his transfer) and Bishop Kozlowski of Milwaukee. The meeting of the Association of Polish Priests, held in Buffalo in January 1915, led to the formation of the Polish Clergy Association Number One of Chicago, to which nearly every Polish priest in the archdiocese belonged. From the Chicago Polish clergy local came Mundelein's most serious challenge on issues related to the process of Americanization in the Catholic Church. The Polish Clergy Association Number One initiated a five-year campaign designed to put an end to Mundelein's Americanization program in the archdiocese of Chicago, a campaign that eventually would call for direct intervention by the Vatican.[37]

But as in all the other Polish campaigns in the 1870–1908 period, the major issues were almost always camouflaged by a host of seemingly insignificant ones. The first of such tests between Mundelein and Polonia had to do with the introduction of a particular edition of a catechism into the parochial schools in August 1916. Just prior to the opening of the school term that year, the Diocesan Commission on Education, members of whom were directly appointed by Mundelein, introduced a Polish translation of Deharbe's *Catechism* for use in Polish schools. The move to introduce the Deharbe version was prompted by Mundelein's insistence that uniform standards of instruction be applied to all parochial schools in the Catholic system. The Deharbe *Catechism* had already been widely used in Europe, particularly in Germany, and had been used in many dioceses in the United States ever since its introduction in 1850. Written by Joseph Deharbe, the famed Jesuit theologian (1800–1871), the *Catechism* was noted for its clarity, precision, and orthodox theology. Despite the fact that later catechists would criticize the work for its rather heavy use of theological abstractions, which often created a good deal of confusion in the minds of young children, the *Catechism* nevertheless was approved by the Diocesan Commission on Education and given Mundelein's formal stamp of approval. Unfortunately, the Commission membership, either through oversight or design, never included the leading Resurrectionist theologian and catechist Reverend Felix Ladon.

Father Ladon had devoted his entire priestly career to catechetical instruction of Polonia's second generation. Of all the Resurrectionists in the Chicago province, Ladon was by far the most competent to deal with matters relating to the religious curriculum in schools. In any event, when the Deharbe *Catechism* was issued for use that autumn, Ladon, no doubt miffed at being left off the Education Commission, challenged the *Catechism*'s use in the Catholic parochial schools. Ladon charged that the Deharbe Polish version was replete "with errors and mistakes." The angry Resurrectionist then produced his own edition and had it privately printed and circulated in the Polish Catholic schools. Ladon included in each copy of his revised edition a letter to the effect that the Commission's selection of the Deharbe *Catechism* had been a serious and horrendous mistake. As he later explained: "When news was announced that the School Commission had made such unfortunate selection [*sic*], my fondest hopes were blasted. I could not realize how such a selection could be made. I was as shocked [*sic*], and this of course drove me to an act which might be judged indiscreet and perhaps would not be done on mature consideration."[38] But this contrite explanation came only after Mundelein brought pressure to bear on the Resurrectionists.

What had really provoked the archbishop was the fact that Ladon had enclosed his explanatory letter with the revised texts *prior* to the time Mundelein received a text of the letter. Furthermore, it later came out that Ladon had acted unilaterally, never consulting anyone either in his own congregation or in the chancery office. For this breach of ecclesiastical discipline, Mundelein informed Archbishop Weber, Ladon's superior, that the Resurrectionist catechist was to be suspended from his priestly faculties until he "recalled the circular letter . . . , made proper reparation for the scandal caused, and [made an] apology for the disrespect he has shown to ecclesiastical authority."[39] To this communiqué from Mundelein, Weber calmly responded that Ladon had indeed apologized for his disrespect to the ordinary, and that he (Weber) awaited further instructions on the matter.[40] The incident was brought to a close when Ladon personally apologized to Mundelein for his improprieties. Ladon stated that "the action was not proper, still it was done with the best of intentions for the good of Polish schools and the Church without the slightest intent of disrespect." He then offered his "profound apology" and assured Mundelein of his "sincere and profound respect, loyalty and submission."[41]

The most significant effect of the Ladon affair, aside from the catechetical implications, was that Mundelein, without warning, had challenged a leading member of the Congregation of the Resurrection, and had dismissed Ladon without having consulted first with Weber. Despite Weber's prompt and courteous reply, Mundelein's stern stance could be interpreted as a major shift in the chancery's dealings with the Resurrectionists. To Feehan or Quigley, such a matter as the suspension, however temporary, of a Resurrectionist priest would not have come about had not the Superior-General of the Congregation first been notified and then agreed to such a drastic penalty. The Ladon *Catechism* incident leads one to the inescapable conclusion that Chicago's new archbishop was not going to take seriously any previous "pacts" made by his predecessors.

But the Ladon incident, which occurred within six months of Mundelein's installation, was only the beginning of a silent, bureaucratic war between Polonia's pastors and the archbishop, a war that quite understandably was never brought to the public's attention via the pages of *The New World*. An even more severe challenge to Mundelein's supremacy and authority came in the early spring of 1917 over an issue that was more directly related to the survival of the community-parishes—the issue of money. In March, Mundelein became involved in a campaign to subsidize orphanages. The public side of his campaign, as we have seen, met with general approval. Beneath the surface of the fund-raising drive, however, there was an intense power struggle over which funds or sources of funds the archdiocese might tap. Since one of the largest orphanages in the archdiocese, the St. Hedwig's Home for Dependent Children, was administered by the Polish community-parish network, Mundelein felt that some of the revenue to run the home should be raised in Polish quarters. But since Chicago Polonia was already so heavily engaged in the *Fundusz Narodowy Polski* and the Liberty Loan drives, both of which Mundelein deeply supported, the archbishop was already looking to other sources of funding. He chose the archdiocesan surplus cemetery fund, a fund to which Polonia had always contributed heavily, as the Polish parishes maintained their own cemetary in Niles, Illinois. Mundelein also, perhaps ill-advisedly, suggested a three percent tax to be levied on all gross incomes of the Polish parishes in Chicago. Mundelein might have expected this move to be opposed by the larger Polish parishes, who were already heavy contributors to their parishes via Sunday collections. In any event, the chairman of the archdiocesan cemetery fund was none other than Father Francis Wojtalewicz, pastor of the powerful Immaculate Conception parish on the far south side. In a meeting which the archbishop was unable to attend, Wojtalewicz used his veto powers to overturn a motion which would have allowed the archdiocese to use the surplus cemetery funds. Furthermore, Father Francis Gordon and Father John Obyrtacz of the Resurrectionist Congregation strongly opposed and defeated a motion to impose the three percent tax. The Resurrectionists argued that since taxes on gross incomes ordinarily included separate building funds then being collected at St. Stanislaus Kostka, St. Hedwig's, St. Mary of the Angels, and St. Stanislaus Bishop and Martyr, the archdiocesan revenue project would seriously interfere with Resurrectionist expansion. Besides, the Resurrectionists argued that building funds had been considered by previous administrations in the diocese to be ineligible for taxation, since if parishioners discovered that contributions were being taxed they might be discouraged from contributing at all. Other complaints registered by pastors in poorer parishes supported the Resurrectionist motion, but for different reasons. The pastors of Immaculate Heart of Mary and of St. Stephan claimed that their parishioners could "scarcely breathe from the burden of debts and the struggles for existence" already imposed on them. However, these pastors argued that the larger parishes, such as St. Mary of Perpetual Help in Bridgeport or Immaculate Conception in South Chicago, should make some effort to share in the cost of running the orphanage.[42]

How the matter was eventually resolved was never made public. Some parishes arrived at a compromise. Holy Trinity, under Casimir Sztuczko, pledged to support a certain number of orphans each month.[43] Whether the other parishes followed the Trinitarian suggestion is largely speculative. But to put the seemingly minor surplus cemetery fund in perspective, it was an accumulation of just these kinds of issues which provoked the Polish pastors into taking even stronger action on more relevant concerns of theirs in the near future.

The first major explosion between the archbishop and Polonia's clergy came on 9 July 1917, when sixty-eight prominent Polish clergymen submitted a lengthy list of grievances to Mundelein. The group of sixty-eight, mostly pastors or assistant pastors, were all members of the Polish Clergy Association Number One of Chicago. Included were such prominent Resurrectionists as Francis Gordon of St. Stanislaus Kostka, Ladislaus Zapala, who by 1920 was elevated to Superior-General of the Congregation, Felix Ladon, and Leo Jasinski, Novice-Master of the Chicago Province and later rector of St. Stanislaus College. Signatories from the Holy Cross Congregation included Casimir Sztuczko, still the pastor of Holy Trinity, A. J. Rozewicz, and Sylvester Hosinski; prominent diocesan pastors included Stanley Nawrocki, an irremovable rector and diocesan consultor, Francis Wojtalewicz of Immaculate Conception, Anthony Furman, a pioneer in Polonia's battle for labor reform, and Francis Kulinski, the war-hero chaplain who would take over as pastor of St. Florian's.

The first grievance spelled out in the petition had to do with the archbishop approving the transfer of "young Polish priests as curates in English speaking parishes." At the time of the petition, the three such actual transfers were said to have "evoked a deep feeling of displeasure and even resentment among the Polish Catholics in the Archdiocese." The Association argued that the transferred Polish priests had indeed "devoted long years of tedious study to master the Polish language and thus be of service to the Polish people, thousands of whom even now are deprived of proper spiritual ministrations." The Association also argued that Mundelein ought to "open up new parishes where Polish priests shall find ample field for sacerdotal labors among their countrymen." Another line of attack pursued by the Association had to do with combatting the pervasive influence of

Americanism in the schools, for only if "efficient schooling facilities [could] be provided to liberate our children from the influence of Public Schools" could "the faith and morals of our children" be preserved. Next, the petitioners called attention to the practice of "non-Polish neighboring pastors" who were conducting both marriage and funeral ceremonies in their respective parishes for Poles "whose catholicity [was] seriously questioned." This "undermining of the faith," the petitioners claimed, "leads undoubtedly to religious indifference." Furthermore, many of the accused priests "would marry and bury even beasts for the sake of filthy lucre." Besides, such "bannless and impromptu weddings . . . are direct roads to the divorce courts."[44]

At this point the petitioners turned their attack on policies initiated by the archbishop. They were particularly upset about the practice "requiring all candidates for the priesthood to continue their studies at the Cathedral College" instead of at their own congregation seminaries. The Association was quick to point out that "while this may be a link in the welding of the chain for so-called Americanization of the youth, it will certainly militate against vocations among Poles, a condition that should not be invited." Next in the long list of grievances was the unanimous dissatisfaction with the way the archdiocesan council was being run. The Polish clergy were annoyed that their official representative on the council, the Reverend Louis Grudzinski, was relegated to being "a mere figurehead." The Association pointedly suggested to the archbishop that "this dreamland creation," referring to the council, be "relegated to the scrapheap." In its conclusion, the petition got to the point: the Rhode transfer was still a festering wound in Catholic Polonia:

> We therefore confidently hoped that your Grace would deign to see this need, as it was seen by the late lamented Supreme Pontiff, or Holy Father Pius the Tenth, and procure the appointment of a Polish suffragan Bishop. In place of this however we hear wafted to us from over the far Atlantic the amazing news—that "among the Polish Clergy of Chicago there is no fit candidate who could properly represent them in the hierarchy of the Church." Need we add that this wantonly inflicted wound pains us almost beyond endurement?

Closing the letter, the sixty-eight signers stated that "it is not the spirit of insubordination but the deplorable neglect of the Polish Catholics that prompted their clergy to bring these things to your notice."[45]

Archbishop Mundelein did not respond to the 9 July appeal of the Polish Clergy Association Number One. There is no record in Mundelein's papers as to why he chose to ignore the matter, but judging from later developments stemming from the original petition, Mundelein only served to exacerbate the tempest in Polonia. A month later, the Association mailed the archbishop a second petition, this one signed by more than one hundred priests. The fact that the second petition picked up more supporters certainly indicates that Mundelein was not handling the situation diplomatically. But when this second petition, too, was ignored, it was followed by a third formally stated appeal, which was accompanied by a personal letter from Father Francis Wojtalewicz, executive secretary of the Polish Clergy Association Number One. Wojtalewicz couched the urgency of the matter in rather diplomatic fashion: "The clergy feel keenly the delicacy of the situation and whilst Your Grace has not yet seen fit to act, they most respectfully pray through their Secretary to learn if possible, whether Your Grace will find it convenient to act on this matter in the near future."[46]

To this third appeal Mundelein finally replied, more than four months after the first petition submitted by the Polish Clergy Association. To show his deep displeasure with the Association, he curtly responded to Wojtalewicz by hurriedly scratching a note on an old calendar pad, as if intentionally to insult Wojtalewicz and the Association. Mundelein's 13 November 1917 response was without question in the same authoritarian spirit of his inaugural message:

> I beg to acknowledge receipt of your letter of yesterday. If a certain petition signed by you and your other members of the clergy did not obtain just the specific results anticipated by them, that does not mean that it has not received due consideration from the archbishop to whom it was addressed. Moreover, some of the principal points touched on in the petition have evidently been disposed of by the Holy See in the new "Codex Juris Canonici", if we may judge from the preliminary notices of the same that have come to us and of which I had been informed at the time.
>
> Finally, you won't mind me saying that I consider it rather indelicate for a portion of the clergy, unmasked, to direct the head of the diocese as to his action with regard to some of his people, for it would argue that he had not the welfare of his people of Polish birth and descent at heart, which I do not think you would for a moment admit.[47]

It is clear from Mundelein's note to Wojtalewicz that the archbishop was going to use his full authority as outlined in the New Code of Canon Law, especially Canon Number 216, to force a showdown with the Polish pastors on the question of continuing national parishes in the face of new regulations regarding the formation of territorial parishes. By February 1918, Mundelein wrote to Weber explaining how he would carry out the revised *Codex* in the Chicago archdiocese. Canon 216 required that "the area of each diocese be subdivided into definite portions or districts. For the Catholic population of each district, there shall be assigned a parish church, and a priest shall govern the district as its proper pastor and take charge of the care of the souls therein."[48] In other words, parishes in the *territorial* sense were seen as "portions or divisions of a diocese, separated one from another by well defined lines or boundaries."[49] On the other hand, in the sense of *coetus fidelium*, or *ecclesia populi*—that is, the principle of a parish church belonging to the people, a principle going back to the Council of Trent— exceptions to the territorial principle could be made. Canon 216 also specified that "without special incult of the Holy See, parishes for the faithful of different languages or nations in the same district shall not be established."[50] However, those national parishes that desired to maintain their *national* status could do so if granted special permission to retain that status by the Vatican. Nevertheless, the ordinary in the diocese still maintained powers within the new *Codex* to recommend whether or not the Vatican should pass favorably on such exceptional petitions submitted by the national parishes. The bishop could still "study the situation, [and] interpret and apply the Roman legislation" as the pastor of his flock. Under the accepted principle that "the bishop is Pope in his diocese," the ordinary could in no way legislate contrary to the new *Codex*, but he still maintained wide powers of interpreting specific circumstances which might be viewed as exceptional.[51] Lastly, and of crucial importance to our discussion here, the ordinary could reassign pastors from national parishes to territorial ones if he so desired.[52] In effect, then, even if a Polish parish managed to maintain its national status (as was the case for Father Grudzinski at St. John of God in the Back of the Yards), the archbishop could still maintain the upper hand in the parish's affairs by threatening to remove "strong" pastors and replace them with more compliant or obedient ones. This is precisely what Mundelein may have had in mind when he communicated his desire to transfer Resurrectionist priests in February 1918.

Francis Gordon, who had been one of the prime movers behind the petition and who had signed all three appeals to Mundelein, was now recommended for transfer to St. Mary of the Angels; Stanislaus Siatka, who had written the only biography of Vincent Barzynski, was transferred to St. John Cantius; Father Obyrtacz was moved to St. Hedwig's; Father Zdechlik to St. Hyacinth's; and Father Swierczek to St. Stanislaus Bishop and Martyr. At the same time the transfers were being approved, Mundelein reminded Weber that each of these pastors was to be held directly responsible for the behavior of his assistants. He expected each Polish priest to demonstrate "the spirit of loyalty that they are expected to show at all times to their superiors, to our Holy Father, to the Ordinary of the diocese and to yourself, their immediate superior." Mundelein closed his letter to Weber with a warning: "Nor will I hesitate to summarily visit any encouragement or even toleration of any spirit of disloyalty in a house by the Rector even to the extent of removal from office."[53] The tone of Mundelein's letter and the fact that it was submitted to the Resurrectionist's Delegate-General, indicate that he was prepared to take a hard line toward any independent movement emanating from the headquarters of the Polish Clergy Association Number One.

In another related move designed to put the independent Polish pastors in line,

Mundelein issued, in 1919, another directive aimed at breaking the conspiracy in Polonia. The archdiocese of Chicago by the end of the war had grown to the point where the archbishop, even if he visited one parish each day, would not be able to visit all the parishes in one year. Accordingly, in order to meet all of the priests at one time, the archbishop depended on a good attendance at the annual retreats. Here the archbishop was able to make known his personal views to his charges in private. Since Polish attendance at these clergy conferences and retreats had been notedly sparse since his arrival, Mundelein informed Weber that he expected one Resurrectionist from each parish to attend the annual retreats. His explanation was that he wanted "to impress on them in my name that they are Religious, and therefore called to a more perfect state of life and for that reason they are expected to be exemplars to their brethren of the secular clergy."[54] It was another way of informing Weber that Mundelein was disappointed with the poor discipline and judgment displayed recently by the Resurrectionists.

Mundelein's letter to Weber, which of course was never made public, was significant not only for the substantive issues it raised but also because it signified that Mundelein was preparing to exert his full authority over and above the influence which had been traditionally exerted by Weber. Of course, as long as Weber lived, Mundelein knew that he would have to deal cautiously with the Polish pastors, especially the Resurrectionists. The reforms calling for the phasing out of national parishes could never be carried out fully without at least the tacit support of Weber. And Mundelein knew this. Despite Mundelein's all too obvious missives to Weber, which were worded so as to convey a feeling of authority, even superiority, the gentleman in Weber's temperament and character never appeared to get ruffled. His return correspondence to Mundelein never contained even a hint of hostility and always stripped the issues at hand of any superficiality and emotion. In one sense Weber may have realized even more than his adversary that Mundelein had been a victim of the historical accident which brought Weber to Chicago in the first place. Although Weber never once boasted about the fact that Chicago Polonia was in effect administered by two archbishops, both he and Mundelein were no doubt conscious of an arrangement which was unique to any diocese in America where Poles predominated. It was mainly for this reason— that Chicago indeed had two *de facto* heads—that both Mundelein and Weber, at least until the passage of the new *Codex*, went out of their ways to defer to each other.

But Mundelein, as always in the past, had youth on his side. When the new *Codex* was being implemented in 1918, Mundelein was only 46 years old, but Weber was 71. The February 1918 exchange of letters between the two archbishops was to be the last; a month later, on 24 March, Weber was dead. His solemn pontifical funeral mass was celebrated by Archbishop Mundelein himself. Weber was buried at the Resurrectionist monastery in the Cragin community area of

Chicago where he had first built the Resurrectionist's North American chapter novitiate. His remains were laid to rest alongside those of Vincent Barzynski, and as the coffin was lowered into the ground Mundelein must have known that most of the national parish system erected by these two dedicated Resurrectionists was likewise going to be buried. The death of Weber indeed was a turning point in the already severely strained relationship between Polonia and Mundelein.[55]

Several months after the funeral, two related incidents, both having to do with parish finances, revealed that Mundelein was making an attempt to tighten the reins on previous archdiocesan policies which had traditionally granted Polonia's parishes a good deal of autonomy in raising funds. The first incident occurred in July 1918, during the peak of the *Fundusz Narodowy Polski* drive. Casimir Sztuczko, whose parish of Holy Trinity remained a national headquarters of sorts for the drive, complained bitterly to the Reverend Edward Hoban, the archdiocesan Chancellor, about the timing of the Archdiocesan Associated Charities Drive, then in full swing, to which all parishes in the archdiocese were expected to contribute. Prior to Weber's death, and prior to the submission of the 9 July 1917 petition, Mundelein allowed parishes in Polonia to handle at their own discretion any archdiocesan fund drives which might have interfered with the favored war drives. But by mid-1918 such was no longer the case. When Sztuczko failed to report results for the Associated Charities Drive, he was reprimanded by Hoban. Sztuczko, in turn, complained that "the majority of our church-going people are too poor to contribute $5.00 annually," which had been the assessment made for Holy Trinity. With nearly 4,000 families, Holy Trinity was expected to contribute nearly $20,000. Sztuczko went on to explain that "lately their poverty was increased by the high cost of living" and that the parish's "able-bodied sons—about 500 in all—serving in the army render them no financial help." Sztuczko also intimated that the vaunted Liberty Bond drives initiated by the archdiocese had been forced on the parishes. "Our church going people are poor," he reiterated, "and they are required, nay, almost forced to purchase the Liberty Bonds." Sztuczko then offered the same explanation regarding the Red Cross and thrift stamp drives, arguing that if his parishioners had not participated in them they would have been branded as "very unpatriotic" or even "unamerican."[56] Sztuczko's position, as the Annual Reports of the Chicago Archdiocese show, was well intentioned and well grounded. In the 1917 fiscal year, for example, Holy Trinity's income was listed at $272,017.98, or roughly $13.00 per parishioner; expenditures were listed as $262,471.66. Thus, even though Holy Trinity had managed a $10,000 surplus for the previous fiscal year, it was undoubtedly in no position to contribute another $20,000 to the Associated Charities Drive.[57]

But charity drives were not the only archdiocesan means for extracting capital from the community-parishes (and all other parishes in the archdiocese, we might add). The tax levy system also took its toll on the hard-pressed community-parishes during the war. In one angry tirade directed at the Chancellor, Casimir

Gronkowski, pastor of St. Adalbert's, attempted to expose inequities in the tax system:

> I suppose you are anxious to know why St. Adalbert's is slow in paying taxes this year? I used to pay them promptly. It is impossible for me to figure out on what bases the parish is taxed, and why this parish consisting mostly of poor people, should pay a higher tax than a larger and richer parish.

Gronkowski further charged that the alleged inequities put him "in a bad light," since he was the one who was actually charged with filing annual reports for the archdiocese.[58]

The Gronkowski charges could of course be documented very easily, as the St. Adalbert pastor had access to all the privileged financial information in the archdiocese. He also knew that the Polish group, although contributing only slightly higher than other ethnic groups per capita, was contributing much higher on a community basis than other ethnic groups in the archdiocese, if only because the Poles were the largest foreign-born group in the archdiocese at the time. It has been estimated that the Poles at the time of the Rhode consecration (1908) were contributing about three and one-half dollars per capita, or over one million dollars per annum, to the support of the church.[59] By 1917, using the taxes paid at *Stanisławowo-Trójcowo* as a base, the contributions were probably well over two million dollars a year. Of course, much of this financial support was derived from the immense fraternal society/church sodality network which had been nurtured by the Polish pastors over the years: St. Stanislaus Kostka had 74 such parish groups by the end of the war, and Holy Trinity had another 70. Most of these also contributed, aside from Sunday collections, through their bingo parties, bake sales, parish bazaars, gift "showers" for the support of teaching nuns, special Easter and Christmas offerings, and a host of other fund-raising functions. Thus, when Sztuczko and Gronkowski used the "poor peoples" argument in their dealings with the archdiocese, despite the heavy working-class population in the Polish parish areas, the Chancellor may not have been convinced. Nevertheless, all available evidence on the subject to this day suggests that the proverbial generosity of the Poles for the church existed only in a *collective* sense. As both Gronkowski and Sztuczko pointed out, even generous Polonia, at least in 1918, was at the limits of its endurance when it came to church contributions. In fact, both the Polish pastors were already articulating what was now commonly circulated by radical socialist groups in Chicago—that Polish priests were getting too "money hungry."[60]

In any event, Mundelein chose not to debate with the pastors of Holy Trinity and St. Adalbert's on this subject at this time. For the meantime, he left these sensitive issues to Hoban, the Chancellor. Mundelein's *laissez-faire* position at this time did not mean, however, that he would not come back another day. Yet, the tone of the Sztuczko-Gronkowski charges should have been sufficient warning to Mundelein that the Polish priests were headed for full-scale revolt. The "Polish Question" in Chicago was near the showdown stage.

Whether the archbishop anticipated a widespread revolt against his administration is still debatable, but Mundelein was always careful to fight the Polish insurgents on his own turf. Just prior to the 1919 annual retreat for the diocesan clergy, he reiterated his earlier position to Weber that "all priests of the Congregation [of the Resurrection] having faculties in this diocese must attend the Annual Retreats of the Clergy . . . unless there is a special retreat for the community which in this case they should attend."[61] Accordingly, based on his earlier directive and this one, Mundelein could now speak to all the priests in the archdiocese, including those who had boycotted these proceedings before. In his retreat address, after having disposed of the subject of the required canonical visitation of all parishes, the archbishop decided to instruct some of the rebels present on the correct interpretations attached to the vow of obedience:

> We must never forget that the Lord fashioned His Church on the pattern of any army. Even the sacraments demonstrate this. The baby that is born becomes a child in Baptism, and is made a soldier, when it grows up in Confirmation. After long training young men become captains in the army in Holy Orders, and in each diocese the head is the bishop, who receives his commission and his authority from above, and not from the priests and people.[62]

Mundelein then stated that by virtue of ordination the priestly candidate gave "a public and solemn pledge of his obedience and loyalty to the bishop." This was a point "we must never lose sight of, [for] the Archbishop or bishop is the spiritual leader, and others must follow him. There must be no individual or group of priests or laymen in the Church, who may depart from the general discipline laid down by him. If they do so contumaciously, that constitutes mutiny, rebellion, and treason to the general body of the Church." The Polish pastors present knew that they were the objects of the archbishop's remarks. But in the very next breath, perhaps hoping to put an end to Polonia's mutiny which had originated with the Rhode transfer, Mundelein tersely announced that the Holy Father was sending "to the Poles, here in their newly made country" his personal representative whom he raised to the rank of nuncio, "something given only to the very old Catholic Kingdoms and empires."[63] If there ever had been a clear signal for a truce, this was it, for the Vatican knew what was going on in Chicago.

Sunday, 4 June 1920, was a very special day for the northwest side Polonia, for on this afternoon Archbishop Mundelein was coming to Polonia to dedicate the church that the Resurrectionists had dedicated to St. Mary of the Angels. It was said to be "one of the grandest in Illinois." Located on the city block bounded by Hermitage, Cortland, Wood, and Bloomingdale, the church was designed to project the awesome strength and boldest aspirations of the Congregation of the Resurrection. The Romanesque structure was in the form of a gigantic cross 230 feet long by 125 feet wide. At the base of the cross was a massive entrance supported by four immense columns and flanked by two steeples which were visible for miles. At the head of the cross stood a huge dome basilica set between two smaller domes. Built for a parish of 12,000, more than ninety percent of whom were Poles, the church was supposed to seat comfortably the entire congregation during a series of six masses which were to be offered each Sunday morning. The pastor of the parish was the indefatigable Francis Gordon, who certainly rivalled the organizational genius of Vincent Barzynski. Bishop Rhode once remarked of Gordon that he was "a Scotsman by name, a Pole by birth, an American by adoption, a priest by vocation, and a persistent, hard worker by his own effort, assisted by Divine Grace."[64] The Rhode tribute could hardly be disputed, for the tenacious Gordon initiated the construction of this showpiece Polish cathedral back in September 1911, during the Quigley administration.

And now, nine years later, the work was finished, and every one of the several thousand Poles who lined the streets outside the church on this cool, cloudy June afternoon was waiting to hear what a German-American archbishop was going to say about a Polish-American church which was certainly more fancy than any church in which the archbishop had ever celebrated a mass. The thousands were hushed as the archbishop moved to the podium, and what they heard was an absolutely magnificent tribute to the Polish Catholic spirit:

> The people in this neighborhood were satisfied to contribute from their slender earnings in order that God's house might rise gigantic, majestic and beautiful, while about it clustered their poorer and unpretentious homes. . . . I congratulate the people of this parish, for among all the churches in this great city, they have added one of the most beautiful. It will stand here as a monument of the zeal, the deep faith and the generous spirit of self-sacrifice of the children of the Polish race in this great city. But more than all we congratulate today the pastor, Father Gordon. It is perhaps the happiest day of his life. . . . There is no man in this diocese that has been more heartily congratulated on such an occasion and there are few indeed who have merited it as much as he. In the few years he has spent here, his record has been one of devotion to his church, love for his fatherland and loyalty to his ecclesiastical superior. But first and above all was his church! . . . You can always know where he stands, he is as solid as a rock. . . . We trust of the future harmonious relations that bind this our country to the Sister Republic of Poland; for which people have indeed given proof of "hands across the sea. . . ."[65]

The archbishop's oratory had never been this splendid, nor had his praise ever been so lavish for Father Gordon, the Resurrectionists, and Polish Catholic priests in general. But what Mundelein did not know that afternoon was that each of the subjects of his affection was already putting the finishing touches on an extensive document outlining the abuses against Polish Catholics in Chicago and the United States, a document which would in another week be mailed off to the Vatican. Prepared by the General Union of the Polish Clergy in America, the same organization which had been reconvened by Bishop Rhode in January 1915, this memorial to the Vatican was the most severe critique of the Americanist hierarchy, Mundelein included, ever submitted by any nationality group in the history of American Catholicism. The secret document, entitled *I Pollachi Negli Stati Uniti Dell' America Del Nord* ("The Poles in the United States of North America") and dated 28 June 1920, was a collaborative effort by the General Union of Polish Clergy and the Polish Embassy at the Holy See. In effect, the *I Pollachi* statement was an attempt by Polonia's clergy to get the Polish government to put pressure on the Vatican to submit to Polonia's demands. At the time *I Pollachi* was delivered, the General Union of Polish Clergy was headed by Reverend Ladislaus Zapala, a leading theologian in the Congregation of the Resurrection and a close personal friend of Gordon, and Reverend Bronislaus Celichowski, a Milwaukee pastor. Working closely with the Polish Embassy, the General Union issued what amounted to a landmark summary of all grievances festering in Polonia since the transfer of Bishop Rhode to Green Bay.[66]

The *I Pollachi* memorial was a highly technical document, containing five major sections, each of which was further subdivided into numerous other categories which carefully delineated the substance of Polonia's complaint. In order to analyze this watershed testament, it becomes necessary to examine each portion of the text separately so as to convey the exact sense and thrust of the whole.

In Section One—the "Introduction" to *I Pollachi*—the drafters first called to the attention of the Vatican an earlier memorial submitted to the Holy See in 1890 which initiated the campaign to select Polish bishops in the United States. So in order "to keep the faith alive" in Polonia and to persist "in the national sentiment which preserves the faith in Poland," the General Union of Polish Clergy in America, thirty years later, was finding it necessary to reinstitute that original demand. *I Pollachi* claimed that despite the fact that Edward Kozlowski and Paul Rhode had been consecrated auxiliaries in Milwaukee and Chicago respectively, the effect of those two decisions "had been minimized" by Rhode's transfer to Green Bay and Kozlowski's death. Furthermore, the impact of immigration on Polonia before and during the war had placed the Poles in America "in a desperate situation." Laying claim to four million Poles in the United States, the General Union and the Polish Embassy demanded that more Polish bishops be consecrated in America "if the faith was to be preserved" and if Poles were in any way to be assisted in adjusting to their new culture.[67]

In Section Two, entitled "The Present Situation," the drafters appeared to adopt almost the same tactic used by Peter Cahensly in his German-American petition to the Vatican; they concentrated on the issue of leakage, perhaps using the issue as a wedge to pry the Vatican loose on some of the demands. It was admitted that since most Poles "had not used the language of the land [English]," they had "to be treated in a very special way by the clergy" or else the Polish masses "would be lost to the Church." The "more than 1000 priests" serving in the "more than 700 Polish parishes in the United States" were not only conscious of the language barriers but also the cultural barriers that made any Polish transition into an "Americanized Church" all the more difficult. The memorial took the position that "the churches built by the Poles were meant for the exclusive use by Poles for their religious, national and social life." This extremely ethnocentric position, whether or not the drafters were aware of it, nearly paralleled that taken by Ladislaus Dyniewicz and the *Gmina Polska* at Holy Trinity in 1873. Nevertheless, the drafters qualified their position when they stated that "the registration of property by the local ordinaries was accomplished without the Polish people realizing that these [their] parishes could serve Catholics of other nationalities." The same held true "for all other real estate" linked to the community parishes.

Next, the memorial launched an attack against "American schools which separate children from their families and their language." Because this was so, Polonia was forced "to establish a Polish Catholic school system which, despite the great sacrifices made . . . did not free the Polish immigrant from paying taxes on the public schools." The memorial then reminded the Holy See that the cost of administering the Polish Catholic school system was in the vicinity of two million dollars per annum, or approximately fifty cents per capita per year. This total cost was cut by some two-thirds due only to "the dedication of Polish teaching nuns . . . who sacrifice their lives for teaching"; were it not for this dedication by the nuns and male religious, the true cost of operating the schools "would be closer to six million dollars per annum." But the sacrifices by the Polish parishioners were made anyway in order "to preserve the faith, the language, the spirit of the family and national customs of Poland" for the 400,000 students in Polonia, 40,000 of whom came from Chicago alone. These students were also required to learn the history of the United States as well as the English language "so that they may become good and intelligent American citizens," but any schoolchildren separated from such vital parish organizations and parochial schools "were usually lost to the Nation and to the Church." The remainder of the section on education contained miscellaneous remarks on Polonia's overall educational and cultural contributions: seven colleges had been instituted at a cost of $750,000 per annum; parishes often offered scholarship programs for these institutions of higher learning; the Poles maintained a national seminary at Orchard Lake, Michigan, for the training of Polish priests, a seminary made necessary "because few Polish candidates were ever sent to Rome"; the Polish parochial organizations maintained a national network of 275 libraries; and all of the educational and cultural institutions were kept alive by a healthy spirit of voluntarism.

Polonia also administered numerous homes for the aged, orphanages, nurseries, and homes for newly arrived immigrants. In addition, Poles buried their dead "in their own cemeteries" where "the poor are even buried for free." These cemeteries were all solvent due to the numerous charitable collections taken up each year, contributions which amounted to more than $100,000 per annum.

In the concluding segment of Section Two, the drafters called attention to the central role played by the Polish Roman Catholic Union in America, which they hailed as a bulwark against "Socialistic elements" that had made frequent attempts to infiltrate the community-parishes; furthermore, the PRCU served as a counterforce to any number of secular organizations which had arisen during the First World War, many of which were "liberal, radical, anti-clerical and schismatic." It was largely to the credit of the PRCU that Poles "were still faithful to the Holy See."[68]

Section Three of *I Pollachi*, entitled "Serious Misunderstandings Between Catholic Poles and the American Clergy," lashed out at the Americanists. Since "American Bishops do not have a clear understanding of the situation of American Poles," the Polish clergy found it necessary to compile a list of "serious misunderstandings": first, the "Americanism of the American episcopate disposes them to look upon Poles with less benevolence"; next, the American bishops were neglecting the education of the Polish clergy by creating difficulties for their entrance into diocesan seminaries, or by failing to institute courses in the Polish language or the history of Poland; third, the "most recent actions of the American bishops are founded on the new Code of Canon Law which recognizes only territorial parishes." In addition, "the various charitable parochial organizations created an intimate spiritual and moral bond with the pastor" whereby "the pastor was acknowledged as the moral leader," but the "Americanization process" worked to the detriment of this bond; instead, the bishops organized charities "into huge diocesan organizations . . . thereby cutting the bond between the pastor and his people." The pastors were thus forced "to administrate a bureaucratic action, totally American"; hence, "poor Poles were cut off from Polonia society" which saw the pastor "lose his moral authority among the people." Because of all this, "relations between the priest and his bishop became all the more material."[69]

Section Four of *I Pollachi* refers to a letter written by Mundelein to his old classmate at the North American College, Archbishop Giovanni Bonzano. The drafters claimed that this letter made their memorial "complete," since it "confirmed complaints made by the Polish clergy." The memorial charged that the letter outlined the entire position of the Americanist hierarchy, one which they feared would soon be implemented. In reference to the Mundelein-Bonzano communiqué, the Polish Embassy in the Vatican wished to make two observations: first, "it is evident that the archbishop in question is *American* to excess and that he does not see why a government which has proclaimed the separation of church and state should have the right to become involved in the question of nominating bishops. It should be stated that the duty of the archbishop is to defend rather than oppose the nomination of a Pole." Next, after arguing strongly that the Polish government should bring pressure to bear on the Holy See in order to have Polish-American candidates consecrated bishops, the Embassy lashed out at some of the comparisons made by Mundelein which put the Poles in an unfavorable light. "The nations cited [Irish and German] are hostile to Poles," the Embassy charged. Perhaps it would be best if Mundelein overcame his fears and chose a Pole as suffragan for the archdiocese of Chicago. Then the Embassy denounced Mundelein for taking the position that Poles had indeed been guilty of pogroms in the Ukraine during the war years. The Embassy concluded this segment of its argument with the claim that Mundelein's charges against the Polish clergy in Chicago "had nothing to do with the issue at stake" in the memorial, for the only important matter was "the fate of 4,000,000 Poles in the United States." Besides, the Embassy pointed out, there was "nothing extraordinary about dissent among 1,000 priests."[70]

Section Five of *I Pollachi* contained the "Postulates of the General Union of Polish Clergy in America." Here the General Union stated that "the theory broadcast . . . that after the Resurrection of Poland, the Poles be Americanized . . . be categorically denied as unjust." Under no circumstances was the "Catholic Church through its bishops to become the instrument of Americanization among the Polish immigrants." But to assure that such efforts at Americanization be brought to a halt, the General Union was advocating the direct intervention of the Polish government in these critical matters because "the supreme authority of the Catholic Church comes over the actual politics of the American hierarchy concerning the welfare of the Polish clergy and immigrants." Accordingly, the Union was authorizing the Reverends Celichowski and Zapala to bring to the attention of the Holy See four demands:

1) that Bishop Rhode be assured an appointment to an archdiocese where a great number of Poles reside.
2) that auxiliary bishops be named in Chicago, Boston, Detroit, Philadelphia, Scranton, Pittsburgh, Buffalo and Milwaukee.
3) that in seminaries in archdioceses where there are great numbers of Poles, a curriculum of Polish literature, culture, and history be instituted, for priests and nuns.
4) that the American hierarchy ought to be "scrupulous" in its application of the new *Codex*, maintaining the rights of immigrants and taking into regard the foreseeable exceptions to this Code.

These conditions, once granted, would "contribute much to the amelioration of differences between the American hierarchy and the Polish parishes."[71]

Despite the fact that *I Pollachi* was the most comprehensive statement ever issued by the clergy in American Polonia, that it was supported by a strong consensus in both the clerical and lay constituencies in Polonia, that it was well researched, adequately written, and supported by documentary evidence with which even the Polish Embassy in the Holy See was much impressed, and that both the General Union and the Polish Embassy wielded a good deal of political clout, the testimonial failed on all counts. Perhaps the failure of the document was due to its uncompromising ethnocentrism, or its embarrassing use of the Mundelein-Bonzano communiqué which hinted at conspiracy in high places in the church, or its perhaps unreasonable call for the immediate consecration of Polish-American bishops in eight dioceses, or its call for the return of Rhode to Chicago ("an archdiocese where a great number of Poles reside")—or a combination of all these factors. But more than anything else, the issuance of the *I Pollachi* memorial to the Holy See in June of 1920 must be judged as a serious blunder. The timing of the memorial is what, in the end, most probably defeated it. Except during his elevation to the College of Cardinals in 1924, Archbishop Mundelein was never more popular in the eyes of the hierarchy and the general Catholic populace (outside Polonia, of course) than in June 1920. It was during this particular month and year that his achievements were genuinely and almost universally recognized.

It was in June 1920 that the archdiocese of Chicago celebrated its diamond jubilee anniversary. The event brought to Mundelein's "western metropolis" a host of church celebrities—James Cardinal Gibbons, fourteen archbishops, and forty bishops and distinguished clergymen from all over the United States and Canada.[72] This alone was enough to center the spotlight on the embattled German-American archbishop. But this was not all. Mundelein, that June, was also celebrating his twenty-fifth year in the priesthood; accordingly, the diamond jubilee celebration of the archdiocese became directly tied to festivities having to do with Mundelein's silver jubilee. Why the General Union of Polish Clergy chose to submit the *I Pollachi* to the Holy See even while Archbishop Hayes was praising Mundelein "in this his hour of transcendent glory" remains a mystery.[73] One possible explanation is that the General Union was hoping to embarrass the archbishop of Chicago at a time when all American Catholic eyes would be drawn to Chicago. Nevertheless, during this fateful month of June, Mundelein was exploding his boundless energy all over the archdiocese: he attended the St. Mary of Angels consecration; he dedicated Rosary College for women; he announced his intention to build a major theology school, St. Mary of the Lake Seminary, in a posh north suburban area that would one day name its town after the archbishop himself; he authorized a major Associated Catholic Charities drive, the largest ever in Chicago; he was interviewed by the Catholic and secular press on dozens of occasions; he was, more or less, the "darling of the media" during this month. The prelate who was once described as "never having lost a battle" appeared destined not to lose this coming fight with all of Chicago and all of American Polonia.[74]

When Mundelein learned of *I Pollachi*, and with his friend Bonzano closely following every move by the Polish Embassy it could not have been long after the June celebrations, he prepared himself for a no-holds-barred counterattack. Co-ordinating his efforts with the highest levels of the American hierarchy—Gibbons, Archbishop Dougherty of Philadelphia, and Bishop Messmer of Milwaukee—Mundelein issued a blistering rebuttal to *I Pollachi*. In November 1920, a lengthy piece of correspondence reached the desk of Cardinal Gasparri, Secretary of State to His Holiness, Benedict XV: "We the members of the American hierarchy unanimously enter protest," the letter began, "against the interference of any foreign government in the ecclesiastical affairs of the United States." And what followed was a comprehensive attempt to demolish *I Pollachi*:

> The American people in general, and the government of the United States in particular . . . expect the various nationalities, which seek a home here, to become one people, one race, loyal to the government of this country, which welcomes them, protects them, gives them liberty, and. affords them the means of an honest livelihood.
>
> For generations the Catholics of the United States have repelled the unjust accusation of disloyalty to the American Government and of subserviency to foreign potentates. Should it become known that the Polish priests of the United States appealed to the Polish Government to bring pressure on the Holy See in favor of their pretensions . . . the Poles of this country would be accused of unfaithfulness to our Government; and the American Church would be charged with subjection to foreign powers. Non-Catholics would calumniate us as hindering the unification of the Nation, and as cooperating in the political aims of foreign nations, with whom our country may one day be at war. The consequences would be serious for the Catholic Religion.[75]

The rebuttal went on to deny that there had ever been "a single case where any discrimination was ever shown by an American Bishop or Bishops against any Polish priest or layman. . . ." It then charged that Poles had operated a propaganda bureau in Washington, D.C., during and after the war designed to mute protests regarding pogroms in the Ukraine, and when public protests were organized in Jewish quarters protesting the bureau, "not a single American Bishop was warned by the Poles or asked to participate. It almost seems that they were willing that the bishops should fall into this trap and that they were not interested in what the bishops might say." Moreover, the rebuttal stated that "the Poles only form one element of the Catholic population in the United States. . . . The greatest danger, however, for the future would threaten the Church in this country did we ever attempt to propagate the study of the history and traditions of every element that goes to make up our population, and even greater danger lies in any attempt to show favoritism to one people like the Poles." The hierarchy then flatly denied that there had ever been a "disposition on the part of any American Bishops to "Americanize" any of the existing Polish parishes." They also refuted the notion that all Poles in America were immigrants; the second generation, the rebuttal emphasized, "was American born." If any leakage from the Church was now occurring, it was coming not from the first generation but from the second; and it was due to "the spirit of foreign nationalism" which was costing "the loss of many souls" in that second generation. This was followed by an attack on ethnocentrism in Polonia and on exclusive national parishes which, according to the hierarchy, were in clear violation of the spirit and the law of the Third Plenary Council; furthermore, this exclusivism in Polonia was responsible for the Polish National Catholic Church schism.

Then, in response to the charge of "Americanism" raised in *I Pollachi*, it was claimed that "the so-called Americanism of the American Bishops proved of tremendous value to the cause of Religion during the late war." They, the bishops, in fact "silenced the accusations . . . flung at the Church as a foreign and anti-American institution by bigoted non-Catholics." Because of the bishops' "prudent and united efforts, the Church is more respected in America than ever before."

Next, the demand by the General Union for Polish auxiliary bishops in the eight dioceses was dismissed by the hierarchy on the grounds that this would positively be "a movement toward the complete isolation of Polish Catholics from the American Catholic brethren"; in addition, it would be viewed by Catholics at large as "an attempt to preserve a distinct and separate Polish nationality in the United States." Closing its argument, the hierarchy stated that:

> It will be a disaster for the Catholic Church in the United States if it were ever to become known that the Polish Catholics are determined to preserve their Polish nationality and that there is among the clergy and leaders a pronounced movement of Polonization. . . . In the face of the continual hatred and hostility against the Church manifested by thousands of American citizens, this Polish movement is, to say the least, fraught with great danger to the present peaceful and happy relations between the Church and the American people and government.[76]

If *I Pollachi* was a watershed document in favor of cultural pluralism, then the response of the hierarchy to Cardinal Gasparri was without question as powerful a defense of Americanization as ever submitted to the Vatican up to that time. The *I Pollachi*-Americanization debate reflected just how deep the division was in the "immigrant Catholic Church" over the issue of assimilation. The Mundelein critique was as strong a defense of American homogeneity as the General Union memorial was of ethnic persistence in American life. The General Union, anticipating perhaps the thesis of the historian Handlin, argued that all the "American people" were in effect all immigrants, whereas the hierarchical position clearly stated that the "American people" were somehow distinct from the immigrants.

When set against the broad panorama of events which constituted the "Tribal Twenties," the hierarchy's position likewise clearly indicated the extreme sensitivity of the hierarchy to the forces of nativism in American life. The fact that the hierarchy's statement was largely drafted by a German-American archbishop who must have been bending over backwards to display his own personal loyalty to America against the backdrop of the "war guilt" debate concerning Germany at Versailles is equally significant. Then, too, the Palmer raids and the ensuing "Red Scare," all of which demonstrated a powerful nativist resentment of foreign radicals, surely swayed the judgment and the course of action pursued by Mundelein and the rest of the hierarchy.

But in the final analysis, *I Pollachi* must be viewed as having ended in defeat. To have submitted the memorial in June 1920 was indeed a calculated gamble, and Chicago Polonia and the rest of American Polonia had lost. In no way could this staunch defense of their heritage be perceived as a victory, even a moral victory, for when Archbishop Mundelein received the red hat in 1924, it was only because the Vatican had finally come to endorse the policies of the Americanists. The new *Codex*, with its decided emphasis on the territorial parish, was intended as the cutting edge for forging a church which would let go, however painfully, of its immigrant moorings.

Yet Chicago Polonia was in no position in 1920 to face the inevitable. The price simply was too high. How could the community-parishes simply choose to allow for uprootedness a *second* time? Had the uprootedness of the first generation not been painful enough? Without community-parishes based on a national parish system, it was all too clear to Zapala, Sztuczko, Gordon, and the others that the day was near when the Old World values would collapse under the weight of territorialism. For in a territorial parish structure, most of Polonia's clergy truly believed that the national parish could never survive; and without the national parish, the community-parish, in every sense of the term *community*, would likewise die off. To view all of the preceding as mere ecclesiastical bickering, then, would be a mistake. For the "war against Mundelein" was nothing less than a fight to maintain the ideals of Janski, Semenenko, and Kajsiewicz. The irony in this major clerical struggle of early twentieth-century Catholic America lies in the fact that both sides—Mundelein and the Americanist hierarchy, and the *I Pollachi* supporters—moved with a sense of conviction that they represented the very best in American Catholicism. To Mundelein, the wave of the future was Americanization; to Polonia, there could be no Catholic future without a Polish past.

Polonia's Religious Origins:
The Search for Meaning

The great things of the past which filled our fathers with enthusiasm
do not excite the same ardour in us, either because they have come
into common usage to such an extent that we are unconscious of
them, or else because they no longer answer to our actual aspirations;
but as yet there is nothing to replace them.

Emile Durkheim
The Elementary Forms of the Religious Life

The Polish Catholic Church in Chicago was the end product of a wide variety
of social processes: its powerful immigrant pastors and vigorous, assertive laymen founded the largest urban-ethnic parishes in America and then proceeded to
do battle in most of them; it became associated with the only major schism in
American Catholicism, one which seemed to wreak greater devastation in Polonia
than within the Church; it participated in a massive national campaign for episcopal recognition and an exhilarating and triumphal wartime crusade for an Old
World cause which led to widespread Americanization; and, finally, it drafted a
celebrated, hard-line memorial to the Holy See for a New World cause which
ended in widespread Polonization.

But at the end of two generations of life (and death), what would the religious
turmoil of the 1870–1920 period in Chicago Polonia mean for future generations?
What did all of Polonia's crusades amount to? Which elements coming from this
stormy era would persist into an equally turbulent post–Vatican II generation?
And which elements of Polonia's formative years would remain a throwback to
the era and spirit of Vatican I, when "authority" is said to have reigned supreme?
Finally, how can the many conflicting voices of the Polish, Catholic, urban-
immigrant past still speak to the present—to the more than 150,000 Poles, parents
and grandparents all, who still fight to survive, socially, economically, and spiritually, in the now fading community-parish centers of inner-city Chicago? For
there is no question that this past generation of parents, grandparents, and great-

grandparents have always been true believers in the neighborhood churches they raised up. These "past generations" have given their all to survive in the city, even when fighting daily against the so-called "urban crisis" of the present generation. But their children and grandchildren, nearly 450,000 strong, have long since moved out of the neighborhood. The fourth and fifth generation have abandoned South Chicago, the Back of the Yards, West 19th Street, Hegewisch, and *Stanisławowo-Trójcowo*. They have joined thousands upon thousands of other Old and New Immigration peoples in Niles, Skokie, and Park Ridge, in Evergreen Park, Oak Lawn, and Orland Township, and in dozens more of those post–World War II suburbs where nearly everyone frantically chases about in search of meaning to life in the shopping centers of tarnished affluence. How does a Reverend Vincent Barzynski or a Reverend Casimir Sztuczko speak to fourth and fifth generation Polonia? Just how does an aging president of a local Polish Women's Alliance, or a Holy Rosary Sodality member in *Trójcowo*, reach out to a generation of Polonia whose ties to an immigrant Catholic Church have all but been severed by a pervasive secularism which tempts the young in ways radically different from those in the 1870–1920 period? Indeed, the questions one might pose are endless, for each of America's six million inhabitants of Polish descent formulates them in his or her own way.

In any case, we have reached a point in the narrative where it might be beneficial to outline the general characteristics that made up the essence of the Polish Catholic way of life.

In any Polish Catholic grammar school at the turn of the century, it would have been customary for the teaching nuns to ask students attending catechism or confirmation classes to identify the so-called "marks" or properties of the "true Church." Almost every student, by the time he or she entered the sixth grade, could rattle off the four marks: the "true Church" was "One, Holy, Catholic, and Apostolic." We might adopt here the tactic of Polonia's teaching nuns and outline those marks of the Polish Catholic Church in Chicago and elsewhere in American Polonia which made it somewhat distinctive, or at least partially distinguishable, from other New Immigrant, Old Immigrant, and native-born American churches.[1]

First, it should now be reasonably clear to the reader that, despite the spirit and substance of accommodation to the Irish hierarchy in Chicago that arose from the Foley-Kajsiewicz pact, the Polish Catholics of Chicago, the laity in particular, formed a church of resistance in the 1870–1920 period. This powerful resistance outlook, largely channelled by the national party in Polonia, was directed toward the Americanizers in the hierarchy who remained unsympathetic to a national parish structure in particular, and to the idea of a pluralistic church in general. This spirit of resistance, inadvertently bolstered by the Rhode transfer to Green Bay, even came to envelop, by 1915, the Congregation of the Resurrection, which up to that time had been the bulwark of orthodoxy in Chicago Polonia. This element of resistance to hierarchical and clerical authority, which in many ways was the fountainhead of the radical lay movement at *Trójcowo* and within Independent forces at *Jadwigowo*, in turn dug the foundations for a deeply ethnocentric community-parish structure. One might even hazard the proposition that the numerous religious subsocieties making up the community-parish network in Polonia were among the most ethnocentric ever developed in American immigrant life. Of course, the origins of these elements of resistance and ethnocentrism are traceable to the Catholic Church in Poland, which for more than two centuries has remained a solid bastion of nationalism as well as resistance to secular or governmental authorities which impose their political and cultural will from outside Poland. To use a present-day example, the challenge to authority laid down by the parishioners of the embattled parish of Our Lady Queen of Heaven in Nowa Huta, which has caused no end of embarrassment and difficulty for the Polish regime, is not substantially different from that spirit of resistance which guided the laity at *Stanisławowo-Trójcowo* in 1870–1900. In both instances, the Polish laity, although separated by a century of historical experience, have insisted on a *national* church, in the truest sense of that nineteenth-century term. Furthermore, despite the obvious one-hundred-year separation in architectural styles, the churches in late nineteenth- and early twentieth-century Polonia and the church of Our Lady Queen of Heaven in Nowa Huta still express that unshakable faith of Poles in a religious presence—that mysterious Divine Presence to which humble Polish peasants invariably resigned themselves when all appeared lost. Whether one observes the dramatic, ultramodern lines of the church of Our Lady Queen of Heaven, which absolutely dominates the drab, cold industrial "suburb" built by the government in Nowa Huta, or one drives today along the Kennedy Expressway in Chicago, passing those many aging but impressive church steeples which still manage to dominate the roadway skyline, the message remains the same: the eye, the mind, and the soul of the observer are at least momentarily reminded of something that was once believed to be of primary importance in the life of Polish immigrants. That is, the church was truly the spiritual *and* social center of Polonia (as it still is in Nowa Huta today). To borrow from Durkheim, one might even conclude that these gigantic Polish "cathedrals" in Chicago were the *totems* erected by the Polish immigrant community to separate that which was sacred from that which was profane.[2]

All of these elements, or "marks," of the Polish immigrant church in Chicago and in America—resistance to authority, deep ethnocentrism, and a dominant religious presence—are also interrelated with another significant characteristic which calls for comment here. All of the evidence unearthed so far by historians and sociologists points to the fact that the Polish Catholic Church in Chicago and in other urban-industrial centers of the Northeast and Midwest was primarily a church of the economic underclass in American society between 1870 and 1920. Whereas Riverside can be said to still symbolize Protestant "respectability" in

Holy Trinity Church today (Chicago Historical Society, photo by Sigmund J. Osty)

American religious life, and whereas St. Patrick's in Manhattan has traditionally retained that same aura of "respectability" in American Catholicism (even for the "lace-curtain Irish"), the Polish community-parishes of Chicago and nearby Cicero and Berwyn, especially those which stand on the outer edges of what is today known as the inner city, still retain that primordial character of "working class Catholicism."

Perhaps we are already anticipating findings from a forthcoming volume to this study which will examine the connection between religion and society in immigrant Chicago, but it is not premature to state here that the Polish immigrant in Chicago, especially in the 1860–1900 period, formed the largest underclass of any nationality group in the city and in the archdiocese of Chicago. In the federal census of 1870, for example, out of the entire parish area of *Stanisławowo-Trójcowo* we find that there is no professional class whatsoever; in fact, out of a total work force of 381 workers, only 2 individuals claimed occupations which might be even vaguely termed "professional." One adult male listed his occupation as "architect," the other as "builder-contractor." On the other hand, the most common occupational category listed in the 1870 census, which was not at all surprising, was that of "common laborer," a category within which the majority of adult Polish males would remain for the rest of the nineteenth century (and for the rest of their working lives). Only 14 percent of the total work force in 1870 Polonia was even considered "skilled": there were a few carpenters, cigarmakers, tailors, and clerks. The Polish female work force was no better off: out of a total of 249 "workers," 219 were classified as housewives; the remaining few working outside the home were employed in the garment trade as seamstresses. By contrast, in 1870, 34 percent of the Irish males in Bridgeport were working in skilled occupations, and 60 percent of the German males in Lincoln Park, on the near north side (and across the Chicago River from Polonia), were skilled. By 1900, an entire generation removed from the Smarzewski-Schermann period, the ratio of unskilled to skilled workers had improved considerably in Polonia; but because of the increase in immigration, Poles in *Stanisławowo*, on the near west side in *Wojciechowo*, in the Back-of-the-Yards parish of St. John of God, and in South Chicago still remained at the bottom rungs of the occupational ladder. Based on a comprehensive census sample for each of these primary Polish areas of settlement in 1900, the three highest occupations for Polish males were as follows: laborers (22 percent); garment workers (9 percent); and factory or foundry workers (4 percent). Nor was there much occupational mobility among Polish females in these community areas either; for the sample areas in 1900, the leading occupations listed were garment workers (59 percent), domestic servants (9 percent), and tobacco workers (6 percent). In fact, the census tabulations for 1900 (the last census for which manuscript schedules are currently available) indicate that the Polish working-class was only in the initial stages of entering what might be termed lower-middle-class occupations for that time, such as tanners, moulders, and machinists. But the overall benefits of higher wage rates associated with some of these skilled occupations were not enjoyed until the 1920s, when the fledgling Polish middle class began the process of geographic mobility, or "population succession." It was not until the 1920s that Poles were able substantially to better their housing conditions, which up to this time had been among the worst in all Chicago, by moving up Milwaukee Avenue on the northwest side and down Archer Avenue on the southwest side.[3] But despite social and economic mobility, Polish Catholicism in Chicago would always retain the working-class character of the sweatshops, the steelmills, and the stockyards. Aside from a few Polish parishes built after 1920, the overwhelming majority of community-parishes built by the Poles still stand in the midst of industrial-urban blight and still offer living testimony to the urban underclass origins of Chicago Polonia.

This predominantly working-class character of Polish Catholicism in Chicago was, of course, directly related to its largely foreign-born character, for the Polish Catholic Church, well into the 1950s, was a foreign-born and foreign-stock church. In 1900, a sample study based on 15,100 Polish immigrants in Chicago showed that nearly 3 out of every 5 Poles in Chicago emigrated to the United States *after* 1885. In other words, 60 percent of the Polish population in Chicago at the time of the Independent schism could be classified as newcomers.[4] By 1920, the foreign-born element in Polonia still prevailed in every major community area: in West Town, the heart of the northwest side Polonia, the total Polish foreign stock was 115,000 out of a total foreign stock of 210,000; in the Back of the Yards, the Polish foreign stock was 31,000 out of a total 75,000; in South Chicago, it was 18,000 out of a total 32,000. As for the city-wide totals in 1920, Poles made up 280,000 out of a total foreign stock of 650,000. In fact, as late as 1960, each of the four primary areas of settlement in Polonia (those founded before 1900) as well as the nine other secondary areas of settlement (those founded after 1900) still retained their predominantly Polish foreign-born and foreign-stock character.[5]

There is no question that the predominantly foreign-born and working-class "marks" of Polish Catholicism in Chicago were directly related to the forms of religious worship that were adopted by the "urban villagers" in each of their community-parishes. The rhythm of the liturgical calendar to which all of Chicago Polonia marched was solidly Old World until the time of Vatican II. Whereas the Irish Catholics had been the recipients of a "devotional revolution" *prior* to their emigration to the United States,[6] the Poles on the other hand were exposed to a devotional revolution *after* arriving in this country. This is not to say that the Poles were not "devotional" in Poland. Thomas and Znaniecki have already demonstrated in most convincing fashion that the religious outlook of the immigrant was decided long before the nineteenth-century migrations. But what we are saying here is that this religious outlook was given a unique devotional shape by Polonia's social structure; that is, the intensely personal side of the peasant's Old World religious ways was given a unique collective expression by the religious fraternals and parish societies which proliferated throughout Chicago Polonia. It is a point that calls for a brief explanation.

Thomas and Znaniecki tell us that when the Polish peasant was still gleaning the fields in *kraju* his religious outlook was shaped largely by the concrete and the personal, by that which could be sensed. Heaven could only be made understandable if it was brought down to earth. Thus, the Polish peasant, like millions of his counterparts in Southern Italy, Yugoslavia, or even rural France, developed highly anthropomorphic religious habits and ways. This was to have a tremendous impact on the Polish Catholic liturgy and the peasant's liturgical rhythm of life. Since the abstractions of religion (such matters as the essence of the Divine Being) were simply incomprehensible, the peasant was content to leave this aspect of religion to others—to the theologians and mystics. But the torments of Christ on Calvary, this was worth contemplating. This could even be re-enacted in the *Gorzkie Żale* ("Bitter Lamentations") Lenten liturgy. It could be sensed, it could be felt. Or to use another example, the Polish peasant was intensely devoted to the Blessed Mother. The singing of *Serdeczna Matko* ("Beloved Mother") has always been one of Poland's favorite ways of expressing her devotion to a lady who is not only the Mother of God but also the Mother of Poland. The *Serdeczna Matko* is also a mother who suffered on earth, just like the peasants who worked their fields or the factory workers who toiled in the mills of South Chicago. This devotion to Mary, Queen of Poland, and other favorite patron saints demonstrated a hunger for the personal, human side of religion.[7]

The intense devotional quality of the Old World religious ways was transplanted on American soil. The Old World liturgical calendar, or "rhythm of life," formed the basis of spiritual movement in the community-parishes of Chicago. In the liturgical way of life of the typical Polish immigrant parish, there was always something happening. The Advent season was always climaxed by the traditional Christmas Vigil dinner (the *Wigilia*) at which the entire family sampled dishes having a religious symbolism and significance. In January, the feasts of the Circumcision and the Epiphany signalled the arrival of another cherished custom, the blessing of homes by the parish priest and the exchange of gifts between parishioner and priest. In February, the feasts of the Purification and of St. Blaise were accompanied by the blessing of sacramentals used during the year and by the blessing of throats; the Lenten season was accompanied by the *Gorzkie Żale*, the stations of the cross, and the celebration of the feasts of St. Casimir and St. Joseph. In late March and early April, one could expect the Holy Week services, the blessing of baskets (*Święcone*), and the Resurrection sunrise mass; in May came the Marian devotions, when Holy Rosary sodalities throughout Polonia conducted their candlelight ceremonies at which time the "living rosary" was prayed; in June, on the feast of St. John the Baptist, the priest would even go out and bless swimming areas; in August, on the feast of the Assumption, thousands of Polish schoolchildren brought bouquets of flowers before the altar of Mary, their innocence matching the freshness of their handpicked treasures. In September, these same schoolchildren could thaw the hardest of hearts singing "Happy Birthday" to the Blessed Mother; in October, many parishes conducted their "Forty Hours" devotions in honor of the Blessed Sacrament; in November, All Saints and All Souls days reminded all of the world to come. All of these feasts in the liturgical year in Polonia were given a distinctly Polish flavor in whatever community-parish one chose to worship. There were thousands of distinctly Pol-

Polish children playing on Noble Street, 1903 (Chicago Historical Society)

ish ceremonies, religious practices, and devotional touches that formed the basis of Polonia's spiritual life. The *Zbiór Pieśni Nabożnych Katolikich*, a collection of religious songs and ceremonies that was heavily used in late nineteenth-century Polonia, contained 1,142 Polish religious songs and 36 different masses.[8] Some of these pieces—such as *Serdeczna Matko* at the Marian devotions, *Twoja Czesz*

Polish wedding party, 1919 (Chicago Historical Society)

Chwała at "Forty Hours," or *Witaj Królowa Nieba* at Requiem masses—were intensely moving and emotional. Entire congregations, within the first few bars, were known to weep or be uplifted as one, as if to express that mass *collective* sense of either joy or sorrow which was at the heart of the Polish Catholic liturgy.[9]

There is no question that the entire Polish Catholic way of life steered the worshipper toward the collective instincts of man. As Durkheim has reminded all students of religious behavior, the man of faith always and everywhere will abandon "his isolation" in order to "approach others," for his faith would "quickly weaken if he remained alone."[10] The immense religious fraternal and parish society network in Polonia forged this collective religious sense for the isolated immigrant. In a study published nearly three decades ago in *Polish American Studies*, Sister Mary Andrea describes six types of religious fraternal organizations at St. Stanislaus Kostka parish, which were more or less typical of many thousands of religious societies that once existed throughout American Polonia. The earliest of these societies, such as the St. Stanislaus Kostka Society and the St. Joseph Society founded in *Stanisławowo* in 1866–1871, were largely organized in order to establish the parish church in the first place. Each, by virtue of its social composition, was oriented toward the clerical party or the national party, the implications of which we have already discussed. A second type of parish society were those which one might call "salvation-oriented." These societies promoted the daily practice of doing spiritual and corporal works of mercy, which, if conducted faithfully, would lead one toward greater virtue and, it was hoped, sanctity. Many Stanislawian societies were formed around the idea of caring for the poor, visiting the sick, and burying the dead; others, like the Society of the Living Rosary, devoted themselves to prayer and other devotional practices. Extremely popular because they catered to Old World religious needs, many of these salvation-oriented societies grew to monumental proportions, far exceeding the expectations of their founders. By 1908, the Living Rosary Society at St. Stanislaus Kostka had an active membership of 4,000 young ladies. The same Society opened a chapter at Holy Trinity and by the end of World War I listed 1,140 members. The Living Rosary Sodality then spread to nearly all Polish parishes in the city. The Society's total membership at St. Stanislaus Kostka was equal to the entire membership of most *parishes* in Chicago at the time, and the combined membership of all Living Rosary Sodality members in all the Polish parishes in the archdiocese was equivalent to some of America's smaller Roman Catholic dioceses. The highlight of the year for Sodality members normally came during Marian devotions held each Sunday during the month of May. During these impressive church ceremonies, a "living rosary" was formed by young ladies, dressed in white, passing a flame from candle to candle, or from "bead to bead," around an already darkened church until the rosary was completed. Another variation of the living rosary sodality was the Society of Virgins of the Most Holy Rosary, founded by Reverend Felix Zwiardowski and Miss Frances Kowalska on the feast of the Immaculate Conception in 1874. Concerned about the temptations lurking in the surrounding environs of Chicago Polonia, the founders encouraged young ladies to pledge their virginity as "roses" in the Society of Virgins. Since the first group of young ladies pledged to the Society of Virgins totalled fifteen in 1874, that figure was determined to be the base unit for one "rose," which would eventually bloom into a full "tree." By 1898, 22 "roses"—a total of 330 young ladies—were active in the original "tree." Other "trees" were organized in 1883 and 1886 to handle new memberships. By 1917, more than 1500 young ladies had publicly professed their chastity during Marian devotion ceremonies as "roses" at St. Stanislaus Kostka.[11]

A third type of parish society, which was to serve as a model for hundreds of imitators, was devoted to "humanitarian, educational and charitable undertakings." Some of these, like the *Macierz Polska* ("Polish Alma Mater"), were founded to assist young males to make the transition from adolescence to adulthood. The *Macierz Polska* maintained a cadet corps, a choir, and athletic teams, and even offered theatre productions. By 1915, the *Macierz Polska*, like so many fraternals in Chicago Polonia, initiated the practice of selling life insurance policies to members of marriage age.

Other parish groups at St. Stanislaus Kostka were founded solely to promote the material welfare of the parish. The Polish Women's Association of Our Lady of Częstochowa, founded by Pastor Jan Kasprzycki in 1900, provided parish ladies age 14 to 45 with the opportunity to promote "friendship, unity and sisterly love" and to propagate "the Christian and national spirit." In what must have been an early Polonia version of present-day "sisterhood," these parish ladies threw themselves into hundreds of fund-raising tasks which were absolutely vital to the continuance of parish programs. The *Dziennik Chicagoski*, in the 1890–1920 period, is replete with hundreds of advertisements for parish fund-raising efforts: bake sales, bazaars, bingos, sodality "bunco parties," and raffles.

A fifth type of parish society devoted itself solely to dramatic and literary activities, all of which were designed to provide a proper Romantic blend of religiosity and patriotism. On the one hundredth anniversary of Poland's Constitution, for example, the Literary and Dramatic Circle of St. Stanislaus Kostka put on a production of Sienkiewicz's *The Deluge* (*Potop*) before an audience of 5,000 at the parish hall. And in 1893, the Trinitarian Literary Circle played Anczyc's *Peasant Aristocrats*, with the world-renowned Helena Modjeska taking to the stage before an audience of 6,000.

Finally, the sixth type of parish society that achieved prominence was what Thomas and Znaniecki termed the "supra-territorial" fraternals, such national organizations as the PRCU, the PNA, the Polish Women's Alliance, and Polish Falcons, which by 1900 had branches in at least 520 parishes throughout American Polonia. Each of these four supraterritorial fraternals maintained its national headquarters in Chicago, and each by 1920 was directly tied to the organizational leadership of the local parish level. In fact, much of the leadership in Polonia's parish societies and in the national fraternals was interlocking. Most of the national officers of the fraternals also played leadership roles on a daily basis in parish societies.[12]

The parish societies and fraternals in Polonia expressed that collective principle in man's religious behavior which Durkheim felt was so essential to a community's well-being. What the Polish liturgy did for Polonia in a spiritual sense, the parish society network accomplished in a social sense. The Polish Catholic "way" in Chicago was never that of a pilgrimage travelled by lonely, isolated individuals.[13] The collective forms of liturgy and the collective social order outlined by the parish societies staved off any widespread *anomie* in Chicago Polonia. To the immigrants in 1900 Chicago Polonia who were certainly as vulnerable to the experience of uprootedness as anyone else, this collective mark of the Polish Catholic way was a major contribution toward arriving at what sociologists would later call community mental health.

Yet no liturgical or devotional transformation, collective or otherwise, could ever have been undertaken without the direction of the clergy in Chicago Polonia. The "immigrant pastor" was always at the center of activity leading to the formation of any parish society, any religious fraternal, any parochial school, or any parish welfare organization.[14] Thus, in addition to the Old World liturgical character of the Polish Catholic Church, we can say that, at least on its Roman Catholic side (which we carefully distinguish from the Polish National Catholic side), Polonia was markedly "priest-centered." The awesome powers held by immigrant pastors like Vincent Barzynski or Francis Gordon or Casimir Sztuczko were the result of a centuries-old process by which the Polish peasant came to first accept and then totally depend on the powers of the priesthood for his or her salvation. In many ways the unsophisticated peasantry of medieval Poland came to view the *ksiądz* (the priest) in the same way that it had viewed the *wiedzący* (the wise one, the magician). The sacramental powers possessed by the priest, then, over the centuries, certainly contributed to the raising of the priest's social status. In fact, Thomas and Znaniecki tell us that Polish families (like Irish ones) considered it an obligation to send at least one son to the seminary. With the sacramental powers accorded him by virtue of Holy Orders, the priest in many Old World villages came to represent that which was sacred, mysterious, and divine. He was in a sense a social "untouchable," and he always retained the aura of the *wiedzący*. For who else but the priest could absolve one of mortal sin on a Saturday afternoon and then consecrate the Eucharist the following morning?[15] On the other hand, we also know that immigrant pastors at times, unfortunately, measured the religious spirit of their flock by the crudest of economic indicators such as the total number of raffle tickets sold, or the proceeds from the Sunday collections— indicators which the post–Vatican II Catholic readily scorns. At times, the demands of the managerial-style priest could get out of hand, as happened during the *Bank Parafialny* fiasco at St. Stanislaus Kostka. Fortunately, Chicago Polonia never again witnessed any of the dimensions of a total parish bank collapse, but the ensuing Independent Revolt in Chicago did point to the fact that Polonia was headed in the direction of what post–Vatican II scholars term the "institutional Church."

Chicago Catholic Polonia was the institutional church *par excellence*. The wide-ranging religious, social, educational, and cultural activities administered by the community-parish system owed their existence to a long-term financial commitment and investment. In June 1918, the *Dziennik Chicagoski* published a census of the community-parish network in Chicago which provides solid evidence as to just how deep that financial commitment to the community-parishes had been. Table One, adapted from that census, gives a parish-by-parish breakdown.[16]

Given the predominantly working-class composition of these thirty-eight Polish parishes, the ten million dollar figure (in 1918 dollars) given for the total real estate valuation of church property is indeed phenomenal. These parishes also maintained elementary schools and contributed to the support of five Polish high schools and one college. They also pooled their resources to sustain several orphanages, welfare agencies, a hospital, several newspapers, various cultural centers and libraries, the national offices of the major fraternals, and even a cemetery—property which was not incorporated into the 1918 census. This massive financial commitment on the part of Chicago Polonia was directly responsible for the creation of a comprehensive community-parish complex providing cradle-to-

Table One: Valuation of Polish Parishes in Chicago in 1918

PARISH	TOTAL PARISHIONERS	VALUE OF PARISH PROPERTY
St. Ann's	8,000	$175,000.00
St. Barbara's	7,000	250,000.00
Good Shepherd	3,200	150,000.00
St. Florian's	3,900	80,000.00
St. Francis of Assisi	2,500	75,000.00
St. Helen's	7,000	150,000.00
St. Hyacinth's (C.R.)	12,000	250,000.00
St. Hedwig's (C.R.)	20,000	400,000.00
St. James	1,500	20,000.00
St. John of God	10,000	200,000.00
St. John Cantius (C.R.)	25,000	750,000.00
St. Joseph's (C.R. to C.A.)	18,000	800,000.00
St. Josaphat's (C.R. to C.A.)	9,000	350,000.00
St. Casimir's	17,000	250,000.00
St. Constantia's	2,000	35,000.00
Holy Innocents	15,000	550,000.00
St. Michael's (C.R. to C.A.)	17,000	600,000.00
St. Mary Magdalene	5,000	150,000.00
St. Mary of Perpetual Help (C.R. to C.A.)	14,000	350,000.00
St. Mary of the Angels (C.R.)	12,000	750,000.00
Immaculate Conception (C.R. to C.A.)	14,000	275,000.00
Immaculate Heart of Mary	5,000	150,000.00
Sacred Heart of Jesus	10,000	161,300.00
Five Holy Martyrs	5,000	45,000.00
SS. Peter and Paul	7,000	204,000.00
Transfiguration	1,200	35,000.00
Blessed Salomea	6,000	120,000.00
St. Stanislaus Bishop & Martyr (C.R.)	5,000	120,000.00
St. Stanislaus Kostka (C.R.)	30,000	800,000.00
St. Stephan's	4,000	125,000.00
Holy Trinity (C.R. to C.A.)	25,000	732,700.00
St. Wenceslaus	5,000	150,000.00
St. Ladislaus	1,300	15,000.00
Assumption	6,000	160,000.00
St. Adalbert's (C.R.)	20,000	550,000.00

Table One (*cont.*)

| | | VALUE OF |
PARISH	TOTAL PARISHIONERS	PARISH PROPERTY
Our Lady of Czestochowa (Cicero)	15,000	350,000.00
St. Valentine's (Cicero)	1,200	65,000.00
All Saints (Polish National Catholic Church)	6,000	Unknown
Totals	375,800	$10,393,000.00

Note: C.R. refers to the "Big Seven" Resurrectionist parishes.
C.R. to C.A. refers to Resurrectionist parishes turned over to the Chicago archdiocese.
The totals exclude the three "mixed nationality" parishes of St. Boniface, Our Lady of Victory, and St. Wenceslaus.

grave services and assistance. Furthermore, the community-parish complexes, especially in West Town, the Back of the Yards, *Wojciechowo*, and South Chicago, were geographically compact. Often numerous services and institutions maintained operations within a few square city blocks, which made the adjacent neighborhood areas extremely attractive to Poles, despite some of the poor housing conditions at the turn of the century. This religious, social, and cultural institutional concentration is no doubt what made the "Polish ghetto" a shock absorber of sorts for the uprooted, unattached, or unassimilated immigrant. In some ways the Polish ghetto was hard to leave. Everything was there (with the exception of new housing): church, school, jobs, family, neighborhood, and organizational life. With so much time, money, and effort invested in the primary areas of settlement, it is no mystery why the Poles moved away ever so slowly from these primary settlements. After all, who really wanted to be uprooted a second time? Leaving the homeland in 1880 had been traumatic enough.[17]

The point here is that the solidity of the community-parish complex helps explain why so many Poles, in comparison to all other white ethnic groups in Chicago, were hesitant about abandoning their neighborhood roots even in exchange for promises of a better economic and social future somewhere else. The powerful magnet of the community-parish complex often proved to have more drawing power than the often vague political slogans thrown the way of Poles by "Progressive era" politicians and reformers, however well-meaning they might be. On the other hand, the heavy Polish investment in the community-parishes was to have some powerful negative social consequences. The very ethnocentric strength of the community-parishes helps explain why Poles in later years were so resistant to sharing these all-Polish resources with Blacks and Hispanics. The ethnocentric drawing power of these parishes was also its greatest weakness. By the end of World War I, and on the eve of the Chicago race riot of 1919, the community-parishes by their capitulation to the national party on any number of Polish patriotic issues had devised a most elaborate, diversified, and sophisticated network which was in principle, if not in practice, intended "to serve Poles only." In many ways, by 1920 the community-parish network in Chicago Polonia had become the ultimate embodiment of the basic *Gmina Polska* principle which it had originally fought so hard against.[18]

Thus we have completed an outline of the basic characteristics, or "marks," of the Polish Catholic Church in Chicago: it was essentially a church of resistance; it was deeply ethnocentric, containing all those Old World Romantic elements that would fuel a national parish structure far into the historical future; it was a church that strived in every way to create and foster a religious presence in an alien land; it was a working-class church that retained its predominantly foreign-born and foreign-stock origins until the eve of Vatican II; it was a devotional and liturgical church which kept the religious spirit alive by utilizing the organizational genius of hundreds of parish fraternal groups and societies; it was in every way a church which could draw every man, woman, and child toward the best of man's collective instincts; it was without doubt a priest-centered church and without doubt a prime example of what the pre–Vatican II institutional church was all about.

Accordingly, we have now reached the point in our analysis where it would be appropriate to place the *I Pollachi* memorial and controversy into some perspective. First, there should be no hesitation on the reader's part to assume that the preservation of the entire community-parish system, with all its socio-religious implications, was the prime force behind Polonia's hard-line stance against Archbishop Mundelein and his Americanist colleagues in the Catholic hierarchy. While the Americanizers were obviously concerned with the overall progress of the Catholic Church as a minority group in American life, they, and especially Cardinal Gibbons, were also deeply concerned with the quality of catholicity in every diocese. Thus the Gibbons-Mundelein rebuttal to the *I Pollachi* memorial must be viewed not only in an assimilationist context whereby the hierarchy was bent only on Americanization of the church but also in a deeply religious context, since it was all-important for the future vitality of the church that it maintain its Catholic identity. On the other hand, the immigrant pastors of Polonia were insisting on the preservation of nationality in the American church. To these immigrant pastors there could be no Catholic Church without the comprehensive incorporation of Old World religious, social, cultural, and structural ways. Accordingly, the fight over the incorporation of territorial parishes, as against the continued maintenance and growth of national parishes in Chicago, unfortunately became entangled in the political controversies surrounding Americanization rather than concerning itself with the more vital spiritual and religious issues of catholicity.

This development and controversy, which occupied the collective thought of both Polonia's ethnocentric pastors and the American Catholic hierarchy over an entire generation, had serious consequences for the future growth of American

Catholicism. In the territorial parish context, the Americanizers, to be sure, could focus their concerns in favor of catholicity even in so polyglot an archdiocese as Chicago. Only in the territorial parish was there any hope for inviting peoples of all nationalities and races. In a national parish, this was not necessarily so. This is not to say that Polish pastors prevented other ethnic groups from entering their parishes. However, in a parish where everything of spiritual *and* social relevance was "done in Polish," it was most discouraging for outsiders to become an integral part of Polish parish life. Of course, when the new *Codex* was enforced in the Mundelein era in Chicago and when territorial parishes were imposed on Polish pastors on the basis of proper implementation of canon law, the Polish pastors were forced to make adjustments. In effect, they decided to conduct a long guerrilla war with the archdiocese in order to maintain the semblance and, in some instances, the substance of national parishes.[19]

How was this accomplished? Just how did the Polish pastors maintain a national parish structure within the new canonical guidelines calling for territorial parishes? Evidently, they did so by discouraging movement out of the parish or the parish neighborhood. If definite territorial boundaries were drawn by the archdiocese which encompassed areas predominantly Polish, the only alternative for the pastors then was to keep these territories solidly Polish.[20] In effect, the retention of Poles in the original community-parish areas became a vested interest for the Polish clergy who were known to lament whenever young people got married and left the neighborhood.

Despite some of these negative features and consequences, there is little doubt, at least in institutional terms, that the "Big Seven" Resurrectionist parishes in the city of Chicago, the other parishes founded by the Resurrectionists that were eventually turned over to the archdiocese, and all the remaining Polish parishes in the greater metropolitan area of Chicago (there were fifty-seven "Polish" parishes in all by 1950) were highly successful. They were certainly successful when measured by the traditional immigrant church yardstick called "brick and mortar." And they were also highly successful in the long battles fought against the perpetual spiritual enemies of the Polish Catholic flock. After the spirit of Independentism subsided, the forces of "anarchy" were never again to make any inroads into Chicago Polonia; "socialism" was indeed checked, as the Polish Socialists in Chicago never once gained access to the community-parish network by the time-honored Polish method of forming a parish fraternal or society; and "Masonry" dissolved away long before 1920 (if it ever indeed was anything more than a "phantom" menace in the first place, used only by the clerical party to scare unwary newcomers away from national party strongholds). As for "liberalism," which in Barzynski's sermonizing was only understood as "indifferentism" to the Catholic faith, this too was checked. In fact, by 1920, only one of the perennial Resurrectionist enemies remained—the force of secularism.[21]

Thus, if one views the community-parish structure within its own terms—that is, from the framework of Janski, Semenenko, and Kajsiewicz—the community-parish and the overall Resurrectionist contribution to the religious life of Polish-American Catholics becomes more apparent. Even from a present-day standpoint, one can view with great admiration the courageous attempts by the still viable community-parishes to adjust to a multiracial city and archdiocese. For today the influence of the Resurrectionists and other clergy in Chicago Polonia extends far beyond the walls of *Stanisławowo* and *Trójcowo*. The Polish clergy in Chicago were able to do on a parish level what the vaunted Irish and German hierarchy did on a diocesan level; they organized hundreds of thousands of foreign-born immigrants into a truly living church. The Polish pastors of Chicago and American Polonia at least deserve credit for being the "organization men" of their time.

But the period following *I Pollachi* would test the best of the immigrant pastors. Whether Polish Roman Catholic or Polish National Catholic, each pastor in Polonia faced a basic problem common to all other immigrant groups in the post–World War I period—survival. Resting on an exclusively Polish base had its drawbacks. When immigration quotas were imposed and when the floodgates of immigration were shut to Eastern and Southern Europeans, Polonia's pastors had to grapple with the problem of "generations." Unlike the Puritans of Massachusetts Bay, the Poles were unable to devise some "half-way covenant" to keep the third and fourth generation Polish-Americans inside the community-parish bastions. With the prospect of better housing, more educational and job opportunities, a more affluent life-style, and all those other secular forces which always appeared to be beyond the control of the clergy and the community-parishes, the way was paved for the grandchildren of the founders of Polonia to move to Belmont-Cragin, to Avondale, to Brighton Park, to Archer Heights, to Marquette Park, and beyond—farther and farther toward the "secular city" horizon.[22]

To be sure, the Polish clergy, after the defeat of the *I Pollachi* memorial, attempted valiantly to stem the tide of mobility. Under the leadership of the Reverend Thomas Bona, who was designated by Archbishop Mundelein to be Polonia's prime spokesman after *I Pollachi*, every effort was made to sustain the dynamism of the community-parishes. But despite the fact that every institution within the community parish complex worked mightily to prevent leakage to the outer areas of the city and the suburbs, the Polish Catholic Church in Chicago, at least by the time John XXIII called for an ecumenical council, came to realize that it was destined to lose to forces well beyond the powers of the original institutions. The population peak for Chicago Polonia was reached in 1930. Bolstered by a brief post–World War II immigration boom, the community-parishes managed to maintain their national character until the late fifties.[23] Judging from Resurrectionist mission records from the post–1930 period, the liturgical peak (that is, the active involvement of large numbers of Poles in the Old World devotional ways) was reached around 1950.[24] Thus, the Polish Catholic Church in Chicago had reached its apex and had already begun the inevitable process of decline just prior to the opening of Vatican II.

The argument that Vatican II assisted in the process of destroying the immigrant church in Chicago, therefore, calls for careful and cautious reexamination. If anything, Vatican II, by making way for the greater participation of the laity in the liturgy and by calling for the use of the vernacular, nurtured the immigrant church somewhat even after the original pioneers and their children had long since departed. If *I Pollachi*, then, was a defeat for the forces of ethnocentrism and Old World nationalism in the American Catholic church, Vatican II was a victory for the catholicity in the immigrant-ethnic church, a church which still throbs with life. When John Paul II came to Chicago in October of 1979, he paid tribute to the magnanimous spirit of Chicago's Polish Catholic community during a late evening address before a crowd gathered in Holy Name Cathedral; the next day in Grant Park, at an outdoor ecumenical mass attended by at least one million celebrants, this Polish Pope acknowledged the blessings of pluralism in the American church and the American nation.

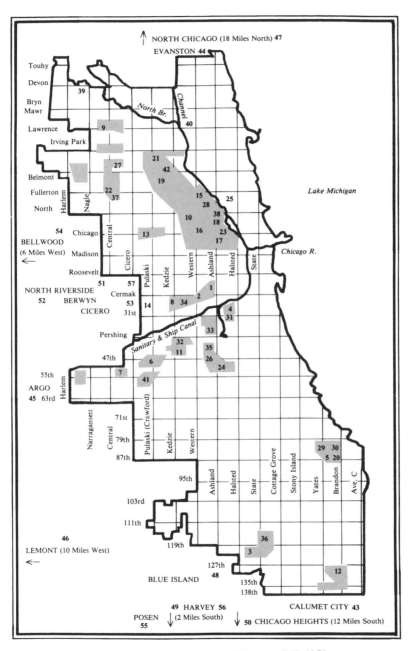

Map Four: Polish Parishes in Chicago, 1867–1950

MAP NO.	PARISH ADDRESS	DATE	ADMINISTRATION	TEACHING ORDER OF NUNS
1	St. Adalbert 1650 W. 17th St. Lower West Side	1873	Diocesan	Holy Family of Nazareth
2	St. Ann 1814 S. Leavitt Lower West Side	1903	Diocesan	Holy Family of Nazareth
3	Assumption B.V.M. 544 W. 123rd St. West Pullman	1902	Diocesan	Holy Family of Nazareth
4	St. Barbara 2859 S. Throop Bridgeport	1910	Diocesan	St. Joseph (of the Third Order of St. Francis)
5	St. Bronislaus 8708 S. Colfax South Chicago	1920	Franciscan (O.F.M. Conv.)	Felicians
6	St. Bruno 4749 S. Harding Archer Heights	1925	Diocesan	Felicians
7	St. Camillus 5430 S. Lockwood Garfield Ridge	1928	Diocesan	Holy Family of Nazareth
8	St. Casimir 2226 S. Whipple Lower West Side	1890	Diocesan	Resurrectionists
9	St. Constance 5843 Strong Jefferson Park	1916	Diocesan	School Sisters of Notre Dame (S.S.N.D.)
10	St. Fidelis 1406 N. Washtenaw West Town	1920	Diocesan	St. Joseph
11	Five Holy Martyrs 4327 S. Richmond Brighton Park	1908	Diocesan	Franciscan Sisters of B. K.
12	St. Florian 13145 S. Houston Hegewisch	1906	Diocesan	Franciscan Sisters of B. K.
13	St. Francis of Assisi 932 N. Kostner Humboldt Park	1909	Diocesan	Franciscan Sisters of Our Lady of Perpetual Help

MAP NO.	PARISH ADDRESS	DATE	ADMINISTRATION	TEACHING ORDER OF NUNS
14	Good Shepherd 2719 S. Kolin South Lawndale	1907	Diocesan	Felicians
15	St. Hedwig 2226 N. Hoyne Logan Square	1888	Congregation of the Resurrection (C.R.)	Holy Family of Nazareth
16	St. Helen 2315 W. Augusta Blvd. West Town	1914	Diocesan	Felicians
17	Holy Innocents 743 Armour St. West Town	1905	Diocesan	Felicians
18	Holy Trinity 1118 Noble St. West Town	1872	Holy Cross Fathers (C.S.C.)	Holy Family of Nazareth
19	St. Hyacinth 3636 W. Wolfram Avondale	1894	C.R.	Holy Family of Nazareth
20	Immaculate Conception 2944 E. 88th South Chicago	1882	Diocesan	St. Joseph
21	Immaculate Heart of Mary 3834 N. Spaulding Irving Park	1912	Diocesan	Holy Family of Nazareth
22	St. James 5730 W. Fullerton Belmont-Cragin	1914	Diocesan	Felicians
23	St. John Cantius 825 N. Carpenter West Town	1893	C.R.	S.S.N.D.
24	St. John of God 1234 W. 52nd Back of the Yards	1906	Diocesan	Felicians
25	St. Josaphat 2311 Southport Ave. Lincoln Park	1884	Diocesan	Holy Family of Nazareth
26	St. Joseph 4821 S. Hermitage Back of the Yards	1887	Diocesan	Felicians

MAP NO.	PARISH ADDRESS	DATE	ADMINISTRATION	TEACHING ORDER OF NUNS
27	St. Ladislaus 5345 W. Roscoe Irving Park	1914	Diocesan	Holy Family of Nazareth
28	St. Mary of the Angels 1825 N. Wood Logan Square	1897	C.R.	Resurrectionists
29	St. Mary Magdalene 8426 Marquette Ave. South Chicago	1910	Diocesan	Felicians
30	St. Michael 8237 South Shore Drive South Chicago	1892	Diocesan	Holy Family of Nazareth
31	Our Lady of Perpetual Help (St. Mary of Perpetual Help) 1039 W. 32nd St. Bridgeport	1883	Diocesan	St. Joseph
32	St. Pancratius 4025 S. Sacramento Brighton Park	1924	Diocesan	Franciscan Sisters of B. K.
33	SS. Peter and Paul 3745 S. Paulina McKinley Park	1895	Diocesan	Felicians
34	St. Roman 2311 S. Washtenaw South Lawndale	1928	Diocesan	St. Joseph
35	Sacred Heart 4600 S. Honore Back of the Yards	1910	Diocesan	Felicians
36	St. Salomea 11824 S. Indiana Pullman	1898	Diocesan	St. Joseph
37	St. Stanislaus Bishop and Martyr 5352 W. Belden Belmont-Cragin	1893	C.R.	Franciscan Sisters of B. K.

MAP NO.	PARISH ADDRESS	DATE	ADMINISTRATION	TEACHING ORDER OF NUNS
38	St. Stanislaus Kostka 1351 W. Evergreen West Town	1867	C.R.	S.S.N.D.
39	St. Thecla 6725 W. Devon Norwood Park	1928	Diocesan	Resurrectionists
40	Transfiguration 2609 W. Carmen Lincoln Square	1911	Diocesan	St. Joseph
41	St. Turibius 5646 S. Karlov West Elsdon	1927	Diocesan	Felicians
42	St. Wenceslaus 3400 N. Monticello Avondale	1912	Diocesan	Felicians

Suburban Polish Roman Catholic Parishes, 1883–1950

MAP NO.	PARISH ADDRESS	DATE	ADMINISTRATION	TEACHING ORDER OF NUNS
43	St. Andrew the Apostle Calumet City	1891	Diocesan	Holy Family of Nazareth
44	Ascension Evanston	1912	Diocesan	Felicians
45	St. Blaise Argo		Diocesan	Holy Family of Nazareth
46	SS. Cyril and Methodius Lemont	1883	Diocesan	Felicians
47	Holy Rosary North Chicago	1904	Diocesan	Felicians
48	St. Isidore Blue Island	1900	Diocesan	Felicians
49	St. John the Baptist Harvey		Diocesan	Holy Family of Nazareth
50	St. Joseph Chicago Heights		Diocesan	Franciscan Sisters of O.L.P.H.
51	St. Mary of Celle Berwyn	1909	Benedictine (O.S.B.)	Benedictine Sisters of the Sacred Heart
52	Mater Christi North Riverside		Diocesan	Sisters of St. Francis of the Holy Family

MAP NO.	PARISH ADDRESS	DATE	ADMINISTRATION	TEACHING ORDER OF NUNS
53	Our Lady (St. Mary) of Czestochowa Cicero	1895	Diocesan	St. Joseph
54	St. Simeon Bellwood		Diocesan	St. Joseph
55	St. Stanislaus Bishop and Martyr	1894	Diocesan	Felicians
56	St. Susanna Harvey		Diocesan	Holy Family of Nazareth
57	St. Valentine Cicero	1912	Diocesan	St. Joseph

Note: A Polish Roman Catholic parish is defined here as follows: 1) The parish was founded, organized, and administered on a predominantly Polish basis; 2) the parish was ministered to by Polish priests for the greater part of 1867–1950; 3) the parish school was administered by Polish orders of teaching nuns or Polish nuns belonging to other orders: 4) the parish population was predominantly Polish up to 1950 (i.e., the Poles were the largest nationality group belonging to the parish); 5) as late as 1950, the parish was ministered to by priests with Polish surnames and by Polish teaching nuns.

A number of "Polish" parishes were omitted from the list: St. Boniface (1864) in West Town, and St. Wenceslaus (1863) on the near west side, because they were mixed nationality parishes; St. Mary of Mount Carmel (1892), a Resurrectionist parish, because it was largely Italian; All Saints, in West Town, because it belonged to the Polish National Catholic Church; St. Stephan on the Lower West Side, because it was heavily Bohemian (Czech); St. Szczepan, in West Town, because it was closed during the period; and Ascension, in Harvey, because it did not maintain its original Polish base.

The scale has been distorted on the map so as to include all the suburban parishes. The distortion is minimal for those suburbs immediately surrounding Chicago and greater for suburbs on the far periphery of the city (e.g. Lemont). Where dates for suburban parishes were questionable they were omitted.

Sources for the map: *The New World*, 26 November 1976, pp. 15–18; Swastek, "Contribution of the Poles"; Thompson, *Diamond Jubilee*; Iwicki, *Resurrectionist Studies*; *Local Community Factbooks*; the *Official Catholic Directory*.

Notes

CHAPTER ONE

1. Chapter One is largely synthetical and is only intended as a broad survey; consequently, I have depended upon what I feel are the best secondary sources for the period. Some of the principal sources include William F. Reddaway, ed., *The Cambridge History of Poland*, 2 vols. (London: Cambridge University Press, 1941–50); Stefan Kieniewicz, ed., *A History of Poland* (Warsaw: Scientific Publishers, 1968); Oscar Halecki, *A History of Poland* (New York: Roy, 1943); Piotr Wandycz, *The Lands of Partitioned Poland, 1795–1918*, vol. 7 of Peter F. Sugar and Donald W. Treadgold, eds. *A History of East Central Europe* (Seattle: University of Washington Press, 1974); Stefan Kieniewicz, *The Emancipation of the Polish Peasantry* (Chicago: University of Chicago Press, 1969); and Piotr Wandycz, *The United States and Poland*, American Foreign Policy Library (Cambridge, Mass.: Harvard University Press, 1980), especially chaps. 1 and 2.

2. Wandycz, *Partitioned Poland*, pp. 3–23; Wandycz, *United States and Poland*, pp. 14–27; Herbert H. Kaplan, *The First Partition of Poland* (New York: Columbia University Press, 1962), pp. 182–89.

3. The "death sentence" quote is from Robert Howard Lord, *The Second Partition of Poland: A Study in Diplomatic History* (Cambridge, Mass.: Harvard University Press, 1915), p. 484. Note, also, Lord's extensive conclusions, pp. 484–505. For other viewpoints, see *Cambridge History of Poland*, 2: 88–176; Halecki, *History of Poland*, pp. 176–213; R. Nesbit Bain, *The Last King of Poland and His Contemporaries* (New York: Putnam, 1909).

4. See Halecki, *History of Poland*, passim; *Cambridge History of Poland*, 2: 88–176.

5. See Wandycz, *Partitioned Poland*, passim, for the latest comprehensive treatment, in English, on the overall impact of the Partitions. For a discussion of "regional separatism," see Carole Golab, *Immigrant Destinations* (Philadelphia: Temple University Press, 1977), pp. 75–100; Helena Znaniecki Lopata, *Polish Americans: Status Competition in an Ethnic Community* (Englewood Cliffs, N.J.: Prentice-Hall, 1976), pp. 33–47 in particular, which covers the impact of separatism on neighborhood development; and Joseph J. Parot, "Sources of Community Conflict in Chicago Polonia: A Comparative Analysis and Historiographical Appraisal," *Ethnicity* 7 (December 1980): 333–48.

6. Wandycz, *Partitioned Poland*, p. 11, and my personal calculations.

7. See Lord, *The Second Partition*, pp. 8–25, for a well-seasoned but still reliable treatment of the *szlachta*. I have also depended heavily on Paul W. Knoll, *The Rise of the Polish Monarchy* (Chicago: University of Chicago Press, 1972). For extensive discussion of the *chłopi*, see Kieniewicz, *Emancipation*, pp. 1–153. For the relationship of Old World divisions to the clerical-nationalist dispute in Chicago Polonia, see Parot, "Sources of Community Conflict," pp. 333–48.

8. Knoll, *Rise of the Polish Monarchy*, passim; *Cambridge History of Poland*, 1: 188–299; Jerzy Kloczowski, "The Polish Church," in *Church and Society in Catholic Europe of the Eighteenth Century*, ed. William J. Callahan and David Higgs (Cambridge: Cambridge University Press, 1979), pp. 131–35.

9. Kloczowski, "Polish Church," pp. 124–25. My estimate is based on a study of statistics provided by Kloczowski and by: Henry Mucha, ed., *The Polish American Parish* (Orchard Lake, Michigan: St. Mary's Seminary, 1963), which lists all the Polish-American

parishes in the United States; and, Joseph Swastek, "The Contribution of the Poles to the Growth of Catholicism in the United States," *Sacrum Poloniae Millenium*, VI (Rome, 1959), pp. 261–71 and passim.

10. Kaplan, *First Partition*, pp. 2–12; Wandycz, *Partitioned Poland*, p. 6 and n. 2; Kloczowski, "Polish Church," pp. 125–37.

11. William I. Thomas and Florian Znaniecki, *The Polish Peasant in Europe and America*, 2 vols. (New York: Knopf, 1927), 1: 87–105, 128–35, 205–87; Kloczowski, "Polish Church," p. 129; Kaplan, *First Partition*, pp. 38–92.

12. Kloczowski, "Polish Church," pp. 136–37; Thomas and Znaniecki, *Polish Peasant*, 2: 1511–1646; Adam Zoltowski and Zbigniew M. Ossowski, "Catholicism and Christian Democracy in Poland," in *Church and Society: Catholic Social and Political Thought and Movements, 1789–1950*, ed. Joseph N. Moody (New York: Arts Incorporated, 1953), pp. 587–631.

13. The Dissident question is examined in Kaplan, *First Partition*, pp. 49–181.

14. Ibid., p. 58.

15. Ibid., pp. 57–90.

16. For a viewpoint more sympathetic to Roman Catholicism, see Oscar Halecki, "Problems of Ecumenism in Poland's Millenium," *Catholic Historical Review* 52 (January 1967): 477–93. The full text of Catherine's "Declaration" is in Kaplan, *First Partition*, pp. 191–95.

17. Wandycz, *Partitioned Poland*, pp. 20–21.

18. Lech Trzeciakowski, "The Prussian State and the Catholic Church in Prussian Poland, 1871–1914," *Slavic Review* 26 (December 1967): 618–37.

19. Harry Kenneth Rosenthal, "The Election of Archbishop Stablewski," *Slavic Review* 28 (June 1969): 265–75.

20. Wandycz, *Partitioned Poland*, p. 196. The literature dealing with the Partition is, of course, too lengthy for summary here. The reader should consult Wandycz's excellent bibliographical essay on pp. 381–411.

21. R. F. Leslie, *Polish Politics and the Revolution of November 1830* (London: Athlone Press, 1956); see also, Colonel Br. Pawlowski, "The November Insurrection," in *Cambridge History of Poland*, 2: 295–310.

22. A. P. Coleman, "The Great Emigration," in *Cambridge History of Poland*, 2: 311–23.

23. Monica Gardner, *Adam Mickiewicz: The National Poet of Poland* (London: Dent; New York: Dutton, 1911), pp. 126–54; see also, Wiktor Weintraub, *The Poetry of Adam Mickiewicz* (The Hague: Mouton, 1954), pp. 194–207; Waclaw Lednicki, *Life and Culture of Poland* (New York: Roy, 1944), pp. 158–211; and, Monica Gardner, "The Great Emigration and Polish Romanticism," *Cambridge History of Poland*, 2: 324–35.

24. The translation of "Dawn" is from Coleman, "Great Emigration," p. 323.

25. Kieniewicz, *Emancipation*, pp. 120–23.

26. The best English-language interpretation of the 1863 Insurrection remains R. F. Leslie, *Reform and Insurrection in Russian Poland, 1856–1865* (London: Athlone Press, 1963). See also W. J. Rose, "Russian Poland in the Later Nineteenth Century," *Cambridge History of Poland*, 2: 391–96.

27. Wandycz, *Partitioned Poland*, pp. 260–72, provides a good summary of Positivism for the general reader.

28. Statistical materials are from *Statistical View of the United States . . . being a Compendium of the Seventh Census . . .*, comp. J. D. B. DeBow (Washington, D.C.: Superintendent of the U.S. Census, 1854), pp. 347, 399. Also see U.S. Department of Commerce, Bureau of the Census, *1970 Census of Population and Housing. Census Tracts: Chicago,*

Illinois Standard Metropolitan Statistical Area, Part One—Social Characteristics of the Population, 1970 (Washington, D. C.: G. P. O., 1970), p. 119.

29. Milo M. Quaife, *Chicago's Highways Old and New: From Indian Trail to Motor Road* (Chicago: D.F. Keller, 1923), pp. 33–42; "Commercial Cities and Towns of the United States, Number VII: City of Chicago, Illinois," *Hunt's Merchants' Magazine and Commercial Review* 26 (April 1852): 164–71; Bessie Louise Pierce, *History of Chicago*, 3 vols. (Chicago: University of Chicago Press, 1937–57), 1: 81–97, 119; 2: 35–76.

30. "Commercial Cities and Towns of the United States, Number XXXI: Chicago: Its Trade and Growth in 1851," *Hunt's Merchants' Magazine and Commercial Review* 18 (February 1848): 424–43; Pierce, *History of Chicago*, 1: 275, 512.

31. Harold M. Mayer and Richard C. Wade, *Chicago: Growth of a Metropolis* (Chicago: University of Chicago Press, 1969), pp. 35–44. For attitudes of big business in this period, see the following: Cyrus McCormick, *The Century of the Reaper: An Account of Cyrus Hall McCormick* (Boston: Houghton Mifflin, 1931); William T. Hutchison, *Cyrus Hall McCormick*, 2 vols. (New York: Appleton-Century, 1935); Frank C. Waldrop, *McCormick of Chicago: An Unconventional Portrait of a Controversial Figure* (Englewood Cliffs, N.J.: Prentice-Hall, 1966); Harper Leech and John Charles Carroll, *Armour and His Times* (New York: Appleton, 1938); Louis Franklin Swift, *The Yankee of the Yards: The Biography of Gustavus Adolphus Swift* (New York: A. W. Shaw, 1936). For the impact of corporate policies on immigrant labor within the German community during the Haymarket Affair, see Henry David, *A History of the Haymarket Affair: A Study of American Social Revolution and Labor Movements* (New York: Farrar and Rinehart, 1936). Note that numerous Poles were employed at the McCormick Works, International Harvester, and the Union Stockyards throughout the 1870–1920 period.

32. For the incorporation of Chicago, see Edmund J. James, *The Charters of the City of Chicago* (Chicago: University of Chicago Press, 1898–99), pp. 20–49. For political developments, see Pierce, *History of Chicago*, 1: 317–63, 383, 421–24. For the later development of Polish politics, see Edward Kantowicz, *Polish-American Politics in Chicago, 1888–1940* (Chicago: University of Chicago Press, 1975).

33. Pierce, *History of Chicago*, 2: 354, 511; Evelyn M. Kitagawa and Karl E. Taeuber, eds., *Local Community Fact Book: Chicago Metropolitan Area, 1960* (Chicago: University of Chicago Press, 1963), p. 8. For individual historics of various Protestant churches, see A. T. Andreas, *History of Chicago From the Earliest Period to the Present Time*, 3 vols. (Chicago: A. T. Andreas, 1884–86), 1: 299–356. Other miscellaneous statistics for Chicago and Illinois are derived from U.S., Department of Commerce, Bureau of the Census, *Historical Statistics of the United States, Colonial Times to 1957* (Washington, D.C.: G.P.O., 1960), p. 13.

34. Morris Gutstein, *A Priceless Heritage: The Epic Growth of Nineteenth Century Chicago Jewry* (New York: Bloch Publishing 1953), pp. 24–28.

35. Andreas, *History of Chicago*, 1: 289.

36. Gilbert J. Garraghan, *The Catholic Church in Chicago, 1673–1871* (Chicago: Loyola University Press, 1921), pp. 108–36. See also Joseph J. Thompson, *Diamond Jubilee of the Archdiocese of Chicago, 1920* (Des Plaines, Ill.: St. Mary's Training School Press, 1920), pp. 19–39; Pierce, *History of Chicago*, 2: 359–60.

37. Pierce, *History of Chicago* 2: 379–80; Garraghan, *Catholic Church*, pp. 137–66; Thompson, *Diamond Jubilee*, pp. 31–34; Timothy Walch, "Catholic Social Institutions and Urban Development: The View from Nineteenth Century Chicago and Milwaukee," *Catholic Historical Review* 64 (January 1978): 16–32.

38. Henry De Couray and John Gilmary Shea, *History of the Catholic Church in the United States* (New York: P. J. Kenedy, 1879), p. 574.

39. Walter F. Willcox, ed., *International Migrations*, 2 vols. (New York: National Bureau of Economic Research, 1929–31), 1: 126–28, 401–17. For more on the Polish population, see Miecislaus Haiman, *The Polish Past in America, 1608–1865* (Chicago: Polish Roman Catholic Union, 1939), pp. 152–59. Note that Haiman challenges Census Bureau statistics.

40. M. Inviolata Ficht, S.S.J., "Noble Street in Chicago," *Polish American Studies* 9 (January-June 1954): 1–8; Miecislaus Haiman, "The Poles in Chicago," in *Poles of Chicago, 1837–1937: A History of One Century of Polish Contribution to the City of Chicago*, (Chicago: Polish Pageant, 1937), pp. 1–10; *Album Pamiątkowe z Okazji Złotego Jubileuszu Parafii Św. Stanisława K(ostki) Chicago, Illinois 1867–1917* (Chicago: St. Stanislaus Kostka Parish, 1917), p. 8 (hereafter cited as *Album SSK*); M. Inviolata Ficht, S.S.J., "Noble Street in Chicago" (M.A. thesis, DePaul University, 1952), p. 46; Mrs. Isaac Rawlings, "Polish Exiles in Illinois," *Transactions of the Illinois Historical Society* 20 (12–13 May 1927): 83–103; Waclaw Kruszka, *Historya Polska w Ameryce*, 13 vols. (Milwaukee: Kuryer Polski, 1905–08), 8: 135. For distinctions regarding the controversial use of the term "Polonia," see Stefan Wloszczewski, "The Polish 'Sociological Group' in America," *American Slavic and Eastern European Review* 4 (August 1945): 142–57.

Anthony Smarzewski-Schermann is listed as Antoni Sherman in the 1860 Federal Census manuscript schedules. The Census lists his age as 28, although Francis Bolek, ed., *Who's Who in Polish America*, 3rd ed. (New York: Harbinger House, 1943), claims that Schermann was 42 years old at the time of the 1860 Census. Bolek also lists Smarzewski-Schermann's original Polish name as Smagorzewski-Schermann. I have noted numerous misspelled names in the 1860, 1870, 1880, and 1900 manuscript schedules, as well as numerous other errors. This was no doubt due to carelessness on the part of house canvassers, who in many instances did not understand Polish. Misunderstandings by Polish immigrants, who did not know how to formulate proper answers to questions, also contributed to the errors. Note that Smarzewski-Schermann's family, however, is listed as follows: Frederica, age 26, wife; and children, Loisa, age 14; Dora, 13; Antoni, 12; Julia, 7; Charles, 4; and Francis, 9 months. Smarzewski-Schermann listed his occupation in 1860 as carpenter. See the U.S. Census Bureau, *Federal Population Census, 1860. Illinois: Cook County, City of Chicago, Ward Six* (National Archives Microfilm Edition, Reel 166, House Number 303, Family Number 311).

41. See maps of this territory in Mayer and Wade, *Chicago*, pp. 13, 64. For other descriptions, see *Album SSK*, p. 8, and Kruszka, *Historya*, 8: 137. For the 1900 population, see City Homes Association, *Tenement Conditions in Chicago: Report by the Investigating Committee of the City Homes Association* (Chicago: City Homes Association, 1901), pp. 195–96.

42. The Dąbrowski letter is translated and cited in John Iwicki, *Resurrectionist Studies, The First One Hundred Years: A Study of the Apostolate of the Congregation of the Resurrection in the United States, 1866–1966* (Rome: Gregorian University Press, 1966), p. 53.

43. *Album SSK*, p. 9ff.; Kruszka, *Historya*, 8: 135; Helen Busyn, "Peter Kiolbassa— Maker of Polish America," *Polish American Studies* 8 (July-December 1951): 71. For the relationship of religion and society in Poland, see Sula Benet, *Song, Dance and Customs of Peasant Poland* (New York: Roy, 1951), pp. 28–29 and passim. For etymological distinctions and derivations, see *Cambridge History of Poland*, 1: 80; see also Joshua Fishman et al., *Language Loyalty in the United States: The Maintenance and Perpetuation of Non-English Mother Tongues by American Ethnic and Religious Groups* (The Hague: Mouton, 1966). For songs in the Polish liturgy, see *Zbiór Pieśni Nabożnych Katolickich do Użytku Kościelnego i Domowego* (Chicago: Polish American Publishing Company, n.d.; *imprimatur* dated July 1868), pp. 223, 449, 556.

44. Leonard Covello, "Language as a Factor in Social Adjustment," in *Our Racial and National Minorities*, ed. Francis J. Brown and Joseph S. Roucek (New York: Prentice-Hall, 1939), p. 683; Victor Greene, "For God and Country: The Origins of Slavic Self-Consciousness in America," *Church History* 35 (December 1966): 446.

For tensions in the stockyards, see, e.g., Alma Herbst, *The Negro in the Slaughtering and Meat-Packing Industry in Chicago* (Boston: Houghton Mifflin, 1932), p. 16 and passim; Sperling D. Spero and Abram L. Harris, *The Black Worker: The Negro and the Labor Movement* (1931; reprint ed., Port Washington, N.Y.: Kennikat Press, 1966), pp. 128–33; Paul Taylor, *Mexican Labor in the United States*, 2 vols., University of California Publications in Economics, vols. 6, 7 (Berkeley: University of California Press, 1928–34), especially VII, pp. 165, 180–81, 221, 271; and Joseph J. Parot, "Ethnic Versus Black Metropolis: The Origins of Polish-Black Housing Tensions in Chicago," *Polish American Studies* 29 (Spring-Autumn, 1972), pp. 5–34.

45. See the commentary by Thomas and Znaniecki to letter No. 349 (27 January 1908) of the Rzepkowski Series, in *Polish Peasant*, 1: 667.

46. *Album SSK*, p. 9. The quotation is attributed to Dr. Karl Wachtel, longtime resident of *Stanisławowo*. For general problems facing the national parishes, see Joseph Ciesluk, *National Parishes in the United States* (Washington, D.C.: Catholic University of America, 1944). For an excellent comparison between Polish and Italian anticlericalism in Chicago, see Rudolph J. Vecoli, "Prelates and Peasants: Italian Immigrants and the Catholic Church," *Journal of Social History* 2 (Spring 1969): 222–23.

47. Bishop Duggan was eventually removed from the Chicago diocese and sent to a sanitarium in St. Louis in 1869. He suffered a complete mental breakdown. See Thompson, *Diamond Jubilee*, p. 43.

48. For biographical details on Kiolbassa, see Busyn, "Maker of Polish America"; see also Helen Busyn, "The Political Career of Peter Kiolbassa," *Polish American Studies* 7 (January–June 1950): 7–8 and passim; Andreas, *History of Chicago*, 3: 563; *Naród Polski*, 28 June 1905; *The New World* (Official Newspaper of the Roman Catholic Archdiocese of Chicago, now *The Chicago Catholic*), 27 October 1900. The best work on Kiolbassa and the Panna Marya settlement in general is T. Lindsay Baker, *The First Polish Americans: Silesian Settlements in Texas* (College Station, Tex.: Texas A & M University Press, 1979). Baker also gives details on the Reverend Leopold Moczygemba, who directed the Franciscan missions in Texas. Note that Kiolbassa's name is correctly spelled with the diacritical bar across the letter l (Kiołbassa), which I omit in the text.

49. *Album SSK*, p. 9.

50. Ibid.

51. Kruszka, *Historya*, 3: 140; *Dziennik Chicagoski*, 17 June 1918.

CHAPTER TWO

1. Ray Billington, *The Protestant Crusade, 1800–1860: A Study of the Origins of American Nativism* (1938; reprint ed., Gloucester, Mass.: Peter Smith, 1963).

2. John Higham, *Strangers in the Land: Patterns of American Nativism, 1860–1925* (New York: Atheneum, 1963).

3. On the Irish immigration, see Carl Wittke, *The Irish in America* (Baton Rouge: Louisiana State University Press, 1956), pp. 150–60, 196–97, 221–22, and Wittke's *We Who Built America: The Saga of the Immigrant* (New York: Prentice-Hall, 1940), p. 140. The most complete calendar outlining the activities of the A.O.H. in this period may be in *The New World*, which carried weekly accounts of the A.O.H. and numerous other Irish fraternal societies between 1890 and 1920.

4. Theodore Saloutos, *The Greeks in the United States* (Cambridge, Mass.: Harvard University Press, 1964), pp. 138–59, 185–209, 254–56.

5. Robert Foerster, *The Italian Emigration of Our Times* (1919; reprint ed., New York: Russell and Russell, 1968), pp. 47–126, 392–93; see also Phyllis H. Williams, *South Italian Folkways in Europe and America* (New Haven, Conn.: Yale University Press, 1938).

6. Humbert Nelli, *The Italians in Chicago, 1880–1930* (New York: Oxford University Press, 1970), pp. 172–75.

7. Moses Rischin, *The Promised City: New York's Jews, 1870–1914* (Cambridge, Mass.: Harvard University Press, 1962), pp. 97–98, 103–11.

8. George Prpic, *The Croatians in America* (New York: Philosophical Library, 1971), pp. 178–82.

9. Quoted in Nelli, *Italians*, p. 178.

10. Thomas Capek, *The Čechs (Bohemians) in America* (Boston: Houghton Mifflin, 1920), pp. 254–64; Joseph Cada, "Czechs of Chicago," in *Panorama: A Historical Review of Czechs and Slovaks in the United States of America* (Cicero, Ill.: Czechoslovak National Council of America, 1970), pp. 30–34; and "One Hundred Years of the Bohemian Free-thinkers in Chicago," ibid., pp. 82–84.

11. For my account of the Insurrection and the events surrounding the Miliutin Decrees I have depended heavily on Leslie, *Reform and Insurrection*, especially pp. 232–51. The quotation is from A.P. Coleman, "Poland Under Alexander II: The Insurrection of 1863," in *Cambridge History of Poland*, 2: 383.

12. Coleman, "Poland Under Alexander," p. 383. For a detailed description of these *ukase* issued by the Czar, see Kieniewicz, *Emancipation*, pp. 172–79.

13. Franciszek Bujak, *Poland's Economic Development: A Short Sketch*, trans. K. Zuk Skarszewska (London: G. Allen & Unwin, 1926), p. 39; Richard Wonser Tims, *Germanizing Prussian Poland* (1941; reprint ed., New York: AMS, 1966), pp. 108–9; W.J. Rose, "Prussian Poland, 1850–1914," in *Cambridge History of Poland*, 2: 409–31.

14. For a complete translation of Giller's remarks, see Frank Renkiewicz, ed., *The Poles in America, 1608–1972: A Chronology and Factbook* (Dobbs Ferry, N.Y.: Oceana, 1973), pp. 64–65. Also see Thomas and Znaniecki, *Polish Peasant* 2: 1629–30.

15. See "Polish Organizations in Chicago," in *Poles of Chicago*, p. 149. See also Kruszka, *Historya*, 3: 140.

16. Wladislaw Dyniewicz, *Ustawy Gminy Polskiej* (Chicago: W. Dyniewicz, 1877).

17. For other material on Dyniewicz, see the *Dziennik Chicagoski*, 28 February 1929, p. 10, and 22 January 1947, p. 3; John Drury, *Old Chicago Houses* (Chicago: University of Chicago Press, 1941), pp. 384–87, which includes a brief sketch of the *Gmina* founder based in part on an interview with Mrs. Stanley Kuflewski, granddaughter of Dyniewicz; *Who's Who in Polish America*, p. 3; Helena Chrzanowska, "Polish Book Publishing in Chicago," *Polish American Studies* 4 (January–June 1947): 37–39; Eugene P. Willging and Herta Hatzfield, "Nineteenth Century Polish Catholic Periodical Publications," *Polish American Studies* 12 (July–December 1955): 95–96. On the origins of the *Gmina Polska*, see Dyniewicz, *Ustawy*, passim; Stanley Osada, *Historya Związku Narodowego Polskiego i Rozwój Ruchu Narodowego w Ameryce Północnej* (Chicago: Polish National Alliance, 1905), pp. 34–36, 58–66; S.M. Ancilla, F.S.S.J., "Catholic Polish Book Publishing in the United States, 1871–1900," *Polish American Studies* 16 (January–June 1959): 1–11.

18. Dyniewicz, *Ustawy*, passim; Osada, *Historya ZNP*, pp. 58–66; Kruszka, *Historya*, 1: 567–68; *Album SSK*, p. 9; Busyn, "Maker of Polish America," pp. 73–74; Greene, "Slavic Self-Consciousness," pp. 449–51.

19. Dyniewicz, *Ustawy*, p. 5.

20. Miecislaus Haiman, *Zjednoczenie Polskie Rzymsko-Katolickie w Ameryce, 1873–*

1948 (Chicago: Polish Roman Catholic Union, 1948), p. 25 (hereafter cited as *ZPRK*); M. Andrea, "The Societies of Saint Stanislaus Kostka Parish, Chicago," *Polish American Studies* 9 (January-June 1952): 28; Peter Kiolbassa to Reverend Jelowicki, C.R., 14 June 1869 in Kruszka, *Historya*, 1: 575–76. Wage computations and comparisons were drawn from *Historical Statistics . . . to 1957*, pp. 90–92.

21. Bishop Duggan was taken to a sanitarium in St. Louis in the spring of 1869. Thomas Foley, having had previous experience as chancellor and vicar-general in Baltimore, was appointed Coadjutor Bishop and Administrator of the Chicago diocese and Titular Bishop of Pergamus. Foley was offered rights of succession to Duggan, which he later accepted. He was consecrated on 27 February 1871. See Thompson, *Diamond Jubilee*, pp. 45–46; Busyn, "Maker of Polish America," p. 73; *Album SSK*, pp. 9–10; *Chicago Tribune*, 6 September 1874, p. 11. The most complete account of the administrative chaos in the diocesan chancery in this period is James P. Gaffey, "Patterns of Ecclesiastical Authority: The Problem of Chicago Succession, 1865–1881," *Church History* 42 (June 1973): 257–70.

22. *Chicago Tribune*, 6 September 1874, p. 11. Peter Kiolbassa, "The Polish Element," in *History of the Catholic Church in Illinois in the XIX Century*, a special issue of *The New World*, 14 April 1900, p. 140. *Album SSK* speaks of the eventual church site as "a beautiful location among shady trees." An artist's conception of the area in the *St. Stanislaus Kostka Diamond Jubilee Book* (Chicago: St. Stanislaus Kostka Parish, 1942) reveals a heavily wooded location. Today, all the poplars are gone.

23. Kiolbassa, "The Polish Element," p. 140.

24. *Album SSK*, p. 10; Iwicki, *Resurrectionist Studies*, p. 51.

25. Peter Kiolbassa to Reverend Jerome Kajsiewicz, 6 May 1869, in Iwicki, *Resurrectionist Studies*, p. 49. See also Kruszka, *Historya*, 1: 575–76, quoting from a letter from Kiolbassa to Reverend Alexander Jelowicki, C.R., 14 June 1869; Busyn, "Maker of Polish America," p. 75; Greene, "Slavic Self-Consciousness," pp. 449–50.

26. The "For Poles Only" statement is cited in Busyn, "Maker of Polish America," p. 75. Kruszka also discusses some of the implications of this ethnocentric stance in *Historya*, 1: 577–78; 8: 135–38. See also Osada, *Historya ZNP*, pp. 58–66; *Album SSK*, p. 10; Brat Maxymus, *Pamiątka Złotego Jubileuszu Kapłaństwa Wielebnego Ks. Kazimierza Sztuczki, C.S.C., Proboszcza Parafii Świętej Trójcy w Chicago* (Chicago: Holy Trinity Parish, 1941), pp. 29–30 for a discussion of trusteeship; F. Niklewicz, *Historya Polaków w Stanie Illinois* (Green Bay, 1931), p. 9. For a thorough discussion of the trusteeship issue in American Catholicism, see Thomas T. McAvoy, *A History of the Catholic Church in the United States* (Notre Dame, Ind.: University of Notre Dame Press, 1969), pp. 92–122 and passim.

27. Busyn, "Maker of Polish America," p. 75.

28. Gaffey, "Patterns of Ecclesiastical Authority," passim; Iwicki, *Resurrectionist Studies*, p. 50.

29. The letter is printed in Kruszka, *Historya*, 8: 145. Kruszka's thesis is that the Resurrectionists and the Jesuits were competing for the Chicago Polonia mission. Based on Szulak's action, one might be tempted to accept the Kruszka hypothesis. The manuscript "Proceedings of the General Chapters: Reports of the American Delegates, Congregation of the Resurrection of Our Lord Jesus Christ, 1871," in the St. Joseph Novitiate Library, Woodstock, Ill., reveals that the Reverend Eugene Funcken was unaware of Halligan's decision when he (Funcken) sent Fathers Wollowski and Elena to Chicago. See also *Album SSK*, pp. 11–12. Władysław Kwiatkowski, *Historia Zgromadzenia Zmartwychwstania Pańskiego Na Stuletnią Rocznicę Jego Założenia 1842–1942* (Albano: Nakładem Księży Zmartwychwstania Pańskiego, 1942), strangely, ignores the entire sequence of events.

30. Kruszka, *Historya*, 8: 147.

31. *Album SSK*, p. 11.
32. *Dziennik Chicagoski*, 10 July 1916; Kruszka, *Historya*, 8: 150–52.
33. Busyn, "Maker of Polish America," p. 77.
34. Ks. Adolph Bakanowski, *Moje Wspomnienia, 1840–1863–1913* (Lwow: Nakładem XX. Zmartwychwstańców Drukiem Jakubowskiego i Sp., 1913), pp. 75–76.
35. *Album SSK*, p. 11.
36. Bakanowski, *Moje Wspomnienia*, p. 76.
37. Ibid.
38. "Proceedings of the General Chapters . . . 1871"; Kwiatkowski, *Historia Zgromadzenia*, p. 287. Kajsiewicz did receive a report from Bakanowski on the Juszkiewicz incident. Kajsiewicz stands by the Bakanowski account claiming that Bakanowski "was totally unaware of the citizen reaction" to Juszkiewicz. Kruszka (*Historya*, 8) accuses the Resurrectionists of conspiracy to dominate the Chicago mission. The Resurrectionists in later writings (e.g., Bakanowski's *Moje Wspomnienia*) deny this. For more on this controversy, see Chapter Seven, "A Bishop for Polonia."

CHAPTER THREE

1. Edward T. Janas, "Father Peter Semenenko, C.R. and His Message," *Polish American Studies* 13 (January–June 1956): 2. The literature dealing with the history of the Congregation of the Resurrection is enormous. The most complete bibliography dealing with the Resurrectionists in Chicago is in Iwicki, pp. 223–26, 265–82. Microfilmed copies of the manuscript records referred to by Iwicki are housed at the St. Joseph Novitiate in Woodstock, Illinois. A very valuable part of the collection are the microfilmed copies of the *Listy z Ameryki (Letters from America)* by the Reverends Adolph Bakanowski, Vincent Barzynski, Francis Gordon, Jan Kasprzycki, Simon Kobrzynski, and Felix Zwiardowski. The letters detail the daily activities of each of the Resurrectionists, all of whom served in the Chicago Polonia mission between 1871 and 1926. See also note 5 below for interpretations of community-parish life by Superior-General Kajsiewicz.
2. Janas, "Semenenko," p. 7; Iwicki, *Resurrectionist Studies*, p. 263.
3. Iwicki, *Resurrectionist Studies*, p. 253; Janas, "Semenenko," pp. 7–18; Kwiatkowski, *Historia Zgromadzenia*, p. 287. Note that the Congregation of the Resurrection technically was not a religious *order*, but a religious *society*. The *Decretum Laudis* (Degree of Praise) is the first step taken by the Holy See when granting approval of a religious missionary society.
4. The Reverend Julian Felinski, Assistant Superior-General of the Resurrectionists at the time, strongly advocated the curtailment of foreign missions and desired that the society devote its full efforts to Poland. Iwicki claims that Felinski was strongly influenced by Mother Marcelline Darowska, Superior-General of the Immaculate Conception Sisters. Mother Darowska is reputed to have based her convictions on spiritual revelations. See Iwicki, *Resurrectionist Studies*, pp. 256–57.
5. For information on the Foley-Kajsiewicz pact, see Hieronym Kajsiewicz, *Pisma: Rozprawy, Listy z Podróży, Pamiętnik o Zgromadzenia*, 3 vols. (Berlin: B. Behra, 1872), 3: 350. Outside of Kajsiewicz's *Writings*, no other primary source exists which would confirm the exact nature of the pact. The only remaining document dealing with the Foley administration still housed in the Archives of the Roman Catholic Archdiocese of Chicago is Bishop Thomas Foley's "Last Will and Testament, 1879," which is of little use to the historian. According to the Reverend Dr. Menceslaus J. Madaj, Archivist of the Chicago Archdiocese, this huge source gap for the Foley administration makes a thorough analysis of the pact virtually impossible. Iwicki notes that Father Adolph Bakanowski's letter to the

Central House in Rome, dated 1 February 1872, makes mention of the recently approved pact; see *Resurrectionist Studies*, p. 8, n. 36.

6. Greene, "Slavic Self-Consciousness," p. 450.

7. Iwicki, *Resurrectionist Studies*, pp. 167–70.

8. Ficht, "Noble Street in Chicago" (M.A. thesis), p. 86; Andrea, "Societies of Saint Stanislaus," pp. 28–29; Kwiatkowski, *Historia Zgromadzenia*, p. 294. The classic study of Polish parish society remains Thomas and Znaniecki, *Polish Peasant*, which is based on letters, parish albums, and interviews.

9. For the extent of the Chicago Fire, see the map provided in Mayer and Wade, *Chicago*, p. 108. For a brief analysis of the *kulturkampf* on Polish emigration, see Joseph Wytrwal, *America's Polish Heritage* (Detroit: Endurance Press, 1961), pp. 125–30. Also see *St. Stanislaus Kostka Diamond Jubilee Book*, p. 64. Note that emigration from Posen was 531 per 100,000 in 1871–1874 as compared to Pomerania's rate of 695 per 100,000 for the same period. For these and additional statistics, see National Bureau of Economic Research, *International Migrations* (New York: National Bureau of Economic Research, 1931), 2: 349.

10. *Album SSK*, passim. Also see *Pamiętnik Parafii Święti Trójcy w Chicago* (Chicago: American Catalog Printing Co., 1918), p. 8; Kruszka, *Historya*, 10: 7–13; Maxymus, *Pamiątka . . . Ks. Sztuczki*, p. 29. The quotation attributed to Peter Kiolbassa comes from Kiolbassa, "The Polish Element," p. 140.

11. For a comprehensive study of the origins of *Pielgrzym* and other contemporary Polish newspapers, see Edmund Olszyk, *The Polish Press in America* (Milwaukee: Marquette University Press, 1940), p. 53 and passim. For the *Gmina* position, see Chapter Four of this study, especially note 24. The "good Yankee" quote comes from a letter of Barzynski to Reverend Father General Jerome Kajsiewicz, 10 June 1872, as quoted in Iwicki, *Resurrectionist Studies*, p. 198; the italics are those of the original.

12. Barzynski to Semenenko, 2 March 1872, Barzynski MSS, microfilm copy of the original, Archives of the Congregation of the Resurrection (hereafter, ACR), St. Joseph Novitiate, Woodstock, Ill. Also see Kruszka, *Historya*, 4: 3, and Olszyk, *Polish Press*, passim.

13. Haiman, *ZPRK*, pp. 25–32. See also, Karol Wachtel, *Z.P.R.K. Dzieje Zjednoczenia Polskiego Rzymsko-Katolickiego w Ameryce* (Chicago: L. J. Winiecki, 1913), p. 213, and Wytrwal, *America's Polish Heritage*, p. 208. A complete text of the original constitution of the PRCU is in Iwicki, *Resurrectionist Studies*, pp. 232–37.

14. Vincent Barzynski to Semenenko, 14 August 1872 in Iwicki, *Resurrectionist Studies*.

15. Karol Wachtel, *Polonia w Ameryce* (Philadelphia: The author, 1944), pp. 164–65; Haiman, *ZPRK*, pp. 32–33; Wytrwal, *America's Polish Heritage*, p. 168.

16. Iwicki, *Resurrectionist Studies*, pp. 232–37. In all probability the document was written by Bakanowski himself. See Iwicki, p. 232, n. 19.

17. Maxymus, *Pamiątka . . . Ks. Sztuczki*, p. 30; Bakanowski, *Moje Wspomnienia*, pp. 88–93; Kruszka, *Historya*, 10: 6–11. The St. Joseph Society originally requested of Bishop Foley that the parish be named after its patron, but Foley instead recommended the name of Holy Trinity so as to avoid confusion with St. Joseph Parish in Chicago, founded in 1846. For an interesting discussion of the relationship of nationalism to Catholicism in Irish quarters, see Lawrence J. McCaffrey, "Irish Nationalism and Irish Catholicism: A Study in Cultural Identity," *Church History* 42 (December 1973): 524–34.

18. *Pamiętnik . . . Św. Trójcy*, p. 6; *Album SSK*, p. 15; Kruszka, *Historya*, 10: 11; Edward Kantowicz, "Polish Chicago: Survival Through Solidarity," in *The Ethnic Frontier: Essays in the History of Group Survival in Chicago and the Midwest*, ed. Melvin G. Holli

and Peter d'A Jones (Grand Rapids, Mich.: Eerdmans, 1977), p. 193. Kantowicz, in turn, depends upon the findings of Galush and Stolarik, who have discussed *jus patronatus* in some detail: see William Galush, "The Polish National Catholic Church," *Records of the Catholic Historical Society of Philadelphia* 83 (Sept.–Dec. 1972): 131–49, and Mark Stolarik, "Lay Initiative in American Slovak Parishes, 1880–1930," *Records of the Catholic Historical Society of Philadelphia* 83 (Sept.–Dec. 1972): 151–58.

19. *Album SSK*, p. 15.
20. Kruszka, *Historya*, 10: 15.
21. Kiolbassa, "The Polish Element," p. 140.
22. The German Catholic attempt to organize a national parish at Holy Trinity in Philadelphia in 1789 is remarkably similar in separatist and trusteeship characteristics to the situation at Holy Trinity in Chicago in the 1870s. The prime mover for separation in Philadelphia was the German Religious Society; see Sidney E. Ahlstrom, *A Religious History of the American People* (New Haven, Conn.: Yale University Press, 1972), pp. 531–32. For similarities with the situation in the German-Irish parishes in New York, see Jay Dolan, "Immigrants in the City: New York's Irish and German Catholics," *Church History* 41 (September 1972): 354–68.

CHAPTER FOUR

1. Kruszka, *Historya*, 10: 84. John J. Rolbiecki, "Vincent Barzynski," *Dictionary of American Biography*, 1, part 2: 30, attributes the comparison between Barzynski and Pope Gregory VII to a writer for the *Illinois Staats-Zeitung*, 20 January 1879. The epigraph for this chapter is from Kruszka, *Historya*, 4: 32.
2. *Dziennik Chicagoski*, 3 January 1895, p. 2; Stanislaus Siatka, *Krótkie Wspomnienie o życiu i Działalności Ks. M. Wincentego Barzynskiego, C.R., napisane ku uczczenia pamiątki odsłoniecia pomnika w drugą rocznicę jego śmierci* (Chicago: Dziennik Chicagoski, 1901), p. 29.
3. Editorial, *Dziennik Chicagoski*, 20 April 1892, p. 2.
4. As quoted in T. Lindsay Baker, "The Early Years of Rev. Wincenty Barzynski," *Polish American Studies* 32 (Spring 1975): 43.
5. Ibid., p. 42.
6. Siatka, *Krótkie Wspomnienie . . . Barzynskiego*, pp. 7–16; Iwicki, *Resurrectionist Studies*, pp. 26–45; Baker, "Early Years," pp. 29–52.
7. Kruszka, *Historya*, 10: 15–16.
8. Ibid.; Maxymus, *Pamiątka . . . Ks. Sztuczki*, pp. 29–30; *Pamiętnik . . . Św. Trójcy*, p. 7; Iwicki, *Resurrectionist Studies*, p. 70.
9. Kruszka, *Historya*, 10: 16–22; Iwicki, *Resurrectionist Studies*, pp. 68–70; *Pamiętnik . . . Święti Trojcy*, p. 7; Maxymus, *Pamiątka . . . Ks. Sztuczki*, p. 29; Greene, "Slavic Self-Consciousness," pp. 450–52.
10. Siatka, *Krótkie Wspomnienie . . . Barzynskiego*, p. 18.
11. Thompson, *Diamond Jubilee*, p. 381. Also see the photographs in Iwicki, *Resurrectionist Studies*, opposite p. 49, for a view of the parish in 1869 and a design submitted for the building in 1877, and opposite p. 64, for a photograph of the building in its final form (completed in 1892 with alterations to the steeples).
12. Siatka, *Krótkie Wspomnienie . . . Barzynskiego*, p. 17.
13. Ibid., p. 18. Siatka does not date the speech, but the text indicates an approximate date of November 1876.
14. Ibid., p. 19.
15. See, for example, Thomas and Znaniecki, *Polish Peasant* 1: 349, 354.

16. For brief histories of each of these thirteen parishes and other Resurrectionist parishes in Chicago and Cook County, see Thompson, *Diamond Jubilee*, passim, and Iwicki, *Resurrectionist Studies*, pp. 46–110.

17. Henryk Sienkiewicz, *Portrait of America: Letters of Henryk Sienkiewicz*, ed., trans. Charles Morley (New York: Columbia University Press, 1959), pp. 284–85.

18. Ibid., p. 282. For substantiation of Sienkiewicz's charge see Paul Fox, *The Poles in America* (New York: George H. Doran, 1922).

19. Kruszka, *Historya*, 10: 22–32.

20. Ibid. See also the letter signed by Vincent Barzynski, Francis Breitkopf, and Joseph Barzynski to the Resurrectionist Central House in Rome, dated 1883 (no month or day), in the Barzynski MSS (ACR); *Pamiętnik . . .Święci Trójcy*, pp. 10–11; Greene, "Slavic Self-Consciousness," p. 453; McAvoy, *History*, p. 260, especially regarding Title VIII of the decrees of the 1884 Plenary Council.

21. *Chicago Tribune*, 3 June 1881, p. 5.

22. Ibid; see also the letter from Joseph Grajczyk and other members of the Trinitarian delegation to Cardinal Simeoni, 2 April 1891, copy of the original in the Barzynski File, Archives of the Roman Catholic Archdiocese of Chicago (hereafter, AAC), St. Mary of the Lake Seminary, Mundelein, Ill.; Thompson, *Diamond Jubilee*, p. 49; Kruszka, *Historya*, 10: 32–37; Ficht, "Noble Street in Chicago" (M.A. thesis), p. 88.

23. *Chicago Tribune*, 3 June 1881, p. 5.

24. Thompson, *Diamond Jubilee*, p. 53; Kruszka, *Historya*, 10: 38–39; Vincent Barzynski to Peter Semenenko, letter dated 1883 (no month or day), in Barzynski MSS (ACR). The Vatican apparently failed to use the statistical information on immigrants to the United States available from the U.S. Census Bureau. This oversight was the cause of much misinformation. Of the thirteen proposals to the Council of 1884, only the Italian emigration was mentioned, to the exclusion of all other groups. See McAvoy, *History*, p. 256.

25 *Pamiętnik . . . Święci Trójcy*, pp. 11–12; Kruszka, *Historya*, 10: 40–41. Note, too, the strong Americanization theme in Gibbons's Milwaukee address of 20 August 1891. Referring to the Cahensly affair, Gibbons stated: "Let us glory in the title of American citizen. We owe our allegiance to one country, and that country is America." See McAvoy, *History*, p. 296.

26. *Dziennik Chicagoski*, 17 June 1918. For an examination of population movements during and after this period, see Parot, "Ethnic Versus Black Metropolis," pp. 18–22, and Joseph J. Parot, "The Racial Dilemma in Chicago's Polish Neighborhoods," *Polish American Studies* 32 (Autumn 1975): 27–37. *The Official Catholic Directory* (New York: P. J. Kenedy, 1886–); for the years 1886–1890 this work was known as *Hoffman's Catholic Directory, Almanac and Clergy List*, and for 1900–1905 as *The Catholic Directory, Almanac and Clergy List*. See also, Iwicki, *Resurrectionist Studies*, pp. 46–110, and Thompson, *Diamond Jubilee*, passim.

27. The problem of leakage is discussed by Gerald Shaughnessy, *Has the Immigrant Kept the Faith? A Study of Immigration and Catholic Growth in the United States, 1790–1920* (New York: Macmillan, 1925). Shaughnessy's statistics are not altogether reliable.

28. Barzynski to Przewlocki, 18 October 1887, in the Barzynski MSS (ACR). See also Kwiatkowski, *Historia Zgromadzenia*, p. 517.

29. Iwicki, *Resurrectionist Studies*, pp. 72–79. I have also examined the extensive parish album collection for numerous parishes listed in Map Three. See the Parish Album File in the Polish Roman Catholic Union Museum and Archives, Chicago, Ill.; many of the albums discuss Barzynski's difficulties with the selection of pastors.

30. St. Adalbert's Parish was organized in 1873. Its first pastor was a certain Reverend Klimecki, about which little is known. Klimecki was succeeded by: Reverend Dominic

Majer, later to become active in the Polish National Alliance, who served until 1878; Reverend Adolph Snigurski, who resigned in 1884 due to poor health; Reverend Radziejewski, who was pastor until his death in 1904. Note that Majer's tenure at St. Adalbert's coincides with Dyniewicz's renewed efforts there to initiate the *Gmina Polska*. See "Polish Churches of Chicago and Vicinity," in *Poles of Chicago, 1837–1937*, p. 98.

The Radziejewski edicts gained some notoriety, as even the *New York Times* carried the story (in addition to similar coverage in various Chicago newspapers). See, for example, "A Priest's Dictation—Chicago's Polish Catholics in Open Rebellion," *New York Times*, 26 September 1888, p. 6. The *Times* also carried stories on the Trinitarian conflict of the 1890s in addition to reporting the nationalist party activities in other urban Polish settlements outside Chicago. For more secondary information on the *Wojciechowo* conflict, see the *St. Adalbert Parish Diamond Jubilee Book* (Chicago: St. Adalbert Parish, 1947).

31. *Chicago Tribune*, 4 September 1889, p. 2; *New York Times*, 4 September 1889, p. 8; Kruszka, *Historya*, 10: 42–48; *Pamiętnik . . . Święti Trójcy*, passim. Archbishop Feehan states the chancery position in his letter to Father Simon Kobrzynski, June 1889, in the Kobrzynski MSS (microfilmed copy of the original in the ACR, St. Joseph Novitiate, Woodstock, Ill.).

32. Giller's letter is quoted in Renkiewicz, *Poles in America*, pp. 64–65.

33. Editorial, *Zgoda*, 23 November 1881. This was the first issue of *Zgoda*, a copy of which is preserved at the editorial office of the *Dziennik Związkowy* (Chicago Daily Zgoda), Chicago, Ill.

34. The Chicago *Gmina Polska* became *Grupa N. 2* (Group Number Two) of the Polish National Alliance's 711 such local groups; see Osada, *Historya ZNP*, p. 639. Osada's work is the standard history of the PNA, as Haiman, *ZPRK*, is of the PRCU. PRCU statistics are from *65 Lat Zjednoczenia Polskiego Rzymsko-Katolickiego w Ameryce, 1873–1938* (Chicago: PRCU, 1938), pp. 82–85, 88, 106, 112, 114–16, 120. See also Kruszka, *Historya*, 4: 32ff.

35. Osada, *Historya ZNP*, pp. 624–27.

36. "Our Polish Citizens," *Chicago Tribune*, 14 March 1886, p. 3. For a detailed discussion of Polonia's press, see Olszyk, *Polish Press in America*. I have also depended upon a series of articles by Eugene P. Willging and Herta Hatzfield, "Nineteenth Century Polish Catholic Publications in the United States," *Polish American Studies* 12 (July–December 1955): 88–100; 13 (January–June 1956): 19–35; 13 (July-December 1956): 89–101. Also see the editorial in the first issue of the *Dziennik Chicagoski*, 15 December 1890.

37. Kruszka, *Historya*, 10: 50–57.

38. Grajczyk, Binkowski, and Bartoszewicz to Simeoni, 12 April 1891, Polish Parish File, AAC, St. Mary of the Lake Seminary, Mundelein, Ill. My translation.

39. Kwiatkowski, *Historia Zgromadzenia*, pp. 347–48.

40. "Proceedings of the General Chapters: Congregation of the Resurrection of Our Lord Jesus Christ, 1901," ACR, St. Joseph Novitiate, Woodstock, Ill.; see also the "Rendiconto della missione d'e Chicago, 1901," signed by Jan Kasprzycki, Provincial, 10 June 1901, which lists Resurrectionist assets in Chicago as of 1 January 1901, in Kasprzycki MSS, ACR, St. Joseph Novitiate, Woodstock, Ill. Smolikowski's directives and other material on the Parish Bank is covered in Kwiatkowski, *Historia Zgromadzenia*, pp. 340, 347–48, 353, 362, 373, 389.

41. The quotation regarding the Title Six Plenary decree is from McAvoy, *History*, p. 260. For assets of the PRCU, see Haiman, *ZPRK*, p. 549, and *65 Lat ZPRK*, pp. 84, 88–116.

The social and economic mobility of Dyniewicz and Kiolbassa indicates that Chicago Polonia's leadership elite was by this time beginning to prosper. Dyniewicz, in the 1880s, purchased ten acres of land and built a 16-room mansion at 5917 West Diversey. It was said "to be his country house, similar to the country house of his ancestors in Poland." In addition to owning the *Gazeta Polska* and its allied printshop, Dyniewicz also owned a bookstore and was consultant to several savings and loan associations. Before long, he was to form friendships with Joseph Medill, J. Ogden Armour, and Victor F. Lawson (founder of the *Chicago Daily News*). See the interview with Dyniewicz's granddaughter in Drury, *Old Chicago Houses*, pp. 384–86. Kiolbassa was elected to the Illinois House of Representatives in 1877 and to the post of City Treasurer of the city of Chicago in 1891. His law practice and real estate dealings also subsidized his political career. See *The New World*, 27 October 1900, p. 4.

42. Gibbons to Mundelein, 18 November 1920, Mundelein MSS, AAC, St. Mary of the Lake Seminary, Mundelein, Ill. For statistics on other dioceses in Illinois, see U.S., Department of Commerce and Labor, Bureau of the Census, *Special Reports of the United States Census Bureau: Religious Bodies, 1906* part 2, pp. 611–12.

43. The total population of East St. Louis in 1890 was 27,655; of Springfield, 34,159; of Rockford, 31,051; of Quincy, 36,252; of Peoria, 56,100. See U.S., Department of Commerce and Labor, Bureau of the Census, *Thirteenth Census of the United States, 1910 Abstract with Supplement for Illinois* (Washington, D.C.: G.P.O., 1913), p. 569.

44. *Książka Jubileuszowa Parafii Św. Trójcy, 1893–1943* (Chicago: Holy Trinity Parish, 1943), pp. 23–24; Maxymus, *Pamiątka . . . Ks. Sztuczki*, p. 32; Kruszka, *Historya*, 10: 50–57. *The New World*, 14 September 1895, p. 4, indicates that despite Barzynski's anger, he was still the only Polish priest to concelebrate the Pontifical Mass with Archbishop Satolli at Holy Name Cathedral on 8 September 1895. See also, *The New World*, 19 October 1901, for Sztuczko's subsequent involvement at the Polish National Alliance Convention of 1901.

45. The aims of the Polish League are listed in Haiman, *ZPRK*, pp. 139–43. For the PNA's reaction to the Polish League, see Osada, *Historya ZNP*, pp. 387–89. For an interesting discussion of the interdenominational interchange taking place at the Columbian Exposition, see Paul Carter, "The Meeting of East and West," *The Spiritual Crisis of the Gilded Age* (DeKalb, Ill.: Northern Illinois University Press, 1971), pp. 199–221. Carter's presentation does not cover Polonia but does offer challenging insights into the ecumenical activities of the Exposition. For other expressions of Polish American unity in 1893 Polonia, see the *Dziennik Chicagoski*, 17 August 1893. For events involving a direct Catholic contribution, see the *Chicago Tribune*, 5 September 1893, p. 12. The "Pax Dei" quotation is from Haiman, *ZPRK*, p. 129. See also, Victor Greene, *For God and Country: The Rise of Polish and Lithuanian Ethnic Consciousness in America, 1860–1910* (Madison: State Historical Society of Wisconsin, 1975), pp. 90–95.

CHAPTER FIVE

1. For a thorough discussion of the Third Plenary Council of Baltimore, see McAvoy, *History*, pp. 253–274. For a brilliant analysis of the entire Americanization question and the relationship of the hierarchy to the lay immigrant Catholic, see Philip Gleason, "The Crisis of Americanization," in *Contemporary Catholicism in the United States*, ed. Philip Gleason (Notre Dame, Ind.: University of Notre Dame Press, 1969), pp. 3–31. McAvoy synthesizes much Catholic scholarship pre-dating Vatican II, while the Gleason volume summarizes post-Vatican II perspectives on numerous historical topics. See also Moses Rischin, "The New American Catholic History," *Church History* 41 (June 1972): 225–29.

For statistical references regarding immigration during 1884–1914, see U.S. Bureau of the Census, *Historical Statistics . . . to 1957*, pp. 56–57; for religious statistics, see ibid., pp. 228–29. The total number of immigrants to the United States for the 1884–1919 period is given as 19,802,949, the total number of Catholics for 1891 as 8,277,000, and for 1914 as 16,068,000.

2. John Tracy Ellis, *The Life of James Cardinal Gibbons, Archbishop of Baltimore: 1834–1921*, 2 vols. (Milwaukee: Bruce, 1952), 1: 373–74. For a definitive treatment of the liberal versus conservative debate, see Robert D. Cross, *The Emergence of Liberal Catholicism in America* (Cambridge, Mass.: Harvard University Press, 1958), especially pp. 22–50. Another account which covers the debate over assimilation is Richard M. Linkh, *American Catholicism and European Immigrants (1900–1924)* (Staten Island, N.Y.: Center for Migration Studies, 1975), pp. 1–33. The most complete treatments of the relationship of Catholicism to the German immigration are Colman Barry, *The Catholic Church and the German Americans* (Washington, D.C.: Catholic University Press, 1953), and Philip Gleason, *The Conservative Reformers: German-American Catholics and the Social Order* (Notre Dame, Ind.: University of Notre Dame Press, 1968). Barry's book includes texts of the Abbelen Memorial and other memorials submitted to the Vatican and the hierarchy.

The best survey of developments in the Polish and Lithuanian communities regarding the twin issues of national parishes and national bishops is Greene, *Polish and Lithuanian Ethnic Consciousness*. For similar conflicts among other ethnic groups, see Henry B. Leonard, "Ethnic Conflict and Episcopal Power: The Diocese of Cleveland, 1847–1870," *Catholic Historical Review* 62 (July 1976): 388–407, and Bohdan Procko, "Soter Ortynsky: First Ruthenian Bishop in the United States, 1907–1916," *Catholic Historical Review* 58 (January 1973): 513–33.

3. Shaughnessy, *Has the Immigrant Kept the Faith?*, passim.

4. For an excellent treatment of the Cahensly movement, see John H. Meng, "Cahenslyism: The First Stage, 1883–1891," *Catholic Historical Review* 31 (January 1946): 389–413, and "Cahenslyism: The Second Chapter, 1891–1910," *Catholic Historical Review* 33 (October 1946): 302–40. I have also depended heavily upon McAvoy, *History*, pp. 263–302, and Cross, *Emergence*, passim.

5. See McAvoy, *History*, pp. 300–305 for an account on Leo's decision to select Satolli. For the evolving Americanist debate and the challenge to the "heresy" of Americanism, see Cross, *Emergence*, pp. 182–205, and Meng, "Second Chapter," passim. The most comprehensive treatment is still Thomas T. McAvoy, *The Americanist Heresy in Roman Catholicism, 1895–1900* (Notre Dame, Ind.: University of Notre Dame Press, 1963), and McAvoy's, "Americanism, Fact and Fiction," *Catholic Historical Review*, 31 (July 1945): 133–53.

6. *Historical Statistics . . . to 1957*, p. 56; Wandycz, *Partitioned Poland*, pp. 276–95. For crowded tenement conditions, see City Homes Association, *Tenement Conditions in Chicago*, pp. 55–61 and passim; also Parot, "Ethnic Versus Black Metropolis," pp. 5–34.

7. *Złoty Jubileusz Parafii Św. Jadwigi* (Chicago, 1938), the parish jubilee album of St. Hedwig's parish, carries a hazy account of the origins of the Independent movement.

8. Ibid.

9. *Dziennik Chicagoski*, 17 January 1895, p. 2; Kruszka, *Historya*, 10: 97–98.

10. "Recent Schismatical Movements Among Catholics of the United States," *American Ecclesiastical Review*, 21 (July 1899): 1–13; Theodore Andrews, *The Polish National Catholic Church in America and Poland* (London: S.P.C.K., 1953), p. 18. The standard work on the Old Catholic Church is C. B. Moss, *The Old Catholic Movement: Its Origins and History*, 2nd ed. (London: S.P.C.K., 1964).

11. Anthony Kozlowski is not to be confused with Reverend Edward Kozlowski, later the Auxiliary Bishop of Milwaukee.

For details on the Old Catholic-Independent connection, see Chas. C. Grafton, *A Journey Godward* (Milwaukee: Morehouse-Young-Churchman, 1910). Grafton's reminiscences include a description of the Old Catholic Church in the United States, especially in Wisconsin. For another view, see S. J. Tonsor, "Old Catholics," *New Catholic Encyclopedia*, 10: 672–73; also, T. Horgan, "The Polish National Catholic Church," ibid., 11: 505–6. The *Chicago Tribune*, 15 January 1907, p. 1, has brief biographical material on Kozlowski.

The relationship of the Independents to the rise of the Polish National Catholic Church has attracted serious professional study in recent years. A pioneer work in the field, which unfortunately has gone unpublished, is Menceslaus J. Madaj's "A Study of the Polish National Catholic Church." Professor Madaj, Archivist of the Chicago Roman Catholic Archdiocese and pioneer-scholar in the Polish American Historical Association, is a leading authority on Polish schismatics. His work and insightful suggestions are summarized in "The Polish National Catholic Church: Bibliographic Suggestions," *Polish American Studies* 25 (January–June 1968): 10–15. Also see Andrews, *Polish National Catholic Church*, and Greene, "The Rise of Independentism" *Polish and Lithuanian Ethnic Consciousness*, pp. 100–121. I endorse Professor Greene's conclusion that the Independent party rose in response to the clerical-nationalist deadlock. For the Resurrectionist side of the story, see Iwicki, *Resurrectionist Studies*, pp. 79–95. Readers of Polish can consult Hieronym Kubiak, *Polski Narodowy Kościół Katolicki w Stanach Zjednoczonych Ameryki w latach 1897–1965* (Cracow: Polish Academy of Science, 1970); *Złoty Jubileusz . . . Św. Jadwigi*; and Kruszka's *Historya* as well as his *Siedm Siedmioleci Czyli Pół Wieku Życia: Pamiętnik i Przyczynek do Historji Polskiej w Ameryce*, 2 vols. (Milwaukee: The author, and the press of St. Adalbert's, 1924). The periodical literature on the subject is too vast to include here, but readers can consult my article, "Bishop Francis Hodur," in supplement 5 of the *Dictionary of American Biography*, Supp. 5, ed., John A. Garraty (New York: Charles Scribner's Sons, 1977), pp. 304–6, and the accompanying bibliographic note. Finally, the comprehensive Jagiellonian University bibliography *Materiały Do Bibliografii Dziejów Emigracji Oraz Skupisk Polonijnych W Ameryce Północnej I Południowej W XIX I XX Wieku*, ed. Irene Paczynska and Andrew Pilch (Cracow: Jagiellonian University, 1979), contains numerous entries on the Polish National Catholic Church.

12. Tonsor, "Old Catholics," p. 672; "Recent Schismatical Movements," p. 1–13; Moss, *Old Catholic Movement*, passim.

13. *Dziennik Chicagoski*, 13 June 1893 (Chicago Foreign Language Press Survey, hereafter CFLPS). Translations made by the author in this chapter and elsewhere will carry the standard bibliographic citation; translations coming from the CFLPS will be specifically indicated.

14. *Dziennik Chicagoski*, 2 January 1894 (CFLPS); *Książka Jubileuszowa Parafii Św. Trójcy*, pp. 23–24; Maxymus, *Pamiątka . . . Ks. Sztuczki*, p. 32; Greene, *Polish and Lithuanian Ethnic Consciousness*, pp. 100–112.

15. A complete text of the Polish League Constitution is in the *Dziennik Chicagoski*, 23 April 1894. The *Dziennik Chicagoski* carried initial revisions of the constitution in its 10 May 1894 issue (see note 16 below). For details of the new clerical-nationalist harmony, see Greene, *Polish and Lithuanian Ethnic Consciousness*, pp. 91–95. For material on the original Polish League founded by Polish émigrés in *kraju*, see Wandycz, *Partitioned Poland*, p. 152.

16. Further constitutional revisions and other League resolutions were printed in the *Dziennik Chicagoski*, 11–12 May 1894.

17. "Father Barzynski and Jacob Tamillo," *Dziennik Chicagoski*, 16 January 1892 (CFLPS).

18. Both the quotation and the questions are in ibid.

19. *Zgoda*, 17 February 1892 (CFLPS); Greene, *Polish and Lithuanian Ethnic Consciousness*, p. 76.

20. *Dziennik Chicagoski*, 29 February 1892 and 28 July 1892 (CFLPS).

21. "Polish Priests and National Affairs," *Dziennik Chicagoski*, 20 August 1892 (CFLPS).

22. Ibid.

23. For example, see *Dziennik Chicagoski*, 27 March 1894 (CFLPS) for editorial remarks on the liberal pamphlet entitled "The Polish League Is A Political Work Of Father Vincent Barzynski, Pastor Of St. Stanislaus Kostka Parish."

24. "Schismatics Invade Chicago," *Dziennik Chicagoski*, 23 October 1894 (CFLPS); letter, "Tamillo, Chrestowski and Company Are In Chicago," *Dziennik Chicagoski*, 23 October 1894, signed "A Catholic Priest From Chicago" (Vincent Barzynski?). See also, the editorial " 'Messiah' For The Poles," *Dziennik Chicagoski*, 6 February 1894 (CFLPS). The *Chicago Tribune*, 14 March 1895, has an account of the Omaha incident involving Kaminski. For an account of the Scranton movement, see Kubiak, *Polski Narodowy Kościoł*, pp. 112–14, and Kruszka, *Historya*, 12: 87–89. For Greene's interpretations of Independentism, see *Polish and Lithuanian Ethnic Consciousness*, pp. 102–3, 110–14.

25. *Dziennik Chicagoski*, 17 January 1895 (CFLPS); Iwicki, *Resurrectionist Studies*, pp. 79–82.

26. Szczesny Zahajkiewicz to Reverend John Kasprzycki, C.R., 2 May 1907, Provincial Archives of the Chicago Province of the Congregation of the Resurrection of Our Lord Jesus Christ, Woodstock, Ill. A translation of the entire text is provided in Iwicki, *Resurrectionist Studies*, pp. 82–83.

27. *Chicago Tribune*, 15 January 1895, p. 1.

28. *Dziennik Chicagoski*, 19 January 1895 (CFLPS).

29. A lengthy account of the riot is given in the *Chicago Tribune*, 9 February 1895, p. 3; see also the *Dziennik Chicagoski*, 9 February 1895.

30. *Dziennik Chicagoski*, 12 February 1895.

31. Zahajkiewicz to Kasprzycki, 2 May 1907 (see note 26 above); *Chicago Tribune*, 20 February 1895, p. 1.

32. For various accounts of the Muldoon meeting, see "Recalcitrant Poles," *The New World*, 2 March 1895; *Chicago Tribune*, 26 February 1895, p. 11; Iwicki, *Resurrectionist Studies*, p. 87.

33. *Dziennik Chicagoski*, 1 March 1895 (CFLPS).

34. *Chicago Daily News*, 15 March 1895.

35. *Chicago Tribune*, 16 March 1895, p. 1.

36. Ibid.

37. *Dziennik Chicagoski*, 25 March 1895 (CFLPS).

38. *Dziennik Chicagoski*, 24 March 1895 (CFLPS).

39. *The New World*, 1 January 1898, p. 9; Iwicki, *Resurrectionist Studies*, p. 94. For the eventual union of the Chicago Independents and the Polish National Catholic Church under Hodur, see Andrews, *Polish National Catholic Church*, pp. 18–19, and John Hardon, S.J., "The Polish National Catholic Church," *Homiletic and Pastoral Review* 56 (April 1956): 552–61.

40. *Dziennik Chicagoski*, 24 May 1895, p. 2.

41. Siatka, *Krótkie Wspomnienie . . . Barzynskiego*, pp. 20, 22, 25.

42. For particulars regarding this case, see *The New World*, 22 June 1895, p. 4; *Dziennik Chicagoski*, 21 June 1895, p. 1; 22 June 1895, p. 1; *Chicago Tribune*, 16 June 1895, p. 6.

43. *Dziennik Chicagoski*, 22 June 1895 (CFLPS).

44. *Chicago Tribune*, 12 August 1895, p. 7; *Dziennik Chicagoski*, 12 August 1895 (CFLPS).

45. *Dziennik Chicagoski*, 26 August 1895 (CFLPS).

46. *Chicago Tribune*, 29 September 1895, p. 1.
47. *The New World*, 5 October 1895, p. 8.
48. *Chicago Tribune*, 29 September 1895, p. 1.
49. H. J. Heuser, "European Priests Applying For Admission To American Dioceses," *The Ecclesiastical Review* 30 (March 1904): 293–95.
50. *Chicago Tribune*, 29 September 1895, p. 1.
51. Yet *The New World* tactfully praised "Poland's Catholicism" in an editorial four weeks later, 2 November 1895, p. 8.
52. Andrews, *Polish National Catholic Church*, p. 19.
53. *The New World*, 1 January 1898, p. 1.
54. *The New World*, 9 July 1898, p. 9.
55. *The New World*, 2 September 1899, p. 8.
56. *The New World*, 19 January 1907, p. 5. For an account of the events surrounding the death of Kozlowski, see the *Chicago Tribune*, 15 January 1907.
57. *Dziennik Chicagoski*, 11 November 1895 (CFLPS).
58. *Dziennik Chicagoski*, 13 November 1895 (CFLPS).
59. "Letters to the Editor," *Dziennik Chicagoski*, 4 January 1896.
60. Siatka, *Krótkie Wspomnienie . . . Barzynskiego*, p. 27.
61. Barzynski concluded that the Independents had rejected their Polish heritage in their rejection of Roman Catholicism. See ibid.; also see "Mowa Patryotyczna" *Dziennik Chicagoski*, 3 January 1895, p. 1.
62. *The New World*, 2 January 1897, p. 10.
63. Greene, *Polish and Lithuanian Ethnic Consciousness*, pp. 119–20.
64. "Recent Schismatical Movements," pp. 1–13; Greene, *Polish and Lithuanian Ethnic Consciousness*, pp. 108–9. The most complete doctrinal statement of the Polish National Catholic Church is given in *Księga Pamiątkowa "33" Polsko Narodowego Katolickiego Kościoła w Ameryce i Dwudziestą Rocznicę Pierwszego Sejmu Polsko Narodowej Spójni* (Scranton: Drukiem Straży, 1930).
65. W. Kruszka, "Let There Be Smaller Congregations," *American Ecclesiastical Review* 21 (August 1899): 202–3.
66. Ibid.
67. The call for the Congress was made in the *Dziennik Chicagoski*, 11 February 1896; the quotation is from the *Dziennik Chicagoski*, 27 February 1896 (CFLPS).
68. *Dziennik Chicagoski*, 18 March 1896 (CFLPS).
69. *Dziennik Chicagoski*, 20 March 1896; 11 May 1896 (CFLPS).
70. For details of the ceremonies, see the *Dziennik Chicagoski*, 3–5 May 1899; all are page one stories. For other details, see Siatka, *Krótkie Wspomnienie . . . Barzynskiego*, pp. 53–56.
71. *The New World*, 9 July 1898, p. 9.
72. *The New World*, 19 September 1908, p. 1.
73. Ibid.; see also the instructions for the readmission of Independents to the Roman Catholic Church contained in two letters from M. Cardinal Rampolla to Archbishop Quigley, 31 July 1911 and 14 June 1912, in the Quigley MSS, AAC, St. Mary of the Lake Seminary, Mundelein, Ill. The term "schismatic" was used by clerical loyalists but not by the Independents themselves; see Greene, *Polish and Lithuanian Ethnic Consciousness*, pp. 115–21.
74. The Polish National Catholic Church suffered an Independent movement of its own in Poland, one known as the Faron movement. By the outbreak of World War II, the PNCC claimed only 50,000 converts in Poland, less than a fraction of one percent of all Catholics in Poland; see Andrews, *Polish National Catholic Church*, p. 82.

75. *Dziennik Ludowy*, 20 May 1907 (CFLPS).

76. *Dziennik Ludowy*, 19 March 1908 (CFLPS).

77. *Dziennik Ludowy*, 30 July 1908 (CFLPS). Items of a similar nature may be found in *Bicz Boży*, 1 January 1912; 16 June 1912; 15 November 1913 (CFLPS).

78. See the published findings of a symposium of Polish-American scholars held at St. Mary's College, Orchard Lake, Mich., 19 March 1967 in *Polish American Studies* 24 (January-June 1967). For the Resurrectionist rebuttal to the initial volumes of Kruszka's *Historya*, see Pawel Smolikowski, "Ks. Kruszka i Jego Dokumenty," *Dziennik Chicagoski*, 9 February 1907.

79. Greene, *Polish and Lithuanian Ethnic Consciousness*, pp. 100–101, 108–9, 119–20.

CHAPTER SIX

1. H. J. Heuser, "American Bishops and Polish Catholics," *The Ecclesiastical Review* 29 (October 1903): 347–52; see also H. J. Heuser, "European Priests Applying for Admission," pp. 293–95.

2. "The Cardinal Prefect on the Election of American Bishops," *The Ecclesiastical Review* 7 (July 1892): 15–19.

3. Ibid., p. 17. For the most complete, up-to-date discussion of Polonia's drive for *równouprawnienie*, see Greene, *Polish and Lithuanian Ethnic Consciousness*, pp. 122–42.

4. Joseph J. Parot, "The American Faith and the Persistence of Chicago Polonia, 1870–1920" (Ph.D. diss. Northern Illinois University, 1971), pp. 53–54; on the "Irish Catholic Church" in America, see Wittke, *The Irish in America*, p. 190.

5. "Constitution of the Association of Polish Catholic Priests in the United States of America, Under the Patronage of the Most Sacred Heart of Jesus, and the Protection of the Blessed Virgin Mary, Immaculately Conceived," in Iwicki, *Resurrectionist Studies*, pp. 243–44.

6. Ibid., p. 245.

7. Ibid. See also Thomas and Znaniecki, *Polish Peasant*, 2: 1576.

8. For more details, see Haiman, *ZPRK*, p. 79. Haiman lists the names of the eleven priests who supported Father Majer. For other Alliancist activity, see *Zgoda*, 2 March 1887, p. 4.

9. Haiman, *ZPRK* p. 80; Iwicki, *Resurrectionist Studies*, p. 246 and passim. For an Alliancist standpoint, see Osada, *Historya ZNP*, pp. 277–79. The fraternal alliance founded by Majer was the Polish Union of America.

10. Haiman, *ZPRK*, pp. 80–81.

11. Quoted in Osada, *Historya ZNP*, pp. 278–79.

12. Parot, "The American Faith," pp. 64–65; Iwicki, *Resurrectionist Studies*, pp. 206, 246.

13. Regarding Archbishop Ireland's resistance to ethnic pluralism in the church, see, e.g., James H. Moynihan, "Resisting Nationalism in the Church," *The Life of Archbishop John Ireland* (New York: Harper, 1953), pp. 54–78. The Irish bishops in the United States were hardly a monolithic force in the American church; they engaged in bitter intragroup feuds which often dwarfed many of Polonia's internal clashes, especially in the crisis over the Americanist and Modernist "heresies"; see McAvoy, *Americanist Heresy*. The bibliography dealing with both of these "phantom" heresies (McAvoy's terminology) is extensive. The blackballing of Bishop John Lancaster Spalding, head of the Peoria, Illinois, diocese, indicates the degree of intensity of the feud among Irish Americanists within the hierarchy; for more on this and related incidents, see David Francis Sweeney, *The Life of John Lan-*

caster Spalding, First Bishop of Peoria: 1840–1916 (New York: Herder and Herder, 1965), p. 286.

14. In his correspondence with Archbishop Mundelein thirty years later, Gibbons admits that he had received a request to install a Polish American bishop in the United States in 1890 but gives no other particulars regarding the request. See Gibbons to Mundelein, 18 November 1920, in Mundelein MSS (AAC).

15. For a later summary of arguments regarding the question of Polish bishops in America, see *The New World*, 12 September 1903, pp. 14–15. Robert Trisco, "Apostolic Delegation in the U.S.," *New Catholic Encyclopedia* (New York: McGraw-Hill, 1967), 1: 690–93, covers the transition period from missionary status to the administration by the Apostolic Delegate. For the installation of German-American bishops, see McAvoy, *History*, pp. 306–07. For interethnic conflict in the Cleveland diocese leading to the selection of Bishop Horstmann, see Leonard, "Ethnic Conflict and Episcopal Power," pp. 388–407. For corresponding movements to organize a national diocese in the Byzantine-Slavic Rite for Ruthenians in the United States, see Procko, "Soter Ortynsky," pp. 513–33.

16. "The Cardinal Prefect," pp. 15–19. The Cardinal-Prefect's directives were translated from Latin (the *Epistola ad Episcopos Stat. Foeder. Americae*) to English by the editor of *The Ecclesiastical Review* in the "Analecta" section, a regular feature outlining recent changes in Canon Law.

17. Sweeney, *Spalding*, pp. 194–98.

18. Wandycz, *Partitioned Poland*, p. 234.

19. Rose, "Prussian Poland," p. 416. Ledochowski's zeal led to his directive forbidding the singing of "Boże Coś Polskę," the religious version of the Polish anthem, during church ceremonies in Poland.

20. Edward Wakin and Joseph F. Scheuer, *The De-Romanization of the American Catholic Church* (New York: Macmillan, 1966), p. 27.

21. Jay P. Dolan, *The Immigrant Church: New York's Irish and German Catholics, 1815–1865* (Baltimore: Johns Hopkins University Press, 1975), p. 165.

22. Ibid.

23. Greene, *Polish and Lithuanian Ethnic Consciousness*, pp. 122–28. For another viewpoint, see Warren C. Platt, "The Polish National Catholic Church: An Inquiry into Its Origins," *Church History* 46 (December 1977): 474–89. Platt discusses the numerous theological implications of the term "schism." For the line of succession of Polish National Catholic Church bishops, see Gregory Swiderski, "Polish-American Polish National Catholic Bishops," *Polish American Studies* 24 (January-June 1967): 27–41, and Edward Zukowski, "Polish-American Old Catholic Bishops," *Polish American Studies* 24 (January-June 1967): 41–44. See also M. J. Madaj, "The Polish Immigrant, the American Catholic Hierarchy, and Father Wenceslaus Kruszka," *Polish American Studies* 26 (1969): 16–29.

24. The most complete account of Kruszka's life is his autobiography, *Siedm Siedmioleci*. For a brief English language sketch, see Bolek, *Who's Who in Polish America*, p. 239; Alexander Syski, "The Nestor of Polish Historians in America: Reverend Waclaw Kruszka," *Polish American Studies* 1 (January-December 1944): 69; and Madaj, "Polish Immigrant," pp. 16–29. Finally, as with all other major figures in the history of American Polonia, a brief sketch can be found in the *Polski Słownik Biograficzny* (Wroclaw, Warszawa, Krakow, Gdansk: Zakład Narodowy Imienia Ossolińskich Wydawnictwo Polskiej Akademii Nauk, 1935–), 23 vols. to date.

25. The passage in Polish reads as follows: "Że po dziś dzień w Stanach Zjednoczonych, Ktokolwiek (kandydat) śmie przyjąc na siebie obowiązki biskupa w diecezji polyglotycznej sam nie będąc polyglytem, ten przymuje na barki obowiązki, o których wie, że nie może

ich wypełnic, *a przez to popelnia grzech śmiertelny*" (my italics). See Kruszka, *Siedm Siedmioleći*, 1: 394. *The Freeman's Journal* was a popular sounding board for clerical opinions; see McAvoy, *History*, p. 253.

26. Kruszka unashamedly includes in *Siedm Siedmioleci* full texts of all criticisms of his position; for Heuser's critique, see 1: 396.

27. Ibid.

28. Ibid., p. 402. Kruszka's response to Horstmann was clearly sarcastic: "Jak gdyby ich nie mieli! To jusz szczyt pychy i obłudy!" ("As if they didn't have any [bishops]! This is the epitomy of conceit and hypocrisy!").

29. Kruszka, "Smaller Congregations," pp. 202–3.

30. The Proceedings of the First Catholic Congress were chronicled in *Polak w Ameryce* 22–25 September 1896. *Polak w Ameryce* (later *The Buffalo Telegram*, 1920–1933) was an irregularly published newspaper emanating from the Buffalo Polonia; a microfilm copy of this scarce item is housed at the University Library of the State University of New York at Buffalo. Greene, *Polish and Lithuanian Ethnic Consciousness*, p. 125, also cites the *Sprawozdanie z Pierwszego Polsko-Katolickiego Kongresu . . . Buffalo* (Buffalo, 1897), an item I did not see. For other secondary accounts, see Daniel Buczek, "Polish-Americans and the Catholic Church," *The Polish Review* 21 (bicentennial issue, 1976): 50–53, and Joseph Swastek, "The Formative Years of the Polish Seminary in the United States," *Sacrum Poloniae Millenium* 6 (1956): 127–29. Issues of the *Sacrum* are available at the PRCU in Chicago. Haiman, *ZPRK*, and Osada, *Historya ZNP*, also discuss the Congresses.

31. See note 30 above. I have depended primarily on Buczek and Greene; I do not agree, however, with Professor Greene's interpretation of the Barzynski resolution, calling for an adviser to the Apostolic Delegate, as necessarily "moderate." All archbishops in the United States, with the exception of Archbishop Ireland, expressed opposition to the appointment of an Apostolic Delegate on the grounds that foreign influence in the American Church would only be more pronounced. Most were greatly concerned about losing their discretionary powers that had been traditionally exercised within a "missionary church" arrangement. Accordingly, I feel that Barzynski's resolution was far more radical. A Polish-American "adviser" to the Apostolic Delegate—given the times—could conceivably have wielded far more power than a single bishop within a single diocese. Of course all of this is conjecture since no adviser was ever appointed. For more discussion of this issue, see Trisco, "Apostolic Delegation," p. 691.

32. For a complete text of the Congress Memorial, see Kruszka, *Siedm Siedmioleci*, 1: 441–44.

33. Ibid, p. 445.

34. Trisco, "Apostolic Delegation," p. 692. See also a series of articles in the *New Catholic Encyclopedia*, 2: 590–94, on the selection of bishops and the rights of auxiliary, monastic, and coadjutor bishops; Buczek, "Polish-Americans," pp. 44–46; and Greene, *Polish and Lithuanian Ethnic Consciousness*, pp. 132–34.

35. *Zgoda*, 28 March 1901 (CFLPS).

36. For example, see *Zgoda*, 20 December 1900. The anglicanization argument is also forcefully expressed in Greene, *Polish and Lithuanian Ethnic Consciousness*, p. 133.

37. Greene, *Polish and Lithuanian Ethnic Consciousness*, p. 141; *Dziennik Chicagoski*, 10 February 1906.

38. The Archives of the Chicago Roman Catholic Archdiocese maintains a partial set of the Minutes of the Annual Meeting of the Archbishops in the United States, St. Mary of the Lake Seminary, Mundelein, Ill. See, in particular, folders for 1901 and 1904 meetings, which include notes taken by Archbishop Keane. Both these meetings addressed the issues of cultural and ethnic pluralism and racism in the American Church.

39. See *The New World*, 13 September 1903 for a brief report on the petition.

40. Kruszka gives a detailed account of the Katzer mission in *Siedm Siedmioleci*, 1: 448–51 and passim.

41. Ibid., pp. 542–43. Contrast Kruszka's position with that of Iwicki, *Resurrectionist Studies*, p. 107. Other Resurrectionist accounts by Ladislaus Kwiatkowski and Leonard Long ignore the charges.

42. Kruszka, *Siedm Siedmioleci*, 1: 552–54. Kruszka gives a 12 October 1902 date for *The Freeman's Journal* letter.

43. The text authorizing the mission is in Latin. It is addressed "Quorum interest" ("To whomever is interested"). Francis Wojtalewicz, Casimir Sztuczko, and three laymen, Leon Szopinski, Steven Czaplewski, and Stanislaus Lipowicz, signed the Congress authorization, dated 18 May 1903. See ibid., 1: 597; the texts of the affidavits are on pp. 605–16. Also see *The New World*, 12 September 1903; Madaj, "Polish Immigrant," pp. 22–25; and Syski, "Nestor of Polish Historians," pp. 69–70.

44. Kruszka, *Siedm Siedmioleci*, 1: 665–66. Kruszka gives a detailed diary of his activities in the interim period in 1: 660–97.

45. Heuser, "American Bishops," pp. 348–49.

46. Ibid., pp. 350–52.

47. H. J. Heuser, "Slav Catholics in the United States," *American Ecclesiastical Review* 29 (November 1903): 501–8. Cf. Heuser, "Polish Religious Communities," *American Ecclesiastical Review* 26 (February 1902): 215–16, an article in which Polish teaching nuns are reprimanded for their ignorance of the English language. On the other hand, the hierarchy and the editors of *AER* failed to grasp the significance of the use of Polish in the liturgy and in the educational system. For this discussion, see Platt, "Polish National Catholic Church," pp. 474–89, and Joseph Swastek, "The Contribution of the Catholic Church in Poland," *Sacrum Poloniae Millenium* 6 (1956): 20–26.

48. For various interpretations of the relationship of the hierarchy to liberal crosscurrents in the church, to the issue of Americanization, and the institutionalization of the immigrant church, see Philip A. Gleason, ed., *Catholicism in America* (New York: Harper & Row, 1970), especially the essays by McAvoy, Barry, O'Brien, and Gleason. The most perceptive and comprehensive treatment of these subjects, in my judgement, is David O'Brien, *The Renewal of American Catholicism* (New York: Oxford University Press, 1972), pp. 51–162. See also Cross, *Emergence*, pp. 182–205.

49. Kruszka, *Siedm Siedmioleci*, 1: 745. Brief sketches of each of the candidates can be found in Bolek, *Who's Who in Polish America*.

50. A full text of the petition is in Kruszka, *Siedm Siedmioleci*, 1: 798–99.

51. The audience with Pius X was carefully recorded in ibid., 1: 804–06. Kruszka's first audience with the Pontiff, on 11 September 1903, was without significance.

52. Ibid., 2: 28–29. For a detailed analysis of Hodur's movement, see Andrews, *Polish National Catholic Church*; Kubiak, *Polski Narodowy Kościół*; Joseph Przudzik, "Schism in America," *Homiletic and Pastoral Review* 47 (September 1947): 982–88, and Platt, "Polish National Catholic Church," pp. 474–89.

53. Madaj, "Polish Immigrant," p. 22.

54. There is no biography of Joseph Weber. However, a typescript biography (ca. 20 pp.) was included in the Weber Folio of the editorial office of the now defunct *Dziennik Chicagoski*, materials of which were moved to several locations after 1971. For more information on Weber, see Kwiatkowski, *Historia Zgromadzenia*, pp. 383–86; Iwicki, *Resurrectionist Studies*, p. 172; *Dziennik Chicagoski*, 18–20 March 1918; *The New World*, 29 March 1918; and a special issue of the *Dziennik Chicagoski*, 15 June 1946, devoted to the life of Weber.

55. See Kruszka, *Siedm Siedmioleci*, 2: 104–7, 209–10; Buczek, "Polish Americans," pp. 52–53; *Album SSK*, passim; *Dziennik Chicagoski*, 25 June 1905. Peter Kiolbassa died three weeks before the arrival of Symon in Chicago; see *Dziennik Chicagoski*, 27 June 1905, p. 1.

56. Kruszka, *Siedm Siedmioleci*, 2: 171–74.

57. Ibid., pp. 192–95.

58. The most stinging criticism of Kruszka's *Historya* was published by Superior-General Paul Smolikowski of the Congregation of the Resurrection; see "Ks. Kruszka i Jego Dokumenty," *Dziennik Chicagoski*, 9 February 1907. I count nineteen other articles on the Kruszka-Resurrectionist feud published in the *Dziennik Chicagoski* between 28 January and 3 December 1907; most of them elaborate on points raised by Smolikowski in addition to raising new evidence. The best critique in English of the *Historya* was published on the fiftieth anniversary of the controversy; see Joseph Swastek, "A Critical Examination of Father Kruszka's *Historya Polska w Ameryce*," *Polish American Studies* 14 (July-December 1957): 103–10. Also see Syski, "Nestor of Polish Historians," pp. 62–70. Father Francis Gordon's criticisms were printed in the *Dziennik Chicagoski*, 10 December 1906.

59. A substantial portion of Volume Two of Kruszka's *Siedm Siedmioleci* is devoted to the Milwaukee controversy. The most thorough and scholarly study of the Messmer-Kruszka feud and of the adultery charges leveled at Kruszka is Anthony J. Kuzniewski, *Faith and Fatherland: The Polish Church War in Wisconsin, 1896–1918* (Notre Dame, Ind.: University of Notre Dame Press, 1980), pp. 60–61 and passim. Kuzniewski's study is based on much new evidence coming from archival sources throughout Milwaukee and Wisconsin. See also Thaddeus Borun, *We, The Milwaukee Poles: 1846–1946* (Milwaukee: n.p., 1946), pp. 63–66, and Bayrd Still, *Milwaukee, The History of a City* (Madison: State Historical Society of Wisconsin, 1965), pp. 270–72, 464–65.

60. Kruszka, *Siedm Siedmioleci*, 2: 611–12; *Chicago Tribune*, 20 July 1908, p. 5; *The New World*, 25 July 1905, p. 1; 1 August 1908, pp. 1–8.

61. *Dziennik Chicagoski*, 20 June 1908, p. 1; *Album SSK*, passim; *Chicago Tribune*, 28 July 1908, pp. 1, 4; 29 July 1908, p. 5; *Dziennik Chicagoski*, 25–28 July 1908. Rhode was born in Werowo in Prussian Poland on 16 September 1870 to Augustine and Christine Rhode. He attended St. Stanislaus Kostka school in Chicago during his youth. Rhode was ordained by Archbishop Katzer in Milwaukee on 16 June 1894 and shortly thereafter assumed his pastoral duties at St. Michael's Parish. He died on 3 March 1945. The best biographical sketches of Rhode appear in commemorative form in the *Dziennik Chicagoski*, 3–6 March 1945.

CHAPTER SEVEN

1. Greene, *Polish and Lithuanian Ethnic Consciousness*, pp. 168–69.

2. Kantowicz, "Polish Chicago," pp. 179–209.

3. Joseph J. Parot, "Immigrant Labor and the Paradox of Pluralism in American Urban Society, 1860–1930: A Comparative Study and Census Analysis of Polish, Irish, German, Bohemian, Italian and Jewish Workers in Chicago," paper presented at the International Congress of Scholars of Polish Descent, Cracow, Poland, 21–24 July 1979, forthcoming in a publication of Congress papers by the Polish Research Institute, Jagiellonian University, in a Polish edition published by Ossolineum and an English edition published by Macmillan.

4. Rose, "Prussian Poland," pp. 409–31.

5. *Dziennik Związkowy*, 25 January 1919, p. 8. For an excellent comparison of Poles to German-Americans in the war period, see Frederick C. Luebke, *Bonds of Loyalty: German*

Americans and World War I (DeKalb, Ill.: Northern Illinois University Press, 1974), pp. 115–266.

6. *Dziennik Związkowy*, 3 October 1914 (CFLPS). Also, note earlier such attempts at unification by the *Liga Polska* in the 1890s; see *Dziennik Chicagoski*, 10 June 1895.

7. Louis L. Gerson, *Woodrow Wilson and the Rebirth of Poland, 1914–1920* (New Haven, Conn.: Yale University Press, 1953), pp. 55–85; *Cambridge History of Poland*, 2: 478–89. Note the opposition to the Dmowski-Paderewski group by Polish Socialists supporting Pilsudski; for this story, see Kantowicz, *Polish-American Politics*, p. 111.

8. Kantowicz, *Polish-American Politics*, p. 116; Gerson, *Woodrow Wilson*, pp. 61–62, 156–58; John M. Allswang, *A House for All Peoples: Ethnic Politics in Chicago, 1890–1936* (Lexington: University of Kentucky Press, 1971), pp. 112–18.

9. *Dziennik Chicagoski*, 13 October 1917, p. 1; 16 October 1917, p. 1; 17 October 1917, p. 1; and nearly all page-one political cartoons in December 1917. Also see *Dziennik Związkowy*, 9 June 1920.

10. Wachtel's letter is reprinted in the *Dziennik Chicagoski*, 16 April 1918, p. 5.

11. *Report of the Industrial Commission: Chicago Labor Disputes of 1900, With Especial Reference to the Disputes in the Building and Machinery Trades* (Washington, D.C., 1901), 8: cliv; Allswang, *House for All Peoples*, p. 22, 42–46.

12. *Dziennik Chicagoski*, 12 March 1918, p. 6; 9 September 1918, p. 3; *Chicago Tribune*, 29 April 1914; *The New World*, 30 January 1914, pp. 1, 4. Polonia's voting record, on the whole, remained dismal in comparison to other white ethnic groups in the city, largely due to the slow pace of naturalization. Only Lithuanian males and Italian females recorded a slower naturalization rate than the Poles.

13. Editorial, *Dziennik Związkowy*, 31 July 1918 (CFLPS).

14. *Naród Polski*, 25 April 1917 (CFLPS).

15. *Dziennik Chicagoski*, 4 February 1918, p. 4; 11 February 1918, p. 7; 26 February 1918, p. 2; 11 March 1918 for numerous details concerning the flag ceremonies; see *Dziennik Związkowy*, 27 September 1918 for the ceremony at St. Michael's.

16. *Dziennik Związkowy*, 27 September 1918.

17. *Dziennik Związkowy*, 9 April 1918 and 2 May 1917 (CFLPS).

18. *Dziennik Związkowy*, 7 February 1918 (CFLPS).

19. *Dziennik Chicagoski*, 17 June 1918, p. 3. Each parish was assessed directly by the Chicago Central Loan Committee. The highest assessment was levied against St. John of God Parish at $1350 per month; next highest came the parishes of St. Stanislaus Kostka, Sacred Heart, and St. Hedwig at $1200 per month; St. Joseph Parish was assessed at $1000 per month.

20. *Dziennik Chicagoski*, 22 April 1918, p. 5; 26 April 1918, p. 4; *Dziennik Związkowy*, 27 April 1918, p. 1. For circulation statistics, consult *N. W. Ayer and Son's Directory of Newspapers and Periodicals* (Philadelphia: Ayer, 1880–) for the post-war period.

21. *Dziennik Chicagoski*, 5 September 1917, p. 6.

22. Gerson, *Woodrow Wilson*, p. 80; Kantowicz, *Polish-American Politics*, pp. 111–12; Irwin Edman, "The Fourth Part of Poland," *Nation* 107 (1918): 342; Haiman, *ZPRK*, pp. 314–15.

23. Haiman, *ZPRK*, p. 315. Haiman concluded that the Polish National Fund was successful, if only because the final total averaged out to more than six dollars per family in American Polonia. The Polish National Fund was not the only war fund. Others, like the Paderewski Fund for "Hungry Polish War Children," were initiated at the local level; see *Dziennik Chicagoski* 22 April 1918, p. 6. Likewise, note that another $275,000,000 in direct loans were made to Poland from a variety of Polish-American sources; see H. H. Fisher, *America and the Other Poland* (New York: Macmillan, 1928), p. 342.

For a complete list of monthly assessments leveled against individual parishes in Chicago, see *Dziennik Chicagoski*, 17 June 1918, p. 3. The PRCU was reported to have contributed $98,252 in 1918 and $30,775 in 1920 "for national and humanitarian purposes." Compare this to the paltry $2000 amount in 1921, when the Polish Relief Fund was drastically cut. See *65 Lat ZPRK*, p. 106.

24. *Dziennik Chicagoski*, 17 June 1918, p. 3.

25. Paderewski's Chicago Coliseum address was carried in both the *Dziennik Chicagoski* and *Dziennik Związkowy* on 18 March 1918. I depended upon the *Związkowy* account.

26. For the Morrison Hotel address, see *Dziennik Związkowy*, 5 March 1918, p. 6, and *Dziennik Chicagoski*, 5 March 1918, p. 5. The *Związkowy* carried the full text in English. But note the Paderewski turnabout in his Detroit address of September 1918, when he stated that "the Poles in America do not need any Americanization"; see Gerson, *Woodrow Wilson*, p. 90.

27. *Dziennik Chicagoski*, 3 June 1918, p. 10.

28. *Dziennik Chicagoski*, 8–16 November 1918, page-one stories and headlines, which can be compared to the *Dziennik Związkowy* for the same time period.

29. *Dziennik Chicagoski*, 23 January 1919, p. 8; 30 January 1919, p. 4; 21 July 1919, p. 6; 28 July 1919, p. 6.

30. *Dziennik Związkowy*, 4 December 1918, p. 5.

31. *Dziennik Związkowy*, 9 December 1918, p. 4; 18 December 1918, p. 4.

32. The *New York Times*, 22 May 1919, p. 5; 27 May 1919, p. 6.

33. "Żydzi a Amerykanizacya," *Dziennik Chicagoski*, 3 February 1919, p. 4.

34. *Naród Polski*, 6 August 1919 (CFLPS).

35. Kantowicz, *Polish-American Politics*, p. 118.

36. Edward C. Hill, "The Americanization of the Immigrant," *American Journal of Sociology* 24 (May 1919): 614. Cf. Joseph Roucek, "The Image of the Slav in U.S. History and Immigration Policy," *American Journal of Economics and Sociology* 28 (January 1969): 29–48; Edward R. Saveth, "Race and Nationalism in American Historiography; the Late Nineteenth Century," *Political Science Quarterly* 54 (September 1939): 421–41; A. McLaughlin, "The Slavic Immigrant," *Popular Science* 63 (May 1903): 25–32; Lawrence Fleck, "What America Has Gotten Out Of The Melting Pot," *Catholic Historical Review* 11 (October 1925): 407–30. Finally, note John Higham's trenchant analysis of the period in *Strangers in the Land*.

37. *Dziennik Chicagoski*, 17 April 1918, p. 4.

38. *Dziennik Chicagoski*, 18 July 1918, p. 4.

39. *Dziennik Związkowy*, 25 January 1919, p. 8.

40. *Dziennik Chicagoski*, 6 May 1919, p. 4. The Chicago Polish community was indeed grateful to Creel for his efforts on behalf of the Division of Work Among the Foreign Born, which did much to publicize Polonia's relief work during the war. See George Creel, *Rebel at Large: Recollections of Fifty Crowded Years* (New York: Putnam's, 1947), pp. 194–202.

41. *Dziennik Związkowy* ran numerous editorials on the subject during January-June 1920. Also see the *New York Times*, 1 February 1920, p. 6; the *Times* claimed that Poles were leaving the United States over the issue of Prohibition!

42. *Dziennik Chicagoski*, 3 February 1919, p. 4.

43. *Dziennik Chicagoski*, 24 March 1919, p. 4.

44. This set of editorials was widely publicized by the sociologist Robert Park; see his *The Immigrant Press and Its Control* (New York: Harper, 1922), pp. 210–13, for translations of the Polish text and adjacent English version.

45. Higham, *Strangers in the Land*, pp. 264–330.

CHAPTER EIGHT

1. Editorial, "Home Rule For Poland Deferred," *The New World*, 2 December 1905, p. 14.

2. It is significant that the Holy Cross Fathers were stationed only at Holy Trinity Parish at the turn of the century in Chicago. The remainder of the Polish parishes in Chicago were administered either by Resurrectionist priests or by diocesan priests who were normally assigned only after Vincent Barzynski or John Kasprzycki had been consulted. But this policy of accommodation had its drawbacks, especially during the height of the Independent Revolt in 1894–1897; see *The New World*, 2 January 1897, p. 10.

3. *Chicago Tribune*, 11 July 1915, p. 11. That Archbishop Quigley had consistently led an unpretentious way of life is further corroborated by numerous tributes paid him at his funeral mass, most of which called attention to his simple tastes.

4. James E. Quigley, pastoral letter, 26 September 1907, Quigley MSS (AAC).

5. For additional commentary on archdiocesan growth during the Quigley years, see Thompson, *Diamond Jubilee*, pp. 73–85; *The New World*, 16 July 1915, p. 11; *Chicago Tribune*, 11 July 1915, p. 11; 12 July 1915, p. 6; 14 July 1915, p. 11.

6. *The New World*, 16 May 1908, p. 11.

7. Ibid.

8. Cardinal Rampolla to Quigley, 3 July 1911, Quigley MSS (AAC); *The New World*, 19 September 1908, p. 1.

9. Weber was already seventy years old at the time of Quigley's death. For this and other details related to Weber, see Kwiatkowski, *Historia Zgromadzenia*, pp. 383–95.

10. See note 5 above; see also *Dziennik Chicagoski*, 17 June 1918.

11. For brief sketches of each potential successor to Quigley, see Thompson, *Diamond Jubilee*, p. 69, for McGavick; pp. 71–72, for Muldoon; pp. 87–88, for Rhode. For other details on Rhode's candidacy, see *Dziennik Chicagoski*, 3 March 1945, .p. 1; 6 March 1945, p. 4. Also, note speculation in *Chicago Tribune*, 16 July 1945, p. 9.

It is significant that McGavick was also a diocesan consultor, although once the selection of Mundelein was made this becomes a moot point. No biographies exist, as yet, for any of the other candidates; however, the Archives of the Roman Catholic Archdiocese of Chicago at St. Mary of the Lake Seminary, Mundelein, Illinois, maintains unpublished sets of papers relating to the lives of each candidate.

12. *The New World*, 16 July 1915, pp. 7, 11; *New York Times*, 11 July 1915, p. 8. Also see numerous reactions to the transfer in the *Dziennik Chicagoski* and *Dziennik Związkowy*, 11–15 July 1915.

13. *Chicago Tribune*, 14 July 1915, p. 5.

14. For a sequence of stories on Quigley's illness, see the *New York Times*, 1 July 1915, p. 11; 2 July 1915, p. 11; 3 July 1915, p. 7; 4 July 1915, Part Two, p. 11; 9 July 1915, p. 11. The *Times* also carried stories on the funeral and related events taking place in Chicago: note items on 11 July 1915, pp. 1, 11; 12 July 1915, pp. 5, 6; 14 July 1915, p. 5; 15 July 1915, p. 2; 16 July 1915, p. 5; 17 July 1915, p. 9. Many of these stories also provide details concerning the canonical proceedings for the succession. *The New World*, of course, carried additional stories and details throughout the funeral period. For materials relating to Bishop Spalding, see notes 13 and 17 to Chapter Six.

15. *Chicago Tribune*, 11 July 1915, p. 11.

16. See note 12 above.

17. *Chicago Tribune*, 14 July 1915, p. 5; 17 July 1915, p. 9.

18. *Chicago Tribune*, 3 October 1939, p. 3; Thompson, *Diamond Jubilee*, pp. 89–123.

19. *Naród Polski*, 28 July 1915 (CFLPS).

20. My choice of the term "structural pluralism" is intentional, and is used in the sense defined by Milton Gordon, *Assimilation in American Life: The Role of Race, Religion, and National Origins* (New York: Oxford University Press, 1964).

21. Thompson, *Diamond Jubilee*, pp. 89–102; *Chicago Tribune*, 3 October 1939, pp. 10–14.

22. Thompson, *Diamond Jubilee*, p. 191.

23. *Chicago Tribune*, 3 October 1939, p. 10.

24. Thompson, *Diamond Jubilee*, p. 101. Thompson prints a complete text of Mundelein's address.

25. Ibid.

26. *The New World*, 12 February and 22 February 1916, lead stories; the *Chicago Tribune*, 13, 15, 16 February 1916, devoted page one coverage to details of the bizarre reception dinner.

27. *The New World*, 24 March 1916, p. 1.

28. Ibid., pp. 1–3.

29. *The New World*, 21 April 1916, pp. 2–4.

30. Zapala to Mundelein, 9 December 1916, Mundelein MSS (AAC).

31. George Mundelein, pastoral letter, 9 February 1917, Mundelein MSS (AAC).

32. *The New World*, 1 June 1917, p. 1.

33. *The New World*, 31 May 1918, pp. 1–3.

34. Mundelein to Reverend Lewis J. O'Hern, C.S.P., 1 November 1917, Mundelein MSS (AAC).

35. Mundelein to Reverend Casimir I. Gronkowski, undated, Mundelein MSS (AAC). The letter was probably sent in December 1917.

36. Mundelein to Ledvina, 11 April 1918, Mundelein MSS (AAC).

37. *The New World*, 12 February 1915, p. 3. The Polish clergy passed a resolution in favor of "Polonia Semper Fidelis"; however, the general purpose of the meeting, i.e., "the spiritual uplift of four million Poles," can also be construed to be an unofficial declaration of war against the archdiocese.

38. Ladon to Mundelein, 29 August 1916, Mundelein MSS (AAC). For a discussion of the work of Joseph Deharbe, see J. E. Koehler, "Deharbe, Joseph," *New Catholic Encyclopedia*, 15 vols. (New York: McGraw-Hill, 1967), 4: 720–21.

39. Mundelein to Weber, 19 August 1916, Mundelein MSS (AAC).

40. Weber to Mundelein, 20 August 1916, Mundelein MSS (AAC).

41. Ladon to Mundelein, 29 August 1916, Mundelein MSS (AAC).

42. Anonymous letter addressed from "The Other Side of the Medal" to Mundelein, 23 March 1917, Mundelein MSS (AAC).

43. Sztuczko to Mundelein, 1 March 1917, Mundelein MSS (AAC).

44. Letter in the Archives of the Polish Roman Catholic Union of America (Chicago). The letter is typed and contains 68 handwritten signatures.

45. Ibid.

46. Wojtalewicz to Mundelein, 10 November 1917, Mundelein MSS (AAC).

47. Mundelein to Wojtalewicz, 13 November 1917, Mundelein MSS (AAC).

48. Stanislaus Waygood, "Changes Made By The New Code Of Canon Law," *American Ecclesiastical Review* 57 (October 1917): 373.

49. E. Rucupis, "The Canonical Formation of Parishes and Missions," *American Ecclesiastical Review* 55 (September 1916): 239.

50. Ibid.; see also, Waygood, "Changes," p. 373.

51. "The Establishment of Canonical Parishes in the United States," *American Ecclesi-*

astical Review 63 (October 1920): 346–48; see also Jos. Selinger, "Boundaries of the Parishes in the New Code," *American Ecclesiastical Review* 60 (June 1919): 691–93.

52. See Selinger, "Boundaries of the Parishes," pp. 691–93, as well as the companion article "Removability of Pastors of National Parishes," *American Ecclesiastical Review* 60 (June 1919): 693–94. For comparison with previous attempts to govern national parishes through diocesan councils made up of pastors from the national parishes, see "Diocesan Bureaux for the Care of Italian, Slav, Ruthenian and Asiatic Catholics," *American Ecclesiastical Review* 48 (February 1913): 221–22. The numerous citations in the *American Ecclesiastical Review* during 1913–1919 reflect the immense interest and concern of the church over the problem of national as against territorial parishes.

53. Mundelein to Weber, 15 February 1918, Mundelein MSS (AAC).

54. Ibid.

55. *Dziennik Chicagoski*, 25 March 1918; the entire issue is devoted to biographical sketches of Weber. See also *The New World*, 29 March 1918, p. 1.

56. Sztuczko to Hoban, 13 July 1918, Hoban MSS (AAC). For a good example of Mundelein's appeal for funds for Catholic Charities (Associated Charities), see *The New World*, 16 April 1920, p. 1.

57. Roman Catholic Archdiocese of Chicago. Annual Reports: Holy Trinity Parish, 1917 (AAC).

58. Gronkowski to Hoban, 11 October 1918, Hoban MSS (AAC). Both Gronkowski and Sztuczko were by this time addressing all correspondence to Hoban rather than to Mundelein directly.

59. Kantowicz, "Polish Chicago," pp. 188–89. The *per capita* church donations are for parishes in the year 1908. The German average was $6.27 *per capita*; the Slovaks, $3.89; the Poles, $3.51; the Lithuanians, $3.12; the Bohemians, $1.81; and the Italians, $0.38.

60. *Roman Catholic Archdiocese of Chicago. Annual Reports. St. Stanislaus Kostka Parish, 1917; Holy Trinity Parish, 1917.* For material on parish societies, consult *Album SSK*; the *St. Stanislaus Kostka Diamond Jubilee Book*; and the *Pamiętnik . . . Św. Trójcy*. For a brief analysis of these societies, see Andrea, "Societies of St. Stanislaus," pp. 27–37, and Thomas and Znaniecki, *Polish Peasant*, 2: 1525–74. The most vocal critics of Polonia's priests and their alleged worldly ways were Polish socialists writing for the *Dziennik Ludowy*; see, for example, *Dziennik Ludowy*, 3 July 1908 (CFLPS). But the *Dziennik Ludowy* was hardly representative of public opinion in Chicago Polonia, nor was its circulation even close to that of the *Dziennik Chicagoski* or *Dziennik Związkowy*.

61. See note 53 above.

62. Undated autograph copy at AAC, St. Mary of the Lake Seminary, Mundelein, Ill.

63. Ibid.

64. *Dziennik Chicagoski*, 4 April 1942. A detailed description and photograph of St. Mary of the Angels church can be found in Thompson, *Diamond Jubilee*, pp. 368, 574. See also the parish album *Pamiątka Srebrnego Jubileuszu Parafii Naświętszej Maryi Panny Anielskiej, 1899–1924* (Chicago, 1924), for more details and a brief history of that parish.

65. *Pamiątka Srebrnego.* Thompson, *Diamond Jubilee*, p. 574. The address "Sermon at St. Mary of the Angels, June 4, 1920," is in the Mundelein MSS (AAC). For other news on the dedication service, see *The New World*, 4 June 1920, Part One, p. 9.

66. Polish Legation at the Holy See, *I Pollachi Negli Stati Uniti Dell' America Del Nord*, 28 June 1920. A copy of the original is at the AAC, St. Mary of the Lake Seminary, Mundelein, Illinois, Document Number 6–1920–H–264. Succeeding citations refer to pagination in the original.

67. Ibid., p. 1.

68. Ibid., pp. 2–6.

69. Ibid., pp. 7–12.

70. Ibid., pp. 12–13. Note that Mundelein is never mentioned by name in *I Pollachi*; he is referred to, instead, as the "Archbishop of said diocese."

71. Ibid., pp. 13–14.

72. See the special issue of *The New World*, 4 June 1920, Parts One and Two.

73. For the complete text of Hayes's speech, see *The New World*, 11 June 1920, p. 1. The *Chicago Tribune* also covered the festivities of June 1920 thoroughly.

74. *The New World*, 18 June 1920; 25 June 1920; for the week in between, see the *Chicago Tribune* for coverage.

75. The rebuttal letter to *I Pollachi* was actually signed by James Cardinal Gibbons, speaking "For The Hierarchy of the United States." The letter to Gasparri was acknowledged in another piece of correspondence from Gibbons to Mundelein, 18 November 1920, stating that the Gasparri letter was "signed by me and mailed to Rome." Gibbons also told Mundelein in his 18 November letter that the rebuttal "is an admirable document and I hope it will have a salutary effect on the Holy See." For a final draft of the Gibbons to Gasparri rebuttal letter, see Mundelein MSS (AAC), Document No. 6–1920–G–1, which also contains Mundelein's handwritten commentary to the final draft, many points of which made their way into the final text of the rebuttal. Also, see the Mundelein-Gibbons exchange of letters, 16 November 1920, and the Gibbons-Mundelein exchange dated 18 November 1920 in the Mundelein MSS (AAC), Document Nos. 6–1920–G–1 and 6–1920–M–144, respectively.

76. Gibbons to Gasparri.

CHAPTER NINE

1. I do not wish to imply that this turn-of-the-century catechetical exercise is in any way obsolete or that the theology of *ecclesia*, from a Catholic standpoint, has been substantively changed. See *New Catholic Encyclopedia*, s.v. "Marks of the Church (Properties)."

2. Emile Durkheim, *The Elementary Forms of the Religious Life* (New York: Free Press paperback ed., 1965), pp. 52–56, 122–26, 475. As for the Church of Our Lady Queen of Poland as a symbol of resistance, see Peter Hebblethwaite, *The Year of the Three Popes* (London: Collins, 1978), pp. 169–70. Hebblethwaite states that Pope Paul VI sent the foundation stone, actually carved from St. Peter's tomb in Rome, to Nowa Huta for the church building. With the stone, he sent the following message: "Take this stone to Poland, and may it be the corner-stone on which a church will stand in Nowa Huta, dedicated to the Queen of Poland."

3. Data are from Parot, "Immigrant Labor and the Paradox of Pluralism." The study is based on a total sample of 47,000 immigrants in this period. I have also traced the population movement of Poles in two separate articles done from a totally different vantage point; see Parot, "Ethnic Versus Black Metropolis," and "Racial Dilemma."

4. Parot, "Immigrant Labor," p. 70.

5. Parot, "Racial Dilemma," pp. 33–36, which is based on Ernest Watson Burgess and Charles Newcomb, *Census Data for the City of Chicago, 1920* (Chicago: University of Chicago Press, 1931).

6. See Emmet Larkin, "The Devotional Revolution in Ireland, 1850–1875," *American Historical Review* 77 (June 1972): 625–52.

7. Thomas and Znaniecki, *Polish Peasant*, 1: 205–88.

8. *Zbiór Pieśni Nabożnych Katolickich do Użytku Kościelnego i Domowego*; see also the devotional booklet, *Wianek Nabożeństw odprawianych w ciągu roku kościelnego*, comp. S. Siatka (Chicago: Drukiem Spółki Wydawniczej Polskiej, 1904).

For the most thorough study of Polish religious customs and folkways done to date, see the remarkable series of articles by Helen Stankiewicz Zand in *Polish American Studies*. Especially of note for some of the contentions raised is "Polish Folkways in America," *PAS* 6 (January-June 1949): 33–41; see also "Polish Folkways in the United States," *PAS* 12 (July-December 1955): 65–72; "Polish Family Folkways in the United States," *PAS* 13 (July-December 1958): 81–90; and, "Polish American Folkways (Cures-Burials-Superstitions)," *PAS* 17 (July-December 1960): 100–104. Zand's work should be supplemented by Fr. Basil Janasik, "Polish American Lenten Customs," *PAS* 20 (July-December 1963): 97–101.

9. See the scholarship of Zand cited in note 8. I also base this observation on my experiences as an altar boy during the late 1940s and early 1950s. The intense emotionalism experienced by parishioners, when singing these three hymns in particular, was probably widely shared throughout Chicago Polonia and American Polonia.

10. Durkheim, *Elementary Forms*, p. 473.

11. Andrea, "Societies of Saint Stanislaus," pp. 27–37. See also Thomas and Znaniecki, *Polish Peasant*, 2: 1558–59, which is based on their translations of the *Album SSK*, p. 100.

12. Andrea, "Societies of St. Stanislaus," pp. 27–37; Thomas and Znaniecki, *Polish Peasant*, 2: 1575–1623.

13. See Paul Wrobel, *Our Way: Family, Parish and Neighborhood in a Polish American Community* (Notre Dame, Ind.: University of Notre Dame Press, 1979). Wrobel's socio-religious analysis of Detroit Polish Catholic parish life speaks to this point better than any other study I have come across.

14. Compare the life of Vincent Barzynski to another well-known "immigrant pastor" in American Polonia, Lucjan Bojnowski; see Daniel Buczek, *Immigrant Pastor: The Life of the Right Reverend Monsignor Lucjan Bojnowski of New Britain, Connecticut* (Waterbury, Conn.: Heminway, 1974).

15. It is the personal feeling of this writer, based on observation of Polish Catholic parish life, that elements of Jansenism persisted in Chicago Polonia up to Vatican II and even beyond.

16. *Dziennik Chicagoski*, 17 June 1918.

17. Parot, "Ethnic Versus Black Metropolis," pp. 19–21.

18. Ibid.

19. Edward R. Kantowicz, "Polish Chicago," pp. 201–4.

20. Joseph J. Parot, "Strangers in the City: Immigrant Catholics and Blacks in Twentieth Century Chicago," paper delivered at the Black History Conference, Lincoln University, Oxford, Pennsylvania, 20 April 1978. The process of gerrymandering diocesan boundaries on the parish level is described by William Gremley, "The Scandal of Cicero," *America* 85 (25 August 1951): 495–98. Gremley's position, one to which I subscribe, is that boundaries were redrawn so as to contain Blacks on the south side of Chicago. For other documentary substantiation for this controversial point of view, see the letter of George Cardinal Mundelein to Reverend P. Fumasoni-Biondi, Apostolic Delegate, 20 November 1930, Mundelein File (AAC). Mundelein justifies the process of gerrymandering for reasons of protecting south side Catholic property interests.

21. For a vivid description of the efforts by Italian American clergymen in Chicago to maintain Old World orthodoxy, see Vecoli, "Prelates and Peasants," pp. 217–68. Also see Vecoli's "*Contadini* in Chicago: A Critique of *The Uprooted*," *Journal of American History* 51 (December 1964): 404–17. Both articles provide numerous details and explanations which can be compared to the Polish situation in Chicago and Poland.

22. For example, note the outward Polish mobility from the primary areas of settlement, adequately documented in Louis Wirth and Eleanor H. Bernert, eds., *Local Community*

Fact Book of Chicago, 1940 (Chicago: University of Chicago Press, 1949), Philip M. Hauser and Evelyn Kitagawa, eds., *Local Community Fact Book of Chicago, 1950* (Chicago: University of Chicago Press, 1953), and Kitagawa and Taeuber, eds. *Local Community Fact Book—Chicago Metropolitan Area: 1960*.

23. See Reverend Thomas Bona to Archbishop George Mundelein, 2 March 1922, Mundelein File (AAC). There is no question that, by this time, Bona had been placed in charge of overseeing Polonia's parishes in Chicago.

24. Note the "devotional" decline for the period September 1934 through December 1962, as documented in parish mission records accumulated by the Chicago Province Mission Band of the Congregation of the Resurrection. For these records, see Iwicki, *Resurrectionist Studies*, pp. 240–41, insert.

Also, note the strenuous efforts by Resurrectionists to maintain devotional orthodoxy. See, in particular, two published collections of sermons by two prominent Resurrectionist preachers: Ks. Tadeusz S. Ligman, *Konferencje* (Chicago: Nakładem Księży Zmartwychstańców, n.d.; *imprimatur* dated 2 March 1945, and Ks. Wladislaw Zapała, *Kazania Okolicznościowe z Moich Prac Kaznodziejskich* (Chicago: Nakładem Księży Zmartwychstańców, 1945). Zapała's remarkable collection of sermons spans nearly a half-century of Polish-American life, not only in Chicago but also throughout American Polonia. I consider his work to be a classic expression of Resurrectionist thinking on the Polish devotional way of life.

Bibliographical Note

The following note makes no attempt to be comprehensive. It lists only those sources which were of primary concern to my research. Furthermore, it only includes items related to the religious history of Chicago Polonia; a separate bibliographic note will include all sources dealing with the social history of Chicago Polonia in a sequel to this volume. I have omitted from this essay numerous secondary materials which have already been fully cited in the notes. One other matter of concern also requires explanation. Since the research for and writing of this book occupied a span of ten years, it is possible that some of the repositories and source collections noted are no longer in their original location. For instance, the Polish National Alliance offices and library have been relocated from the original "Polish triangle" site (Milwaukee, Ashland, and Division Sts.) to new headquarters on North Cicero Avenue; and the *Dziennik Chicagoski* editorial offices, where I first began my work, are no longer in existence, as this Polish daily ceased publication in 1971. The files of the *Dziennik Chicagoski* have been moved to the Immigration History Research Center at the University of Minnesota, currently directed by Professor Rudolph Vecoli. In any event, for items which I feel are central to positions taken in my book, the reader will find locational symbols directing him to such materials. Hopefully, this service will contribute to further research on the Polish immigrant in Chicago and in the United States and to a sustained "revisionism" of American Catholic historiography.

The locational symbols for depositories, libraries, and source material centers are as follows:

ACR —Congregation of the Resurrection, Chicago Province Archives, Winnetka, Illinois; St. Joseph Novitiate Provincial Library, Woodstock, Illinois; Gordon Technical High School, Chicago, Illinois.

AAC —Chicago Roman Catholic Archdiocesan Archives, St. Mary of the Lake Seminary, Mundelein, Illinois.

CHS —Chicago Historical Society

CPL —Chicago Public Library.

CRL —Center for Research Libraries, Chicago, Illinois.

DC —*Dziennik Chicagoski.* Editorial Library, Chicago, Illinois. Disbanded in 1971 with holdings transferred to the Immigration History Research Center at the University of Minnesota; also, a broken run of the newspaper file is now housed in the Center for Research Libraries.

DZ —*Dziennik Związkowy.* Editorial Library, Chicago, Illinois.

HT —Holy Trinity Parish, Chicago, Illinois.

JP	—Personal collection (books, manuscripts, letters) of the author. DeKalb, Illinois.
NIU	—Northern Illinois University, Founders Library, DeKalb, Illinois.
PNA	—Polish National Alliance Library, Chicago, Illinois.
PRCU	—Polish Roman Catholic Union Museum and Archives, Chicago, Illinois.
SSK	—St. Stanislaus Kostka Parish, Chicago, Illinois.
TNW	—*The New World*. Editorial Offices and Library of *The Chicago Catholic*, Chicago, Illinois.
UC	—University of Chicago, Regenstein Library, Chicago, Illinois.
UIC	—University of Illinois Circle Library, Chicago, Illinois.

Manuscript Collections

The major repository for papers dealing with the Congregation of the Resurrection is the St. Joseph Novitiate Provincial Library in Woodstock, Illinois. A majority of the manuscripts in the collection were microfilmed from the originals housed in the Archives of the Congregation's Central House in Rome. The papers, largely the correspondence of Chicago Resurrectionists with superiors in Rome, are of widely varying quality and usefulness. This collection, spanning the 1866–1930 period, is the only sizeable body of primary evidence dealing with the early parish life of Chicago Polonia. Unfortunately, some of the microfilm is unreadable because some of it was filmed in the negative (white script on black background) and because the handwriting of several Resurrectionists (especially that of Vincent Barzynski) is sometimes illegible. On the whole, if the researcher is looking for sociological treatises on the development of the community-parish network, he will be very disappointed; but if he wishes to gain an understanding of the organizational details of day-to-day parish life, his patience will be amply rewarded. The author was given permission to use at the Gordon Technical High School the papers and letters of the following religious figures: Joseph Weber, Adolph Bakanowski, Vincent Barzynski, Eugene Funcken, Francis Gordon, Jan Kasprzycki, Simon Kobrzynski, Andrew Spetz, John Wollowski, and Felix Zwiardowski. I found the Barzynski and Kasprzycki papers the most useful. Of equal importance to a study of the Resurrectionists in Chicago are the *Minutes and Proceedings of the Provincial Board of the Chicago Province of the Congregation of the Resurrection, 1898–1920,* and *Reports of the General Chapters of the North American Delegates, 1857–1920.* A comprehensive list of holdings at various Resurrectionist repositories in Chicago is contained in John Iwicki, *Resurrectionist Studies*, pp. 223–26, 265–82. Father Iwicki's work also contains numerous translations, both from Polish to English and from Latin to English. It was largely through the efforts of Father Iwicki himself, who was then pastor at

St. Hedwig's parish in Chicago, and of Father Joseph Baker, who was then with the *Dziennik Chicagoski* editorial staff, that I was able to first gain access to the Resurrectionist manuscript materials. My biggest disappointments in working with these papers was that I was never able to locate any manuscript material signed by either Superior-General Jerome Kajsiewicz or Bishop Foley attesting to a formal recognition of the Chicago diocesan-Resurrectionist pact, which several secondary sources (written by Resurrectionists) claim was concluded in the year 1871, during the visit of Kajsiewicz to Chicago. Moreover, I was not able to find any new material relating to the demise of the *Bank Parafialny* at St. Stanislaus Kostka. Evidently, all the financial records dealing with subsequent Resurrectionist efforts to amortize their debts are still deposited at the Central Resurrectionist House in Rome, unless they have been destroyed.

The official depository of the Roman Catholic Archdiocese of Chicago is located at the Archdiocesan Archives building on the campus of St. Mary of the Lake Seminary in Mundelein, Illinois. Here the author was given permission to use all papers up to and including the year 1925 for the administrations of Thomas Foley (1870–1879), Patrick Feehan (1880–1902), James Quigley (1902–1915), and George Mundelein (1915–1939). Mundelein's papers were used only for the years 1916–1925. Other sets of papers used here included those of the Reverend Edward Hoban, who was chancellor of the Chicago archdiocese during the Mundelein term, and sparse sets of papers dealing with Vincent Barzynski, Casimir Sztuczko, Louis Grudzinski, Francis Wojtalewicz, Francis Gordon, and Thomas Bona. Included in the Mundelein Papers, of course, is the *I Pollachi Negli Stati Uniti Dell' America Del Nord* Polish memorial of 1920. Also included in the sparse collection of papers dealing with James Cardinal Gibbons is the Gibbons to Gasparri letter of 18 November 1920, which comments on the *I Pollachi* memorial. Also significant is the Grajczyk to Simeoni memorial of 12 April 1891, a photographic copy of which is available in the Feehan administration papers. I was also able to use the *Parish Annual Reports* for Holy Trinity and St. Stanislaus Kostka parishes, which give the complete financial statements for these two parent parishes in Polonia. However, due to an order of the chancery, these *Parish Annual Reports* were closed to researchers while I was still in the initial stages of copying financial statements for the years 1906–1908 and 1917–1919. No reason was given by the Archives or the archdiocese of Chicago for this decision. One can only hope that this decision will one day be rescinded, for it would be next to impossible to relate the overall contribution of the laity to Catholic life in the immigrant parishes without a comprehensive study of these *Reports*. On the other hand, I was given permission to use the Minutes to the Annual Meetings of the American Hierarchy for the 1900–1920 period.

Manuscript holdings at the Polish Roman Catholic Union Museum and Archives were sparse. A major portion of the holdings at the PRCU deal with the origins of that organization and with the origins of *Naród Polski*. The Archives does maintain a letter file containing correspondence of Jan Barzynski. The only other letter in this file which I found useful was the original draft of the Polish Clergy Association Number One to Archbishop Mundelein, dated 9 July 1917. On the other hand, the *Dziennik Chicagoski* editorial offices contained papers dealing with the origins of that newspaper, as well as scrapbooks and bulky clipping files relating to Joseph Weber, Vincent Barzynski, Casimir Sztuczko, and Francis Gordon, among others.

The parishes of St. Stanislaus Kostka and Holy Trinity still maintain baptismal, marriage, and death records, as well as church bulletins and extremely sketchy financial records (most of which were deposited at St. Mary of the Lake Seminary in Mundelein, Illinois).

The Chicago Historical Society maintains major manuscript collections of the Chicago Commons settlement house, the Mary McDowell papers (the "Angel of the Stockyards"), and papers dealing with the hierarchy in Chicago, which are dispersed in many fringe collections. The Society also houses the Oral History Archives of Chicago Polonia, the most extensive collection of interviews on Polonia in existence. However, the Oral History Archives are of limited value for the pre-World War I period, as most of the participants discussed their experiences for the twenties and thirties. The only major clergyman interviewed was Bishop Alfred Abramowicz, Suffragan Bishop of the Chicago Archdiocese and pastor of Five Holy Martyrs parish. His taped remarks say nothing about Independentism, *równouprawnienie*, or the Americanist hierarchy.

Newspapers

As the notes already indicate, I relied very heavily throughout my research on the Polish press in Chicago. By combining the holdings of various depositories, I was able to make use of several important complete runs. One of the most valuable, of course, was the *Dziennik Chicagoski*, which I used for the years 1890–1925 and 1939–1945 (DC, CRL, NIU). The "Polish Daily News," founded by Vincent Barzynski and Francis Gordon in 1890, remained under Resurrectionist auspices until its closing in 1971. It is certainly an indispensable source for any study of Chicago Polonia in the late nineteenth century. I was indeed fortunate to have been able to gain access to the extensive card file index to the *Dziennik Chicagoski* which, according to Father Joseph Bednowicz and Father Joseph Baker of the editorial staff of the *Dziennik*, was meticulously put together by another Resurrectionist colleague, the Reverend Joseph Książek. The "Książek Index" must certainly rank as the "*New York Times Index* of the Polish Press." It notes the dates and pagination for thousands of articles and editorials dealing with the lives of all major and many minor characters introduced in my narrative; furthermore, the Książek subject index can be keyed to any number of topics and events of great concern to the researcher of Polonia—for example, the subject of Independentism in Chicago, or the issue of bishops for Polonia.

Of equal importance for a study of Chicago Polonia from a national party perspective are the holdings of the *Dziennik Związkowy*, which I used for the period 1908–1925 (DZ, CRL, PNA, NIU). The "Alliance Daily" was just that, a detailed record of the activities of the Polish National Alliance in Chicago and in American Polonia. It is especially valuable for the World War I period and for the transition in Polonia during the twenties. I also used the weekly, *Zgoda*, for 1881–1920 (DZ, CRL). Both *Związkowy* and *Zgoda* survive to the present day. I also used *Naród Polski* for 1900–1920 (PRCU) and the *Dziennik Ludowy* for 1907–1908 (CRL).

Throughout, I also made use of the Chicago Foreign Language Press Survey. Done by the Federal Writers Project in the Works Progress Administration in the late 1930s and early 1940s in conjunction with the University of Chicago and the Chicago Public Library, the Chicago Foreign Language Press Survey (UC, CPL, NIU, CHS) contains 120,000 sheets of typescript translations from the immigrant press in the 1880–1930 period. The typescript originals are housed at both the Regenstein Library of the University of Chicago and the Chicago Public Library. Numerous microfilm copies made from the original typescripts have been made available to libraries throughout the United States. The microfilm edition contains 67 rolls, of which roll numbers 49 through 58 contain translations of the Polish press. The CFLPS is indispensable since it allows the researcher to make comparisons with other foreign-language newspapers and groups which he might not be able to read in the native tongue. The CFLPS should be used with its accompanying guide compiled by the U.S. Work Projects Administration, Illinois, entitled *A Guide to the Chicago Foreign Language Press Survey: Microfilm Edition of Newspapers of the Chicago Ethnic Press, 1880–1930* (translated and compiled by the Chicago Public Library Omnibus Project, Chicago, Illinois, 1942). Circulation figures and other information on the Polish press in Chicago and in the United States are obtainable from the annual *N.W. Ayer and Son's American Newspapers Annual and Directory* published in Philadelphia from 1868 to the present. The most thorough study of the nineteenth-century Polish press in America is E. P. Willging and Herta Hatzfield, "Nineteenth Century Polish Catholic Periodical Publications in the United States," *Polish American Studies* 12 (July-December 1955): 88–100; 13 (January-June 1956): 89–101. The reader is also directed to Iwicki, *Resurrectionist Studies*, pp. 196–220, for a thorough survey of the Resurrectionist press in America.

By far, the most useful newspaper run in English which chronicles the history of Catholic Chicago during the period is *The New World*, holdings of which I used for the 1892–1920 period (AAC, TNW). The official organ of the Roman Catholic Archdiocese of Chicago, *The New World* devoted extensive coverage to all ethnic groups in Chicago. *The New World* recently changed its name to *The Chicago Catholic*.

For secular coverage in the period, I depended mainly upon the *Chicago Tribune* (CHS, CPL, CRL, NIU, UC) for the years 1860–1945, the *Chicago Evening Post* (CRL) for 1890–1912, the *Chicago Inter-Ocean* (CRL) for 1880–1890, and the *New York Times* (CRL, NIU) for 1888–1897 and 1914–1920. Surprisingly, the *New York Times* carried several articles of interest dealing with Independentism, the Quigley-Mundelein transition, and the debate over the Lemberg incident.

Periodicals

The most complete introduction to Polish periodicals in America is Jan Wepsiec, *Polish American Serial Publications 1842–1966* (Chicago: The author, 1968). Also valuable is Lubomyr Wynar, *Encyclopedic Directory of Ethnic Newspapers and Periodicals in the United States* (Littleton, Colo.: Libraries Unlimited, 1972).

Periodicals devoted to the study of the history of Poland and Polonia have not only increased in number since World War II but have also been significantly upgraded in stature and quality. I will make no attempt here to include those many journals I have perused over the past ten years. However, I found *The Polish Review*, time and time again, to be of critical importance when formulating concepts having to do with the history of Poland *per se*; as for American Polonia, *Polish American Studies* is indispensable. Published by the Polish American Historical Association since 1944, it contains approximately two hundred articles thus far on all aspects of Polish American life. In addition to both the *TPR* and *PAS* (NIU), I found the following to be of importance for a study of the history of Poland (with the exception of a few missing numbers, all are housed at NIU): *American Slavic and Eastern European Review* (the *Slavic Review* since 1961), *Slavonic and East European Review*, *Slavic and East European Journal*.

Selected Guides and Published Source Materials on Polonia

When I first began this work there were precious few bibliographic sources to guide the way. However, during the past ten years the quantity and quality of bibliographic materials on Polonia has greatly improved. Unfortunately, the most comprehensive effort of all was not available to me until the last three months of my work. I am, of course, referring to the *Materiały Do Bibliografii Dziejów Emigracji Oraz Skupisk Polonijnych w Ameryce Północnej I Południowej W XIX I XX Wieku*, ed. Irene Paczynska and Andrew Pilch, Zeszyty Naukowe Uniwersytetu Jagiełłonskiego, DXI, Prace Polonijne, Zeszyt 3 (Cracow: Jagiellonian University, 1979). The Jagiellonian Bibliography is comprehensive, listing 6,701 items on the emigration of Poles to both North and South America in the 19th and 20th centuries. It will remain the standard bibliography for some time to come. In any event, I had to depend on the following bibliographies for most of my work: Alphonse Wolanin, *Polonica Americana* (Chicago: Polish Roman Catholic Union, 1950), which is an annotated catalogue of holdings at the PRCU library in Chicago; Joseph Zurawski, *Polish American History and Culture: A Classified Bibliography* (Chicago: Polish Museum of America, 1975); Irwin T. Sanders and Ewa T. Morawska, *Polish American Community Life: A Survey of Research*, Community Sociology Monograph Series, vol. 2 (Boston: Dept. of Sociology, Boston University; New York: Polish Institute of Arts and Sciences, 1975); and Stanley B. Kimball, ed., *Slavic American Imprints: A Classified Catalog of the Collection at Lovejoy Library* (Edwardsville: Southern Illinois University, 1972). Wolanin is especially useful for Polish language sources at the PRCU (now the Polish Museum of America); Zurawski is useful for English language sources at the PRCU; Sanders and Morawska are invaluable for integrating research on immigrant religion with all aspects of Polish social, cultural, political, and economic life; Kimball is less useful here because of its concentration on Czech and Czech-American sources.

In addition to these major bibliographic works, one should consult the steady stream of bibliographic essays appearing in *The Polish Review* and *Polish American Studies*. Also extremely useful is volume 463 of the *National Union Catalog of Pre–1956 Imprints* (London: Mansell for the Library of Congress, 1976) and all the *NUC* supplements for volumes on "Poland," "Poles" and the "Polish" for imprints between 1957 and 1980. Just as valuable is the *Dictionary Catalog of the Slavonic Collection of the New York Public Library Reference Department*, 26 vols. (Boston: G.K. Hall, 1959), vol. 17 in particular. The standard bibliography on the history of Poland is Karl Estreicher's *Bibliografia Polska* . . . (Cracow, 1872–1976), which now totals twenty-six volumes.

For a bibliography of materials on Chicago, I depended throughout on the card catalog of the Chicago Historical Society and the extensive bibliography contained in Bessie Louise Pierce, *A History of Chicago*, 3 vols. (New York: Knopf, 1937–57). In the past year, however, all previous efforts on the bibliography of Chicago were superseded by Frank Jewell, *Annotated Bibliography of Chicago History* (Chicago: Chicago Historical Society, 1979). No bibliography of Catholic Chicago is satisfactory at this stage. I largely depended upon the holdings and checklists of the AAC.

Polish Language Sources

The Congregation of the Resurrection faithfully recorded its contributions to the community-parish network in Chicago Polonia. I will call attention here to works which were of vital concern to my work. Of primary importance is Hieronym Kajsiewicz, *Pisma: Rozprawy, Listy z Podróży, Pamiętnik o Zgromadzenia*, 3 vols. (Berlin: B. Behra, 1872). Kajsiewicz's *Writings*, especially vol. 3, are significant, for they form the only substantive primary source material on the diocesan-Resurrectionist pact (see holdings of ACR). I also relied heavily on the microfilm edition of Pawel Smolikowski, *Historia Zgromadzenia Zmartwychwstania Pańskiego*, 4 vols. (Cracow: Księgarnia Spółki Wydawniczej, 1892–96). Smolikowski's *History* of the Resurrectionists is the first of four "official" authorized histories of the Congregation (followed by Kwiatkowski, Long, and Iwicki). The microfilm edition is housed at ACR. I also relied heavily on volume two of Wladislaw Kosinski, *Duch Na Czasie* (Rome: Gregorian University Press, 1966), a multivolume biography of Peter Semenenko (JP). Valuable for material on the first *burza* over *Stanisławowo* in 1869–1871 is Ks. Adolf Bakanowski, *Moje Wspomnienia, 1840–1863–1913* (Lwow: Nakładem XX. Zmartwychwstańców Drukiem Jakubowskiego i Sp., 1913). Bakanowski's *Memoirs* (JP) are one of the few contemporary published accounts left by the Resurrectionists for Polonia's early years. A note on pp. 212–17 makes the volume even more valuable: it contains, in full, Superior-General Smolikowski's rebuttal to Kruszka's *Historya*, entitled "Ks. Kruszka i jego dokumenty," reprinted from the *Dziennik Chicagoski*, 9 February 1907. Other primary sources published by Resurrectionists which I found useful were Stanislaus Siatka, *Krótkie Wspomnienie o Życiu i Działałności Ks. M. Wincentego Barzynskiego* (Chicago: Dziennik Chicagoski, 1901) (JP, ACR). Based largely on articles printed in the *Dziennik Chicagoski*, Siatka's work is the sole biography of Barzynski ever published in book form. In my work on Barzynski, I translated Siatka's biography in full; I still retain the typescript (JP). Throughout the research for this book I also looked, in vain, for published sermons of Vincent Barzynski. Outside of occasional sermons printed in the *Dziennik Chicagoski*, none that I know of have survived. The only two useful collections of sermons I located were Ks. Władisław Zapała, *Kazanie Okolicznościowe* (Chicago: Congregation of the Resurrection, 1945), and Ks. Tadeusz Ligman, *Konferencje* (Chicago: Congregation of the Resurrection, 1945). Both are personal copies (JP); however, both are also available from ACR. Of the two, I found Zapała's to be of more use, only because his sermons go back to 1899, whereas Ligman's are more recent. Surprisingly, Archbishop Weber's publications are quite scarce. During his tenure as a Resurrectionist he made two commentaries on the Resurrectionist rule and published a brief catechism (see Iwicki, *Resurrectionist Studies*, p. 225). In regards to the Ladon *Catechism* incident, in addition to the manuscripts already mentioned, I relied on Reverend Felix Ladon's *Podręcznik dla Nauczycielek Szkół Parafialnych* (Chicago: Congregation of the Resurrection, 1914), available at ACR, and the *Zarys Ogólny Dogmatyki* (Chicago: Dziennik Chicagoski, 1920), a personal copy (JP). The *Podręcznik* and the *Zarys Ogólny Domatyki* provide the researcher with Ladon's catechetical views prior to and after the Mundelein episode. Extremely valuable for synthesizing previous works as well as for carrying the Resurrectionist story up to World War II is Ks. Władisław Kwiatkowski, *Historia Zgromadzenia Zmartwychwstania Pańskiego Na Stuletnią Rocznicę Jego Założenia, 1842–1942* (Albano: Nakładem Kzięży Zmartwychstania Pańskiego, 1942). Kwiatkowski's *History* (JP, ACR) is the second official history done of the Resurrectionists and the last one ever done in Polish (Leonard Long and John Iwicki wrote their histories in English).

A host of sources are available in the Chicago area to assist in the study of the clerical party-nationalist party controversy. Valuable is Wladislaw Dyniewicz's *Ustawy Gminy Polskiej* (Chicago: W. Dyniewicz, 1877), available at DC. Also see his *Wspomnienia z Mojej Młodości* (Chicago: Ladislaus Dyniewicz, 1908). I also perused a handbook on citizenship, *Prawa i Reguły* (Chicago: L. Dyniewicz, 1908) which Dyniewicz wrote for newly arrived immigrants. The *Prawa* (DC) demonstrates clearly the extent of Dyniewicz's "assimilation in American life." It is this particular work which leads me to believe that Ladislaus Dyniewicz was somewhat embarrassed in his later years by all the controversy swirling around him and the Chicago Gmina in the 1870s. Kiolbassa's side in the controversy will always be somewhat obscured, if only because he refused to write anything about his early days in Chicago. The Jagiellonian University bibliography lists nothing by Kiolbassa, and outside of his short history of Polonia appearing in the 14 April 1900 issue of *The New World*, and a few letters in the CR manuscript collections, I was unable to locate anything else.

The PRCU maintains the largest parish album collection I know of in the Chicago area. The Polish parishes, fortunately, assessed their brief pasts in Chicago at periodical intervals, almost always falling on parish anniversary dates— silver, golden, diamond, and centenary. Although most of the albums portray Polonia in a highly defensive posture and thus contribute to the strong ethnocentric positions adopted by unwary scholars today, many were still ably written and fairly well researched. In fact, some of the early controversies still persist in later editions of albums. Most important of all is the *Album Pamiątkowe z Okazji Złotego Jubileuszu Parafii Św. Stanisława K(ostki) Chicago, Illinois, 1867–1917* (Chicago: St. Stanislaus Kostka Parish, 1917) (SSK, PRCU). The St. Stanislaus Golden Jubilee album is the pioneer parish album in Chicago Polonia. So well received was this item that Thomas and Znaniecki adopted the text, came forth with numerous translations of it, and undoubtedly based on it many of their conclusions as to the strength of Polish fraternal and parish sodality life. A Diamond Jubilee edition was published in 1942, in English, and a centennial edition in 1967, also in English (PRCU, SSK, JP). The national party perspective is contained in the *Pamiętnik Parafii Św. Trójcy w Chicago Illinois Z Okazji 25-tej Rocznicy Otwarcia Kościoła Przez J(ego) E(minencję) Ks. Kar(dinała) F. Satol-*

liego Delegata Papieskiego (Chicago: American Catalog Printing Co., 1918) (PRCU). As the title indicates, the official history of Holy Trinity parish considers the parish's 25th anniversary to date from 1893, and not from 1873. The *Pamiętnik* was updated on the golden anniversary date with a revised edition in English, dated 1943. It should be read with Brat Maxymus, *Pamiątka Złotego Jubileuszu Kapłaństwa Wielebnego Ks. Kazimierza Sztuczki, C.S.C., Proboszcza Parafii Świętej Trójcy w Chicago* (Chicago: Holy Trinity Parish, 1941). Maxymus's biography of Sztuczko, done for the Trinitarian pastor's golden anniversary in the priesthood, is the only study we have of Sztuczko's long pastoral career at Holy Trinity. It is comparable in quality to Siatka's biography of Barzynski; both are uncritical and unswerving admirers of their subjects (which is to be expected in a commemorative work). Anthony Mallek's *Dzieje Parafii Św. Trójcy, 1873–1898* (Chicago, 1898), puts the Trinitarian history in a strong pro-PNA light. The Independent uprising at St. Hedwig's is given brief apologetic coverage (from a clerical standpoint) in *Złoty Jubileusz Parafii Św. Jadwigi, Chicago, Illinois. Dnia 8 Grudnia 1938 r.* (Chicago: Cristo, 1938). For St. Mary of the Angels, see *Pamiątka Srebrnego Jubileuszu Parafii Naświętszej Maryi Panny Anielskiej, 1899–1924* (Chicago, 1924). Parish albums similar to the above mentioned also exist for St. Stanislaus Bishop and Martyr, St. John Cantius, St. Josaphat's, St. Mary of Perpetual Help, and numerous other Polish parishes (PRCU).

Supplementing these parish albums, I found the *Odgłos z Trójcowo, Rok IV* (Chicago, 1942), a statement on Trinitarian growth between 1893 and 1912, to be of limited use. The *Odgłos* (DC) only hints at the phenomenal fraternal organization growth in Holy Trinity parish. In order to gain a comprehensive picture of the development of parish fraternal life, one must read some of the standard histories of the organizations. Highly recommended for a study of the PRCU are: Miecislaus Haiman, *Zjednoczenie Polskie Rzymsko-Katolickie w Ameryce, 1873–1948* (Chicago: PRCU, 1948), located at PRCU, DC, and JP. All of the scholarship of Haiman, a pioneer founder of the Polish American Historical Association, is well researched and highly reliable. For an earlier history, see Karol Wachtel, *Z.P.R.K. Dzieje Zjednoczenia Polskiego Rzymsko-Katolickiego w Ameryce* (Chicago: L. J. Winiecki, 1913), at PRCU. I also depended on *65 Lat Zjednoczenia Polskiego Rzymsko-Katolickiego w Ameryce, 1873–1938* (Chicago: PRCU, 1938) for financial statements relating to contributions of the PRCU during World War I. The Jagiellonian University Bibliography lists a lengthy bibliography for the history of the Polish National Alliance on pp. 279–86, but the standard still is Stanley Osada, *Historya Związku Narodowego Polskiego i Rozwój Ruchu Narodowego w Ameryce Północnej* (Chicago: Polish National Alliance, 1905), located at DZ and PNA. For a history of the Polish Women's Alliance, I depended on Jadwiga Karlowicza, *Historya Związku Polek w Ameryce* (Chicago: Polish Women's Alliance, 1938), a personal copy (JP). For the *Liga Polska*, see the pamphlet entitled *Liga Polska w Stanach Zjednoczonych P.A. jako dzieło polityki Wiel(ebnego) Ks. Wincentego Barzynskiego, Proboszcza Parafii Polskiej Św. Stanisława K. w Chicago* (Chicago, 1894), at DC. For the Polish Alma Mater, I used the *Album Jubileuszowy Macierzy Polskiej, 1897–1917* (Chicago, 1917), at the PRCU.

For materials on the Polish Catholic liturgy, I made use of Tomasz Kowaleski, *Liturgika Czyli Wykład Obrzędow Kościoła Katolickiego* (Chicago, 1902); Ks. Stanislaw Siatka, *Wianek Nabożeństw odprawianych w ciągu roku kościelnego* (Chicago: Drukiem Spółki Wydawniczej Polskiej, 1904); and the *Zbiór Pieśni Nabożnych Katolickich Do Użytku Kościelnego i Domowego* (Chicago: Polish American Publishing Company, n.d.; *imprimatur* dated 1868). I assume that each of these items is housed somewhere in Chicago Polonia, but I used copies in my personal collection throughout.

The bibliography of the Polish National Catholic Church is enormous, especially for Polish language materials. But the one single item I found to be of greatest benefit was the *Księga Pamiątkowa '33' Polsko Narodowego Katolickiego Koscioła w Ameryce* (Scranton, Pa.: Polish National Catholic Church of America, 1930). The best professional history of the PNCC is Hieronym Kubiak, *Polski Narodowy Kościoł Katolicki w Stanach Zjednoczonych Ameryki w latach 1897–1965* (Cracow: Polish Academy of Science, 1970). Kubiak puts events in a Marxist perspective, viewing Hodur as a hero of the working-class Poles in the Scranton area, a position I support. See the PNA for both these items.

The only Polish-language source in book form that gives extensive coverage to *równouprawnienie* is Wenceslaus Kruszka, *Siedm Siedmioleci Czyli Pół Wieku Życia: Pamiętnik i Przyczynek do Historji Polskiej w Ameryce*, 2 vols. (Milwaukee: The author and the press of St. Adalbert's, 1924). Kruszka's autobiography (JP) contains numerous documents, letters, memorials, and translations found nowhere else.

The best general histories of American Polonia in Polish are the following: Wacław Kruszka, *Historya Polska w Ameryce*, 13 vols. (Milwaukee: Kuryer Polski, 1905–08), which I have already discussed in the text (PRCU, DC, PNA, JP); Karol Wachtel, *Polonia w Ameryce* (Philadelphia: The author, 1944) (PNA); and the extensive scholarship of Miecislaus Haiman (see the Jagiellonian Bibliography, items 4821–41).

English Language Sources

There are no full-scale biographies in English on any of the major figures introduced in my book. Accordingly the reader must cull biographical information from a variety of sources. The most valuable source by far is the "Książek Index" to the *Dziennik Chicagoski*, which I introduced earlier in this essay. Despite some factual errors, the researcher will also profit from Francis Bolek, *Who's Who in Polish America*, 3rd ed. (New York: Harbinger House, 1943). Even more valuable is Edward Janas, *Dictionary of American Resurrectionists, 1865–1965* (Rome: Gregorian University Press, 1967). Bolek is obtainable at many locations (PRCU, PNA, DC, DZ, NIU, JP); Janas from the ACR. Of great value on a wide variety of topics dealing with Poland and Polonia is the *Polish Encyclopedia*, Vols. 1–3 (New York: Arno Press, 1972); also, Joseph Slabey Roucek, ed., *Slavonic Encyclopedia* (New York: Philosophical Library, 1949), both available at NIU and elsewhere. Beginning scholars wishing to gain a grasp of essential issues and basic controversies in ethnic areas throughout the United States will find extremely valuable the translations in *Makers of America*, ed. Wayne Moquin, 10 vols. (New York: Encyclopedia Britannica, 1971). *Makers of America* forms a basic source collection for comparative studies of immigration groups.

The single most important source for the study of Polish immigration in English is William I. Thomas and Florian Znaniecki, *The Polish Peasant in Europe and America*, 2 vols. (New York: Knopf, 1927). Of equal interest is Emily Green Balch, *Our Slavic Fellow Citizens* (New York: Charities Publication Committee, 1910). For background information on the history of Poland, I still find the *Cambridge History of Poland*, ed. William F. Reddaway, 2 vols. (Cambridge: Cambridge University Press, 1941–50), to be the most reliable. Of more recent vintage, Piotr Wandycz, *The Lands of Partitioned Poland, 1795–1918* (Seattle and London: University of Washington Press, 1974) is invaluable; Wandycz's work, volume 7 of the History of East Central Europe Series, is, I feel, the best and most readable piece of English-language scholarship on the Partitions ever published. It must be read in conjunction with Stefan Kieniewicz, *The Emancipation of the Polish Peasantry* (Chicago: University of Chicago Press, 1969) and the works of the noted scholar of the Insurrections, R. F. Leslie, *Polish Politics and the Revolution of November 1830* (London: Athlone Press, 1956), and *Reform and Insurrection in Russian Poland, 1856–1865* (London: Athlone Press, 1963). The scholarship of Leslie should be read along with M. Kukiel, *Czartoryski and European Unity, 1770–1861* (Princeton, N.J.: Princeton University Press, 1955). Two other surveys of note which supplied me with a framework of ideas dealing with nationalism and religion are Oscar Halecki, *A History of Poland* (New York: Roy, 1943), and Aleksander Gieysztor, et al., *History of Poland* (Warsaw: PWN—Polish Scientific Publishers, 1968). I also found much useful information in Bernadotte E. Schmitt, ed., *Poland* (Berkeley: University of California, 1947), and Hans Roos, *A History of Modern Poland: From the Foundations of the State in the First World War to the Present Day* (New York: Knopf, 1966), especially for the Pilsudski *coup d'etat*. For cultural history, I will always enjoy Manfred Kridl, *A Survey of Polish Literature and Culture* (The Hague: Brill, 1956), and Waclaw

Lednicki, *The Life and Culture of Poland as Reflected in Polish Literature* (New York: Roy, 1944). Each of the above-mentioned titles on Poland is at NIU and in almost every other library mentioned earlier in the essay.

The bibliography of Chicago is, of course, enormous. I have already mentioned Pierce's bibliographical note and the Jewell bibliography as essential guides. In addition to Pierce's *History of Chicago*, I used two well-known nineteenth-century histories: Alfred T. Andreas, *History of Chicago*, 3 vols. (Chicago: A.T. Andreas, 1884–86), and John Moses and Joseph Kirkland, *History of Chicago*, 2 vols. (Chicago and New York: Munsell, 1895). The histories of various nationality and racial groups in Chicago have likewise proliferated. Rather than list these individually, I refer the reader to Jewell's *Annotated Bibliography*, pp. 170–94, for religious, racial, and ethnic groups, and pp. 195–212, for histories of various neighborhoods and community areas. Of special mention, however, are the *Local Community Factbooks* published for 1940, 1950, and 1960 by the University of Chicago under the editorship of Louis Wirth and others (see Jewell, pp. 130–31). The *Factbooks* were essential for the study of Polish mobility in the city of Chicago. Even more critical for the study of population succession are Ernest Watson Burgess and Charles Newcomb, *Census Data for the City of Chicago, 1920* (Chicago: University of Chicago Press, 1931) and *Census Data for the City of Chicago, 1930* (Chicago: University of Chicago Press, 1933). In addition to the quantitative data, the maps of respective community areas in the *Census Data* were indispensable (as were the rich nineteenth-century map collections on Chicago at NIU, UC, and CHS). Throughout my research, I was heavily dependent on the *Federal Population Census Manuscript Schedules* for the city of Chicago for the 1860–1900 period (the 1890 schedules were destroyed in the Commerce Department Fire of 1921 and thus are unavailable today). The Manuscript Census Schedules are available for Illinois and Chicago at NIU, CHS, and the UC. As for the history of Catholic Chicago, I depended upon Joseph J. Thompson, *Diamond Jubilee of the Archdiocese of Chicago, 1920* (Des Plaines, Ill.: St. Mary's Training School Press, 1920), which was far more useful than Gilbert J. Garraghan, *The Catholic Church in Chicago, 1673–1871* (Chicago: Loyola University Press, 1921). Unfortunately, there is still no scholarly history of the Roman Catholic Archdiocese of Chicago—an incredible gap in Catholic scholarship in the United States.

The list of works on which I depended in order to formulate a structure for my treatment of immigrant Catholics would be formidable and long indeed. Nevertheless, I especially cite the following for taking Catholic history out of a routine ecclesiastical history framework and providing scholars with an intellectual history construct: Robert D. Cross, *The Emergence of Liberal Catholicism in America* (Cambridge, Mass.: Harvard University Press, 1958); John Tracy Ellis, *The Life of James Cardinal Gibbons, Archbishop of Baltimore: 1834–1921*, 2 vols. (Milwaukee: Bruce, 1952), which, despite its title, goes well beyond the confines of ecclesiastical history; Colman Barry, *The Catholic Church and German Americans* (Washington, D.C.: Catholic University Press, 1953); Philip Gleason, ed., *Contemporary Catholicism in the United States* (Notre Dame, Ind.: University of Notre Dame Press, 1969); and, especially, David O'Brien, *The Renewal of American Catholicism* (New York: Oxford University Press, 1972), who, along with Gleason, has launched the "New Catholic Historiography."

Prior to his death in 1948, Miecislaus Haiman toiled in relative isolation from the wider community of professional historians in the "establishment" centers of the American Historical Association or the "Mississippi Valley" historians (now the Organization of American Historians). The work of Haiman never was recognized in his lifetime by his peers in the profession. Today, however, Polish-American scholarship is making great strides; accordingly it would be impossible to list the dozens of friends who made some sort of contribution to my work on Chicago Polonia. Nevertheless, it should be quite obvious from the notes that my work could not have progressed very far without the scholarship of several key individuals who are also devoting their academic lives to explaining the experience of Polish immigrants and "ethnics" in American life. One of these is Professor Victor Greene of the University of Wisconsin, Milwaukee, whose work in *For God and Country: The Rise of Polish and Lithuanian Ethnic Consciousness in America, 1860–1910* (Madison: State Historical Society of Wisconsin, 1975) forced me to reconsider some of my previously held positions, especially in regard to Independentism and *równouprawnienie*. Next, I must cite Helena Stankiewicz Zand, for her pioneering efforts in the anthropology of religion and Polish religious folkways, and whose series of articles on Polish folkways and culture, published in *Polish American Studies* in 1955–1961, is of the highest quality I have ever read on this complex and diverse subject.

Along with the work of Greene and Zand, any scholar of Chicago Polonia must read Edward Kantowicz, *Polish-American Politics in Chicago, 1888–1940* (Chicago: University of Chicago Press, 1975). This is the only book-length study in existence which treats not only Polonia's contribution to Chicago politics but also the relationship of the Polish immigrant church to the political process. Kantowicz's study also is valuable since it is the foundation for any study of comparative ethnic politics and voting behavior between Poles and other major immigrant groups in Chicago, work which has been furthered by John M. Allswang, *A House for All Peoples* (Lexington: University of Kentucky Press, 1971). Both Professors Greene and Kantowicz have also written two extremely significant essays of a comparative nature in *The Ethnic Frontier: Essays in the History of Group Survival in Chicago and the Midwest*, ed. Melvin G. Holli and Peter d'A. Jones (Grand Rapids, Mich.: Eerdmans, 1977). Greene's essay in this volume is entitled "'Becoming Americans': The Role of Ethnic Leaders—Swedes, Poles,

Italians, Jews," on pp. 143–75; Kantowicz's essay is "Polish Chicago: Survival Through Solidarity," on pp. 179–209. Both deal with religious topics. The only major studies, aside from these, having to do with the comparative religious development of immigrants in Chicago prior to Vatican II are two unpublished doctoral dissertations, one by Charles H. Shanabruch, "The Catholic Church's Role in the Americanization of Chicago's Immigrants, 1833–1928 (University of Chicago, 1975), the other by Helena Znaniecki Lopata, "The Function of Voluntary Associations in an Ethnic Community: 'Polonia.'" (University of Chicago, 1954). Whereas the study by Shanabruch concentrates on the interrelationship of the archdiocese to specific immigrant groups in Chicago, Lopata instead deals with the interlocking nature of Polonia's major supraterritorial fraternals.

Numerous other secondary studies in English calling attention to the relationship of American Polonia to the Catholic Church and hierarchy in the United States also require further inspection. Foremost among these are the numerous articles published by Menceslaus Madaj, whose association with the Polish American Historical Association both in an executive capacity and as scholar spans more than a quarter-century. I found the following studies by Father Madaj to be the most helpful for the formulation of basic hypotheses and working models: "The Polish Immigrant, the American Catholic Hierarchy, and Reverend Wenceslaus Kruszka," *Polish American Studies* 26 (January–June 1969): 16–29; "The Polish Immigrant and the Catholic Church in America," *Polish American Studies* 6 (January–June 1949): 1–8; "The Polish Community a Ghetto?" *Polish American Studies* 25 (July–December 1968): 65–71. Along with these studies by Father Madaj, the researcher is encouraged to examine Thomas I. Monzell, "The Catholic Church and the Americanization of the Polish Immigrant," *Polish American Studies* 26 (January–June 1969): 1–15. A series of articles specifically outlining the overall contribution of Poles to the city of Chicago, from religious, social, political, and economic standpoints, can be found in *Poles of Chicago 1837–1937: A History of One Century of Polish Contribution to the City of Chicago, Illinois* (Chicago: Polish Pageant, 1937). Numerous translations of key documents on American Polonia can be located in *The Poles in America, 1608–1972: A Chronology and Factbook*, ed. Frank Renkiewicz (Dobbs Ferry, N.Y.: Oceana, 1973). In addition to some of the standard bibliographies on Polonia mentioned earlier, the reader is advised to examine the secondary literature mentioned in *A Bibliography for the Study of American Minorities*, ed. Wayne Charles Miller, et al., 2 vols. (New York: New York University Press, 1976), 1: 613–30. Finally, two works on Polish-American history published during the final stages of my manuscript revision are noteworthy pieces of scholarship: T. Lindsay Baker, *The First Polish Americans: Silesian Settlements in Texas* (College Station, Tex.: Texas A & M University Press, 1979), and Anthony J. Kuzniewski, *Faith and Fatherland: The Polish Church War in Wisconsin, 1896–1918* (Notre Dame, Ind.:

University of Notre Dame Press, 1980). Baker's work on the Panna Marya settlement must henceforth be read by any scholar of American Polonia because of its
precise narration of the history of American Polonia's first permanent settlement.
Kuzniewski's work is the most solid piece of scholarship in English today on both
Wenceslaus and Michael Kruszka; his handling of the "church war" in Wisconsin
includes so many details which parallel the Chicago situation that I consider this
must reading for the Polish-American scholar.

Index